TOURISM, RECREATION AND SUSTAINABILITY

Linking Culture and the Environment

Tourism, Recreation and Sustainability

Linking Culture and the Environment

Edited by

Stephen F. McCool

and

R. Neil Moisey
School of Forestry
University of Montana
Missoula
Montana
USA

CABI *Publishing*

CABI *Publishing* is a division of CAB *International*

CABI Publishing
CAB International
Wallingford
Oxon OX10 8DE
UK

CABI Publishing
10 E 40th Street
Suite 3203
New York, NY 10016
USA

Tel: +44 (0)1491 832111
Fax: +44 (0)1491 833508
Email: cabi@cabi.org
Web site: www.cabi-publishing.org

Tel: +1 212 481 7018
Fax: +1 212 686 7993
Email: cabi-nao@cabi.org

A catalogue record for this book is available from the British Library, London, UK.

Library of Congress Cataloging-in-Publication Data
Tourism, recreation, and sustainability: linking culture and the environment / edited by Stephen F. McCool and R. Neil Moisey.
    p. cm.
  Includes bibliographical references.
  ISBN 0-85199-505-5 (alk. paper)
    1. Tourism. 2. Ecotourism. 3. Sustainable development. I. McCool, Stephen F. II. Moisey, R. Neil.

G155.A1 T59244 2001
338.4'791—dc21

338.4791/MCC

00-062130

ISBN 0 85199 505 5

First printed 2001
Reprinted 2002

Typeset by York House Typographic
Printed and bound in the UK by Biddles Ltd, Guildford and King's Lynn.

Contents

Contributors

S.W. Burr, Institute of Outdoor Recreation and Tourism, Department of Forest Resources, Utah State University, 5215 Old Main Hill, Logan, Utah 84322–5215, USA

B. Carmichael, Department of Geography and Environmental Studies, Wilfrid Laurier University, Waterloo, Ontario, Canada, N2L 3C5

C.P. Dawson, SUNY College of Environmental Science and Forestry, 211 Marshall Hall, One Forestry Drive, Syracuse, NY 13210–2787, USA

S. Evans, Anglia Polytechnic University, School of Design and Communication Systems, South Victoria Road, Chelmsford, Essex, CM1 1LL, UK

T.A. Farrell, School for Field Studies, 16 Broadway, Beverly, MA 01915, USA

K. Horochowski, Department of Parks, Recreation and Tourism, University of Missouri, Columbia, MO 65211, USA

D. Ioannides, Department of Geography, Geology and Planning, Southwest Missouri State University, 901 S. National Avenue, Springfield, MO 65804, USA

U. Jamrozy, Department of Health, Leisure and Exercise Science, Appalachian State University, Post Office Box 32071, Boone, NC 28608–2071, USA

M.E. Johnston, School of Outdoor Recreation, Parks and Tourism, Lakehead University, Thunder Bay, Ontario, Canada, P7B 5E1

B.C. Kaae, Danish Forest and Landscape Research Institute, Hoersholm Kongevej 11, DK–2970 Hoersholm, Denmark

Y.-F. Leung, Department of Parks, Recreation and Tourism Management, North Carolina State University, Box 8004, 4012F Biltmore Hall, Raleigh, NC 27695–8004, USA

J.B. Lewis, Department of HPER, Western Michigan University, 1201 Oliver Street, Kalamazoo, MI 49008, USA

C. Litchfield, Department of Psychology, The University of Adelaide, North Terrace, Adelaide 5000 SA, Australia

J.L. Marion, USGS Cooperative Park Studies Unit, Virginia Tech, 304 Cheatham Hall, Blacksburg, VA 24061–0324, USA

S.F. McCool, School of Forestry, University of Montana, Missoula, MT 59812, USA

J.L. Meyer, Department of Geography, Geology and Planning, Southwest Missouri State University, 901 S. National Avenue, Springfield, MO 65804–0089, USA

R.E. Mitchell, Department of Rural Economy, 515 General Service, University of Alberta, Edmonton, Alberta, Canada, T6G 2HI

R.N. Moisey, School of Forestry, University of Montana, Missoula, MT 59812, USA

J. Neil, School of Leisure, Sport and Tourism, Faculty of Business, University of Technology, Kuring-gai Campus, PO Box 222, Lindfield 2070, Sydney, Australia

R.J. Payne, School of Outdoor Recreation, Parks and Tourism, Lakehead University, Thunder Bay, Ontario, Canada, P7B 5E1

S. Ross, c/o Don Ross, 12 Viburnum, Pointe Claire, Quebec, Canada, H9R 5A7

G.D. Twynam, School of Tourism, Box 3010, University College of the Cariboo, Kamloops, British Columbia, Canada, V2C 5N3

G. Wall, Faculty of Environmental Studies, University of Waterloo, Waterloo, Ontario, Canada, N2L 3G1

J.A. Walsh, 108 Zimmerli Bldg., Lock Haven University, Lock Haven, PA 17745, USA

S. Wearing, School of Leisure, Sport and Tourism, Faculty of Business, University of Technology, Kuring-gai Campus, PO Box 222, Lindfield 2070, Sydney, Australia

Preface

Since the concept of sustainability and its cousin sustainable development was made popular by the publication of the book *Our Common Future* (by the World Commission on Economic Development) in 1987, it has been applied to many areas of economic development and natural resources management. Lying at the intersection of both these important domains is tourism. Tourism, particularly that which is based upon a region's natural and cultural heritage, contains both the promises of a better quality of life and protection of the region's heritage, as well as numerous pitfalls.

Understanding how sustainable tourism has been applied in different locations, and the factors leading to its success as well as its failure, is an important prerequisite to advancing the concept and being more efficient in achieving the goals of sustainability through the use of tourism, not only as an economic development tool but also as a tool of conservation. In this book, we present both analytical frameworks for examining the concept of sustainable tourism (within the context sustainable development) and numerous case studies in a variety of cultural, political and environmental contexts. Our hope is that these case studies and analytical frameworks will assist in creating better understanding of those promises and pitfalls.

The book is organized into several sections. Section I provides an overview and several frameworks from which sustainable tourism can be critiqued and revised. Such analytical frameworks form the foundation for substantive critique of sustainable tourism and help us ask appropriate questions. Section II contains several chapters that address social and environmental consequences of tourism development. These chapters point out how important it is that we understand what it is that tourism should be sustaining. Section III focuses on communities and tourism development, and raises a number of issues concerning the quality-of-life linkages to tourism development, as well as how tourism affects the social fabric and capital of small communities. The final section emphasizes sustainable tourism within the larger context of economic development, and documents the struggles that numerous localities have experienced in using this sometimes controversial tool.

The book is not meant to be read from beginning to end, but rather to be not only a sourcebook for case studies and analytical frameworks, but also for other work that is cited by the chapter authors.

The editors wish to thank the various contributors who have had faith that this project would succeed.

Stephen F. McCool
R. Neil Moisey
June 2000, Missoula, Montana

Introduction: Pathways and Pitfalls in the Search for Sustainable Tourism

Stephen F. McCool and R. Neil Moisey

School of Forestry, University of Montana, Missoula, Montana, USA

Introduction

The growing, even accelerating, concerns about the status of the world environment initially triggered by such publications as Rachel Carson's *Silent Spring* and the Club of Rome report (Meadows *et al.*, 1972) were coalesced by the Brundtland Commission's *Our Common Future*, which argued that survival of the human species depended on adoption of a new paradigm of economic development termed 'sustainable development' (World Commission on Environment and Development, 1987). This paradigm was significantly different from previous calls for environmental protection and economic progress in the sense that it represented a combination of both, while attending to quality-of-life needs. The Commission argued that the only effective method to protecting the environment, addressing economic progress, alleviating poverty and preserving human rights was through a developmental paradigm that 'provided for the needs of the present while ensuring that options for the future were preserved'.

The Brundtland Commission report served as a catalyst for discussing the future of human society and ways of ensuring that development is sustainable over the long term. The report was favourably received in many academic and policy circles around the world, and as a result stimulated a great amount of discussion. Yet, many questions have been left unanswered: How does one conserve the environment, provide a more equitable distribution of income among those living at the present, and ensure that there is equality in access to quality of life? Can we optimize all three goals, or are there trade-offs involved? If so, what are they? How does one provide for the needs of the present while preserving options for future generations? Who represents future generations and their needs in these decisions? What is supposed to be sustained? What is the role of different economic sectors, non-government organizations, and government institutions in seeking sustainability? What is the role of ethics and science in sustainability policy? How can development be sustained? Can sustainability be achieved within existing institutional and political-economy frameworks and processes? How does one develop and apply a science of sustainability while promoting more public participation in government decision-making?

Academic fields such as agriculture, ecology, economics, management, political science, psychology and community development have made progress in developing research and policy on the meaning of sustainability and sustainable development. In this widely scattered search for purpose, a variety of themes have developed, including sustainability as ecosystem maintenance, preservation of natural capital, provision for intergenerational and intragenerational equity, sustainable development, redistribution of political power, and maintenance or restoration of the resiliency of human–environment systems. These different themes have made communicating about sustainability difficult but have also raised important and useful questions about the pathways, interrelationships, and pitfalls to a more sustainable world.

Tourism has not escaped the discussions concerning sustainability. Indeed many texts, including this one, have been challenged to frame the question of sustainable tourism, its dimensions and challenges (e.g. Innskeep, 1991; McCool and Watson, 1995; Stabler, 1997; Wahab and Pigram, 1997; Hall and Lew, 1998; Swarbrooke, 1999; Font and Tribe, 2000). Clearly, tourism has become a global financial power, achieving a planetary presence unequalled by many other economic sectors. As it has grown, so have the criticisms of its environmental, economic, cultural and political consequences (e.g. Cater and Goodall, 1992; McLaren, 1997; Rothman, 1998; Honey, 1999). Tourism is no longer the benign economic development tool that the boosterism of the past purported it to be. Yet, the social and environmental issues associated with tourism development are not necessarily significantly different from those of other methods of development, such as forestry, mining, manufacturing and agriculture.

This book is designed to illustrate many of the issues and approaches associated with sustainable tourism development, policy and research. Included are case studies of tourism development, using both quantitative and qualitative methods; analytical frameworks for managing tourism; and chapters addressing critical questions about the relationship between tourism and sustainability goals. As a whole, the book demonstrates the many dimensions and topics associated with attempts to address the complex issues associated with sustainability and tourism.

In this chapter, we outline several of the pathways and pitfalls confronting tourism as it seeks an appropriate role in the world. These include:

1. The meaning of sustainable tourism – there are several such meanings, which ones are used suggest not only world-views but also have implications for other issues.
2. Integration with the larger economy and linkage with scale of consideration – planners, academics and advocates are increasingly concerned with how tourism development fits in with broader social and economic development goals.
3. The search for indicators – how do we know if sustainable tourism is indeed sustainable without a set of measurable variables that indicate progress?
4. Planning and implementation – sustainable tourism does not just happen, it occurs only with explicit decision-making processes that consider what futures are plausible and desirable and the pathways to them.
5. Forms of knowledge and public participation – achieving sustainable tourism will require a variety of individuals, agencies and programmes, each using different forms of knowledge and each involving those affected by decisions.

We discuss each of these pathways and pitfalls briefly, and then provide an overview of the book.

Sustainable tourism, sustaining tourism or what should tourism sustain? Different meanings, alternative pathways

As with its larger context, the meanings attached to sustainable tourism have varied significantly, with little apparent consensus among authors and government institutions. This leads to two problems. First, sustainable tourism constitutes what is termed a 'guiding fiction': guiding fictions serve socially valuable functions as long as definitions remain vague; they stimulate and organize social discourse around problematic issues, but when individuals seek the more specific definitions needed to guide action, this function breaks down as groups argue over the meaning of terms (Shumway, 1991). The challenge here is to maintain the pathway to sustainable tourism while providing secure venues for public deliberation about meanings and actions.

Secondly, agreement on meanings is a necessary, but not sufficient condition, for making progress on socially problematic challenges. Action in society requires a variety of actors performing in concert (Friedmann, 1973). In tourism development, this includes promotional agencies, governmental planning and zoning institutions, community development groups, local residents, transportation planners, private entrepreneurs and others. Use of different meanings of terminology central to discourse can lead ultimately to conflict and development of mistrust. This lack of consensus on meanings is becoming a significant pitfall in the search for sustainability, for the different meanings result from significantly different perceptions of tourism and its role in society. There are at least three different meanings that relate directly to the notion of sustainable tourism that are used in the literature. These meanings reflect a continuum of world-views, from those that are industry centred to those that are more broadly socially centred.

1. Sustaining tourism: how to maintain tourism industry businesses over a long time frame

This view suggests that the primary task is to build and manage a set of tourism businesses that can maintain themselves over a long period. This view is narrow in the sense that the objective of sustainable tourism is the tourism (and recreation) industry and included business firms. While maintaining the health of individual businesses may be viewed as a worthy social goal, this perspective does not necessarily recognize tourism as a tool to enhance economic opportunity, protecting a community's cultural and natural heritage, and maintaining a desired quality of life. This view of sustainable tourism would place great emphasis on maintaining promotional programmes that ensure that the number of tourists visiting an area continues to rise. In this sense of sustainable tourism, the more tourists, the better. This view, of course, neglects to see tourism as an input, as a method of enhancing social and economic welfare.

2. Sustainable tourism: a kinder, gentler form of tourism that is generally small in scale, sensitive to cultural and environmental impact and respects the involvement of local people in policy decisions

This view comes from an argument that there are finite biophysical and social limits to tourism development. It recognizes that tourism, as any other economic activity, can overwhelm a community with negative social and environmental impacts. Thus, sustainable tourism, closely allied with the notion of ecotourism, is small in scale, designed to benefit local peoples and communities, and protect resources upon which the tourism and recreation industry is built. Within this view, there remains considerable divergence of opinion, with some authors suggesting that sustainable tourism represents the conduct of individual tourists, others maintaining that it is ethical behaviour on the part of tourism- and recreation-based businesses, and still others suggesting that it focuses on the amount of social and environmental impact. A larger question, however, concerns unnecessary, normative and counter-productive distinctions between sustainable tourism and mass tourism that often accompany this meaning. Much of the globe's tourism may qualify as mass tourism, but the central question of sustainability concerns how the negative social and economic impacts of human activity can be reduced. Given that most tourism would probably be defined as mass tourism, it follows that the greatest progress in reducing impacts would be to address mass tourism, not ignore it.

3. What should tourism sustain? Tourism as a tool for development

This view sees tourism as a tool of social and economic development, as a method to enhance economic opportunity, not as an end itself. This question is similar to Gale and Cordray's (1994) question, 'What should be sustained?', in a natural resource management context, to which they gave nine different answers, primarily focusing on various ecosystem characteristics. In this sense, tourism is integrated into broader economic and social development programmes (Hunter, 1995; McCool *et al.*, 2001) and can be viewed as a method – similar to many definitions of ecotourism – to protect the natural and social capital upon which the industry is built. By asking this question, we view tourism as a tool, which at times may be important to a community and other times not so important. In this sense, we are not speaking of protecting cultures for their value to the tourism industry, but because of their value to their peoples (Robinson, 1999). It may be possible under this view that tourism is not sustained over a long period, but is used as a method to accumulate income and government revenue that can be used later for other development tools. Tourism would be viewed as part of a larger policy framework designed to achieve a sustainable society. In addition, the type of tourism in this view may not necessarily be small in scale.

These alternative views of sustainable tourism carry significantly different implications for social and economic policy, selection of indicators, public participation and the planning processes needed to encourage tourism development in the private sector. They reflect differing perspectives on the concept of sustainability.

We prefer to use the third approach to studying sustainability and tourism. It seems that it more properly places tourism as a means and not an end to economic development. It allows tourism to be considered as one of several alternatives that can help a community overcome its weaknesses and preserve its strengths. It views tourism as a tool and not as an end.

Integrating tourism into broader social and economic development processes

To think of tourism in any of these meanings except for the first, means that tourism is integrated into development decisions in the larger social and economic context. Sustainable tourism as a kinder, gentler form embraces not only growing societal concerns over social and environmental impacts but also a moral commitment to future generations. It promotes softer forms of tourism, but fails to address where the largest gains in impact reduction – particularly environmental consequences – can occur. Determining what tourism should sustain requires more explicit consideration of social goals and values.

Tourism is a method that society, in many places, has decided can be used to enhance economic opportunity. Far too often, however, its ultimate goal of enhancing economic opportunity has been neglected in favour of unbridled boosterism, with few acknowledgements of tourism's negative social and environmental consequences. In the US, state-level tourism agencies are generally involved solely in promotion activities, through advertising, 'fam tours' and the like, without significant responsibility in other areas of marketing, such as pricing and product development. This focus on promotion only fails to capture the important positive and negative consequences of tourism in identification of goals and policy implementation.

The fragmented and disjointed nature of tourism development remains an important pitfall in seeking a more sustainable world. State and local promotion agencies (e.g. destination marketing organizations, visitor and convention bureaus), for example, often have little planning relationship with local government agencies, usually are focused on promotion, rather than marketing (which includes 'product protection and development') and generally have little influence over private investment in tourism infrastructure, services and opportunities. The variety of agencies and organizations with competing, if not conflicting, goals makes the coordinated action needed for achieving sustainability difficult. One agency may promote protected areas as a tourism destination while another is responsible for managing the tourists and their impacts when they arrive. Such compartmentalized decision-making remains a great obstacle to integrated planning and development.

Since tourism development and promotion are collective decisions (in the sense that government agencies provide the funding), knowledge and attitudes of the public are important considerations in policy articulation and implementation. Attitude data have been collected for many years in a variety of situations. The data show general support for tourism, but concern about equity in funding the cost of services needed by tourists, about excessive use leading to crowding of favourite recreation areas, and about the ability of tourism to provide jobs that pay good wages. This type of information can assist promotion agencies review the impacts of their advertising efforts and suggest new ways to enhance opportunities for tourism development.

The search for sustainable tourism indicators

Given a goal of sustainability, and a real and legitimate desire to measure progress toward achieving that goal, there is a need for indicators that will suggest the extent to which the goal is being attained. In a sense, we need to know if, indeed, sustainable tourism has become sustainable! We need to know if the things that tourism is supposed to sustain are becoming sustainable. The search for indicators is an important path to sustainability, but the meaning of the term has a critical influence on what path is measured.

There is a growing literature on the concept of sustainability indicators, both in a larger context and with respect to tourism (for excellent discussions of sustainability indicators see Moldan *et al.*, 1997; Bossel, 1999). A number of efforts by the World Tourism Organization, Manning (1996), and other individuals have identified an almost unlimited set of indicator variables. The extent to which these variables (concerning sustainable tourism) relate to broader efforts concerning sustainability (such as those proposed by the International Institute for Sustainable Development, the Montreal Process and others) is unknown. Again, there is the very real possibility of compartmentalization of attention, when sustainability is more of a holistic concept. Selection of indicators in the past has been conducted primarily on an ad hoc basis, without a specific theoretical or conceptual framework of the system in place. A number of authors have argued that ad hoc approaches have a number of dangers in indicator selection (e.g. Bossel, 1999). This suggests a need for further research and description of the tourism–recreation system that would be useful for sustainability questions.

Selecting indicators is constrained by our lack of knowledge of the effects of tourism development at larger scales, such as communities and nations, and over long time frames. Often such effects lag significantly in time from the initial causes. The system may exhibit non-linear dynamics (consequences are not additive) because of the interaction of many variables over time. Effects may be spatially displaced. A resort development near a tropical marine park may eventually lead to reef decline because of excessive nutrients from inappropriately treated sewage, but these effects may not be measurable for a long time. Declines in the quality of the coral may then lead to changes in the resort's clientele, which in turn may result in other developments leading to further insidious and difficult-to-trace impacts.

What indicators might there be that are available at the community and national level, and are data for those indicators available over periods of, say, decades? We need to understand and specify the function of indicators, of which there are at least three: (i) indicating the state or condition of some entity (such as a community or industry); (ii) measuring the effectiveness of a particular management practice (such as a specific advertising programme or development plan); and (iii) providing leading information on changes that may occur in a later time period (McCool and Stankey, 1999).

Indicators must meet certain criteria to be useful. These criteria include such things as containing an output orientation, holding construct validity, being quantitatively measurable, having interobserver reliability, being easy to collect or measure, and sensitive to change across space and time (Livermann et al., 1988).

Planning and implementation of tourism development

Tourism, particularly those forms based on the local cultural and natural heritage, contains great potential to impact negatively the very resources upon which the industry is founded. The literature contains a great outcry about 'tourism destroying tourism'. And, given that the 'friendliness' of community or destination residents may be an important influence on the satisfaction of tourists, understanding the capacity of local residents for tourism and their involvement in development decisions is important for successful tourism implementation. Therefore, planning of tourism developments at both larger and smaller scales must take great care to reduce negative impacts.

Planning and implementation can only be considered as linked activities, for if planning is to change the future, it needs to be linked directly to means of implementing actions. Proceeding with planning without providing for implementation represents an unnecessary compartmentalization of functions without any redeeming value. To paraphrase Wildavsky (1973), the promise of planning must be dignified by its performance. This can only occur if implementation is considered a component of planning processes.

While the basic function of planning is to select a future and find the best path to it, traditional planning processes for tourism development may no longer be appropriate for 21st century contexts. These contexts are likely typified by seemingly competing goals (for example, protecting environmental quality and providing economic opportunity) and lack of scientific agreement on cause–effect relationships, particularly at the larger spatial and temporal scales of interest in sustainability issues. While attaining these types of goals is an apparent purpose of pursuing a sustainable tourism policy, they are not necessarily compatible in all situations. Analyses are needed that suggest what trade-offs between them will occur.

These contexts may be termed 'messy situations' (Ackoff, 1974; McCool and Patterson, 2001). In messy situations, traditional approaches to planning, based on formalized rational–comprehensive planning involving only minimal public participation, quite often lead to hostile and polarized relationships without resolving the problem. In messy situations, where goals conflict or compete and science contains a lot of uncertainty, planning is based on the notion of social learning (Lee, 1993; Stankey *et al.*, 1999), to better understand how things fit together, and consensus building (Krumpe and McCool, 1997; McCool *et al.*, 2000), to organize the societal action needed to implement a plan. Importantly, in these processes, implementation is viewed as an extension of planning rather than compartmentalized from it.

There is a myth in the sustainable tourism literature that suggests that resources responsibly developed in this paradigm will not be negatively impacted. For example, Innskeep (1991) observes that carrying capacity is the level of '. . . use that will not result in environmental or sociocultural deterioration . . .' (p. 144). This, of course, is impossible: any kind of development will result in some change in the social and natural environment, thus tourism development deals with trade-offs. However, the validity of the carrying capacity concept is increasingly contested in the tourism and recreation literature (see especially Getz, 1982; Butler, 1996; Lindberg, *et al.*, 1997). Carrying capacities, as Stankey and McCool (1984) have long argued, lead planners to ask the question 'How many is too many?', when the real issue concerns how we best protect the values, biophysical conditions and social meanings that are important to people.

The question is then, how much change from a pre-existing condition is acceptable, given the benefits provided? For example, a new tourism development may lead to some biophysical impacts on a nearby protected area, but also provide employment for local residents. In a sense, this could be looked at as a conflict, for example, between providing economic opportunity and protection of the natural heritage. If protection is viewed as an ultimately constraining goal, then the question is, how much impact will we permit to gain a certain economic benefit or quality-of-life benefit? While this question can be informed by science, it is not a scientific question but a political and economic one. One of the problems of carrying capacity approaches is that they give the illusion that the question is primarily scientific.

Planning for sustainable tourism represents a redistribution of power, particularly to those living in the future. Given this definition, a number of questions arise: Who represents the future? How well are institutions prepared to consider the needs of future generations or those in the current generations that are not as well off? We cannot predict the future with any level of accuracy, thus we are continually faced with uncertainty. In this context, how can we adapt tourism development strategies to maintain community resiliency in the face of ecological and economic surprises?

Integrating different forms of knowledge into sustainable tourism planning

Given the complexity of tourism sustainability and the current lack of scientific knowledge about cause–effect relationships, it is clear that various forms of knowledge (scientific, emotional and experiential) are all legitimate in making tourism development decisions. While sustainability is often posed as a technical–scientific issue, it actually represents a moral commitment to future generations, because it represents a decision to provide future generations with the same array of options current generations now enjoy (Pearce *et al.*, 1989). Science can inform sustainability decisions, but cannot determine those decisions. In addition to scientific knowledge, experiential and emotional forms of knowledge can contribute to more informed decisions. These forms of knowledge may not only substitute for the lack of scientific knowledge, they frequently inform policy-makers of the importance of various values and places. They suggest where conflicts between tourists and local residents may appear. They indicate how much tolerance for tourism the local community has. They can help identify goals of economic and tourism development and how particular policies may or may not contribute to attaining those goals. They indicate what values are important to a community.

This suggests that policy-makers pay particular attention to the design of public participation programmes and their objectives. The literature of tourism development provides powerful arguments that affected publics have rights to engage in decision-making processes. Such rights, however, are not limited to simply being informed about what an agency or private firm may wish to do, but also involve helping to identify desirable futures and the acceptable pathways to them. However, such processes are often so designed as to make participation such a formality that conflict is often aggravated. In the messy situations that were identified earlier, public participation provides important learning and consensus-building functions that serve to address uncertainty and conflict over goals.

Some suggestions on participation include identifying objectives of participation efforts (Arnstein, 1969), determining whether a consensus is desired, developing the situational conditions to enhance the usefulness of public participation (Shindler and Neburka, 1997), experimenting with new forms of participation and collaboration (Hall, 1999; Ritchie, 1999) and identifying methods for evaluating the success of participation techniques (Marien and Pizam, 1997). Increasingly, authors are calling for planning processes to involve collaboration and negotiation, and to recognize that planning should be adaptive and viewed in a sense as experimental (cf. Reed, 1999).

Organization of this book

These pathways and pitfalls are fundamental to developing and implementing sustainable tourism policy, but are only illustrative of the challenges confronting the industry as it seeks a more sustainable world. That they are complex and demand equally sophisticated responses is an imperative not to be ignored. Tourism and recreation are two aspects of the same phenomenon: society's search for meaningful uses of leisure. What those uses are and their consequences can be understood only within the context of the linkages between culture and the environment. To examine one without considering the other leads to incomplete analyses, for they are both inextricably joined. In many situations, this linkage is neither neat nor pretty, but complex and difficult to describe and understand.

The chapters that follow further illustrate the complexity and messiness of sustainable tourism. This book is designed in part to address the pathways, through a variety of case studies and analytical frameworks, while acknowledging and addressing the pitfalls. The chapters report on sustainable tourism as it is occurring in different areas and at diverse scales throughout the world. We have divided the book into three sections, each of which addresses a different sustainable tourism theme.

In the first section (Integrating Environmental and Social Concerns Over Tourism Development), several authors discuss the needs for

integration of social and environmental issues in tourism development. In so doing, they provide not only frameworks for such
integration, but also illustrate, in several case studies, the inevitable
and intricate relationships between these two major domains. The
fundamental proposition here is that successful tourism development
occurs only within a framework that explicitly considers impacts on
these two domains. The second section of the book (Society,
Recreation and Sustainable Tourism) builds upon these frameworks
and provides the reader with a variety of situations in which recreation
and tourism are related to larger societal needs. In this section, such
concepts as sense of place and public participation are presented.
Tourism development holds many consequences for how residents
and tourists assign and derive meanings from specific communities
and tourism destinations. These studies examine these issues and
significance of place attachment in tourism development decisions.
The call for wider public participation in tourism planning has many
subscribers; such calls are based on ideologies that strive for a
restructuring of political power. The third section (Sustainable
Tourism Development: Some Applications) presents some case-study
examples of places that have attempted to develop sustainable tourism,
with varying degrees of success. These places range from highly
urbanized and rural settings in Europe to relatively empty or
'undeveloped' areas in the Arctic and Asia. What these chapters tell
us is that the pathway to a more sustainable world embraces developed
and undeveloped locations, although the specific parameters, actions
and developments may vary significantly: in a sense, the search for
sustainability forgoes 'cookie-cutter' solutions.

The last chapter summarizes the lessons learned and the
challenges to be met in this bid to discuss sustainable tourism. We
have included this chapter in an attempt to synthesize the underlying
learning that has occurred from these studies of sustainable tourism in
vastly different circumstances. Archiving this learning, then, becomes
an important footstep along the pathway to sustainability and helps
avoid the pitfalls that must have occurred in each of the studies.

Conclusions

If anything, tourism is a complex form of economic development that
has many forward and backward linkages, not only to the economy, but
to the culture and environment as well. Sustainable tourism – in the
sense of what tourism should sustain – links cultures and their
environment, for cultures have developed out of their interaction with
their embedding environment. Ignoring one while dealing with the
other leads to potentially negative and irreversible consequences that

may not be identifiable for a long time. The experience of others, as archived here, is helpful in understanding how we can better link both in our trek to a more sustainable world.

Making tourism sustainable and cultures resilient requires that we properly frame the question of sustainable tourism. Clearly, as we have shown here, there are several possible ways of framing the question; this indicates the importance of asking the right question. The 'answers' depend on how the question is framed.

All too often, solutions are aimed at symptoms and not problems, previous solutions, or problems that have nothing to do with the problem at hand (Bardwell, 1991). The pitfall in discussing sustainable tourism is that we maintain an illusion of knowing what the question is when we really do not. The promise is that we will be better off in the future by examining the concept of sustainability than by not examining it.

The sustainable tourism literature, including the chapters in this book, informs us as to the alternative pathways to the future. They suggest the types of pitfalls one may confront along those pathways, as well as ways of bridging them. They indicate how culture and the environment are inextricably linked in tourism development. The chapters suggest the enormous complexity of tourism development, particularly the type of development that is designed to be softer and oriented toward achieving socially important goals. Which pathways are selected and how the pitfalls are avoided are, of course, political and ethical decisions, not necessarily scientific ones.

References

Ackoff, R.L. (1974) *Redesigning the Future: a Systems Approach to Societal Problems.* John Wiley & Sons, New York.

Arnstein, S.R. (1969) A ladder of citizen participation. *Journal of the American Institute of Planners* 35, 216–224.

Bardwell, L. (1991) Problem framing: a perspective on environmental problem-solving. *Environmental Management* 15, 603–612.

Bossel, H. (1999) *Indicators for Sustainable Development: Theory, Method, Applications.* International Institute for Sustainable Development, Winnipeg, Manitoba, Canada.

Butler, R.W. (1996) The concept of carrying capacity for tourist destinations: dead or merely buried? *Progress in Tourism and Hospitality Research* 2, 283–292.

Cater, E. and Goodall, B. (1992) Must tourism destroy its resource base? In: Mannion, A.M. and Bowlby, S.R. (eds) *Environmental Issues in the 1990s.* John Wiley & Sons, Chichester, UK, pp. 309–323.

Font, X. and Tribe, J. (eds) (2000) *Forest Tourism and Recreation: Case Studies in Environmental Management.* CAB International, Wallingford, UK.

Friedmann, J. (1973) *Retracking America*. Anchor Press/Doubleday, Garden City, New York.

Gale, R.P. and Cordray, S.M. (1994) Making sense of sustainability: nine answers to 'what should be sustained?'. *Rural Sociology* 59, 314–332.

Getz, D. (1982) A rationale and methodology for assessing capacity to absorb tourism. *Ontario Geography* 19, 92–102.

Hall, C.M. (1999) Rethinking collaboration and partnership: a public policy perspective. *Journal of Sustainable Tourism* 7, 274–289.

Hall, C.M. and Lew, A.A. (eds) (1998) *Sustainable Tourism: a Geographical Perspective*. Addison Wesley Longman, Essex, UK.

Honey, M. (1999) *Ecotourism and Sustainable Development: Who Owns Paradise?* Island Press, Washington, DC.

Hunter, C.J. (1995) On the need to re-conceptualize sustainable tourism development. *Journal of Sustainable Tourism* 3, 155–165.

Innskeep, E. (1991) *Tourism Planning: an Integrated and Sustainable Development Approach*. Routledge, London.

Krumpe, E. and McCool, S.F. (1997) Role of public involvement in the Limits of Acceptable Change wilderness planning system. In: McCool, S.F. and Cole, D.N. (eds) *Limits of Acceptable Change and Related Planning Processes: Progress and Future Directions*. USDA Forest Service Intermountain Research Station, Missoula, Montana, pp. 16–20.

Lee, K.N. (1993) *Compass and Gyroscope: Integrating Science and Politics for the Environment*. Island Press, Washington, DC.

Lindberg, K., McCool, S. and Stankey, G. (1997) Rethinking carrying capacity. *Annals of Tourism Research* 24(2), 461–464.

Livermann, D.M., Hanson, M.E., Brown, B.J. and Merideth, R.W. Jr. (1988) Global sustainability: toward measurement. *Environmental Management* 12, 133–143.

Manning, E. (1996) Tourism: where are the limits? *Ecodecision* Spring, 35–39.

Marien, C. and Pizam, A. (1997) Implementing sustainable tourism development through citizen participation in the planning process. In: *Tourism, Development and Growth: the Challenge of Sustainability*. Routledge, London, pp. 164–178.

McCool, S.F. and Patterson, M.E. (2000) Trends in recreation, tourism and protected area planning. In: Gartner, W.C. and Lime, D.W. (eds) *Trends in Outdoor Recreation and Tourism*. CAB International, Wallingford, UK.

McCool, S.F. and Stankey, G.H. (1999) Searching for meaning and purpose in the quest for sustainability. School of Forestry, The University of Montana, Missoula, Montana.

McCool, S.F. and Watson, A.E. (eds.) (1995) *Linking Tourism, the Environment, and Sustainability*. Intermountain Research Station, USDA Forest Service, Ogden, Utah.

McCool, S.F., Guthrie, K. and Kapler-Smith, J. (2000) *Building Consensus: Legitimate Hope or Seductive Paradox?* USDA Forest Service, Rocky Mountain Research Station, Ft Collins, Colorado.

McCool, S.F., Moisey, R.N. and Nickerson, N. (2001) What should tourism sustain? Industry perceptions of useful indicators. *Journal of Travel Research* (in press).

McLaren, D. (1997) *Rethinking Tourism and Ecotravel: the Paving of Paradise and What You Can Do to Stop it.* Kumerian Press, West Hartford, Connecticut.

Meadows, D.H., Meadows, D.L., Randers, J. and Behrans III, W.W. (1972) *The Limits to Growth.* Universe Books, New York.

Moldan, B., Billharz, S. and Matravers, R. (eds) (1997) *SCOPE 58 Sustainability Indicators: a Report on the Project on Indicators of Sustainable Development.* John Wiley & Sons, Chichester, UK.

Pearce, D., Markandya, A. and Barbier, E.B. (1989) *Blueprint for a Green Economy.* Earthscan Publications, London.

Reed, M.G. (1999) Collaborative tourism planning as adaptive experiments in emergent tourism settings. *Journal of Sustainable Tourism* 7, 331–335.

Ritchie, J.R.B. (1999) Interest based formulation of tourism policy for environmentally sensitive destinations. *Journal of Sustainable Tourism* 7, 206–239.

Robinson, M. (1999) Collaboration and cultural consent: refocusing sustainable tourism. *Journal of Sustainable Tourism* 7, 379–397.

Rothman, H.K. (1998) *Devil's Bargains: Tourism in the Twentieth Century American West.* University Press of Kansas, Lawrence, Kansas.

Shindler, B. and Neburka, J. (1997) Public participation in forest planning – 8 attributes of success. *Journal of Forestry* 95, 17–19.

Shumway, N. (1991) *The Invention of Argentina.* University of California Press, Berkeley, California.

Stabler, M.J. (1997) *Tourism and Sustainability: from Principles to Practice.* CAB International, Wallingford, UK.

Stankey, G.H. and McCool, S.F. (1984) Carrying capacity in recreational settings: evolution, appraisal, and application. *Leisure Sciences* 6, 453–473.

Stankey, G.H., McCool, S.F., Clark, R.N. and Brown, P.J. (1999) Institutional and organizational challenges to managing natural resources for recreation: a social learning model. In: Burton, T. and Jackson, E. (eds) *Leisure Studies at the Millenium.* Venture Publishing, State College, Pennsylvania.

Swarbrooke, J. (1999) *Sustainable Tourism Management.* CAB International, Wallingford, UK.

Wahab, S. and Pigram, J.J. (eds) (1997) *Tourism, Development and Growth: the Challenge of Sustainability.* Routledge, New York.

Wildavsky, A. (1973) If planning is everything, maybe its nothing. *Policy Sciences* 4, 127–153.

World Commission on Environment and Development (1987) *Our Common Future.* Oxford University Press, Oxford.

Integrating Environmental and Social Concerns Over Tourism Development

Stephen F. McCool and R. Neil Moisey

School of Forestry, University of Montana, Missoula, Montana, USA

The environment, local social and cultural systems, and tourism development are, in many instances, inextricably linked in a relationship, most often illustrated by our inability to identify this relationship until made evident by manifestations of irreversible change. The authors in this section discuss the need for providing frameworks for the integration of social and environmental issues in tourism development. In so doing, they provide not only frameworks for such integration, but also illustrate, in several case studies, the inevitable and intricate relationships between these two major domains. The fundamental proposition here is that successful tourism development occurs only within a framework that considers explicitly impacts on these two domains.

While the environmental impacts of tourism are well understood and documented, the recent explosive growth of ecotourism has resulted in a shifting of these impacts to more primitive and fragile locations. With this shift, these impacts are more related to tourist activity rather than the development of a tourism superstructure. Leung *et al.* (Chapter 2) propose that the environmental impacts caused by nature-based tourism or ecotourism are similar to those studied in the field of recreation ecology – 'the scientific study of ecological changes associated with visitor activities including the role of influence factors'. They note that the level of impacts is influenced by environmental and use-related factors that are unique to each destination. Understanding these relationships provides information about the ecological sustainability of the tourism resources within ecotourism destinations.

Successful management of the environmental impacts of tourism implies not only an understanding of the relationship between use and the natural environment, but also the development of frameworks for implementing and measuring the outcomes of a variety of management options. Monitoring the outcomes of these options defines the success of each in terms of meeting sustainable objectives. Dawson (Chapter 3) illustrates one such framework, the Tourism Opportunity Spectrum (TOS), that 'considers a wide array of tourism opportunities over (space and) time'. The TOS is a 'rational and comprehensive' planning framework that focuses on what opportunities should be sustained, how success is measured, and can illustrate the potential impacts of alternative development scenarios.

Social and cultural systems can also show the strains of tourism development. Cultural anthropologists, sociologists, geographers and economists have long studied the social impacts of tourism. Again, understanding the implications of tourism development on both developed and developing cultures can guide development to more sustainable options. Based on Butler's resort cycle model, Ioannides (Chapter 4) discusses a longitudinal framework that explains the changing attitudes of various stakeholders toward sustainability objectives in the Mediterranean. Ioannides argues that support for sustainability occurs first in a top-down fashion as tourism develops along the cycle. Paradoxically, Ioannides notes that in the later phase of development, when economic gains decline and social and environmental costs are increasing, the various stakeholders are most likely to agree on adopting 'weak' approaches to sustainability.

For many natural areas, there is a duality of management objectives – the protection of the natural resources and the provision of visitor access. These often conflicting objectives inhibit formulating or meeting goals for sustainability. Popularity leads either to degradation or to access restrictions. Evans (Chapter 5) illustrates a proactive approach to this dilemma by providing a long-term sustainable solution that focuses on the causes of excess demand to Britain's national parks rather than restricting access to these areas. Evans argues that a 'community forest initiative' would create new areas of countryside in currently degraded urban fringe environments that would draw visitors away from the national parks, thereby reducing both social and environmental impacts.

Yellowstone National Park, the first designated national park in the US, provides yet another example of the potentially conflicting goals of resource protection and the provision of visitor experience. Yellowstone has been described as the 'crown jewel' of the national park system in the US and, as such, is one of the country's most visited natural areas. Meyer (Chapter 6) proposes that, in light of increasingly complex management issues and questions, the park, and particularly the 'park experience' might be better sustained by including the concepts of 'sense of place' and 'historical appropriateness' in developing management options. Meyer argues that managers concerned with protecting the 'sense of place' provided uniquely by Yellowstone National Park may be more sensitive to the environmental as well as experiential consequences of management decisions.

In the final chapter in this section (Chapter 7), Litchfield illustrates one paradox of ecotourism. 'Responsible tourism' should protect the resource base. But Litchfield argues that ecotourism in Uganda is exposing the great apes to life-threatening diseases and viruses, even though ecotours are being conducted in otherwise 'responsible' ways with regard to the environment.

The Role of Recreation Ecology in Sustainable Tourism and Ecotourism

2

Yu-Fai Leung[1], Jeffrey L. Marion[2] and Tracy A. Farrell[3]

[1]*Department of Parks, Recreation and Tourism Management, North Carolina State University, Raleigh, North Carolina, USA;* [2]*USGS Cooperative Park Studies Unit, Virginia Tech, Blacksburg, Virginia, USA;* [3]*School for Field Studies, Beverly, Massachusetts, USA*

Introduction

Sustainable tourism and ecotourism are two buzzwords that generate considerable debate in the tourism literature regarding their definitions, attainability, implementation and consequences. Much of this debate has revolved around the issue of sustainability (Butler, 1991; Cater and Lowman, 1994; Hunter and Green, 1995; Wall, 1997; Butler, 1999). Sustainable tourism has been defined, based on the principles of sustainable development, as tourism development that 'meets the needs of present tourists and host regions while protecting and enhancing opportunity for the future' (WTTC *et al.*, 1995, p. 30). Ecotourism, a fast-growing segment within the nature-based tourism industry, is generally believed to be a desired form of sustainable tourism. The Ecotourism Society defines ecotourism as 'responsible travel to natural areas that conserves the environment and sustains the well-being of local people' (Blangy and Wood, 1993, p. 32). This chapter restricts its focus to ecological sustainability in tourism and recreation contexts, although it is recognized that the concept of sustainability also encompasses economic and sociocultural dimensions.

One important criterion for evaluating the ecological sustainability of tourism is the extent to which undesirable environmental effects of tourism development and tourist activities are prevented or minimized. Previous research on the environmental impacts of tourism has demonstrated that tourism, if unchecked, can be as destructive as other industries (Cohen, 1978). Despite its environmentally benign image, ecotourism can also induce substantial ecological changes at protected areas (Wall, 1997).

Recreation ecology is the scientific study of ecological changes associated with visitor (e.g. tourists and recreationists) activities, including the role of influential factors. Knowledge of recreation ecology is therefore most useful in addressing the issue of ecological sustainability of tourism at the site and facility levels. While most components of tourism can result in environmental impacts, the scope of this chapter is limited to visitor-use impacts within protected areas, which play a critical role in sustainable tourism by maintaining biodiversity, protecting land from other more exploitative resource uses, and generating revenue for local people.

The objectives of this chapter are to demonstrate the relevancy of recreation ecology to tourism and ecotourism research and management, and to examine how recreation ecology can contribute to an increased understanding and better evaluation of ecological sustainability of tourism and ecotourism in protected areas. It begins by providing an overview of the environmental impacts of recreation and tourism, followed by a brief synthesis of recreation ecology knowledge. The connections between recreation ecology and tourism research are highlighted and followed by a discussion of some potential contributions recreation ecology can make to sustainable tourism and ecotourism research and management. The chapter concludes with recommendations for further integration between recreation ecology and tourism.

Environmental impacts of recreation and tourism

The linkage between tourism and the environment is well established in the literature (Edington and Edington, 1986; Farrell and Runyan, 1991; Mieczkowski, 1995). Environments provide the resource base essential for many forms of tourism, particularly nature-based tourism and ecotourism. On the other hand, the environment can be impacted positively or negatively by tourism. Tourism development and tourist activities can impact environments positively by facilitating nature conservation efforts. For example, Costa Rica has set aside more than 20% of its total land area as protected areas in response to ecotourism-related earnings (Sweeting et al., 1999).

Conversely, undesirable effects on ecological components, diminished ecological integrity, or degraded natural processes may also result from tourism development and operations. Tourism impacts may take a variety of forms, including habitat fragmentation and loss due to infrastructure development, travel-related air pollution, facility-related water and land pollution, and activity-related soil and vegetation damage and wildlife harassment. Rapid development and growth of tourism facilities in the Galapagos Islands, wildlife disturbance in East African safaris, coral-reef damage in the Great Barrier Reef of Australia, and mountain degradation in the Himalayas are some of the better-known cases of tourism impacts. Reviews of this topic are provided by Mathieson and Wall (1982), Buckley and Pannell (1990), HaySmith and Hunt (1995), and McCool and Watson (1995).

The scope of tourism's environmental impacts may be understood using an opportunity spectrum framework. The recreation opportunity spectrum, developed as a recreation planning tool (Clark and Stankey, 1979), has been adapted to adventure tourism (Butler and Waldbrook, 1991) and ecotourism contexts (Boyd and Butler, 1996; Dawson, Chapter 3 this volume). The common thread of these frameworks is a continuum of recreation or tourism opportunities, ranging from primitive settings and experiences to developed settings and experiences. Management interventions differ according to location along the spectrum. Figure 2.1 represents this continuum in the form of concentric circles, extending from a primitive core zone through an intermediate front-country buffer zone to an outer developed zone (Ceballos-Lascuráin, 1996, p. 184).

Environmental impacts of mass tourism are predominantly caused by infrastructure and facility development within the outer developed zone, where activities most commonly occur on man-made attractions such as resorts and other facilities (Fig. 2.1). Much of the earlier tourism–environment research has focused on impacts within this outer zone. Management interventions to such impacts in this zone primarily involve facility development and direct regulation of visitor activities.

Since nature-based tourism, and particularly ecotourism, has grown in popularity, tourism impacts have begun to shift in type, location and extent. Specifically, impacts are spreading into front-country buffer zones and primitive core zones (Fig. 2.1). Wall (1997) contends that ecotourism can be a damaging force due to its penetration into fragile, protected-area environments. In these primitive zones, tourist activities, rather than facility development, often become the main stressor to ecological communities.

Visitor impacts within protected areas are important management concerns because protected-area mandates typically require managers to protect natural resources or promote certain visitor experiences, such as solitude. Impacts are also socially significant since they compromise the quality of visitor experiences and adversely affect local populations (Ceballos-Lascuráin, 1996). An increasing number of developed and developing countries have attempted to address these

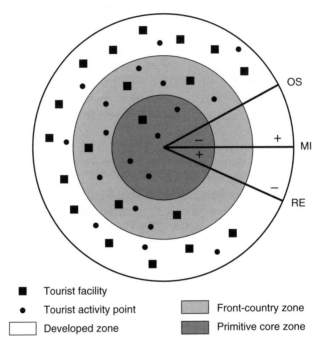

Tourist facility
Tourist activity point
Developed zone
Front-country zone
Primitive core zone

Fig. 2.1. Schematic representation of tourism development zoning and amount of acceptable impacts. OS, opportunity spectrum; MI, management intervention; RE, recreation ecology.

concerns by mandating national tourism or ecotourism strategies (Edwards *et al.*, 1998). Unfortunately, protected-area managers, particularly in developing countries, often have limited funding and expertise to perform ecological planning or implement timely management and maintenance programmes.

Recreation ecology: the scientific study of visitor impacts

Although the scientific study of visitor impacts can be traced back to the 1930s, considerable literature has appeared since the 1960s. In the US, this body of literature was developed in response to rapid growth of outdoor recreation activities and associated resource degradation in protected areas such as national parks and wilderness areas. Studies pertaining to soil and vegetative changes on trails and campsites comprise the majority of the literature (Cole, 1987; Kuss *et al.*, 1990; Leung and Marion, 2000).

Visitor-impact studies have focused on understanding environmental changes resulting from visitor activities and the influence of use-related, environmental and managerial factors. This knowledge has been applied in the selection of visitor- and site-management strategies and actions that prevent or minimize resource impacts. Such knowledge is especially critical in managing backcountry and wilderness areas because facility development and site-hardening practices commonly used in front-country or developed settings are usually considered inappropriate and are too costly in these primitive settings (Fig. 2.1).

Despite the long history of visitor-impact studies, only recently has the term *recreation ecology* been applied consistently to reference this literature. Most definitions refer to recreation ecology as a field of study that seeks to identify, assess, understand and manage resource impacts caused by park and protected-area visitors (Cole, 1989; Marion and Rogers, 1994; Leung and Marion, 1996; Liddle, 1997; Hammitt and Cole, 1998). The field of recreation ecology is multidisciplinary, with studies conducted by researchers from diverse disciplines, such as biology, ecology, forestry, geography, soil science and wildlife science. Only a small group of researchers has devoted their careers to this field of study (Cole, 1987; Leung and Marion, 2000).

Types and causes of visitor impacts

Visitor activities result in a variety of impacts affecting vegetation, soil, water and wildlife resources. For example, trampling by foot traffic, recreational animals or wheeled vehicles can easily damage ground vegetation or cause a change in composition or loss of cover (Hammitt and Cole, 1998). Such traffic quickly pulverizes organic materials such as leaf litter, exposing soil to compaction and erosion by water or wind. Compacted soils inhibit seed germination, root penetration, and water infiltration, increasing water runoff and erosion and decreasing soil moisture (Liddle, 1997). Surface runoff may carry soil, faecal material, soaps and other chemicals from recreation sites to streams, lakes and rivers, increasing sedimentation, nutrients and pathogens that may threaten water quality and human health (Kuss *et al.*, 1990).

The mere presence of visitors may cause animals to flee, temporarily or permanently displacing them from preferred habitats to other, often lower-quality habitats (Muthee, 1992). Displaced animals are greatly disadvantaged in competing with resident animals, are more susceptible to predation, and may have insufficient food or cover. Other animals may be attracted to visitors' food, obtaining food scraps, improperly stored food, or food offered directly by visitors. The development of unnatural food dependencies can alter natural wildlife activities and may cause increased predation, nutritional deficiencies and intestinal problems (Knight and Gutzwiller, 1995).

The type of visitor activity influences the severity of environmental impacts. For instance, trampling from foot traffic is less impacting than trampling from recreational animals, whose impact force per unit area is far greater (Liddle, 1997). Wheeled vehicles create linear depressions that may collect and accelerate water runoff and soil erosion (Wilson and Seney, 1994). The noise associated with motorized activities may displace animals from larger areas than human-powered types of recreation (Knight and Gutzwiller, 1995).

Impacts may occur wherever visitor activities are concentrated: on trails or campsites, along riverbanks and lakeshores, and at attraction features such as waterfalls, coral reefs or wildlife viewing areas. Visitor use is typically distributed unevenly within protected areas, with limited areas of concentrated activity, larger areas of dispersed activity, and the majority of areas with limited or no activity (Cole, 1987; Henry, 1992). Impact may be distributed as linear disturbance along trail corridors which, in turn, connect nodes of disturbance at recreation and attraction sites (Manning, 1979). At the local scale, impacts are also unevenly distributed within a campground and along a trail corridor, reflecting differential amounts of use or environmental durability, respectively.

The influence of environmental and use-related factors

Differences in environmental attributes may modify the type and extent of visitor impacts. For example, the flexible stems and other morphological characteristics of grasses make them far more resistant to trampling than the rigid stems of many broad-leafed herbs (Liddle, 1997). Differences in plant morphology and environmental conditions also create substantial variation in the ability of plants to recover following disturbance. Soil moisture and nutrients, growth rates, and length of growing season are other important factors that influence recovery rates. Similarly, soil types and associated properties vary in their compactability and erodibility, and their susceptibility to muddiness (Leung and Marion, 1996; Hammitt and Cole, 1998).

Substantial attention has been focused on the relationship between amount of use and amount of resource impact (Cole, 1987; Kuss et al., 1990). Previous research consistently documented a curvilinear response pattern for many types of impact, with substantial change occurring at low levels of use followed by diminished increases in impact as use rises to moderate and high levels (Marion and Merriam, 1985; Cole, 1987). For example, most vegetation groundcover is lost on trails and campsites shortly after they are opened for use. Figure 2.2 illustrates this generalized curvilinear use–impact relationship. Different environments or ecological communities may exhibit varying

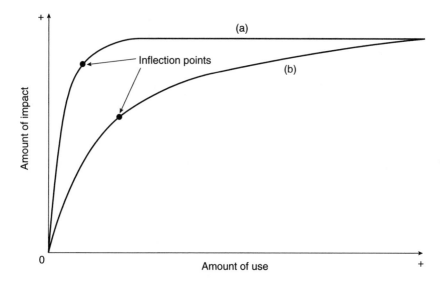

Fig. 2.2. Generalized relationships between visitor use and resultant resource impacts.

responses to impact force, as portrayed by two curves with different degrees of curvilinearity in Fig. 2.2: curve (a) indicates a highly sensitive environment, whereas curve (b) represents a less-sensitive environment with a more gradual response to changes in amount of use. An important management implication of this relationship is that most types of impact can be reduced substantially only if visitor use is limited to extremely low levels. Accordingly, an effective management strategy is to concentrate tourist activities on a small number of established trails and sites where impacts tend to stabilize (Hammitt and Cole, 1998; Leung and Marion, 1999b). This containment strategy is often accompanied by judicious selection of resistant sites to limit the severity and spatial extent of impact.

Visitor behaviour can also influence the type and extent of environmental impacts. Vegetation and soil disturbance may be avoided or minimized by selecting resistant surfaces or vegetation for travel and camping. The area of disturbance is minimized when visitors constrain their activities to existing disturbed surfaces – by staying on established trails, travelling single file in the centre of the tread, or camping within core areas of established sites. Such low-impact travel and camping skills are the focus of the *Leave No Trace* (LNT) outdoor skills and ethics programme, which will be described shortly.

Protected-area managers can avoid or minimize visitor impacts by influencing factors related to both visitation and the environment within which use occurs. Visitation can be shifted from fragile to resistant and resilient locations or away from critical wildlife habitats. Visitor activities can be concentrated on hardened sites or facilities maintained to sustain high levels of use. Higher-impact activities can be prohibited or restricted to areas best able to accommodate such use. Low-impact visitor behaviour can be encouraged through education, or required through regulations. Finally, rehabilitation efforts can facilitate recovery on sites unacceptably degraded by visitor use.

Recreation ecology in sustainable tourism and ecotourism

Recreation and tourism are similar with respect to their potentially undesirable effects on the environment, especially those associated with visitor activities and behaviour. As Mathieson and Wall (1982, p. 8) stated, 'recreationists and tourists may be found together at the same sites doing similar things'. Recreation ecology knowledge may therefore inform tourism and ecotourism resource management about ecological sustainability within protected areas. The dramatic worldwide growth of ecotourism within protected areas has prompted an expansion of environmental impact research, including recreation ecology. There is already evidence of increasing linkages between ecotourism and recreation ecology research.

First, there is an increasing number of empirical studies on ecological impacts of ecotourist activities in destination areas which are situated within the primitive core zone in Fig. 2.1. Table 2.1 illustrates the diversity of recent studies, many of which focused on site deterioration occurring along trails and campsites, the two major topics in the recreation ecology literature.

Secondly, ecotourism impact studies are increasingly applying techniques and procedures developed in the recreation ecology literature. For instance, Obua and Harding (1997) adapted procedures developed by Cole (1987) in their survey of campsite and trail conditions in Kibale National Park in Uganda. Assessment procedures developed by Marion (1991, 1994) for US national parks have recently been adapted for assessing visitor impacts in Torre del Paine National Park in Chile (Farrell and Marion, 2001) and eight protected areas in Belize and Costa Rica (Farrell and Marion, 1999). Similar procedures are also being incorporated into monitoring manuals developed by the National Outdoor Leadership School for application in Central and South American protected areas.

Thirdly, there is increasing cross-fertilization between recreation ecology and tourism literature. This is, in part, reflected by the increasing number of citations of recreation ecology studies in the tourism literature (e.g. Valentine, 1992; Wall, 1997). Furthermore, Liddle's (1997) comprehensive text on recreation ecology added

Table 2.1. Some recent examples of investigations on the ecological impacts of ecotourist activities.

Study area	Stressor activities	Impacted components	Methods	Impact indicators	Source
Kilimanjaro National Park, Tanzania	Hiking; firewood collection	Trail conditions; woody plants	Systematic point sampling; quadrats method	Trail widths and incision depths; damaged trees	Newmark and Nguye (1991)
Tortuguero National Park, Costa Rica	Presence and behaviour of tourists	Nesting turtles	Census of nests and observation of nesting behaviour	Number, location and type of nests	Jacobson and Lopez (1994)
Tikal National Park, Guatemala	Creation and use of trails/ roads	Mammals and birds	Transect surveys; distance sampling	Population densities; animal behaviour	Hidinger (1996)
Costa Rica and Ecuador	Hiking	Trail conditions	Rainfall simulation experiments	Compaction; infiltration; soil erosion rate	Wallin and Harden (1996)
Kibale National Park, Uganda	Camping and hiking	Campsite and trail conditions	Condition assessment surveys	Campsite and trail condition indicators	Obua and Harding (1997)
Kibale National Park, Uganda	Campsite development and activities	Vegetation	Plot sampling	Population and diversity indices; species composition	Obua (1997)
Torres del Paine National Park, Chile	Hiking and camping	Campsite and trail conditions	Condition assessment surveys	Campsite and trail condition indicators	Farrell and Marion (2001)
Loxahatchee National Wildlife Refuge, Florida, USA	Walking; birdwatching	Birds (herons and ibis)	Behaviour observations	Foraging and avoidance behaviour	Burger and Gochfeld (1998)

'ecotourism' in the subtitle and included many ecotourism examples. Finally, book chapters published recently were devoted specifically to recreation ecology research and its application to ecotourism resource management (Marion and Leung, 1998; Marion and Farrell, 2001).

Fourthly, recreation ecologists are increasingly involved in training park staff at ecotourism destinations. For example, recreation ecologists David Cole, Tracy Farrell, Jeffrey Marion and Christopher Monz have been involved in park manager training courses in South America. They and other researchers in this field are increasingly consulted by researchers and professionals in the tourism and ecotourism fields.

Finally, non-government organizations involved in ecotourism and protected-area management (e.g. Conservation International, The Nature Conservancy, the RARE Center for Tropical Education and The Ecotourism Society) are becoming increasingly more interested in research projects and workshops related to visitor-impact planning, assessment and management.

Despite these growing connections, much more can be done to enhance the integration. Following is a discussion of potential contributions recreation ecology can make to sustainable tourism and ecotourism research. Three major contributions identified are: (i) visitor-use planning and management; (ii) impact assessment and monitoring; and (iii) visitor education and communication.

Potential contributions

Visitor-use planning and management

Carrying capacity was once a guiding concept in the recreation and tourism management literature. Due to its conceptual elusiveness, lack of management utility and inconsistent effectiveness in minimizing visitor impacts (Lindberg *et al.*, 1997; Lindberg and McCool, 1998; Buckley, 1999b), it has largely been re-conceptualized into management-by-objectives approaches. The Limits of Acceptable Change (LAC) framework developed by the US Forest Service (Stankey *et al.*, 1985), and the Visitor Experience and Resource Protection (VERP) framework adapted from the LAC concept by the US National Park Service (NPS, 1997), are two planning and management decision-making processes based on this new understanding of carrying capacity. Since its first application in the mid-1980s, the LAC process has been applied to numerous protected areas in the US, and has recently been adapted and modified for use in sustainable tourism and ecotourism contexts (e.g. Wallace, 1993; McCool, 1994; Harroun and Boo, 1995; Borrie *et al.*, 1998; Farrell, 1999).

The LAC and VERP frameworks emphasize setting management goals, for which resource and social condition indicators and standards (or acceptable limits) are developed in consultation with professionals and the concerned public. Recreation ecology studies contribute information about the types and magnitude of resource impacts that occur as a result of visitor use and on the selection of appropriate impact indicators. This research has also produced impact assessment and monitoring (IA&M) procedures that are an integral part of these frameworks, providing baseline and monitoring data for evaluating standards and the effectiveness of management strategies and actions.

Managers can make informed decisions when selecting effective visitor-impact management strategies and actions with recreation ecology knowledge. For example, the merits of visitor containment versus visitor dispersal as an impact management strategy constitute a perpetual debate in the recreation and tourism management literature (Mieczkowski, 1995; Hammitt and Cole, 1998). As previously noted, the curvilinear use–impact relationship (Fig. 2.2) identified in previous studies suggests that visitor-containment strategy is often more effective in minimizing impacts in high-use settings (Cole, 1989; Leung and Marion, 1999b). An understanding of recreation ecology is also useful in supporting certain management actions, such as selecting resistant locations for facilities, trails and campsites, or in formulating effective educational messages (Nelson, 1994). Price (1983) provided an excellent example from Canada's Banff National Park, where trail-route planning decisions were enhanced by research that documented substantial variations in the susceptibility of vegetation types to hikers' trampling impacts.

Impact assessment and monitoring

Impact assessment and monitoring programmes can address the potential and observed impacts related to tourism and ecotourism development and operations. The concepts and procedures of environmental impact assessment (EIA) are incorporated into tourism contexts for their predictive, assessment and monitoring capabilities (Williams, 1994; Hunter and Green, 1995). Methods and procedures for tourism-specific EIAs are still rudimentary in development (Warnken and Buckley, 1998; Warnken and Buckley, 2000). There is also increasing interest in adopting the concept of post-impact environmental auditing (EA) to tourism management (Ding and Pigram, 1995). Tourism's EIAs are primarily oriented toward the potential physical and environmental effects of tourism-related infrastructure and facility development projects. Tourism's EAs, on the other hand, focus on monitoring the broad-scale environmental performance of tourism operations.

IA&M programmes focusing on tourist activities are increasingly recognized as a complementary part of traditional EIAs and EAs. These activity-based IA&M programmes are particularly valuable for ecotourism destinations, as the ecological effects of tourist activities are of particular concern in these areas. Standardized IA&M protocols for monitoring visitor impacts to trails and recreation sites are being developed (Marion, 1995; Leung and Marion, 1999a). Unfortunately, in many ecotourism destinations, particularly in developing countries, insufficient staffing and experience have prevented such programmes from becoming firmly established components of decision-making processes. The integration and continuation of IA&M programmes require that they be low cost, efficient and require minimal specialized knowledge or equipment (Buckley, 1999a).

Another related issue in sustainable tourism is the development of sustainability indicators (McCool and Moisey, Chapter 1 this volume). The World Tourism Organization has proposed a set of indicators for sustainable tourism management (IWGIST, 1993; Manning, 1999). Most of these are *macro-scale* indicators, with none currently included to evaluate tourist activity impacts at the micro-scale or site level. Due to its scale of focus, recreation ecology may complement these efforts by identifying and selecting site-level sustainability indicators that address tourist activity impacts. This contribution is most effective at local scales, and when the impacts are associated directly with tourist activities and behaviour. Nevertheless, the processes and procedures of indicator selection and measurements in recreation ecology research may inform similar processes in selecting macro-scale sustainability indicators.

Visitor education and communication

Education can also play a pivotal role in reducing environmental impacts from tourism. Educational efforts apply to three target groups: tourism developers, tour operators and tourists. Environmental codes of conduct for tourism developers frequently focus on energy saving and waste minimization. Codes of conduct for tour operators and tourists often relate to social-cultural and wildlife protection issues (e.g. Blangy and Wood, 1993; Boo, 1993). In the US, several land management agencies and the National Outdoor Leadership School developed the LNT programme that communicates outdoor skills and ethics targeted to park and wilderness visitors. This programme is based on a set of LNT principles used to communicate low-impact hiking and camping practices. An important component of this programme is the provision of specialized 'Masters' courses, the graduates of which disseminate and promote LNT knowledge and practices in 'Trainer' courses, and through printed literature and personal visitor contacts. The LNT programme is expanding to Mexico, Chile, Puerto Rico and other countries where ecotourism is booming.

Similarly, the Ecotourism Society's Guidelines for Nature Tour Operators instructs operators and guides to encourage less impacting behaviours and practices (Wood, 1993).

Recreation ecology knowledge has, and will, continue to provide a scientific basis for low-impact educational guidelines and practices (Hampton and Cole, 1995). Such knowledge can be applied to inform visitors about selecting resistant travel routes and campsites, building low-impact campfires, and how to dispose of human waste properly. Other important applications include the development of low-impact practices for viewing wildlife, motorized travel, travelling with recreational stock and minimizing visitor crowding and conflict.

Concluding remarks

The growth in nature-based tourism and ecotourism is likely to continue with increased global environmental awareness, improved access to remote portions of the world and an ageing and better-educated population. While the Agenda 21 for Travel and Tourism advocates a global effort devoted to conservation, protection and restoration of the Earth's ecosystem through the power of tourism (WTTC *et al.*, 1995), such effort would be challenged if tourism impacts continue to intensify and proliferate. As tourism professionals and researchers address the issues of ecological sustainability, tourism and ecotourism research from an ecological perspective will become increasingly important (Marion and Leung, 1998; Buckley, 1999b; Tyler and Dangerfield, 1999).

This chapter has introduced the field of recreation ecology to sustainable tourism and ecotourism researchers and practitioners. It demonstrates the close and growing links between recreation ecology and tourism research, and discusses three potential contributions recreation ecology knowledge can make to enhance the symbiotic tourism–environment relationship (Budowski, 1976). Previous recreation ecology studies have identified the diversity of visitor impacts, influential factors and their interactions, indicating the complexity of the carrying capacity concept and fostering its reconceptualization into management-by-objectives frameworks. The curvilinear use–impact model (Fig. 2.2) established in the recreation ecology literature provides important insights for protected-area managers in formulating impact-management strategies and actions. The selection of sustainability indicators for tourism, a critical component of sustainable tourism (McCool and Moisey, Chapter 1 this volume), also benefits from recreation ecology research with respect to site-level and activity-related indicators. Finally, the LNT and other low-impact visitor-education programmes grounded in recreation ecology knowledge provide an excellent model and specific examples for developing tourism/ecotourism guidelines and activity codes.

Several recommendations are provided below to foster further integration between recreation ecology and tourism and ecotourism research, with respect to ecological sustainability:

1. Recreation ecology should be recognized as an integral component in the recreation–tourism–environment research theme. Farrell and Runyan (1991) settled on 'ecological tourism', when they failed to find a term for the tourism–environment research theme. Neither did Potts and Harrill (1998) nor Tyler and Dangerfield (1999) identify the field of recreation ecology in their searches of ecological perspectives for sustainable tourism and ecotourism. In order to facilitate the integration and communication of its knowledge base, tourism students, professionals and researchers should be introduced to recreation ecology as a related and supporting field of study.

2. Recreation ecology should be incorporated into sustainable tourism, and particularly into ecotourism, research agendas. Greater numbers of recreation impact studies with rigorous research designs should be conducted in existing and proposed ecotourism destinations to increase our awareness about visitor impact problems, assessment techniques and appropriate management strategies.

3. As the knowledge base of recreation ecology continues to grow, its findings and techniques should be applied and adapted to tourism and ecotourism contexts whenever appropriate. Areas in which the applications would be fruitful include visitor-use planning and management, carrying-capacity determinations, visitor education and the establishment of visitor-impact assessment and monitoring programmes.

4. Communication among recreation ecologists, tourism researchers and professionals, and protected-area managers should be enhanced through publications, conferences and training. Such communication could help to build a research partnership to further our understanding of recreation and tourism impacts, and to develop the conceptual frameworks needed to guide future research efforts (Andereck, 1995).

References

Andereck, K.L. (1995) Environmental consequences of tourism: a review of recent research. In: McCool, S.F. and Watson, A.E. (comps) *Linking Tourism, the Environment, and Sustainability*. General Technical Report INT-GTR-323, USDA Forest Service, Intermountain Research Station, Ogden, Utah, pp. 77–81.

Blangy, S. and Wood, M.E. (1993) Developing and implementing ecotourism guidelines for wildlands and neighboring communities. In: Lindberg, K.

and Hawkins, D.E. (eds). *Ecotourism: a Guide for Planners and Managers.* The Ecotourism Society, North Bennington, Vermont, pp. 32–54.

Boo, E. (1993) Ecotourism planning for protected areas. In: Lindberg, K. and Hawkins, D.E. (eds) *Ecotourism: a Guide for Planners and Managers.* The Ecotourism Society, North Bennington, Vermont, pp. 15–31.

Borrie, W.T., McCool, S.F. and Stankey, G.H. (1998) Protected area planning principles and strategies. In: Lindberg, K., Wood, M.E. and Engeldrum, D. (eds) *Ecotourism: a Guide for Planners and Managers*, 2nd edn. The Ecotourism Society, North Bennington, Vermont, pp. 133–154.

Boyd, S.W. and Butler, R.W. (1996) Managing ecotourism: an opportunity spectrum approach. *Tourism Management* 17, 557–566.

Buckley, R. (1999a) Tools and indicators for managing tourism in parks. *Annals of Tourism Research* 26, 208–211.

Buckley, R. (1999b) An ecological perspective on carrying capacity. *Annals of Tourism Research* 26, 705–708.

Buckley, R. and Pannell, J. (1990) Environmental impacts of tourism and recreation in national parks and conservation reserves. *Journal of Tourism Studies* 1, 24–32.

Budowski, G. (1976) Tourism and environmental conservation: conflict, coexistence, or symbiosis? *Environmental Conservation* 3, 27–31.

Burger, J. and Gochfeld, M. (1998) Effects of ecotourists on bird behavior at Loxahatchee National Wildlife Refuge, Florida. *Environmental Conservation* 25, 13–21.

Butler, R.W. (1991) Tourism, environment and sustainable development. *Environmental Conservation* 18, 201–209.

Butler, R.W. (1999) Sustainable tourism: a state-of-the-art review. *Tourism Geographies* 1(1), 7–25.

Butler, R.W. and Waldbrook, L.A. (1991) A new planning tool: the tourism opportunity spectrum. *Journal of Tourism Studies* 2(1), 2–14.

Cater, E. and Lowman, G. (eds) (1994) *Ecotourism: a Sustainable Option?* John Wiley & Sons, Chichester.

Ceballos-Lascuráin, H. (1996) *Tourism, Ecotourism, and Protected Areas: the State of Nature-based Tourism Around the World and Guidelines for Its Development.* IUCN, Gland, Switzerland.

Clark, R.N. and Stankey, G.H. (1979) *The Recreation Opportunity Spectrum: a Framework for Planning, Management, and Research.* Research Paper PNW–98, USDA Forest Service, Pacific Northwest Forest Experiment Station, Portland, Oregon.

Cohen, E. (1978) The impact of tourism on the physical environment. *Annals of Tourism Research* 2, 215–237.

Cole, D.N. (1987) Research on soil and vegetation in wilderness: a state-of-knowledge review. In: Lucas, R.C. (ed.) *Proceedings National Wilderness Research Conference: Issues, State-of-Knowledge, Future Directions.* General Technical Report INT–220, USDA Forest Service, Intermountain Research Station, Ogden, Utah, pp. 135–177.

Cole, D.N. (1989) Recreation ecology: what we know, what geographers can contribute. *Professional Geographer* 41, 143–148.

Ding, P. and Pigram, J.J. (1995) Environmental audits: an emerging concept in sustainable tourism development. *Journal of Tourism Studies* 6(2), 2–10.

Edington, J.M. and Edington, M.A. (1986) *Ecology, Recreation and Tourism.* Cambridge University Press, Cambridge, UK.

Edwards, S.N., McLaughlin, W.J. and Ham, S.H. (1998) *Comparative Study of Ecotourism Policy in the Americas–1998.* Inter-Sectoral Unit for Tourism, Organization of American States, Washington, DC.

Farrell, B.H. and Runyan, D. (1991) Ecology and tourism. *Annals of Tourism Research* 18, 26–40.

Farrell, T.A. (1999) Visitor impact assessment and management for protected areas in Central and South America. PhD thesis, Virginia Polytechnic Institute and State University, Blacksburg, Virginia.

Farrell, T.A. and Marion, J.L. (1999) Identification and management of visitor impact problems within protected areas in Costa Rica and Belize. In: Harmon, D. (ed.) *On the Frontiers of Conservation: Proceedings of the 10th Conference on Research and Resource Management in Parks and on Public Lands.* The George Wright Society, Hancock, Michigan, pp. 62–67.

Farrell, T.A. and Marion, J.L. (2001) Trail impacts and trail management related to ecotourism visitation at Torres del Paine, Chile. *Leisure: Journal of the Canadian Association of Leisure Studies* (in press).

Hammitt, W.E. and Cole, D.N. (1998) *Wildland Recreation: Ecology and Management,* 2nd edn. John Wiley & Sons, New York.

Hampton, B. and Cole, D. (1995) *Soft Paths: How to Enjoy the Wilderness without Harming It,* revised and updated. Stackpole Books, Harrisburg, Pennsylvania.

Harroun, L.A. and Boo, E.A. (1995) *The Search for Visitor Carrying Capacity.* World Wildlife Fund, Washington, DC.

HaySmith, L. and Hunt, J.D. (1995) Nature tourism: impacts and management. In: Knight, R.L. and Gutzwiller, K.J. (eds) *Wildlife and Recreationists: Coexistence through Management and Research.* Island Press, Washington, DC, pp. 203–220.

Henry, W.R. (1992) Carrying capacity, ecological impacts and visitor attitudes: applying research to park planning and management. In: Gakahu, C.G. and Goode, B.E. (eds) *Ecotourism and Sustainable Development in Kenya.* Wildlife Conservation International, Nairobi, pp. 49–62.

Hidinger, L.A. (1996) Measuring the impacts of ecotourism on animal populations: a case study of Tikal National Park, Guatemala. In: Malek-Zadeh, E. (ed.) *The Ecotourism Equation: Measuring the Impacts.* Bulletin Series No. 99, Yale University, School of Forestry and Environmental Studies, New Haven, Connecticut, pp. 49–59.

Hunter, C.J. and Green, H. (1995) *Tourism and the Environment: a Sustainable Relationship?* Routledge, London.

IWGIST (International Working Group on Indicators of Sustainable Tourism) (1993) *Indicators for the Sustainable Management of Tourism – Report of the International Working Group on Indicators of Sustainable Tourism to the Environment Committee, World Tourism Organization.* International Institute for Sustainable Development, Winnipeg, Manitoba.

Jacobson, S.K. and Lopez, A.F. (1994) Biological impacts of ecotourism: tourists and nesting turtles in Tortuguero National Park, Costa Rica. *Wildlife Society Bulletin* 22, 414–419.

Knight, R.L. and Gutzwiller, K.J. (eds) (1995) *Wildlife and Recreationists:*

Coexistence through Management and Research. Island Press, Washington, DC.

Kuss, F.R., Graefe, A.R. and Vaske, J.J. (1990) *Visitor Impact Management: a Review of Research.* National Parks and Conservation Association, Washington, DC.

Leung, Y.-F. and Marion, J.L. (1996) Trail degradation as influenced by environmental factors: a state-of-knowledge review. *Journal of Soil and Water Conservation* 51, 130–136.

Leung, Y.-F. and Marion, J.L. (1999a) Assessing trail conditions in protected areas: an application of a problem-assessment method in Great Smoky Mountains National Park, USA. *Environmental Conservation* 26, 270–279.

Leung, Y.-F. and Marion, J.L. (1999b) Spatial strategies for managing visitor impacts in national parks. *Journal of Park and Recreation Administration* 17(4), 20–38.

Leung, Y.-F. and Marion, J.L. (2000) Recreation impacts and management in wilderness: a state-of-knowledge review. In: Cole, D.N., McCool, S.F., Borrie, W.T. and O'Loughlin, J. (eds) *Wilderness Science in a Time of Change Conference, Vol 5, Wilderness Ecosystems, Threats and Managements.* Proceedings RMRS-P-15-Vol-5, USDA Forest Service, Rocky Mountain Research Station, Ogden, Utah, pp. 23–48.

Liddle, M.J. (1997) *Recreation Ecology: the Ecological Impact of Outdoor Recreation and Ecotourism.* Chapman & Hall, London.

Lindberg, K. and McCool, S.F. (1998) A critique of environmental carrying capacity as a means of managing the effects of tourism development. *Environmental Conservation* 25, 291–292.

Lindberg, K., McCool, S.F. and Stankey, G.H. (1997) Rethinking carrying capacity. *Annals of Tourism Research* 24, 461–465.

Manning, R.E. (1979) Impacts of recreation on riparian soils and vegetation. *Water Resources Bulletin* 15, 30–43.

Manning, T. (1999) Indicators of tourism sustainability. *Tourism Management* 20, 179–181.

Marion, J.L. (1991) *Developing a Natural Resource Inventory and Monitoring Program for Visitor Impacts on Recreation Sites: a Procedural Manual.* Natural Resources Report NPS/NRVT/NRR–91/06, USDI National Park Service, Denver, Colorado.

Marion, J.L. (1994) *An Assessment of Trail Conditions in Great Smoky Mountains National Park.* Research/Resources Management Report, USDI National Park Service, Southeast Region, Atlanta, Georgia.

Marion, J.L. (1995) Capabilities and management utility of recreation impact monitoring programs. *Environmental Management* 19, 763–771.

Marion, J.L. and Farrell, T.A. (1998) Managing ecotourism visitation in protected areas. In: Lindberg, K., Wood, M.E. and Engeldrum, D. (eds) *Ecotourism: a Guide for Planners and Managers*, 2nd edn. The Ecotourism Society, North Bennington, Vermont, pp. 155–182.

Marion, J.L. and Leung, Y.-F. (1998) International recreation ecology research and ecotourism resource management. In: Hammitt, W.E. and Cole, D.N. *Wildland Recreation: Ecology and Management*, 2nd edn. John Wiley & Sons, New York, pp. 328–346.

Marion, J.L. and Merriam, L.C. (1985) *Recreational Impacts on Well-*

Established Campsites in the Boundary Waters Canoe Area Wilderness. Station Bulletin AD-SB-2502, University of Minnesota, Agricultural Experiment Station, St. Paul, Minnesota.

Marion, J.L. and Rogers, C.S. (1994) The applicability of terrestrial visitor impact management strategies to the protection of coral reefs. *Ocean and Coastal Management* 22, 153–163.

Mathieson, A. and Wall, G. (1982) *Tourism: Economic, Physical and Social Impacts.* Longman, London.

McCool, S.F. (1994) Planning for sustainable nature dependent tourism development: the limits of acceptable change system. *Tourism Recreation Research* 19(2), 51–55.

McCool, S.F. and Watson, A.E. (eds) (1995) *Linking Tourism, the Environment, and Sustainability.* General Technical Report INT-GTR–323, USDA Forest Service, Intermountain Research Station, Ogden, Utah.

Mieczkowski, Z. (1995) *Environmental Issues of Tourism and Recreation.* University Press of America, Lanham, Maryland.

Muthee, L.W. (1992) Ecological impacts of tourist use on habitats and pressure-point animal species. In: Gakahu, C.G. (ed.) *Tourist Attitudes and Use Impacts in Maasai Mara National Reserve: Proceedings of a Workshop Organized by Wildlife Conservation International.* Wildlife Conservation International, Nairobi, pp. 18–38.

Nelson, J.G. (1994) The spread of ecotourism: some planning implications. *Environmental Conservation* 21, 248–255.

Newmark, W.D. and Nguye, P.A. (1991) Recreational impacts of tourism along the Marangu route in Kilimanjaro National Park. In: Newmark, W.D. (ed.) *The Conservation of Mount Kilimanjaro.* IUCN, Gland, Switzerland, pp. 47–51.

NPS (USDI National Park Service) (1997) *The Visitor Experience and Resource Protection (VERP) Framework: a Handbook for Planners and Managers.* Publication No. NPS D-1215, USDI National Park Service, Denver Service Center, Denver, Colorado.

Obua, J. (1997) The potential, development and ecological impact of ecotourism in Kibale National Park, Uganda. *Journal of Environmental Management* 50, 27–38.

Obua, J. and Harding, D.M. (1997) Environmental impact of ecotourism in Kibale National Park, Uganda. *Journal of Sustainable Tourism* 5, 213–223.

Potts, T.D. and Harrill, R. (1998) Enhancing communities for sustainability: a travel ecology approach. *Tourism Analysis* 3, 133–142.

Price, M.F. (1983) Management planning in the Sunshine Area of Canada's Banff National Park. *Parks* 7(4), 6–10.

Stankey, G.H., Cole, D.N., Lucas, R.C., Petersen, M.E. and Frissell, S.S. (1985) *The Limits of Acceptable Change (LAC) System for Wilderness Planning.* General Technical Report INT-176, USDA Forest Service, Intermountain Research Station, Ogden, Utah.

Sweeting, J.E.N., Bruner, A.J. and Rosenfeld, A.B. (1999) *The Green Host Effect: an Integrated Approach to Sustainable Tourism and Resort Development.* Conservation International, Washington, DC.

Tyler, D. and Dangerfield, J.M. (1999) Ecosystem tourism: a resource-based philosophy for tourism. *Journal of Sustainable Tourism* 7(2), 146–158.

Valentine, P.S. (1992) Nature-based tourism. In: Weiler, B. and Hall, C.M. (eds) *Special Interest Tourism*. Halsted Press, New York, pp. 105–127.

Wall, G. (1997) Is ecotourism sustainable? *Environmental Management* 21, 483–491.

Wallace, G.N. (1993) Visitor management: lessons from Galapagos National Park. In: Lindberg, K. and Hawkins, D.E. (eds) *Ecotourism: a Guide for Planners and Managers*. The Ecotourism Society, North Bennington, Vermont, pp. 55–81.

Wallin, T.R. and Harden, C.P. (1996) Estimating trail-related soil erosion in humid tropics: Jatun Sacha, Ecuador, and La Selva, Costa Rica. *Ambio* 25, 517–522.

Warnken, J. and Buckley, R. (1998) Scientific quality of tourism environmental impact assessment. *Journal of Applied Ecology* 35, 1–8.

Warnken, J. and Buckley, R. (2000) Monitoring diffuse impacts: Australian tourism developments. *Environmental Management* 25, 453–461.

Williams, P.W. (1994) Frameworks for assessing tourism's environmental impacts. In: Ritchie, J.R.B. and Goeldner, C. (eds) *Travel, Tourism, and Hospitality Research: a Handbook for Managers and Researchers*, 2nd edn. John Wiley & Sons, New York, pp. 425–436.

Wilson, J.P. and Seney, J.P. (1994) Erosional impact of hikers, horses, motorcycles, and off-road bicycles on mountain trails of Montana. *Mountain Research and Development* 14, 77–88.

Wood, M.E. (1993) *Ecotourism Guidelines for Nature Tour Operators*. The Ecotourism Society, North Bennington, Vermont.

WTTC (World Travel and Tourism Council), WTO (World Tourism Organization), and EC (Earth Council) (1995) *Agenda 21 for the Travel and Tourism Industry: Towards Environmentally Sustainable Development*. WTTC, London.

Ecotourism and Nature-based Tourism: One End of the Tourism Opportunity Spectrum?

Chad P. Dawson

SUNY College of Environmental Science and Forestry, Syracuse, New York, USA

Introduction

Ecotourism and nature-based tourism can be defined as forms of sustainable development when they are limited in scale and minimize environmental and social impacts. While there is a lack of consensus on the exact meaning of the terms 'ecotourism' and 'nature-based tourism', they will be used here to outline a more systematic approach to regional planning in and around undeveloped environments. For example, consideration of the positive and negative impacts of tourism development can be expressed in ecotourism goals: (i) to benefit local communities without overwhelming their social and economic systems; (ii) to protect the environmental, natural and cultural resource base on which the tourism depends; and (iii) to require the ethical behaviour of recreational users and tourists, as well as the supporting commercial recreation and tourism operators.

Over the past decade, ecotourism and nature-based tourism have been the subject of many conferences, professional journals, books, and project reports (Boo, 1990; Kusler, 1991; Whelan, 1991; Tabata *et al.*, 1992; Crotts, 1994; Hall and Johnston, 1995; McCool and Watson, 1995; Eagles and Nilsen, 1997). There are numerous definitions and varied frames of reference as to what constitutes either ecotourism or nature-based tourism. Generally, the concept of ecotourism or nature-based tourism has focused on environmental considerations for tourism development and management (Lindberg and Hawkins, 1993; Economic and Social Commission for Asia and the Pacific,

1995; Ceballos-Lascuráin, 1996) and codes of conduct for environmental responsibility among tourists, host communities and the tourism industry (United Nations Environmental Programme, 1995). The tourism literature suggests that ecotourism and nature-based tourism, like other types of tourism, need to consider a wide array of social, environmental and economic conditions, along with the capacity to sustain those conditions and the tourism experience or opportunities over time (Murphy, 1985; Mathieson and Wall, 1987; Ziffer, 1989; Boo, 1990; Kusler, 1991; Whelan, 1991; Lindberg and Hawkins, 1993; Gunn, 1994; Muller, 1994; McCool and Watson, 1995; Ceballos-Lascuráin, 1996; Eagles and Nilsen, 1997).

Ecotourism and nature-based tourism have great marketing appeal to travelling publics with environmental interests and concerns. Some operators and tourism areas have used this appeal to attract more tourists and exploit the concept, but without supporting the sustainability of the social, economic and environmental conditions (McLaren, 1998; Honey, 1999). Such exploitation of the mass market appeal of ecotravel and ecotourism, especially to exotic environments, has been termed 'green washing'. McLaren uses the term 'ecotravel' to include both ecotourism and nature-based tourism and notes that:

> They offer a participatory experience in the natural environment. At its best ecotravel promotes environmental conservation, international understanding and cooperation, political and economic empowerment of local populations, and cultural preservation. When ecotravel fulfills its mission, it not only has a minimal impact, but the local environment and community actually benefit from the experience and even own or control it. At its worst ecotravel is environmentally destructive, economically exploitive, culturally insensitive, 'greenwashed' travel
>
> (McLaren, 1998, pp. 97–98)

Wight (1993) warns that the view of ecotourism as a marketing opportunity, or 'eco-sell', misses the key principles of ecotourism to manage conservation and have minimal development in a manner that is compatible, complementary and sustainable. Orams (1995) argues for the formulation of tourism management objectives and indicator measures to monitor the evolution of ecotourism into a more desirable form of tourism. Wight offers eight ecotourism principles for the development and management of ecotourism that may be the basis for such indicators:

- it should not degrade the resource and should be developed in an environmentally sound manner;
- it should provide first-hand, participatory, and enlightened experiences;
- it should involve education among all parties – local communities, government, non-government organizations, industry, and tourists (before, during, and after the trip);

- it should encourage all-party recognition of the intrinsic values of the resource;
- it should involve acceptance of the resource on its own terms, and in recognition of its limits, which involves supply-oriented management;
- it should promote understanding and involve partnerships between many players, which could include government, non-government organizations, industry, scientists, and locals (both before and during operations);
- it should promote moral and ethical responsibilities and behaviors towards the natural and cultural environment, by all players;
- it should provide long-term benefits – to the resource, to the local community, and to industry (benefits may be conservation, scientific, social, cultural, or economic).

(Wight, 1993, p. 3)

Given these types of principles and the reaction against the impacts of mass tourism on natural and cultural environments, ecotourism has been defined as one end of a continuum of tourism development. However, as Wall (1997) points out, ecotourism is not by itself sustainable, rather it should be considered one component of sustainable development, since it must compete with other uses of the social, economic and environmental resources of a region.

Regional planning for tourism, especially sustainable development of tourism, requires a systematic approach that considers what opportunities are provided and their management. Several authors have offered a planning framework that adapts the Recreation Opportunity Spectrum (ROS) to tourism in the form of a Tourism Opportunity Spectrum (TOS) (Butler and Waldbrook, 1991) and to ecotourism in the form of an Ecotourism Opportunity Spectrum (ECOS) (Boyd and Butler, 1996). These frameworks outline tourism opportunities and conceptual management approaches.

This study attempts to further the evolution of the ROS into a TOS using the definitions of ecotourism and nature-based tourism, opportunities to be provided and setting characteristics. The formulation of a TOS creates a system of reference points so that regional planners can compare the type of opportunities to be provided at a site or in an area with the opportunities in another area. Given such a framework, regional planners then have some commonly understood reference points for discussion and comparisons between various levels of development. Currently, the definitions in the literature are very disparate as to what is ecotourism, nature-based tourism, or rural and urban tourism. This chapter outlines this concept for discussion and follows other authors who have started a formulation of a TOS as a means of defining some commonly used terminology and the conceptual relationships between the terms (Butler and Waldbrook, 1991; Robertson *et al.*, 1995; Boyd and Butler, 1996).

The emphasis in this chapter is to illustrate the concept of the TOS using ecotourism and nature-based tourism as examples of reference points within the larger tourism opportunity framework. The objectives of this chapter are to: (i) briefly define ecotourism and nature-based tourism; (ii) outline the ROS and explain the value of an adaptation of this planning concept to tourism; (iii) propose a TOS and suggest the indicators to be measured and monitored if the opportunities are to be sustained over time; and (iv) explain the strengths and weaknesses of such a TOS.

Ecotourism and nature-based tourism definitions

The published literature often uses the terms ecotourism and nature-based tourism interchangeably; however, this chapter indicates through the proposed TOS why these are different terms. Popular tourism literature and marketing materials offer many other terms that are used interchangeably with ecotourism and nature-based tourism (Wall, 1994), such as green tourism, sustainable tourism, alternative tourism, ethical tourism, responsible tourism, conservation tourism and others. While the use of these different terms may have appeal to advertising agencies and various market segments, it creates confusion about what is being described (Wight, 1993). Do each of these terms mean the same thing or do they refer to somewhat different tourism products and opportunities?

Several researchers and planners have attempted to write a definition of ecotourism and nature-based tourism while others have argued against any single overall definition since it would be too restrictive (Buckley, 1994). Ceballos-Lascuráin (1991) has been often quoted as the first author to use the term and to define ecotourism as 'Traveling to relatively undisturbed or uncontaminated natural areas with the specific objective of studying, admiring, and enjoying the scenery and its wild plants and animals, as well as any existing cultural manifestations (both past and present) found in these areas'. Other authors, such as Kusler (1991), have tried to improve on that definition by adding concepts such as protection and sustainability: 'Tourism based principally upon natural and archaeological resources such as birds and other wildlife, scenic areas, reefs, caves, fossil sites, archaeological sites, wetlands, and areas of rare or endangered species . . . Protection of these natural and archaeological resources is essential for sustained ecotourism'. However, Caneday and Duston (1992), in a study of tourism in the Ozark Mountains, used a definition that emphasized conservation but not the concept of protection: 'Ecotourism is a form of tourism that primarily involves observing and exploring the natural history of an area . . . to experience, learn about and help conserve the cultural and natural history of the local ecosystem. Ecotourism trips emphasize minimal impacts on the ecosystem and strongly promote education and conservation themes'.

Some standardization of the terms 'ecotourism' and 'nature-based tourism' would be beneficial to the discussion among researchers, planners and managers, because nomenclature is necessary for accurate and effective communication. Although it is recognized that everyone will never agree on one exact definition, some standardization is helpful to the dialogue. One of the most complete definitions of ecotourism found in the published literature was outlined by Ziffer (1989) and is adapted here (Table 3.1) to include both ecotourism and nature-based tourism. Since these are two closely related reference points on a continuum, the application of these definitions is not exact and requires considerable knowledge of the situation and the setting characteristics. The reason to outline the definitions of these reference points is that it provides a baseline against which professionals can discuss a planning or management situation.

Any definition is a starting or reference point that can be debated and challenged. The purpose of using these two definitions here is to illustrate the potential for development of a more complete TOS. Such a future development will require making operational definitions that help a planner to understand what changes in characteristics shift the area to another type on the TOS. The key advantage is to understand the relative type of tourism opportunity provided and ensure that comparisons between two different areas are made with knowledge of their comparability or differences. The components of the ecotourism and nature-based tourism definitions listed here are not exhaustive and suggest some direction for further development of operational definitions among tourism planners.

With these proposed definitions of ecotourism and nature-based tourism (Table 3.1), the tourism opportunity types can be labelled and a continuum of tourism development levels, extending up to a highly developed urban setting can be outlined. The ROS offers an approach to formulating a parallel TOS, as proposed by Butler and Waldbrook (1991) and Robertson *et al.* (1995). The concept uses characteristics of the setting and the opportunities provided to users to classify the tourism planning area into a position on the continuum.

Recreation Opportunity Spectrum

The ROS has been used by the US Forest Service and the Bureau of Land Management since the 1970s (Clark and Stankey, 1979; Driver *et al.*, 1987; Nilsen and Tayler, 1997). The guiding concept was to develop a rational and comprehensive planning approach for regional

Table 3.1. Definitions of ecotourism and nature-based tourism (adapted from Ziffer, 1989).

Definition components	Ecotourism	Nature-based tourism
Management goals	Preservation and protection of the resource	Conservation and resource management
Primary resource use	Natural resources and natural history of the area, including its indigenous cultures	Natural resources, natural history, and the present and historic cultures of the area
Primary tourist motivation	Visit an ecosystem or undeveloped natural area for appreciation and to experience the environmental conditions	Visit an undeveloped natural area for appreciation and to directly experience the environmental conditions, or indirectly as a background for a consumptive or non-consumptive recreational experience
Recreational activities	Non-consumptive appreciation and study of wildlife and natural resources	Non-consumptive appreciation and study of, and consumptive use of, wildlife and natural resources
Economic contribution of tourism to area	Directly and indirectly contributes to the visited area which supports the protection or preservation of the site and the economic well-being of the local residents	Directly and indirectly contributes to the visited area which supports the conservation of the site and the health of the local economy
Visitor appreciation	The visit should strengthen the tourist's appreciation and dedication to preservation and protection issues at the visited area and in general	The visit should strengthen the tourist's appreciation and dedication to conservation issues at the visited area and in general
Management of the public/ private area	Implies a managed approach by the host country or region which commits to establishing and maintaining the area with the participation of local residents, marketing it appropriately, enforcing regulations, and using the economic benefits to fund the area's land management as well as community development	Implies a managed approach by the public and private sectors which commit to establishing and maintaining the area, marketing it appropriately, enforcing regulations, and using the economic benefits to fund the area's land management

planning and management that provided for a broad array of recreational opportunities for users. The ROS defined 4–6 setting categories of land-use management, from primitive to urban, to help managers better understand physical, biological, social and managerial relationships. The ROS planning product defined the user opportunities for several classes of recreational experience within each setting category. The ROS used several indicators of the recreation setting (e.g. the number of social encounters on trails, ease of access) to monitor the outcomes of the management implementation. The planning products from the ROS process specified the guidelines for managers and the indicators and standards for monitoring results.

The planning premises in the ROS process require that the 4–6 setting categories of land-use management (i.e. opportunities for experiences), from primitive to urban, be defined and agreed upon prior to starting the planning process. Subsequently a further subdivision is outlined of several opportunity classes within each setting category. Then setting and experience indicators are conceptually identified, qualitatively and quantitatively defined, and specific standards developed for monitoring and management decision-making over time. The ROS is a regional planning process that is adapted here to tourism because of concern about growing tourism demand and limited resource supply, especially related to ecotourism and nature-based tourism. The planned and incremental growth of tourism generally continues through various developmental stages from undeveloped rural areas to human-built urban environments (Murphy, 1985; Mathieson and Wall, 1987; Gunn, 1994). The TOS can help to describe this continuum, and by so doing help identify consequences of development and preserve ever-scarcer opportunities for ecotourism. The lack of comprehensive planning for a wide array of tourism opportunities over time is of concern since the distribution of tourism opportunities shifts toward higher development levels (i.e. shifts to the right on the ROS or TOS) but not towards less developed tourism opportunities (i.e. development is rarely removed).

Tourism Opportunity Spectrum

The following discussion and adaptation of the ROS to a proposed TOS is meant to further discussion about the need for a comprehensive planning approach that considers a wide array of tourism opportunities over time. The proposed TOS shown in Table 3.2 lists only five categories and should be thought of as a continuum from ecotourism (e.g. primitive and undeveloped conditions) to an urban environment (e.g. intensively developed and human-built environment). These five reference points are not equally distributed along the TOS continuum since they were chosen as illustrations of this concept, as adapted from the ROS literature. Furthermore, the goals and setting characteristics in the TOS are general conceptual guidelines and not hard and inflexible rules since there is a wide variety of tourism situations and many exceptions and differences between tourism areas. Some of the characteristics of the five reference points on the TOS are listed here for illustration and could be expanded to include other characteristics such as local economic conditions, available infrastructure or acceptable social behaviours.

The management goals and six setting characteristics are used in the TOS to classify the tourism category settings (Table 3.2) and are adapted from the ROS, TOS and ECOS literature (Clark and Stankey, 1979; Driver *et al.*, 1987; Butler and Waldbrook, 1991; Robertson *et al.*, 1995; Boyd and Butler, 1996). The six setting characteristics provide the basis for the formulation of specific indicator variables (e.g. user density per zone or number of user–user encounters per day) and standards. The standards are the quantifiable aspects of the indicator variable that are the baseline against which the existing conditions at a site are judged as acceptable or unacceptable (Stankey and McCool, 1990).

The current or proposed position of a site or area on the TOS can be determined after defining the tourism setting type (e.g. ecotourism), different levels of opportunities (e.g. remote wildlife viewing in a wilderness setting) provided for visitors, and the characteristics and indicators to monitor the provision of those tourism opportunities. Then alternative TOS positions can be evaluated along with the consequences of developing the site to another TOS position. Through the identification of the positive and negative regional social, environmental and economic conditions, the alternatives and consequences of each position on the TOS can be evaluated for a given site. Planners and managers then can decide to: (i) continue to provide the tourism opportunities planned for visitors at a particular ecotourism site or area (i.e. sustain the current opportunity position on the TOS); or (ii) increase the level of development and change the tourism opportunities planned (i.e. move the site to another position on the TOS at a higher level of development). Additionally, measures to mitigate or minimize changes to the characteristics can be considered.

An analysis of the tourism opportunities in an area, using a continuum like the TOS, will help outline an overview of the distribution of what tourism opportunities are being provided and suggest where there is market competition, where market niches could be developed, or what types of new tourism development will be compatible with existing opportunities. Like the ROS, the guiding concept of the TOS is to develop a rational and comprehensive planning approach for regional planning and management that

Table 3.2. A proposed Tourism Opportunity Spectrum and examples of setting characteristics (adapted from Clark and Stankey, 1979).

Setting characteristics	Ecotourism	Nature-based tourism	Rural tourism	Rural–urban tourism	Urban tourism
Management goals	Preservation and protection of the resource	Conservation and resource management	Resource management and some development	Resource management and economic development	Economic development and enterprise
Accessibility factors (difficulty, access type, means of conveyance)	Very difficult or controlled access, mostly by trails or water routes; may be very remote from human habitation	Difficult or controlled access by trails, water routes and secondary roads	Moderately accessible on secondary and primary roads	Accessible on secondary and primary roads; some public transportation	Easy access on highways and roads by vehicles and public transportation
Visual characteristics (acceptability of visitor impacts)	No readily apparent changes to the natural environment or very minimal localized user impacts	Primarily a natural-appearing environment and landscape, but some human impacts are evident	Mix of natural and managed environment and landscape with evidence of human habitation	Moderately managed environment and landscape with evidence of human habitation	Extensively modified and man-altered landscape and environment for human habitation and enterprise
Visitor environmental impact factors	Very minimal user impacts and some concentrated user impacts (e.g. hiking trails and scenic vistas) but with few users	Minimal user impacts and localized to recreation activity areas and facilities (e.g. boat-launch sites, campgrounds) but with low numbers of users	User impacts that are prevalent in small areas due to site development and management, plus some concentrations of users (e.g. marinas, motels)	Moderate user impacts due to site development and management, plus moderate volume of users (e.g. full service resorts, developed attractions)	High degree of user impacts due to extensive site development and management, plus high volume of users (e.g. theme parks, retail store complexes)
On-site management factors (existing infrastructure)	Very limited infrastructure (e.g. hiking trails); most supporting infrastructure is off site but within the region	Minimal infrastructure to support visitor activities on site	Some infrastructure and commercial development	Moderate infrastructure and commercial development	Extensive infrastructure and commercial development
Social interaction factors	Infrequent user–user or group–group interactions; managers expect highly ethical behaviour to other users and environment	Some user–user or group–group interactions; managers expect ethical behaviour to other users and environment	Moderate user–user or group–group interactions; managers expect ethical behaviour to other users and environment	Frequent user–user or group–group interactions; managers expect ethical behaviour to other users	Extensive user–user or group–group interactions; managers expect moderately to minimal ethical behaviour to other users
Visitor-management factors (acceptable regimentation)	Managed for non-motorized uses and non-consumptive recreational activities	Managed for non-motorized and some motorized uses and non-consumptive and consumptive recreational activities	Managed for motorized and non-motorized uses and non-consumptive and consumptive recreational activities	Managed for motorized and non-motorized uses and more consumptive recreational activities.	Managed for motorized and non-motorized uses and more conspicuously consumptive recreational activities

provides for a broad array of tourism opportunities for users, as appropriate to the regional social, environmental and economic conditions. Some of the advantages of using a TOS approach are that: (i) it is a planning and management matrix approach that is rational and comprehensive; (ii) it makes explicit what tourism opportunities are being provided or sustained; (iii) it links supply with demand in a practical planning process; and (iv) it provides a framework to evaluate the regional tourism alternatives and consequences of changing development levels.

One of the potential drawbacks to the TOS analysis approach is that it requires all of the tourism setting types and characteristics on the TOS to be defined and accepted by planners and managers. Lack of general consensus or agreement can affect the entire regional planning process. On site, the TOS approach requires that indicators and standards be specified and accepted by planners and managers for monitoring over time.

Discussion

The TOS, as proposed here and by Butler and Walbrook (1991), is a conceptual approach to a tourism planning tool that enables a rational and comprehensive overview for assessing the tourism opportunities provided within an area. The issue of sustaining the tourism opportunities can be addressed along with the indicators that need to be monitored to measure the experience and resource conditions.

Use of the TOS can help planners and others to understand how ecotourism, nature-based tourism or other types relate to each other. For example, the evolution of ecotourism and nature-based tourism can not continue to be 'old wine in new bottles' as Wall (1994) describes it. Rather, it can be a major contribution to preservation and conservation movements that seek to increase appreciation for the natural environment and educate users, even as demand for natural resources increases to keep pace with world population growth. The concern here is that we understand where and how ecotourism and nature-based tourism fit within a continuum of tourism development opportunities (i.e. what is it and what are the opportunities that we need to sustain). Downs (1994) notes that 'Despite its claims to save the world – or at least small chunks of it – ecotourism is not a panacea. However, with careful management and long-term planning, ecotourism may prove to be one of the most potent tools in the arsenal of the contemporary conservationists'. This warning about the value and importance of ecotourism and nature-based tourism implies that we know where we are on the TOS and how to sustain those opportunities. Boyd and Butler (1996) note that we need to go beyond the general TOS and delineate the subclasses of tourism opportunities within each class, such as their work on ecotourism (ECOS).

Theophile (1995) suggests that ecotourism and nature-based tourism 'is not a panacea for economic or environmental woes in the US or overseas, but if integrated with larger strategies it can be a valuable tool for sustainable development'. We will have greater potential to achieve such important goals if we begin to converse in a nomenclature or typology that we can generally agree upon, like the TOS, rather than tourism definitions that are subject to widespread interpretation and confusion.

References

Boo, E. (1990) *Ecotourism: the Potentials and Pitfalls*, Vols I and II. World Wildlife Fund, Washington, DC.

Boyd, S.W. and Butler, R.W. (1996) Managing ecotourism: an opportunity spectrum approach. *Tourism Management* 17(8), 557–566.

Buckley, R. (1994) A framework for ecotourism. *Annals of Tourism Research* 21(3), 661–669.

Butler, R.W. and Waldbrook, L.A. (1991) A new planning tool: the Tourism Opportunity Spectrum. *Journal of Tourism Studies* 2(1), 2–14.

Caneday, L. and Duston, T. (1992) *Sustainable Tourism Development in South Central Oklahoma: Theory, Case Study and Model*. Oklahoma State University, Oklahoma City, Oklahoma.

Ceballos-Lascuráin, H. (1991) Tourism, ecotourism, and protected areas. In: Kusler, J.A. (ed.) *Ecotourism and Resource Conservation*. Ecotourism and resource conservation project, Berne, New York, pp. 24–30.

Ceballos-Lascuráin, H. (1996) *Tourism, Ecotourism, and Protected Areas: the State of Nature-based Tourism around the World and Guidelines for its Development*. IUCN – The World Conservation Union, Cambridge, UK.

Clark, R.N. and Stankey, G.H. (1979) *The Recreation Opportunity Spectrum: a Framework for Planning, Management, and Research*. General Technical Report PNW-GTR–98. US. Department of Agriculture, Forest Service, Pacific Northwest Forest and Range Experiment Station, Portland, Oregon.

Crotts, J.C. (ed.) (1994) Taking the hype out of ecotourism. *Trends* 31(2), 1–48.

Downs, J. (1994) Protecting paradise is a priority. *Wildlife Conservation* 97(2), 2.

Driver, B.L., Brown, P.J., Stankey, G.H. and Gregiore, T.G. (1987) The ROS planning system: evolution, basic concepts, and research needed. *Leisure Sciences* 9, 201–212.

Eagles, P.F.J. and Nilsen, P. (1997) *Ecotourism: an Annotated Bibliography for Planners and Managers*, 4th edn. The Ecotourism Society, North Bennington, Vermont.

Economic and Social Commission for Asia and the Pacific (1995) *Guidelines for Environmentally Sound Development of Coastal Tourism*. United Nations, New York.

Gunn, C.A. (1994) *Tourism Planning: Basics, Concepts, Cases*, 3rd edn. Taylor and Francis, Washington, DC.

Hall, C.M. and Johnston, M.E. (eds) (1995) *Polar Tourism: Tourism in the Arctic and Antarctic Regions*. John Wiley & Sons, New York.

Honey, M. (1999) *Ecotourism and Sustainable Development: Who Owns Paradise?* Island Press, Washington, DC.

Kusler, J.A. (ed.) (1991) *Ecotourism and Resource Conservation*, Vols I and II. Ecotourism and resource conservation project, Berne, New York.

Lindberg, K. and Hawkins, D.E. (1993) *Ecotourism: a Guide for Planners and Managers*. The Ecotourism Society, North Bennington, Vermont.

Mathieson, A. and Wall, G. (1987) *Tourism: Economic, Physical and Social Impacts*. John Wiley & Sons, New York.

McCool, S.F. and Watson, A.E. (eds) (1995) *Linking Tourism, the Environment, and Sustainability*. General Technical Report INT-GTR–323, US Department of Agriculture, Forest Service, Intermountain Research Station.

McLaren, D. (1998) *Rethinking Tourism and Ecotravel; the Paving of Paradise and What You Can Do to Stop It*. Kumarian Press, West Hartford, Connecticut.

Muller, H. (1994) The thorny path to sustainable tourism development. *Journal of Sustainable Tourism* 2(3), 131–136.

Murphy, P.E. (1985) *Tourism: a Community Approach*. Methuen, New York.

Nilsen, P. and Tayler, G. (1997) A comparative analysis of protected area planning and management frameworks. In: McCool, S.F. and Cole, D.N. (eds) *Proceedings of the Limits of Acceptable Change and Related Planning Processes: Progress and Future Directions; May 20–22; Missoula, Montana*. General Technical Report INT-GTR–371; US Department of Agriculture, Forest Service, Rocky Mountain Research Station; Ogden, Utah, pp. 49–57.

Orams, M.B. (1995) Towards a more desirable form of ecotourism. *Tourism Management* 16 (1), 3–8.

Robertson, R.A., Dawson, C.P., Kuentzel, W. and Selin, S.W. (1995) Trends in university-based education and training programs in ecotourism or nature-based tourism in the USA. In: Thompson, J.L. *et al.* (eds) *Proceedings of the Fourth International Outdoor Recreation and Tourism Trends Symposium and the 1995 National Recreation Resource Planning Conference, May 14–17, 1995, St Paul, Minnesota*. University of Minnesota, College of Natural Resources and Minnesota Extension Service, St Paul, Minnesota, pp. 460–466.

Stankey, G. and McCool, S. (1990) Managing for appropriate wilderness conditions: the carrying capacity issue. In: Hendee, J.C. *et al.* (eds) *Wilderness Management*, 2nd edn. Fulcrum Press, Golden, Colorado, pp. 215–239.

Tabata, R.S., Yamashiro, J. and Cherem, G. (eds) (1992) Joining hands for quality tourism: interpretation, preservation and the travel industry. *Proceedings of the Heritage Interpretation International Third Global Congress, November 3–8, Honolulu, Hawaii.*

Theophile, K. (1995) The forest as a business: is ecotourism the answer? *Journal of Forestry* 93(3), 25–27.

United Nations Environmental Programme (1995) *Environmental Codes of Conduct for Tourism*. Technical report No. 29, Paris, France.

Wall, G. (1994) Ecotourism: old wine in new bottles? *Trends* 31(2), 4–9.

Wall, G. (1997) Is ecotourism sustainable? *Environmental Management* 21(4), 483–491.

Whelan, T. (ed.) (1991) *Nature Tourism: Managing for the Environment*. Island Press, Washington, DC.

Wight, P.A. (1993) Ecotourism: ethics or eco-sell. *Journal of Travel Research* 31(3), 3–9.

Ziffer, K.A. (1989) *Ecotourism: the Uneasy Alliance*. Conservation International and Ernest & Young International Management Consulting Group.

Sustainable Development and the Shifting Attitudes of Tourism Stakeholders: Toward a Dynamic Framework

4

Dimitri Ioannides

Department of Geography, Geology, and Planning, Southwest Missouri State University, Springfield, Missouri, USA

Introduction

During the past decade, sustainable development has become a preoccupation for planning practitioners, policy-makers, and academics (Redclift, 1987; World Commission on Environment and Development, 1987; Gunn, 1994; van den Bergh and van der Straaten, 1994; Berke and Conroy, 2000). Considering that the concept of sustainability strives to reconcile existing conflicts among goals of economic growth, environmental protection and social justice, it is not surprising that this concept has also emerged as a leitmotif of tourism research (McCool, 1995; Wall, 1997; Hall and Lew, 1998; Mowforth and Munt, 1998; Bosselman *et al.*, 1999; Butler, 1999; Williams and Montanari, 1999). Indeed, a whole journal (*Journal of Sustainable Tourism*) is now dedicated to the study of sustainable tourism. However, despite ample rhetoric concerning the merits of adopting the sustainability paradigm in tourist destinations, many authors have criticized the concept for its ambiguity (Butler, 1993; Wahab and Pigram, 1997). This ambiguity makes it hard to transform sustainable development from words into actions (Campbell, 1996; McCool and Stankey, 1999).

The purpose of this chapter is twofold. First, it summarizes the major obstacles to implementing sustainable solutions in touristic environments. A principal impediment is that sustainability is a term fraught with 'imprecision' (Wall, 1997, p. 33), since it holds varying meanings for different stakeholders (see also McCool and Stankey,

© CAB *International* 2001. *Tourism, Recreation and Sustainability* (eds S.F. McCool and R.N. Moisey)

1999; Sauter and Leisen, 1999; Kousis, 2001). Although researchers are well aware of this obstacle, most of them generally assume that for any given tourist destination each group of stakeholders has an agenda which remains static over time. In other words, writers tend to ignore the possibility that in a single locality the same set of players may gradually change its outlook towards tourism and the sector's impacts. For example, a local community may initially regard the tourism sector's potential for economic growth positively, but perceptions could turn increasingly negative as development continues. This makes it practically impossible to prescribe a general agenda for sustainable tourism development without accounting for the context within which this development takes place.

Secondly, the chapter discusses the need for a conceptual framework that recognizes the effect that spatial/geographic and temporal/historic contingencies may have in influencing the attitudes of various stakeholders towards sustainability. A primary aim is to demonstrate the value of adopting a longitudinal model such as Butler's (1980) widely used tourist-area life cycle to investigate the perspectives of different actors towards balanced-oriented growth at each stage of a destination's development. In order to illustrate the use of such a conceptual framework for examining the shifting perceptions of stakeholders over time, the chapter draws on the experiences of insular destinations in the Mediterranean.

Barriers to sustainability in the context of tourism

The idea of sustainable development seems to have gained broad acceptance globally. Campbell (1996, p. 301) argues that this widespread acceptance is inevitable because 'to reject sustainability is to embrace non-sustainability – and who dares to sketch that future?' Therefore, it is not surprising that various groups and individuals, regardless of ideology or political affiliation, have adopted the term 'sustainability' in their everyday vocabulary. Nevertheless, despite the increasing popularity of the term, its transformation into action has thus far proven elusive. The major stumbling block to implementing truly sustainable development options in a variety of contexts, including tourism environments, arises from the notion's malleability, or the fact it means different things to different groups (Butler, 1993, 1999; Burr, 1995; McCool, 1995; McCool and Stankey, 1999; Kousis, 2001).

To achieve sustainable development, communities must find a delicate balance between conflicting economic, environmental, and social equity objectives. Thus, sustainability implies a situation where the economy is growing, the resulting economic growth is distributed equitably, and the environmental impacts of these actions are minimized (Campbell, 1996). In theory, the concept of balancing the 'three Es' of sustainability (environment, economy, and equity) is straightforward. As Berke and Conroy argue it implies that 'current and future generations must strive to achieve a decent standard of living for all people and live within the limits of natural systems' (Berke and Conroy, 2000, p. 22). However, this ideal condition cannot be attained easily because there is no consensus on how the concept of sustainability can be implemented and because the different stake-holders who make up any society have varying agendas regarding development.

Players who prioritize concrete economic growth objectives are often focused on short-term goals compared to those who may give preference to less tangible social justice and environmental protection goals. In the context of tourism, for instance, profit-oriented developers are usually concerned about reaping a fast reward from their investment and will not be too worried about the environmental or societal ramifications of their actions. Unless forced by statutes and other regulatory instruments, these players rarely, if ever, wish to admit responsibility for the externalities generated by their projects (Ioannides, 1994). Similarly, it may be impossible to convince the poor inhabitants of a remote area in the developing world that it is to their long-term advantage to protect their natural environment, especially if these individuals perceive such an objective as an infringement upon their limited opportunities for rapid economic growth. In such settings it becomes a challenge to implement slow growth solutions because 'the poor, whom the transistor radio and the bicycle have wrenched out of their isolation, do not want to be told to discard their aspirations as consumers' (de Kadt, 1990, p. 15). Moreover, in developing countries, the sustainable development concept is commonly regarded as yet another attempt on the part of Western industrialized societies to impose their own agendas on poorer nations (Hitchcock *et al.*, 1993).

The implementation of sustainable development within the context of tourism has proved largely unsuccessful because in most destinations the sector is extremely fragmented and dominated by small businesses. In tourist areas there is a 'constantly shifting mosaic of stakeholders and value systems [and] each of these groups has a different view of the role and future of tourism at the destination, and therefore the adoption of strategies becomes a political process of conflict resolution and consensus' (Cooper, 1997, pp. 82–83). Small-scale entrepreneurs, many of whom depend on the seasonal nature of their business, are usually far more concerned about their next pay cheque than the overall impact their business may have on the environment and the local culture. These players invariably have a short-term perspective and are unlikely to embrace future-oriented issues, especially if they perceive these as a threat to their own priorities. Additionally, when planners and other policy-makers draft slow-growth guidelines for the future development of a resort, these may be hard to implement. Politicians are often wary of enacting strict environmental regulations, since they are more interested about remaining in office and unlikely, therefore, to have an outlook extending beyond the next election. Seeking to stall his waning popularity during the 1993 elections in Cyprus, President Vassiliou made zoning restrictions in the island's sensitive coastal areas less restrictive in order to appease local landowners (Ioannides, 1995a). The following argument highlights such unpredictability in governmental policy:

> Ministers who speak radically, and convincingly, and frequently about protection of the nation's environmental and cultural treasures are the same people who sign agreements which allow transnational companies to build a hotel or tourist complex whose development pays no heed to the environmental, social and cultural impacts caused.
> (Mowforth and Munt, 1998, p. 104).

Another problem making it hard to implement sustainable policy options in tourist destinations is the myopic and fragmented government machinery (de Kadt, 1990; Timothy, 1999). In most non-industrialized nations (but also certain developed nations, including the US) strategies dealing with land-use planning or the environment are commonly isolated from national economic policies. Top-down policies addressing economic, environmental, urban, tourist and transportation-related concerns (among others) have limited influence because they deal with their respective issues in a vertical, sector-specific manner (Richardson, 1987). Within such a vertical system, there are few intersectoral linkages, an obstacle that is accentuated by the tendency of a single professional group to dominate each ministry and governmental organization (Ioannides, 1995b). Isolated strategies mitigate against sustainable development which, by its nature, is inherently integrative.

Inconsistency between the policies of various governmental and quasi-governmental organizations has been documented in the Republic of Cyprus. For example, a few years ago the Cyprus Tourism Organization (CTO) adopted its *New Tourism Policy* (1990), which calls for measures to control the future growth of organized inclusive tours that have fuelled the island's cheap, mass tourist image. Prescribed steps include moratoria on new tourism-related developments, strict policing of informal-sector facilities, and efforts to enhance the destination's appeal to higher-spending individuals and special-interest groups. Nevertheless, other groups, including the national aviation authority and the Cypriot hotel owners' association, have responded to pressure exerted by major northern European tour operators and taken actions contradicting this move towards quality (rather than quantity) tourism. Both these groups have advocated the relaxation of the government's strict restrictions on British charter carriers. The hotel owners, for instance, are concerned about the alarming decline in occupancy rates as a result of an oversupply of tourist accommodation establishments and stagnating numbers of tourist arrivals. The efforts of these entrepreneurs and other groups have led the government to grant an increased number of licences to British charter airlines, in turn resulting in a higher number of low-paying mass tourists visiting the island.

Additionally, it is important to note that national or regional policies geared towards up-market tourism as a means of promoting sustainability can prove counterproductive. Ioannides and Holcomb (2001) indicate that Malta's prescribed attempts to replace mass tourists with up-market visitors are problematic because the necessary luxury-oriented projects consume far more energy, water and land than traditional budget-oriented establishments. Similarly, proposals by the CTO to develop a number of golf courses as a means of diversifying the Cypriot tourism product seem particularly misplaced on an island facing severe water shortages (CTO, 1990).

Conflicting policies are also apparent in Costa Rica, a country often associated with the promotion of alternative tourism, such as ecotourism. For instance, to qualify for incentives to finance hotel construction, developers have to provide at least 20 bathrooms, something that is prohibitively expensive for local entrepreneurs (Place, 1998). Ironically, this measure restricts one of the necessary components for the promotion of sustainability, namely the participation of local community members in the tourist industry (Timothy, 1999), and contradicts national policies geared towards enhancing economic opportunities for the local population (Hill, 1990).

Sustainable tourism or tourism in the context of sustainable development?

Certain authors argue that the concept of sustainable tourism rests on uncertain foundations since it focuses on a single sector, unlike the broader notion of sustainable development that implies a multisectoral approach (Campbell, 1996; Butler, 1997). This single-sector focus (Coccossis, 1996; Butler, 1999) is especially problematic in 'the case of tourism, which is a diffuse activity with far-reaching implications for many other sectors and activities' (Wall, 1997, p. 34). As Buhalis and Diamantis (2001) maintain an emphasis on sustainable tourism alone 'creates "tourism-centric" situations, where most of the approaches become partially divorced from the main principles of the sustainability concept'. According to Buhalis and Diamantis, 'decision-makers concentrate on tourism development as a short-term strategy, tending to neglect . . . the long-term prosperity of regions'. A major stumbling block is that many groups, including tour operators, hotel owners and governmental agencies, often adopt a narrow view of sustainability for a destination without regard to tourism's interconnections with other sectors, such as transportation, housing, employment and the environment. In other words, while these groups may indicate support for sustainable strategies, they are, in fact, far more interested in maintaining the viability of the tourist sector (Butler, 1993).

The fundamental difference between sustainable tourism and tourism within the context of sustainable development is one that few researchers have acknowledged (Wall, 1997). Sustainable tourism can simply mean the development of the sector in a manner that ensures its long-term survival within a destination (Butler, 1993). However, such an interpretation is confusing (Butler, 1999). For instance, one could easily argue that tourism is sustainable in a destination that has managed a steady growth pattern in visitation and spending over an extended period of time. According to this definition there are numerous examples of sites where tourism can be considered sustainable, precisely because they are able to attract a high number of visitors (e.g. Niagara Falls, Disneyworld, Las Vegas, London, Paris) (Butler, 1997). These destinations are not only able consistently to lure large numbers of visitors because of their unique attractions, but also because they can maintain their appeal by constantly diversifying their tourism product. For instance, the Disney Corporation periodically expands its empire in central Florida by adding new theme parks. Nevertheless, while these destinations may be considered sustainable in terms of their ability to maintain their tourist industry, they may not always be thought of as sustainable in an environmental or socio-cultural sense. This is because in these destinations 'tourism is competing for resources and may not [represent] the "best" or wisest use of resources . . . in the long term' (Butler, 1999, p. 11).

Conversely, tourism within the context of sustainable development is a far more complex idea. According to Butler (1993, p. 29) it can be defined as the type of tourism that is developed and maintained in an area (community, environment) in such a manner and at such a scale that it remains viable over an indefinite period and does not degrade or alter the (host) environment to such a degree that it prohibits the successful development and well-being of other activities and processes.

Such a comprehensive interpretation of sustainable development acknowledges that tourism does not occur in a vacuum. Whereas sustainable tourism espouses the long-term survival of the sector regardless of its impacts on a destination's other resources, tourism within a context of sustainability recognizes the need for a comprehensive approach that balances tourism development with that of other activities in order to safeguard the requirements of future generations. Without clearly knowing what these requirements are, however, it is hard to identify the nature of sustainable development in a tourism context.

The conceptual gap between a sector-specific interpretation and one representing a holistic vision of integrated development indicates that the embrace of 'sustainability' in the language of a growing number of groups (e.g. industry representatives) should be regarded cautiously (Mowforth and Munt, 1998). When talking about sustainable tourism, a number of stakeholders are firmly focused on the survival of the sector. Indeed, for many businesses or organizations, terms such as 'sustainable development' or 'green tourism' may be little more than marketing gimmicks to ensure business survival (Butler, 1999, p. 13).

One group that has recently embraced the banner of 'sustainable tourism' is the British-based International Federation of Tour Operators (IFTO), members of which include a number of major mass-oriented tour companies. The IFTO calls for the adoption of 'realistic carrying capacity per destination [and] a sound set of laws to ensure sustainable development' (Brackenbury, 1997, p. 1). As noble as this cause sounds, this lobby group's overriding concern is the continued generation of profits for its members. The tour operators that the IFTO represents are mostly interested in sustaining the appeal of their products among increasingly discerning and sophisticated international travellers, and are not truly worried about the needs of future generations in destination areas (Carey *et al.*, 1997). Thus, these players may talk about sustainable development but their true focus remains on the short-term growth-oriented goals of their business (Ioannides, 1998; Mowforth and Munt, 1998). Environmental and sociocultural concerns are significant to IFTO members only if they have an adverse impact on profits.

Private companies and groups such as the IFTO, which regard the preservation of ecosystems in economic terms, have a 'treadmill' view of sustainability (Kousis, 2001). Similarly, the approach of national and supra-national organizations towards sustainable development tends to be 'weak' since, more often than not, these bodies emphasize economic rather than social or environmental sustainability. In most instances, these organizations are unwilling to implement drastic institutional changes and are anxious to pacify tourism-related producers by responding to their needs. The widespread policy of attracting 'quality' tourists in the Mediterranean, described in the previous section, is an example of a 'weak' approach to sustainable development. In these instances, governments are especially anxious to maintain the economic benefits of the tourist industry by replacing large numbers of low-spending mass tourists with smaller numbers of 'quality' visitors. The only groups that are likely to adopt a 'strong' or 'ideal' perspective of sustainable development, signifying the need for major 'changes in patterns of production and consumption [or even] drastic restructuring of political, legal, social, and economic institutions', are grassroots organizations such as pro-environment, non-government organizations (NGOs) (Kousis, 2001).

In the following section, attention is focused on the manner in which the numerous stakeholders who influence a destination's development have contradictory priorities concerning the role of tourism and, more importantly, varying perspectives of the meaning of sustainable development.

Sustainable development: a longitudinal model

For sustainability to be achieved in any environment it is important for policy-makers to give an opportunity to all stakeholders to become actively involved in collaborative decision-making processes (Bramwell and Sharman, 1999; Burns, 1999; McCool and Stankey, 1999; Sauter and Leisen, 1999; Timothy, 1999). For instance, sustainability cannot be imposed at a tourist destination through top-down physical planning mechanisms alone without accounting for the needs of local communities, tourists, environmental groups, entrepreneurs and other public or private organizations. As McCool and Stankey argue, 'public participation in developmental decisions is a hallmark of many discussions of sustainable development. [It is] viewed as necessary to identifying the distributional consequences of decision-making [and is] also seen as essential to successful implementation of sustainable development projects' (McCool and Stankey, 1999, p. 41).

Ironically, however, the very effort to include all players in the planning process means that their conflicting priorities and expectations can be a major barrier to achieving balanced forms of development, especially since the 'power of stakeholders is often uneven' (Bramwell and Sharman, 1999). Previous authors have recognized this problematic situation, yet most examine the contrasting agendas of different stakeholders at one point in time and ignore geographical contingencies (e.g. Sauter and Leisen, 1999). A fundamental question that needs to be answered is whether the same sustainable development-oriented policies can work in different geographical locations. This, as many authors acknowledge, is highly unlikely (Wall, 1997).

It is easy to claim that sustainable development has a higher chance of success in newly emerging tourist destinations (presumably because the damage has not yet occurred) than in well-established resorts (Butler, 1999). In reality, however, it may be hard to convince certain local stakeholders of the merits of sustainable development, given that they have not witnessed first-hand tourism's long-term negative impacts on the environment and society. By contrast, policy-makers and other players in a mature destination may attempt to institute balanced-growth strategies, only to discover that these are ineffective overall since they often apply to future developments and not existing, unsustainable operations (Butler and Stiakaki, 2001). The moratoria on new tourist accommodation establishments instituted in Cyprus during the late 1980s and early 1990s had negligible impact because they did not apply to a large number of establishments for which building permits had already been secured (Ioannides, 1994).

Studies relating to tourism should account for the overall development of the destination area (Pearce, 1989). A locality's degree of tourism growth and its overall level of development have a bearing on the attitudes and behaviour of different players towards the role of tourism and sustainability practices overall. Cooper argues appropriately that 'the stage of the destination in the life cycle also influences the acceptability of planning and marketing. In the early stages of the life cycle for example, success often obscures the long term view, whilst at the later stages, particularly when a destination is in decline, opposition to long-term planning exercises may be rationalized on the basis of cost' (Cooper, 1997, p. 83). Cooper's statement demonstrates that when devising strategies to promote balanced growth, planners and policy-makers must be sensitive to the temporal context in which tourism development is taking place.

The shifting attitudes of each group of stakeholders towards sustainable development at every stage of a tourist destination's development can be examined through a longitudinal framework. Over the past four decades academics have developed a variety of evolutionary models of tourism development to explain growth and change (Christaller, 1963; Plog, 1973; Miossec, 1976; Stansfield, 1978; Gormsen, 1981). One framework that has received considerable attention in recent years is the resort cycle model (Butler, 1980). Butler hypothesizes that any tourist destination goes through seven consecutive stages of development (exploration, involvement, development, consolidation, stagnation, decline, and rejuvenation).

This simple evolutionary model is attractive because it describes each stage of a destination's development, tourism's impacts, the mechanisms that have caused these impacts, and the identity of key indigenous and foreign actors (Pearce, 1989). Moreover, the resort cycle helps illustrate the market's evolution in terms of changes in the segments and the numbers of visitors (Ioannides, 1994). The model has received criticism, however, because it fails to account for seasonality, it lacks clarity regarding levels of spatial aggregation, and it ignores the fact that carrying capacity thresholds for environmental, social, physical, or perceptual variables are hard to estimate as they all differ from each other (Haywood, 1986). Butler (1997) himself admits that the prescriptive value of the resort cycle is limited because it is a hypothetical development path, dependent upon marketing and managerial actions, rather than an independent mechanical process (Ioannides, 1994).

Despite these shortcomings, a number of authors have adapted Butler's model for a variety of contexts, and some have offered useful extensions (Cooper and Jackson, 1989; Debbage, 1990; Cooper, 1997). Cooper (1997) indicates that the resort cycle can be used in conjunction with strategic planning to develop a framework for implementing 'sustainable principles' (Cooper, 1997, p. 78). He argues that for every stage of a resort's life cycle it is possible to outline the available strategic possibilities that allow the destination to remain competitive. Cooper concludes that only by adopting such an evolutionary perspective will sustainable tourism be approached.

In a similar fashion, the resort cycle can be adapted as a conceptual framework for examining the agendas of various stakeholder groups at each stage of a resort's development. This includes players such as national, regional or local governments, communities (entrepreneurs/developers and inhabitants), tour operators and other industry representatives, NGOs (e.g. environmental groups) and tourists. What follows is an illustration of the observed agendas of different stakeholders at each stage of a tourist destination's evolution. The analysis is influenced by the experiences of various Mediterranean insular regions (Oglethorpe, 1984; Ioannides, 1992; Loukissas and Triantafyllopoulos, 1997). For the sake of simplicity, therefore, the ensuing framework has been labelled 'The Mediterranean isle context'. Nevertheless, it is assumed that this longitudinal conceptual construct, especially the notion that stakeholder attitudes towards tourism and sustainable development may shift according to a destination's development stage, can be tailored for other areas throughout the world.

The Mediterranean isle context

It is impossible to investigate every group of stakeholders involved in a destination's development. Nevertheless, the present analysis accounts for a range of players representing local, regional, national and international concerns. Tables 4.1–4.3 are a series of matrices

Table 4.1. Conflicting development agendas during the exploration/involvement stage (describes a single locality) (after Butler, 1980).

Agenda	Government		Developers/hoteliers	NGOs	Mass tour operators	Inhabitants
	National/regional[a] (relates to parent destination's resort cycle)	Local				
Visibility	Low	High	Emerging	Low	Low	High
Economic	Increase foreign exchange/diversify economy	Fast growth/create jobs	Maximize profits	N/A	Maximize profits	Improve standard of living
Environmental priority	High	Low	Low	High	Low	Low
Social priority	Medium	Low	Low	High	Low	Low–medium
Timeline	Medium–long	Short–medium	Short	Long	Short	Short
Support for regulations	High	Low	Low	High	Low	Low
Tourism strategy	Balance tourism development and environmental protection/diversify tourism product/target 'quality' rather than 'quantity' tourists	Provide incentives/laissez-faire	Support fast growth development/speculative building	Low-impact development	Little involvement at this stage	Support fast growth development
Sustainability approach	Weak	N/A	N/A	Weak/strong	N/A	N/A

[a]In this case it is assumed that national policies are dictated by the overall resort cycle of the hypothetical island and thus remain constant.

Table 4.2. Conflicting development agendas during the development stage (describes a single locality) (after Butler, 1980).

Agenda	Government		Developers/ hoteliers	NGOs	Mass tour operators	Inhabitants
	National/regional[a] (relates to parent destination's resort cycle)	Local				
Visibility	Low	High	High	Low	High	High
Economic	Increase foreign exchange/ diversify economy	Fast growth/ create jobs	Maximize profits	N/A	Maximize profits	Improve standard of living
Environmental priority	High	Emerging concern	Low	High	Low	Mixed
Sociocultural priority	Medium	Emerging concern	Low	High	Low	Mixed
Timeline	Medium–long	Short–medium	Short	Long	Short	Short
Support for regulations	High	Emerging	Low	High	Low	Mixed
Tourism strategy	Balance tourism development and environmental protection/ diversify tourism product/ target 'quality' rather than 'quantity' tourists	Provide incentives/ laissez-faire	Support fast growth development/ speculative building	No more tourism development	Support rapid growth of mass-tourist-oriented infrastructure	Waning support for fast growth development
Sustainability approach	Weak	N/A	N/A	Strong	N/A	Weak

[a]In this case it is assumed that national policies are dictated by the overall resort cycle of the hypothetical island and thus remain constant.

Table 4.3. Conflicting development agendas during consolidation/stagnation (describes a single locality) (after Butler, 1980).

Agenda	Government		Developers/ hoteliers	NGOs	Mass tour operators	Inhabitants
	National/regional[a] (relates to parent destination's resort cycle)	Local				
Visibility	Low	High	High	Moderate	High	High
Economic	Increase foreign exchange/ diversify economy	Maintain growth/ diversification	Business survival	N/A	Maximize profits	Improve standard of living
Environmental priority	High	High	Emerging	High	Emerging	High
Sociocultural priority	Medium	Medium	Low	High	Low	High
Timeline	Medium–long	Short–medium	Short	Long	Short	Short–medium
Support for regulations	High	High	Emerging	High	Moderate	Growing
Tourism strategy	Balance tourism development and environmental protection/ diversify tourism product/ target 'quality' rather than 'quantity' tourists	Limit incentives/ regulate mass tourism development/ impose moratoria	Support moratoria but oppose limits on mass tourist development	No more tourism development	Support regulations to protect product	Limit further tourism development
Sustainability approach	Weak	Weak	Treadmill	Strong/ideal	Treadmill	Weak/strong

[a]In this case it is assumed that national policies are dictated by the overall resort cycle of the hypothetical island and thus remain constant.

reflecting the conflicting economic, sociocultural and environmental agendas, plus the contrasting time perspectives of various actors, according to resort cycle stage. The columns indicate the following stakeholders: national and/or regional governments, local authorities, developers/hoteliers, NGOs, mass tour operators and local inhabitants. The first row represents the visibility of the stakeholders in the tourist destination. Subsequent rows reflect the economic, environmental and sociocultural priorities of these players, their time perspectives, their level of support for regulatory instruments, their respective attitudes towards tourism development and (where appropriate) their overall views on sustainable development.

The conceptual model can either apply longitudinally to a single destination as it progresses through its own life cycle, or describe cross-sectionally, for a single point in time, three separate localities, each of which has reached a distinct stage of tourism development. It is assumed that, regardless of the level of tourism development at an individual locality, the overriding national and/or regional policies are dictated by the present state of the parent destination's resort cycle. For instance, while many Mediterranean islands (e.g. Corfu, Crete, Cyprus, Malta, Mallorca, Rhodes) display overall characteristics placing them in the consolidation, stagnation or early rejuvenation stage (Ioannides, 1994; Bruce and Cantallops, 1996; Loukissas and Triantafyllopoulos, 1997), they each contain localities that have not yet taken off as tourist areas. This implies that the national or regional policies often do not dovetail with objectives in individual communities, especially if the latter are still at an early stage of their individual resort cycle.

The exploration/involvement stage

In a destination that is in this stage, tourism is still in its infancy (Table 4.1). The Akamas peninsula in north-western Cyprus and a few isolated communities in southern Crete fit this description (Ioannides, 1995a; Dagonaki and Kotios, 1998). Certain players, among them the local authority and a small number of private investors, gradually realize (partly based on their experiences from other destinations) that tourism can fuel rapid economic growth. Thus, there is pressure by some stakeholders to create an atmosphere conducive to investment for tourism-related activities. The local government may finance infrastructural projects (e.g. roads, irrigation schemes and airports) and develop incentive packages for attracting private-sector ventures. Moreover, authorities set up a promotional agency to market the locality. Local land-use and building codes (if they exist) are weak and environmental regulations absent, whereas little attention is paid to national or regional policies. Local concern about the sociocultural impacts of tourism is also minimal.

Likewise, the local inhabitants are excited about the prospects of tourism development and demonstrate little opposition to the sector since they commonly associate it with the creation of jobs, wealth creation, and 'progress' or 'modernization'. These local players are not too concerned about environmental issues at this stage. They may be outright hostile towards any attempts by national or regional institutions to implement a regulatory framework or environmental policies, especially if they perceive these measures to directly contradict their own economic growth priorities (Ioannides, 1995a). Exogenous groups (e.g. international organizations such as Friends of the Earth or Greenpeace, or national environmental bodies) show genuine concern about the possible environmental problems generated by the nascent tourist industry. This has occurred in the Akamas peninsula and parts of Zakynthos because of the threat of coastal development on the breeding grounds of rare species of turtles (Ryan, 1991; Ioannides, 1995a). However, as has happened in these areas, there are few supporters of environmental groups in the community. Indeed, local leaders and business concerns may adopt a campaign to depict environmental groups as radical 'tree-huggers' (Ioannides, 1995a).

Development stage

In a destination that has reached this point, mass tourism has set in (Table 4.2). Examples of such areas include certain islands of the Aegean and Ionian archipelago (e.g. Cephalonia, Skiathos) or the area around Polis in north-western Cyprus. Foreign actors (especially tour operators) have discovered the destination and are taking the initiative in its promotion. To these players such a destination presents the opportunity for profit. Meanwhile, local authorities are excited about the sector's rapid growth, especially in terms of its financial returns, and wish to maintain a laissez-faire business atmosphere despite the appearance of some serious environmental or societal problems. At this stage, the priorities of local authorities, businesses, and developers may conflict with those of regional or national planning agencies and other bodies which seek to institute a series of controls (e.g. building moratoria, comprehensive planning and tools such as zoning) for steering tourism's future development.

Meanwhile, local reaction to tourism development is mixed. Although the local residents begin to recognize certain social and environmental problems, they are also willing to put up with tourism in its current mass-market form because of the real and perceived benefits it may provide. Only certain NGOs, including 'fringe' environmental activists, oppose future development to ensure that the physical environment in the destination is not further compromised. The latter are the only group at this stage to adopt a 'strong' perspective of sustainable development.

Consolidation/stagnation/decline stage

This is the phase when a destination will normally begin to demonstrate structural difficulties (Table 4.3). Certain Mediterranean destinations, among them Ayia Napa and Limassol in Cyprus and the north-eastern coast of Rhodes appear to have reached this stage. The growth rate of tourist arrivals and receipts begins to wane. International tourists show increasing dissatisfaction with the quality of the tourism product and eventually find alternative, less-developed destinations (either in other parts of the region or completely new destinations). This situation causes alarm among local policy-makers, leading to a search for strategies to enhance the destination's quality. Like their national or regional counterparts, local authorities adopt a 'weak' approach to sustainability. While economic growth remains the local policy-makers' overriding objective, they also realize the need to introduce strict environmental and land-use regulations. The atmosphere may turn increasingly regulatory and incentives to the private sector are reduced. Ideally, local policies will begin to converge with national priorities and increasingly aim at supporting 'quality' (high-spending) as opposed to 'quantity' (mass-oriented) tourism. This has already happened in a variety of localities on islands such as Malta (Holcomb and Balm, 1996) and Mallorca (Bruce and Cantallops, 1996). Authorities introduce measures to rejuvenate the destination by diversifying the product (e.g. promoting alternative tourism forms such as ecotourism or constructing recreational facilities such as golf courses) and undertaking an aggressive marketing campaign which targets a broad range of market segments (Cooper, 1997). There is a growing realization that failure to intervene in such a manner will lead to decline.

In this scenario, certain local entrepreneurs (e.g. hotel owners) begin to worry about business survival and, thus, support a moratorium on further development in order to protect their existing investments. Nevertheless, they remain reluctant to endorse measures for limiting mass tourism outright because of their concern for declining occupancy rates. Concurrently, the community at large begins to display increasing hostility towards tourists and their activities, because of overcrowding, rising crime, and the perceived dismantling of traditions. Moreover, as has been the case in certain

Mediterranean islands, environmental groups adopt a more active stance within the community ('strong' or 'ideal' approach to sustainability) and their deeds garner increasing local support (Holcomb and Balm, 1996). Finally, foreign tour operators start to exert pressure on local authorities to adopt measures that will protect the quality of the destination but, more importantly, the operators' profits (a 'treadmill' approach to sustainable development). These players know that if the situation does not improve, they will have to search for alternative destinations.

Discussion

The conceptual framework presented in the preceding section demonstrates (based on observations from Mediterranean island destinations) just one possible scenario of stakeholders' varying attitudes according to their respective level of tourism development. The model highlights an extremely important caveat. Even on a small island (e.g. Crete, Majorca, Minorca, Rhodes or Sardinia) it is possible to have a number of communities, each of which currently exhibits a different stage of the resort life cycle which 'may not conform to that of the parent destination' (Cooper, 1997, p. 91). Thus, for example, the Akamas peninsula in Cyprus displays characteristics of the exploration/involvement stage while the island as a whole, including the nearby coastal resort of Paphos, is courting with consolidation/stagnation (Ioannides, 1995a). Similarly, the interior part of Mallorca has only recently witnessed the emergence of low-intensity tourism whereas the parent destination, including many coastal areas, has already progressed through all the stages of its respective tourist life cycles (Bruce and Cantallops, 1996).

This situation reinforces the argument that a single set of top-down comprehensive national or regional policies alone (e.g. national/regional tourism directives, land-use planning and zoning, or environmental restrictions) are most likely unworkable throughout an entire country or region without accounting for the characteristics of individual localities. In the Cypriot context, for example, recent national-level recommendations (based on the advice of World Bank consultants) for improving the island's overall environment through the promotion of quality-oriented tourism ('weak' approach to sustainable development) have generated much hostility among poor inhabitants in certain remote rural areas. The latter are concerned that these national measures are too regulatory and will restrict their bid to improve their quality of life and emulate the economic success witnessed by their counterparts in neighbouring localities. Such a situation does not bode well for attaining the overriding goal of balancing economic, environmental, and societal objectives throughout the island.

The longitudinal model presented in this chapter suggests that the only meaningful way of approaching an overarching goal of sustainability is to ensure a successful marriage of top-down national or regional agendas with bottom-up/community-inspired objectives. In other words, although national or regional policy-makers and other agencies may be guided by a fairly long-term perspective (albeit one gained retrospectively), they should recognize that the best means of attaining this vision is by incrementally and painstakingly working with the constantly changing composite of stakeholders at every locality. In the case of the Mediterranean islands, just as in numerous developing regions, this means that officials representing all levels of government must steer clear of the prevailing perception that the inhabitants of communities lack the expertise to make informed decisions (Timothy, 1999).

An incremental and iterative approach towards the achievement of overall sustainability signifies the need to instigate conflict negotiations in localities representing each stage of the resort cycle. Due to their longer-term vision, national or regional planners and others should take a lead as mediators by seeking to establish a common ground between all stakeholders who have more immediate concerns, instead of creating adversity through the imposition of rigid top-down solutions. This approach necessitates skilful dialogue between all groups in an attempt to draw a distinction between broader ideological clashes from more rudimentary needs (Campbell, 1996). Nevertheless, a mediation process is unlikely to succeed if all concerned parties are unwilling to participate and compromise. There is, however, a higher probability that an agreement will eventually be achieved if the mediators can present all groups with a number of workable alternatives.

Conclusions

Despite considerable ideological debate concerning definitions, it appears that the overall notion of sustainability within a variety of contexts, including tourism, has gained broad acceptance from various quarters. Sustainability can be thought of as a 'policy myth' or 'guiding fiction' which 'serves useful functions in encouraging awareness, debate, and a sense of social purpose at an abstract, conceptual level' (McCool and Stankey, 1999, p. 22). In other words, the concept of sustainable development is valuable in that it allows groups and individuals with divergent ideologies and perspectives to band together around a common theme. Unfortunately, as McCool and Stankey argue, the term's 'intrinsic ambiguity might ultimately constitute an insurmountable barrier to developing consensus on specific actions' (McCool and Stankey, 1999, p. 22). The outstanding problem is how to translate such a fuzzy notion into actions that can be implemented successfully.

In this chapter, our principal aim has been to highlight the value of applying a longitudinal perspective of stakeholder behaviour to the sustainable development concept. Based on Butler's (1980) resort life cycle, our framework has been used to illustrate a hypothetical scenario of various players' changing attitudes according to stage of tourism development. The model is based on observations from one type of destination (i.e. Mediterranean islands) and may not necessarily fit other contexts. A longitudinal viewpoint such as this can either be applied to examine changes in a single locality over time or to concurrently compare communities (each of which has reached a distinct level of tourism development) within the same parent area (e.g. region or nation).

The chapter's major thrust has been a descriptive rather than prescriptive analysis. Nevertheless, a major finding emerging from this investigation is that planners, policy-makers, managers and other professionals need to acknowledge the contingencies dictated by a locality's individual life-cycle stage when attempting to implement overriding sustainable development objectives. This implies that the only *realistic* manner of approaching a future state of balanced development is not through a single holistic giant step but by incrementally adopting distinct measures that are sensitive to a destination's stage in the life cycle. The value of such a framework is that it can be adopted for a variety of strategies, including those directed at maintaining the competitiveness of the tourist product (see Cooper, 1997), but also broader objectives for overall sustainable development. However, the thorny question that remains is how to make this model work.

References

Berke, P.R. and Conroy, M.M. (2000) Are we planning for sustainable development: an evaluation of 30 comprehensive plans. *Journal of the American Planning Association* 66(1), 21–33.

Bosselman, F.B., Peterson, C.A. and McCarthy, C. (1999) *Managing Tourism Growth: Issues and Applications*. Island Press, Washington, DC.

Brackenbury, M. (1997) IFTO's Perspective on Holidays to the Mediterranean. Speech presented at conference on Tourism in the Mediterranean: Challenges and Opportunities, University of Westminster, 2 December.

Bramwell, B. and Sharman, A. (1999) Collaboration in local tourism policy-making. *Annals of Tourism Research* 26(2), 392–415.

Bruce, D. and Cantallops, A.S. (1996) The walled town of Alcudia as a focus for an alternative tourism in Mallorca. In: Briguglio, L., Butler, R., Harrison, D. and Filho, W.L. (eds) *Sustainable Tourism in Islands and Small States: Case Studies*. Pinter, London, pp. 241–261.

Buhalis, D. and Diamantis, D. (2001) Tourism development and sustainability in the Greek archipelagos. In: Ioannides, D., Apostolopoulos, Y. and Sonmez, S. (eds) *Mediterranean Islands and Sustainable Tourism Development*. Cassell, London (in press).

Burns, P. (1999) Paradoxes in planning: tourism elitism or brutalism? *Annals of Tourism Research* 26(2), 329–348.

Burr, S.W. (1995) Sustainable tourism development and use: follies, foibles, and practical applications. In: McCool, S. and Watson, A. (eds) *Linking Tourism, the Environment, and Sustainability*. US Department of Agriculture, Intermountain Research Station, Ogden, Utah, pp. 8–13.

Butler, R. (1980) The concept of a tourist area cycle of evolution: implications for management of resources. *The Canadian Geographer* 24(1), 5–12.

Butler, R. (1993) Tourism: an evolutionary perspective. In Nelson, J.G., Butler, R.W. and Wall, G. (eds) *Tourism and Sustainable Development: Monitoring, Planning, Managing*. University of Waterloo, Waterloo, Canada, pp. 27–43.

Butler, R. (1997) Modelling tourism development: evolution, growth and decline. In: Wahab, S. and Pigram, J.J. (eds) *Tourism Development and Growth: the Challenge of Sustainability*. Routledge, London, pp. 109–125.

Butler, R. (1999) Sustainable tourism: a state-of-the-art review. *Tourism Geographies* 1(1), 7–25.

Butler, R. and Stiakaki, E. (2001) Tourism and sustainability in the Mediterranean: issues and implications from Hydra. In: Ioannides, D., Apostolopoulos, Y. and Sonmez, S. (eds) *Mediterranean Islands and Sustainable Tourism Development*. Cassell, London, (in press).

Campbell, S. (1996) Green cities, growing cities, just cities? Urban planning and the contradictions of sustainable development. *Journal of the American Planning Association* 62(3), 296–312.

Carey, S., Gountas, Y. and Gilbert, D. (1997) Tour operators and destination sustainability. *Tourism Management* 18(7), 425–431.

Christaller, W. (1963) Some considerations of tourism location in Europe. *Paper of the Regional Science Association* 12, 95–105.

Coccossis, H. (1996) Tourism and sustainability: perspectives and implications. In: Priestley, G.K., Edwards, J.A. and Coccossis, H. (eds) *Sustainable Tourism? European Experiences*. CAB International, Wallingford, UK, pp. 1–21.

Cooper, C. (1997) The contribution of life cycle analysis and strategic planning to sustainable tourism. In: Wahab, S. and Pigram, J.J. (eds) *Tourism Development and Growth: the Challenge of Sustainability*. Routledge, London, pp. 78–94.

Cooper, C. and Jackson, S. (1989) Destination life cycle: the Isle of Man case study. *Annals of Tourism Research* 16(3), 377–398.

Cyprus Tourism Organization (1990) *New Tourism Policy.* (In Greek). CTO, Nicosia, Cyprus.

Dagonaki, Z. and Kotios, A. (1998) Cultural tourism and regional development. (In Greek). Paper written at the Department of Planning and Regional Development, University of Thessaly, Greece.

Debbage, K. (1990) Oligopoly and the resort cycle in the Bahamas. *Annals of Tourism Research* 17(4), 513–527.

de Kadt, E. (1990) *Making the Alternative Sustainable: Lessons from Development for Tourism.* Institute of Development Studies, Brighton, UK.

Gormsen, E. (1981) The spatio-temporal development of international tourism: attempt at a center periphery model. *La Consommation d'Espace par le Tourisme et sa Preservation.* Centre des Hautes Etudes to Tourisme, CHET, Aix-En-Provence.

Gunn, C.A. (1994) *Tourism Planning.* Taylor and Francis, New York.

Hall, C.M. and Lew, A.A. (eds) (1998) *Sustainable Tourism: a Geographical Perspective.* Longman, Harlow, Essex.

Haywood, M. (1986) Can the tourist area life cycles be made operational? *Tourism Management* 7, 154–167.

Hill, C. (1990) The paradox of tourism in Costa Rica. *Cultural Survival Quarterly* 14(1), 14–19.

Hitchcock, M., King, V. and Parnwell, M. (eds) (1993) *Tourism in South East Asia.* Routledge, London.

Holcomb, B. and Balm, R. (1996) Upping the ante: environmental and economic implications of Malta's up-market tourism policy. Unpublished paper written at Rutgers University, New Brunswick, New Jersey.

Ioannides, D. (1992) Agents of tourism development and the Cypriot resort cycle. *Annals of Tourism Research* 19, 711–731.

Ioannides, D. (1994) The state, transnationals, and the dynamics of tourism evolution in small island nations. PhD dissertation, Rutgers, State University of New Jersey.

Ioannides, D. (1995a) A flawed implementation of sustainable tourism: the experience of Akamas, Cyprus. *Tourism Management* 16(8), 583–592.

Ioannides, D. (1995b) Planning for international tourism in less developed countries: toward sustainability. *Journal of Planning Literature* 9(3), 235–254.

Ioannides, D. (1998) Tour operators: the gatekeepers of tourism. In: Ioannides, D. and Debbage, K. (eds) *The Economic Geography of the Tourist Industry: a Supply-side Analysis.* Routledge, London, pp. 139–158.

Ioannides, D. and Holcomb, B. (2001) Raising the stakes: implications of up-market tourism policies in Cyprus and Malta. In: Ioannides, D., Apostolopoulos, Y. and Sonmez, S. (eds) *Mediterranean Islands and Sustainable Tourism Development.* Cassell, London (in press).

Kousis, M. (2001) Tourism and the environment in Corsica, Sardinia, Sicily, and Crete. In: Ioannides, D., Apostolopoulos, Y. and Sonmez, S. (eds) *Mediterranean Islands and Sustainable Tourism Development.* Cassell, London (in press).

Loukissas, P. and Triantafyllopoulos, N. (1997) Factores Competitivos en los Destinos Turisticos Traditionales: Los Casos de las Islas Rodas y Myconos

(Grecia). *Papers de Tourisme*, TOURISME Generaliat Valenciana Agencia, Valenciana del Tourisme, 114.

McCool, S.F. (1995) Linking tourism, the environment, and concepts of sustainability: setting the stage. In: McCool, S. and Watson, A. (eds) *Linking Tourism, the Environment, and Sustainability*, US Department of Agriculture, Intermountain Research Station, Ogden, Utah, pp. 3–7.

McCool, S.F. and Stankey, G.H. (1999) *Searching for Meaning and Purpose in the Quest for Sustainability*. School of Forestry, Missoula, Montana.

Miossec, J.M. (1976) Un modele de l' espace touristique. *L' Espace Geographique* 6, 41–48.

Mowforth, M. and Munt, I. (1998) *Tourism and Sustainability: New Tourism in the Third World*. Routledge, London.

Oglethorpe, M. (1984) Tourism in Malta: a crisis of dependence. *Leisure Studies* 3, 147–161.

Pearce, D. (1989) *Tourist Development*. Longman, London.

Place, S.E. (1998) How sustainable is ecotourism in Costa Rica. In: Hall, C.M. and Lew, A.A. (eds) *Sustainable Tourism: a Geographical Perspective*. Longman, Harlow, Essex, pp. 107–118.

Plog, S. (1973) Why destinations rise and fall. *Cornell Hotel and Restaurant Administration Quarterly* 14, 13–16.

Redclift, M. (1987) *Sustainable Development: Exploring the Contradictions*. Routledge, London.

Richardson, H.W. (1987) Whither national urban policy in developing countries? *Urban Studies* 24, 227–244.

Ryan, C. (1991) *Recreational Tourism: a Social Science Perspective*. Routledge, London.

Sauter, E. and Leisen, B. (1999) Managing stakeholders: a tourism planning model. *Annals of Tourism Research* 26(2), 312–328.

Stansfield, C. (1978) Atlantic City and the resort cycle: background to the legalization of gambling. *Annals of Tourism Research* 5, 238–251.

Timothy, D.J. (1999) Participatory planning: a view of tourism in indonesia. *Annals of Tourism Research* 26(2), 371–391.

van den Bergh, J. and van der Straaten, J. (1994) *Towards Sustainable Development: Concepts, Methods, and Policy*. Island Press, Washington, DC.

Wahab, S. and Pigram, J. (eds) (1997) *Tourism Development and Growth: the Challenge of Sustainability*. Routledge, London.

Wall, G. (1997) Sustainable development – unsustainable development. In: Wahab, S. and Pigram, J.J. (eds) *Tourism Development and Growth: the Challenge of Sustainability*. Routledge, London, pp. 33–49.

Williams, A. and Montanari, A. (1999) Sustainability and self-regulation: critical perspectives. *Tourism Geographies* 1(1), 26–40.

World Commission on Environment and Development (1987) *Our Common Future*. Oxford University Press, Oxford.

Community Forestry: Countering Excess Visitor Demands in England's National Parks

5

Simon Evans

Anglia Polytechnic University, School of Design and Communication Systems, Chelmsford, Essex, UK

Introduction

For a relatively small yet densely populated country, demand for tourism and leisure in England's countryside can be extreme. Such demands are not consistent across time and space and, not surprisingly, it is primarily the areas of greatest aesthetic quality which attract the highest number of visitors, particularly in locations in close proximity to major population centres. The designation of certain areas of outstanding natural beauty and heritage as national parks from the early 1950s onwards aimed to preserve their distinctive character while providing opportunities for their enjoyment by the general public. In reality, this relationship between conservation and recreation has proved somewhat conflicting, and the popularity of national parks, as a visitor resource, is currently threatening the continuing protection of their unique qualities.

Viewed by many as an integral element of national heritage, contemporary debates surrounding national parks seek to identify means by which to alleviate much of this excess pressure. Discussions with policy-makers and practitioners involved in national park planning have identified a range of potential solutions currently under proposal. These include levying a charge upon visitation, restricting vehicular access, and zoning visitors away from the more sensitive environments. An overwhelming demand for a free countryside for all, however, is firmly rooted in the national psyche, and this implies that such suggestions are likely to receive little support in practice. Critics may view such attempts as little more than an effort towards exclusivity devised by, and on behalf of, an elitist minority, and therefore unacceptable.

The recent articulation of the principles of sustainable tourism and the concomitant need to view issues holistically has acted to challenge the limited focus of this debate. Instead of forcibly restricting visitation to protected areas, essentially a reactive approach, an alternative method has been identified as the creation of new areas of countryside in currently degraded urban fringe environments, attempting to filter excess demands away from sensitive sites. Instead of challenging the manifestations of problems as and when they occur, this approach favours targeting the causes of excess demand and can be described as a proactive, long-term proposal, consistent with the motivations of sustainable development. This chapter considers a range of potential responses to the decline of valued environments, concentrating on the introduction of the Community Forest initiative as the primary example in which to discuss a particular sustainable tourism solution.

An overview of national parks in England

Historical origins

The origins of national parks in England are diverse and precede their designation under the provisions of the 1949 National Parks and Access to the Countryside Act (the 1949 Act) by many years. Societal values attached to the British countryside reflect an ongoing conflict between town and country, an issue that can be traced back to the Industrial Revolution, when industrialization and centralization of the population were accompanied by declining quality in living and working conditions (Nicholson Lord, 1987). While urban centres have come to be perceived negatively, the countryside has provided their antithesis, considered a place of escape from the everyday pressures and problems associated with urban living (Shoard, 1999). The latter years of the 19th century and the initial decades of the 20th century witnessed a growing organization of specific conservation and recreational interests devoted to protecting the countryside (e.g. National Trust, Royal Society for the Protection of Birds, Ramblers Association, Council for the Protection of Rural England). These organizations ultimately played a pivotal role in developing a network of national parks, mostly through their activities as pressure groups (Matless, 1998).

As populations increased throughout the inter-war years and the countryside came under greater pressure to accommodate urban expansion, societal demands increasingly pointed towards the need for development control as an essential means of protecting valued landscapes and environments. Due to the fact that tenurial structures in the UK have historically been dominated by private ownership, this approach represented a means by which the state could influence and control inappropriate development activity. By the late 1940s a series of reports and studies provided the basis for a framework of planning controls to be introduced nationally. While the 1947 Town and Country Planning Act provided the foundation for green-belt legislation to prevent the lateral spread of cities, the 1949 Act established the powers by which countryside areas could be designated for additional protective controls.

The national parks of England have therefore evolved differently from the majority of international examples, which tend to achieve their protection and appropriate use by retaining the land essentially within the public domain and excluding human habitation within agreed zones. In contrast to this approach, English examples remain as working environments with large internal populations scattered throughout their designated boundaries (Poore and Poore, 1987). Considered in terms of wilderness in many other countries, national parks in England are 'a direct result of man's activities over the centuries' (Goldsmith and Warren, 1993). The British system of protection is therefore based upon influencing the management of land as opposed to excluding human intervention (Edwards, 1991).

The national parks of England

The first national parks in England were designated in 1951 and there are currently nine areas, which cover approximately 10,500 km², around 8% of the land base. Although a feature of the early designations was their focus upon predominantly upland environments, these have been supplemented by the recent addition of the Norfolk Broads and New Forest, both lowland sites. A further similarity between designated sites is their proximity to population centres, which provide a large number of potential day visitors in addition to those tourists who stay longer (Countryside Commission, 1996). The nine national parks of England (Fig. 5.1) currently attract over 70 million day visits per year.

National parks in England have been designated in order to achieve two key stated objectives, to: (i) preserve and enhance their natural beauty; and (ii) promote their enjoyment by the public.

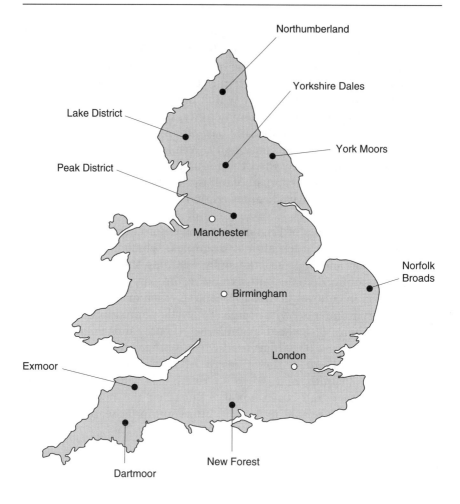

Fig. 5.1. The national parks of England.

Demands upon national parks

Such emphasis upon conservation and recreation as mutually compatible activities and outcomes reflects the relationship between areas of high aesthetic quality and popular landscape appreciation. While the environments contained within the parks undoubtedly represent some of the best examples of countryside in England, their actual designation has identified them as a magnet for visitation. Urry (1995) discusses the existence of a 'place-myth' which can develop around such areas, creating a surfeit of visitor numbers consistent with its enhanced appeal. The national park label in this case can become confused as a certification of excellence, one which is advertised by 'product signs' at all vehicular access points. Not only have national parks proved a magnet to tourists but their popularity has also extended to people wishing to reside within their boundaries. In this case, the designation has produced a premium on house prices and a high number of wealthy incomers have purchased homes and weekend residences, while many indigenous residents have been forced out due to an inability to compete economically. These new 'incomers' tend to be more articulate and vocal in communicating their needs and desires and have thus, in many cases, become the power base upon which local community motivations are judged. At the other end of the spectrum, communities that traditionally have relied on land-based industries as their primary employment sector have become increasingly marginalized as prices have spiralled. It is important to bear in mind throughout the passage of this debate the need to avoid social exclusion of traditionally under-represented groups.

Returning to the issue of visitation from outsiders, such positive expressions of national park attributes can convey a collectable quality to areas as visitors become compelled to spend quality time within their boundaries (Urry, 1990, p. 46). Tresidder (1999) discussed the sacred nature of such landscapes, removed as they are from the profanity of everyday life, attaching an enhanced cultural meaning to valued aesthetic resources, contributing to their popularity and thus their exploitation through mass visitation. As increasing numbers of tourists cross this threshold, so the risk increases that their presence may adversely affect the quality of the resource over the long term. Although not necessarily obvious in terms of significant built development, different forms of urbanization may take place, although these impacts may be highly seasonal and ephemeral in nature. For example, as more visitors seek vehicular access during peak summer months, so traffic congestion on small rural roads reflects many negative aspects traditionally associated with urban environments (p. 137). Additionally, car-parking facilities need to be provided and the visitor exodus from car to attraction can create feelings of over-crowding more akin to town than country.

Many of the ultimate visitor destinations, dictated as they are primarily by aesthetic quality, may coincide with the more sensitive, and therefore threatened, environments (Swarbrooke, 1999). In order to alleviate damaging pressures upon sites of significant value and sensitivity, certain areas have become sacrificed for the greater good of the whole (Newby, 1985), as 'honey-pot' sites, promoted and advertised in a manner designed to filter people into a distinct location where visitor management can be made more effective. Although environmental sensitivity is of central concern in this approach, it is by no means the only factor in determining the location of honey-pot sites. Landscape preference plays a central role also, and decisions in this regard need to reflect visitor perceptions of what actually constitutes a 'popular' attraction. Promoting a site of limited aesthetic or recreational appeal in an attempt to reduce pressures elsewhere is therefore not a viable response, and the relationship between quality, sensitivity and honey-pot attraction is often a close one. Each of these pressures can exacerbate a perceptual loss in feelings of tranquility and remoteness, an issue that has obvious connotations when the appeal of such areas is linked inextricably with a feeling of escape from everyday life and experience.

Further impacts upon heavily used sites include direct physical degradation as a result of visitor-inflicted erosion of footpaths and popular access points (Swarbrooke, 1999). As deterioration compounds, so do calls for remedial activity, which may take the guise of permanent footpath surfaces and straightening and upgrading of winding lanes, negatively affecting their rural character. For example, stretches of the Pennine Way, which fall within the boundaries of the Peak District, have become so overused that footpaths have now spread to some 30 m wide in places. In order to counter this problem, the provision of artificial, weatherproof footpathing materials have been considered the best way to control the erosion. Such factors have contributed to a growing conflict between the twin objectives of conservation and recreation and between visitors and host communities. The 1995 Environment Act recognized the presence of such conflict, prioritizing the conservation element in its statement that 'if it appears that there is a conflict between those [National Park] purposes greater weight shall be attached to the purpose of conserving and enhancing the natural beauty, wildlife and cultural heritage [of those locations]'. According to the Dartmoor National Park Officer, in some locations the point has already been reached where 'not all conflicts can be resolved, where the environment and public enjoyment of it are in danger of being irretrievably damaged and where, even if resource levels were increased, sustainable levels of leisure use are already being exceeded' (Atkinson, 1995). There would appear, therefore, to be a real danger that the national parks are being 'loved to death' (FNNPE, 1993).

Potential responses

The issues discussed previously make it evident that visitor impacts need to be monitored more closely and potential means of alleviating their negative consequences identified and implemented. Discussions with policy-makers and practitioners operating within the national park system have raised a number of proposed solutions in this respect, some of which are articulated and argued in the House of

Commons Environment Committee Report entitled *The Environmental Impact of Leisure Activities* (HM Government, 1995). The following is a summary of the main responses generated by the specific question 'How can we best reduce the damaging impacts of overvisitation in England's National Parks?' In order to set these responses in context, it should be pointed out that not all respondents accepted that a problem existed in reality and, indeed, a minority of those approached claimed that current management regimes were more than sufficient for protecting the national parks' unique qualities into the future. A summary of the main recurring responses from those who recognized the existence of overuse problems includes:

- the closure of specified roads and other vehicular access points;
- limiting car-parking spaces and introducing restrictive car-park pricing mechanisms;
- levying a charge upon entry to sensitive sites; and
- increased investment into resources for more appropriate visitor management techniques.

Although at first glance each of these suggestions would appear to offer certain resolutions, closer inspection identifies a number of limitations to their achievement in reality. First, the issue of road closures is firmly dependent upon highways legislation, which covers the entire country as opposed to individual locations. Additionally, levying a charge upon access would need to operate within an existing legal framework relating to public rights of way, and there is a perceived danger that the introduction of such charges may set a precedent for limited access to all countryside areas. This situation would be contrary to the notion of countryside access for all, a long-standing and popularly defended concept (Shoard, 1999). The restriction of car-parking spaces would be unlikely to achieve a significant downturn in demand and, if anything, would be more likely to increase the incidence of illegal parking on roadsides and verges. The same arguments could be attached to restrictive pricing mechanisms, which may also be seen as contrary to social equity and therefore elitist and divisive in terms of access to resources. Finally, increased investment into visitor management techniques may in itself entail a loss of rural character by its emphasis upon artificial features such as fencing and permanent surfacing. These approaches may also be seen as essentially reactive in nature, in contrast to the principles of sustainability which indicate a need for proactivity, where prevention is better than cure.

Sustainable development and tourism

The quest for sustainable tourism as an important adjunct of broader development activity has been discussed and debated widely by a range of academic and professional interests (e.g. Cater and Goodall, 1992; Burns and Holden, 1995; Hall and Page, 2000). The tendency to theorize rather than provide an unambiguous framework for achieving beneficial change has been an argument levelled widely against the sustainability lobby, with multiple interpretations of sustainability being adopted by different interests. Although the scope of the sustainable tourism debate remains broad, the focus of this chapter is less concerned with the sustaining of tourism itself, but rather considers tourism within the context of sustainable development. Much has been written and debated around the subject of sustainable development in recent years, with the Agenda 21 documentation allocating some 500 pages and 40 chapters to its general description (UNCED, 1992). While such a weight of literature precludes any full assessment of the principles within the limited scope of this chapter, the following sentences aim to provide a general overview of the issues impacting directly upon this study. As little consensus has been achieved in the way individuals view sustainability (Bowers, 1997), and in light of the generally adopted definition from the Brundtland Commission (WCED, 1987) being vague and open to significant interpretation, the following passages represent a somewhat personal reading of the sustainability debate.

The fundamental basis of sustainable development surrounds the need for prudence in the use of finite resources. This requirement necessitates a reappraisal of the traditional structures that underpin development activity. In simple terms, this includes the need to consider outcomes from a number of perspectives, identifying and simultaneously assessing a range of consequences from a variety of economic, social and physical viewpoints. This requires a holistic understanding, identifying the causal influences of change emanating from primary developments as well as the effects of externalities upon those developments. This demands a coordinated approach, one that is supported by quality research and greater accessibility to the generated information. Current research being undertaken at Anglia Polytechnic University suggests that although many interests share common goals in achieving change, their specialist interests lead them to pursue those goals in different ways. While some may advocate the achievement of beneficial change within existing structures, so others call for an overhaul of many traditional practices that they consider to be outmoded and unsustainable in their own right. The issue of green-belt legislation can be considered within this context. While visitor demands upon the national parks may ultimately prove restrictively high, the green belts may represent a wasted asset in alleviating surplus pressure.

Green belt philosophy, introduced under the provisions of the 1947 Town and Country Planning Act, is based upon two simple principles. First that limits to urban growth and sprawl need to be established, and, secondly, that an open area of land surrounding a town or city will convey a range of benefits upon city dwellers. In short, the green belt is perceived by many to be the 'lungs of the city', its immediate countryside. While retaining significant support in principle, the reality is that the green belt, in many cases, represents a degraded resource. The fact that the green belt is often regarded more negatively as 'urban fringe' illustrates many of the problems experienced within this zone. The urban fringe, and hence large areas of green belt, have been described as containing a range of pressures and uses that set it aside from conventionally visualized countryside.

This zone contains the 'attributes of modern society – sewerage works, waste disposal . . . litter, trespass, vandalism, etc.', activities which 'mingle and interact with agriculture, often in inappropriate and detrimental ways' (UFSAG, 1994). Urban dwellers seeking an escape from the city consequently attach a lower priority to their immediate countryside in favour of the more cherished vistas of the deeper countryside. In order for the green belts to play a role as a filter for surplus visitors to more sensitive environments, a general upgrading of this zone becomes imperative.

The Community Forest initiative

Conceived and introduced as a joint venture between the Countryside and Forestry commissions, the Community Forest initiative is proposed within this chapter as a potentially sustainable response to countering overvisitation in England's national parks. As with national parks, community forestry in England is not consistent with other programmes operating globally and therefore requires brief explanation of its distinct characteristics. Focused upon the urban fringes of 12 towns and cities across England (Fig. 5.2), the national initiative, in similar terms to the national parks, is contained within predominantly privately owned landownership systems. Much of this land coincides with the designation of green belts, a high proportion of it despoiled (Fig. 5.2).

The Community Forest concept is based upon the achievement of multiple objectives (e.g. recreation, conservation, education) with the focus of development based around the creation of a woodland resource in areas currently suffering a paucity of existing tree cover. In

Fig. 5.2. Proposed Community Forests in England.

sustainable terms, it is important that this land becomes more accessible and welcoming to short-term visitors who currently penetrate the deeper countryside, reducing travelling times for leisure purposes while educating people, through interpretation, the values of responsible tourism and leisure. For this reason, the role of local communities at all levels of the development process represents a fundamental aim of the programme.

As the label suggests, the Community Forest concept is based upon the union between a range of social (community) and physical (forest) factors, aiming to provide the community with a resource that reflects its needs, consistent with the motivations of sustainable development. Unlike many community forestry activities operating globally, however, this does not mean that the initiative is operated in a bottom-up manner, but rather that a number of partnerships are established between the public, private and voluntary sectors, and that these are expected to determine the scope and character of the ultimate project achievements. In reality this is proving difficult to achieve (Evans and Davies, 1993), both in terms of the levels of planting currently attained and in the full representation of all community interests present in designated localities (Tiffin and Burton, 1996). Initial research findings do suggest that where projects have proved successful, those involved in their development have tended to visit individual sites more frequently, rather than travelling farther afield for their leisure activities. The number of people that this applies to remains small in statistical terms, however, reflecting the early phase of what is, by necessity, a long-term programme, involving as it does the establishment of trees.

The ultimate potential of the Community Forest initiative, if implemented successfully to envisaged targets, does involve the deflection of visitors away from the deeper countryside in favour of positively managed open land on their 'doorsteps'. How then do the two approaches articulated in this chapter (reactive activity within national park boundaries/proactive activity within Community Forestry boundaries) react to the application of sustainable development criteria?

Conclusions

The application of conventional thought to national parks in England appears to be problematic. In physical terms, the protection of the resource is accorded high priority, yet it is the high quality of the resource that attracts increasing numbers of tourists, who, in turn, create greater physical impacts. This visitation provides economic benefits for the locations, yet with a philosophy of a 'free countryside for all' much of this income bypasses the land managers in favour of other businesses directly involved in the leisure/tourism industry (e.g. hoteliers, restauranteurs). While social equity considerations suggest a greater voice for the host community and a greater stake in the generated income (Countryside Commission, 1996), population transience has created a situation where elite internal communities have sometimes developed, often to the detriment of indigenous residents. Furthermore, visitors to the area are often less wealthy than those residing within the national parks and therefore the increased filtering of income to local providers may ultimately lead to deepening social inequity. The future of national parks is open to considerable debate, which has become centred primarily upon physical considerations.

Although the need to protect certain areas against excessive use is an axiom of both arguments expressed in this chapter, the way in which this should be achieved is the issue under question. Should the focus of remedial activity be upon the national parks themselves, or upon the external centres from which the majority of the demand is derived? It is the contention of this chapter, one that incidentally appears to raise more questions than proffer solutions, that the answer lies in a combination of the two. While visitor control within national parks remains essential, ignorance of the reasons for surplus demand can create a series of short-term, reactive responses contrary to the broad rationale behind sustainability.

In contrast, by creating areas of new countryside in proximity to major demand centres, an essentially long-term, proactive approach, policy-makers can seek to reduce visitor pressure in the future. This may enable more effective controls to be implemented within the national parks themselves as the ratio between day and longer-term visitors diminishes. Perhaps the key to success rests with achieving the right balance in achieving a coordinated response both internally and externally. This, however, requires strong communication between national park and Community Forest officers, a situation that is not currently obvious. While, in theory, sustainable tourism strongly promotes partnership and stakeholder participation, this is not necessarily translated into effective practice. In spatial terms, cooperation and communication within the national parks and within the Community Forests may be improving, yet focused integration between the two designations remains sparse.

Perhaps the final word in this respect rests with the forward thinking of Robert Byron, a noted traveller and writer in the 1930s, who described a specialist as 'one who grows to know more and more about less and less' (Byron, 1933), a phrase which could just as easily be applied to problems encountered with sustainability. Holism requires integration not disintegration, whereas current expert panels appear dominated by individual interest, with priorities determined accordingly. The move towards sustainable tourism is not a simple one, and differences in political, socio-economic and cultural values may dictate a range of responses to negative impacts, depending upon location and circumstance.

Establishing guidelines for tourism in terms of its sustainable performance is important, yet to undertake this without reference to broader development issues may be folly. Equally, to regard tourism as an activity distinctly separate from recreation would ignore the fact that in many cases the two groups of visitors display similar demands in the way that they consume environments. There may be no easy answer to overvisitation of popular areas, and improvement of currently degraded green belt/urban fringes should not be viewed as a panacea in this regard. Perhaps a composite model drawn from a variety of current and projected approaches may ultimately prove successful in reducing negative impacts. Of key importance to this ongoing debate is, however, the need to favour proactivity over reactivity, and to produce and communicate high-quality research in order to enable the application of innovative responses to overuse of national parks. Although the tendency to restrict development activity within existing structures may make short-term sense, it needs to be appreciated that sustainability implies long-term solutions to declining environments and that certain conventional approaches may prove outmoded and inconsistent with sustainable tourism objectives. Perhaps the greatest task in this respect is the need to challenge conventional hegemonic mindsets in order to progress sustainability from policy into practice. The experiences gained from the national park/Community Forest union may prove instrumental in this regard, depending on the willingness of decision-makers to adapt and change their processes to reflect current realities.

References

Atkinson, N. (1995) Evidence to House of Commons Environment Committee. In: *The Environmental Impact of Leisure Activities*, Vol. 3. HMSO, London.

Bowers, J. (1997) *Sustainability and Environmental Economics: an Alternative Text*. Longman, London.

Burns, P. and Holden, A. (1995) Alternative and sustainable tourism development – the way forward? In: Burns, P. and Holden, A. *Tourism: a New Perspective*. Prentice Hall, Hemel Hempstead, pp. 218–221.

Byron, R. (1933) *First Russia, then Tibet*. Reprint 1994, Penguin Books, London.

Cater, E. and Goodall, B. (1992) Must tourism destroy its resource base? In: Bowlby, S. and Mannion, A. *Environmental Issues in the 1990s*. John Wiley, Chichester, pp. 317–321.

Countryside Commission (1996) *Visitors to National Parks: Summary of the 1994 Survey Findings*. Countryside Commission, Cheltenham.

Edwards, R. (1991) *Fit for the Future: Report of the National Parks Review Panel*. Countryside Commission, Cheltenham.

Evans, S. and Davies, D. (1993) A review of Community Forest policy and the constraints on its implementation. In: *Environmental Policy and Practice*, Vol. 2, No. 2. EPP, Surrey.

FNNPE (Federation of Nature and National Parks of Europe) (1993) *Loving to Death? Sustainable Tourism in Europe's Nature and National Parks*. FNNPE, Grafenau.

Goldsmith, F. and Warren, A. (1993) *Conservation in Progress*. John Wiley & Sons, Chichester.

Hall, C. and Page, S. (2000) *The Geography of Recreation and Tourism*. Routledge, London.

HM Government (1995) *The Environmental Impact of Leisure Activities*, Vol. 1. HMSO, London.

Matless, D. (1998) *Landscape and Englishness*. Reaktion Books, London.

Newby, H. (1985) *Green and Pleasant Land: Social change in rural England*. Hutchinson, London.

Nicholson Lord, D. (1987) *The Greening of Cities*. Routledge and Keegan Paul, London.

Page, S. (1998) *Transport and Tourism*. Longman, Harlow.

Poore, D. and Poore, J. (1987) *Protected Landscapes: the United Kingdom Experience*. International Symposium on Protected Landscapes, Lake District, 5–10 October.

Shoard, M. (1999) *A Right to Roam*. Oxford University Press, Oxford.

Swarbrooke, J. (1999) *Sustainable Tourism Management*. CAB International, Wallingford, UK.

Tiffin, R. and Burton, R. (1996) Seeing the woods for the trees. *Forestry* June.

Tresidder, R. (1999) Tourism and sacred landscapes. In: Crouch, D. (ed.) *Leisure/Tourism Geographies: Practices and Geographical Knowledge*. Routledge, London, pp. 137–152.

UFSAG (Urban Fringe Special Advisory Group) (1994) *Planning in the Urban Fringe*. Association of Metropolitan Authorities, London.

UNCED (United Nations Commission on Environment and Development) (1992) Agenda 21 Documentation.

Urry, J. (1990) *The Tourist Gaze*. Sage, London.

Urry, J. (1995) *Consuming Places*. Routledge, London.

WCED (World Commission on Environment and Development) (1987) *Our Common Future*. Oxford University Press, Oxford.

Nature Preservation, Sense of Place and Sustainable Tourism: Can the 'Yellowstone Experience' Survive?

6

Judith L. Meyer

Department of Geography, Geology and Planning, Southwest Missouri State University, Springfield, Missouri, USA

At first glance, Yellowstone National Park appears to be a perfect example of 'sustainable tourism'. After all, the park celebrated its 125th anniversary in 1997. Hence, for generations, Yellowstone has sustained its appeal, audience and luxury-resort-in-the-wilderness image, despite the grizzly bear scares of the 1970s and 1980s, the wildfires of 1988, and the 'bison slaughter' of 1997. Each of these events – and other, less publicized events – as well as the management decisions that led to them, caused national uproar and criticism of the park's administrators and managers. This criticism was especially loud and sharp in Yellowstone's bordering states and gateway communities, and was aimed at administrators as far away as Washington, DC. Any policy changes, it seems, that deviate from 'the way it's always been done round here' are followed by a fear that tourists will stay away, sales of rooms, meals, gasoline and other necessities purchased in the communities and outposts surrounding the park will plummet, and jobs will be lost. However, these predicted devastating drops in tourist visitation rates never materialize.

As an example, during the Yellowstone wildfires of 1988, businesses in the park's gateway communities clamoured for immediate fire-fighting efforts, claiming that tourist numbers would drop if the park burned. However, although park visitation did decrease by 400,000 people in 1988 (about 16% of expected totals for the year), visitation in October of 1988 was up 39% over previous years (Wuerthner, 1988).

Despite these losses, some establishments did a brisk business in
supplying the army of firefighters with everything from motel space to
food. For many establishments, the summer fires were a gold mine that
provided an unexpected boom, helping to mitigate the loss of tourist
dollars.

(Wuerthner, 1988, p. 55)

And, if visitation figures from Yellowstone entrance gates are
considered, the minor drop during the fires themselves did not, as
fears suggested, continue into later years. Tourist numbers are
measured at entrance gates in persons per vehicle (PPV), and PPV
figures for 1988, 1989 and 1990 were 2.2 million, 2.7 million and 2.8
million, respectively (T. Wert, Yellowstone National Park, Wyoming,
2000, personal communication).

Obviously, Yellowstone National Park is doing fine. But is it? From
a scientific perspective, where the goal is a functioning, self-sustaining
ecosystem, Yellowstone is faring well. From an economic perspective,
where the goal is a tourist destination with a sustained high-visitor-
satisfaction level, Yellowstone is doing fine. But if one considers the
traditional Yellowstone experience, one rich in history and meaning
and one unique to this particular park, Yellowstone may not be living
up to expectations. Management practices that outwardly achieve both
nature preservation and sustainable tourism may not necessarily
maintain the integrity of the traditional tourist experience. In Yellowstone, proper management may not be a question of saving a resource
or 'tourist product' from stagnation or depletion so much as saving a
tourist experience from being forgotten. This chapter suggests that by
including the concepts of 'sense of place' and 'historical appropriateness' alongside science and cost–benefit analyses, managers might be
able to make decisions that are more sensitive to the broader public
and private interests in places like Yellowstone that serve the dual
purpose of being both nature preserves and 'public pleasuring
grounds'.

This broader, more holistic management perspective provides two
benefits. First, it frees managers from considering only the negative
environmental impacts of tourism by making the tourist experience
itself a central concern. Decision-makers, thereby, are placed in a more
proactive rather than reactive role. Managers begin with a solid
understanding of the park's sense of place or traditional tourist
product and then base management decisions and practices on how to
enhance this site-specific experience without replacing it with something less meaningful, generic or both.

The second benefit of this approach is that it recognizes and
incorporates the interests of the area surrounding the park into the
totality of the park experience. In many instances, the tourist
experience may actually begin well outside the borders of the park

(Meyer, 1996). Few tourists arrive at a Yellowstone National Park entrance without having driven across the western plains or mountains en route to the park. (Despite claims of 'visual blight', signs for Wall Drug do serve as mile-markers and anticipation-builders for sports utility vehicles full of families headed for the western national parks.) If managers expand the scope of the perceived tourist destination, they can broaden and intensify the excitement and wonder of the place. Managers should be willing and eager to elicit advice, ideas and support from surrounding communities, so that the latter might feel a part of the tourist experience rather than apart from it.

Site and situation

Typical descriptions of Yellowstone National Park's establishment (1 March 1872), location (in the north-west corner of Wyoming, but including a narrow strip of land in Montana to the north and Idaho to the west), size (approximately 880,000 ha or 2.2 million acres) and superlative characteristics ('birthplace' of the national park idea; largest national park in the lower 48 states; largest concentration of elk in the USA; more geothermal features than everywhere else in the world combined; and so on) often fail to include information concerning the area surrounding the park. Yet, Yellowstone is literally the 'heart' – geographically, biologically, geologically, economically, politically, even emotionally – of a 5–10 million ha (depending on whose definition of the ecosystem's boundaries one uses) Greater Yellowstone Region (Vale and Vale, 1989; Glick *et al.*, 1991; Schullery, 1997; Pritchard, 1999), composed of publicly and privately owned land surrounding Yellowstone National Park itself. The Greater Yellowstone is home to movie stars, mining and logging camps, new ranchettes and suburban sprawl, working farms and ranches that have been 'in the family for generations', national parks, national forests, national wildlife refuges, state parks, city parks, new and historic resorts, chequerboard acreage owned by railroad corporations, and gateway communities hoping to continue to 'cash in' on Yellowstone's name and reputation.

Because of Yellowstone National Park's size and the even greater expanse of the Greater Yellowstone Region, the park's gateway communities include those immediately adjoining the park, such as West Yellowstone and Gardiner, Montana, as well as those cities as far away as Bozeman and Livingston, Montana, to the north; Cody, Wyoming, to the east; Jackson, Wyoming, to the south; and Big Sky, Montana, to the north and west. Some of these towns were established well before Yellowstone became a national park, but none would attract the number of tourists they do today were it not for their relationship and proximity to the park.

In a perfect world, Yellowstone would be all things to all people. It would be a wilderness, a place with little or no sign of a lasting human presence. It would be a wildlife sanctuary where animals could graze, prowl or migrate without human interruption or intervention. It would be a laboratory where scientists could record these natural cycles and measure, sample, catalogue and theorize about the natural world. It would be an amusement park where people could relive the Wild West by riding a horse or watching a herd of bison graze. It would be a park with plenty of parking spaces, flush toilets, campsites, hotel rooms and souvenir shops.

In this world, however, those in charge of Yellowstone face two problems not typically associated with a nature preserve. First, they must contend not only with the park's international image as an icon of nature preservation, but also with the park's reputation and reality as a world-class tourist destination, bringing over 3 million people into the region annually. Secondly, management decisions made by the National Park Service (NPS) in Yellowstone National Park do not end there. Instead, management decisions reverberate throughout the Greater Yellowstone and have an impact on individuals, communities and resources hundreds of miles away. Some communities or enterprises cannot quickly adjust to, or easily absorb, the impact of such changes. How can park managers be responsive and considerate of so many and such varied stakeholders? Reconciling these oft-conflicting objectives has not been easy or non-contentious.

Ecosystems management and the idea of 'place'

Over the past several decades, in response to American society's growing environmental awareness and concern that began in the 1960s, the NPS has used ecosystem-based management as a tool for achieving and maintaining some illusion, if not actual state, of wildness in the natural parks of the national park system (Houston, 1971; Despain et al., 1986; Schullery, 1997; Pritchard, 1999). For example, in celebration of Yellowstone's centennial in 1972, the NPS introduced a new management strategy based on letting nature run its course. Backcountry rubbish dumps where grizzly bears had fed for generations were closed, radio collars used to monitor bears and other wildlife were removed, and a 'let burn' policy toward naturally occurring forest fires was instituted. The dump closures were followed by several years of 'bear incidents' or 'bear encounters' that resulted in the injury or death of tourists and bears. Ultimately, the NPS had to 'remove', 'destroy' or 'relocate' a portion of the park's grizzly population. Some believe the NPS reduced the Yellowstone grizzly population to near extinction in a misguided attempt to force bears to return to more 'natural' diets and foraging behaviours (Craighead, 1979). Others argued that the NPS's removal programme merely restored a more natural balance between the grizzly bear population and available habitat (Schullery, 1980; Pritchard, 1999). Regardless of the finger-pointing and name-calling, Yellowstone is no longer the Jellystone National Park of the Yogi Bear era, and bears do not line the roads begging for hand-outs. The bears of Yellowstone have apparently returned to their natural, wild ways, and bear sightings along Yellowstone roads are infrequent. However, more than 25 years after the change in management policy, tourists still travel to Yellowstone to see bears and express disappointment when they do not see them.

The public's response to the change in bear-management policies was both swift and persistent, but it took almost two decades for the implications of the let-burn policy to be realized. In 1988, naturally and artificially started backcountry fires, both in and outside Yellowstone, were allowed to burn, but they soon burned out of control. To protect human lives, the NPS escorted tourists and park staff out of the park, locked doors, and closed the park in the middle of the tourist season. The public's critical response – fuelled by emotional hyperbole and exaggeration by the mass media – to the 'ecologically correct' wildfires made park managers realize that Yellowstone was more than a representative bit of wild nature. The 'ecological value' of wildfire may have been acceptable *in theory* but not *in reality*; at least not here, not in Yellowstone National Park. Local residents and members of surrounding communities felt betrayed by administrators who appeared to place more value on science and scientific principles than on their needs and interests. John Barbee, Yellowstone's superintendent during the summer of fires, commented after the fires were out and some semblance of peace had returned to the region that the NPS's ecosystem-based management programme was an 'uneasy truce between what science tells us is possible and what our value system tells us is appropriate' (Barbee and Schullery, 1989, p. 18). He and others realized that, to many of Yellowstone's supporters, the park is not a laboratory, it is a *place*.

More than 20 years ago, humanist geographer Yi-Fu Tuan introduced geographers to the role of 'place' and 'sense of place' in geography as a discipline and as a perspective (1977). Tuan suggested that 'place' 'is not only a fact to be explained in the broader frame of space, but it is also a reality to be clarified and understood from the perspectives of the people who have given it meaning' (1979, p. 387). Since then, geographers and scholars from various academic backgrounds have described how people not only 'socially construct' places and the landscapes that enclose them (Olwig, 1996; Oakes, 1997; Schein, 1997; Proctor, 1998), but then identify themselves and their values with these particular places (Greider and Garkovich, 1994).

Hence, as 'place' – rather than as 'national park' or 'nature preserve' – Yellowstone is a humanized landscape, the product of generations of people interacting with its landscape and assigning meanings beyond its physical setting. Two outcomes of my own work on the evolution of Yellowstone's sense of place (Meyer, 1996) are especially pertinent to the idea of sustainable tourism. First is the role of the tourist in contributing to, articulating and sustaining a sense of place. Earl Pomeroy (1957), historian of tourism in the American West, understood the importance of tourists to the establishment and continued success of western parks and resorts, because, he noted, the tourist not only observed and recorded experiences but became an 'ingredient' of the experience as well. Tourists describe their experiences and create expectations of an experience for others.

My second point is that sense of place is not a subjective, personal, amorphous entity without substance, that can easily be dismissed as peripheral to the tourist experience. Indeed, sense of place can be understood, investigated and quantified (Shamai, 1991). And, the sense of place for Yellowstone is central to the unique 'Yellowstone experience' that differentiates Yellowstone from other national park experiences. Further, this sense of place can serve as a standard or guideline for management strategies today. I offer two examples where policy decisions based on ecosystem-based management conflicted directly with the traditional sense-of-place-based tourist experience.

Winter tourism

Winter has typically been Yellowstone's off-season: a time for the park – and park employees – to rest, recuperate and rejuvenate from the short but intense summer tourist season (Bartlett, 1985). However, over the past two decades, Yellowstone's winter tourist numbers have soared, mostly as a result of increased snowmobile use. An increase in the number of tourists has led to an accompanying increase in winter services and facilities available to them, and modern winter tourists need these services; they are not as self-sufficient as their predecessors.

Historically, winter travel to and through Yellowstone was slow, deliberate and quiet. Visitors had to travel on skis or snowshoes and make camp in the snow. A century ago, a young private in the army stationed on winter duty in Yellowstone wrote the following in a letter to his sister: 'everything is so quiet that one can almost hear the solitude' (Kelsey, 1898). Now, those who come to the park expecting solitude and silence find crowds of people and the roar of snowmobiles. Today's winter tourists arrive on snowmobiles, sleep in hotels, eat in restaurants, and warm themselves and fuel their machines at warming huts and petrol stations. Winter tourism in Yellowstone may have changed, but the situation is not unique to this park. 'Many wildlands have thus experienced a progressive shift from values focused on a natural environment to more socially-oriented, facility dependent values' (Knopf, 1988, p. 6).

Certainly, at the turn of the century, when automobiles replaced horse-drawn carriages as the park's main form of transportation, many must have decried the eventual ruination of the Yellowstone experience. How is the intrusion of snowmobiles different from the earlier intrusion of horseless carriages? First, the exhaust and sound of snowmobiles precludes others from experiencing the traditional Yellowstone winter. Recently, two organizations who oversee national parks in general and Yellowstone in particular, the National Parks and Conservation Association and the Greater Yellowstone Coalition, reported that over the course of a day, the drone of snowmobiles in Yellowstone is now nearly constant, especially at popular places like Old Faithful Geyser. Hence, the use of snowmobiles is 'locking out other users' (Milstein, 2000). Others have pointed out that 'silence' or at least an environment 'uncorrupted by the beeping, pounding, whining, roaring, growling, and screaming of civilization' may be a valid reason for preserving natural places (Watkins, 1999, p. 41). In other words, snowmobiles and the noise and pollution they bring are not a new dimension in Yellowstone's evolving sense of place so much as they are an interruption and replacement of one sense of place for another.

The second way in which the introduction and increased use of snowmobiles in Yellowstone is different from the introduction of the automobile is that it is still possible to consider what we want the Yellowstone experience to be. It is still possible to restrict or channel winter use of the park so as to maintain the traditional sense of place. 'Yellowstone is not supposed to be Disneyland, and the Park Service doesn't have to open it up to snowmobiles', noted a wildlife biologist working for the Fund for Animals (Schubert, in Daerr, 1999, p. 11).

Originally, scientists argued that snowmobiles were a benign presence in the park, because their ecological impact was minimal. It was assumed that because bears hibernate, many of the park's elk herds move to lower elevations outside the park, and much of the park lies hidden and protected under many feet of snow, winter tourism would have little impact on the environment. More recently, however, attention has focused not only the noise but also the air pollution caused by snowmobiles. The two-cycle engine on a snowmobile produces exhaust containing a thousand times more hydrocarbon and nitrous oxide pollutants than that of a car (Greater Yellowstone Coalition, 1996, p. 5). Also, snowmobilers do not necessarily stay on groomed roads and have been found chasing bison and other wildlife as well as competing with cross-country skiers on backcountry ski-only trails. However, the rub lies in the fact that snowmobilers spend more money in local and regional communities than do cross-country skiers, so concessionaires do not want snowmobile numbers reduced or their access restricted.

As the NPS makes plans to deal with the higher number of tourists projected to arrive in the coming years, it might be helpful to consider using Yellowstone's sense of place as a standard for what sort and number of winter facilities to provide. Perhaps future winter tourists will arrive on skis or will avail themselves of the transportation services provided by organized snow coach tours. It may still be possible to sustain what is uncommon about Yellowstone – what makes it unique. The alternative is for Yellowstone to become a generic winter outdoor-recreation experience.

Hot springs and hot tubs

Far and away, it is Yellowstone's geothermal features that make this place unique. The place 'where Hell bubbled up' continues to fascinate people from around the world who come to watch an eruption of Old Faithful, admire the blue of Morning Glory Pool, and dip a finger in one of the many hot springs pockmarking the Yellowstone landscape. But few activities intrigue visitors more than the idea of bathing, wading or swimming in these pools. The park's discoverers soaked in some springs and cooked potatoes in others. Later, tourists used the springs to bathe, brew coffee and wash clothes and dishes. The park's early concessionaires constructed canals and pipelines to bring water from hot springs to swimming pools and soaking chambers where the water temperature could be regulated. For a time, public bathing facilities were operated at Mammoth Hot Springs and near Old Faithful. Fees were charged accordingly: 50 cents for the large pool at Old Faithful and Mammoth Hot Springs, US$1 for the private pool at Old Faithful, and wading was free and was engaged in enthusiastically (a fact to which old photos attest). For therapeutic or purely recreational purposes, swimming and soaking in Yellowstone springs quickly became an important part of the Yellowstone experience. Everyone had to do it.

Initially, the NPS began to dissuade tourists from swimming and wading in the springs, because, rather than being therapeutic, hot spring water could be dangerous. Water temperatures could change without warning from tepid to boiling in a matter of minutes. With this information in hand, hot springs suddenly became, legally, an attractive nuisance, and the NPS did not want to have to monitor and patrol all of the park's 10,000 thermal features in order to keep the public safe.

As the keep-it-natural movement began gaining popularity, however, institutionalized swimming in the park ended once and for all. The private pool at Old Faithful (designed by Robert Reamer, the architect who built the marvellous Old Faithful Inn) was dismantled, since the full-size pool drew water from Solitary Geyser, and drawing hot water from a natural geyser was considered a disruption to a natural system. Further, in an attempt to preserve even the tiniest of Yellowstone's ecosystems, protection was extended to the colonies of bacteria and algae living in the hot springs and runoff channels. These colonies of microscopic organisms would be destroyed if people walked, sat or swam in the water. Hence, swimming is still legal in the rivers, streams and lakes in the park, but the era of soaking in the springs is over.

However, while tourists are prohibited from soaking in Yellowstone's hot springs, they are allowed to soak in hot tubs that come with some room/cabin rentals at park hotels. Hot tubs are safe because the water temperature can be controlled. And hot tubs are ecologically correct, since they use treated, heated hotel water rather than water from a natural thermal feature. How disappointing, however, to the tourist who merely wanted to wade in a warm pool to be told that he or she must rent a room with a hot tub! Ecologically, hot tubs make sense, but in terms of the traditional Yellowstone experience, wading in a real spring is a part of experiencing the real Yellowstone.

Implications of using Yellowstone as a case study

At first glance, Yellowstone National Park would seem to provide fertile ground as a case study for sustainability, whether the focus is on sustaining an ecosystem, one element of the ecosystem, the local or regional tourist economy, or the park's sense of place. After 125 years, Yellowstone's popularity remains high and, except for the years during the world wars, visitation rates have never been through the typical resort cycle of initial boom and eventual stagnation and demise. Also, Yellowstone's gateway communities have thrived, some experiencing renewed vigour as retired and/or wealthy urban dwellers rediscover the American West and buy up ranches to build second homes or retirement homes in the Greater Yellowstone area.

However, there are limitations to using Yellowstone as a blanket example of 'what could be' elsewhere; almost all of these limitations stem from the fact that Yellowstone is one of only a handful of parks considered the 'crown jewels' of the US National Park system. Included in this exclusive club are Yosemite, Mount Rainier, Glacier and Grand Canyon. These parks are old and therefore well established in terms of international recognition, transportation linkages, tourist facilities and administration. They are geographically large and environmentally diverse, hence they can, physically and economically, accommodate large numbers of tourists, support staff and gateway facilities and attractions. Their size and geographic characteristics allow them to absorb large numbers of visitors without straining resources and appearing 'crowded', because there is always the option of dispersing people throughout the park rather than concentrating them in one small area (see Chapter 2, this volume).

These parks are immensely popular, both nationally and internationally, with nature enthusiasts as well as tourists seeking luxury resorts. Further, with few exceptions, parks such as Yellowstone do not need to deal with properly representing the rights and concerns of indigenous peoples as a part of their management programmes. Another limitation to using Yellowstone as a model for other parks is that it is well known and in no danger of disappearing if it isn't publicized and marketed. However, these limitations may serve as lessons for both lesser-known and newly created parks and resorts. Perhaps Yellowstone and Yosemite have been so successful *because* of their size, biological and geographical diversity, and the meanings associated with their sense of place and tourist traditions.

Size

One lesson that might be drawn from the Yellowstone example is that, whenever possible, new nature parks or preserves should be as big as is economically and politically possible. The larger a park's geographic extent, the easier it is to maintain at least a semblance of wildness – if only in the backcountry, interior, highest elevations or densest jungles – while still providing for some amount of modern tourist amenities to sustain the park economically. Larger areas can allow for, and can more easily absorb, macro-scale natural processes, such as volcanic eruptions, wildfire and floods, whereas smaller reserves cannot. Typically, the aftermath of these major, landscape-altering events acts as a tourist draw as curious tourists and scientists rush in to assess the situation. Hence, if a destination hopes to attract both nature-lovers and mainstream tourists, the greater the areal extent of the park means a greater chance for acceptance of its wilderness character and initial popularity, continued support and long-term survival.

Also, the larger the park, the better the chance for more biological diversity within its borders; and, the more diversity or variation in wildlife or landforms, the broader the park's appeal among different interest groups. For example, a single park can attract anglers, photographers, birdwatchers, wildflower enthusiasts and rock climbers only if it has something to offer each of those groups. In Yellowstone, when the wolf was removed as a predator, the grizzly bear took over as the park's main carnivore *perceptually*, if not ecologically, as evidence of the park's naturalness. Certainly, the bear did not fill the same ecological niche as the wolf, but in terms of sustaining the tourists' perception of the park as a place where there are predators and prey, the wolf was not really missed. Today, tourists come to Yellowstone to see and hear wolves not so much because they are an integral part of cycles of life and death, but the wolf and its reintroduction is an attraction itself. Or, when atypical weather conditions cause a river to flood or dry up, a large park most likely has other attractions upon which to fall back, whereas a smaller park might not. When epidemics or other natural (or human-caused) disasters devastate one wildlife population, the viewing of other, different species can be heralded as reasons for visiting the park. Hence, the more opportunities encompassed in a single destination, the greater is the potential as an attractive force.

Another reason for setting aside a large area is that the larger the park, the larger the region dependent on and responsible for its success. Communities geographically distant from the actual border of the park will not be as likely to support the park, nor will these communities feel as responsible for its success. In the Greater Yellowstone Region, different gateway communities emphasize different aspects of their association with the park. Jackson, Wyoming, for example, promotes itself as a part of the 'Wild West' and the 'era of the cowboy', with nightly shoot-outs and 'saloons' instead of bars. Virginia City, Montana is a restored mining town and hopes to draw in visitors interested in the Rockies' gold rush and the settlement of the 'frontier'. Both towns are hours' drive from Yellowstone National Park, and both draw on and profit from their association with the greater Yellowstone-generated tourist region.

Marketing/publicizing the sense of place

Another lesson for other parks is the importance of not only having a sense of place but marketing that image as well. Everyone has heard of Yellowstone (although not everyone knows where it is; for most, it is simply 'out west' somewhere), and everyone wants to see a grizzly, feed a marmot or ground squirrel, swim in a hot spring, and hear a wolf howl. Yellowstone is an old park and a famous park with a well-established and well-known tourist experience. People visit Yellowstone because they know of it. Although Yellowstone historians may describe the 'commodification' of the park (Majoc, 1999) and point out how the Yellowstone experience can be understood as the result of capitalist-driven schemes to 'sell' the park to the public, this 'selling' scheme worked. Yellowstone has survived. It is assumed that in other parks, the 'place' would be intelligently marketed and compassionately promoted in such a way that sustains the resources, the local culture and the regional economy.

Since not all parks can be as large as Yellowstone, park managers might consider ways in which they can market and interpret different parts of their parks as separate and individual elements of the whole. As Hudson's work in Jamaica shows (1999), tourists are easily routed from one natural attraction to another simply through promoting each site as a 'must see' attraction. Hence, for smaller parks, the visitor experience can be enriched or enlarged without actually increasing the size of the park. A park can be 'enlarged' and can serve a broader tourist base without necessarily increasing crowding simply by making the park available to different user groups in different seasons: hikers or bikers in summer and cross-country skiers in winter, for example.

Or, park managers can choose to emphasize certain historical, cultural or environmental aspects or features through interpretation, thereby slowing down the pace of visitation and emphasizing the educational aspect of a park's sense of place. For example, in Yellowstone, near the park's north entrance, there is a small cliff (called Eagle's Nest Rock) on top of which is an osprey's nest. This was an important and regular stop on a tour of the park during the park's early decades. For post-Civil War and First World War tourists, Eagle's Nest Rock represented America and American ideals and how they came together in the creation of this national park. At the turn of the century, John Stoddard, essayist, orator and travel writer, described Eagle's Nest Rock:

> On three sides this is guarded by lofty, well-nigh inaccessible mountains, as though the Infinite Himself would not allow mankind to rashly enter its sublime enclosure. In this respect our Government has wisely imitated the Creator. It has proclaimed to all the world the sanctity of this peculiar area. It has received it as a gift from God and, as His trustee, holds it for the welfare of humanity.
>
> (Stoddard, 1898, p. 208)

After the nation-dividing horror of the Civil War and then the shock of a 'war to end all wars', it was reassuring to think the American eagle (although it was really an osprey) guarded the world's first national park – a symbol of democracy and a democratic government. No one stops at Eagle's Nest Rock today. Its former symbolism or meaning is not important to the tourist experience nowadays, but Eagle's Nest

Rock does serve as an example of how managers might work with local historians and indigenous peoples to learn of and interpret the historical significance of various places within parks. Such information could be used to market the park to particular audiences, help disperse tourist groups within the park, save indigenous knowledge and incorporate locals into the park experience, and provide a more complete, culturally integrative and historically appropriate park experience. Attention to a park's sense of place and traditions – as well as attention to preserving, restoring and maintaining the natural ecosystems – might provide managers with a better understanding of what the public expects, can provide and what they should expect of themselves as administrators and advisors. Only by truly understanding the sense of a place of a park can managers intelligently, comprehensively and appropriately manage the tourist experience. Although the answer may always elude us, it is important to continue to ask what it is we are sustaining, what should we give up, what should we leave in, and at what cost.

References

Barbee, R. and Schullery, P. (1989) Yellowstone: after the smoke clears. *National Parks* 63, 18–19.

Bartlett, R.A. (1985) *Yellowstone: a Wilderness Besieged*. The University of Arizona Press, Tucson.

Craighead, F.C. Jr. (1979) *Track of the Grizzly*. Sierra Club Books, San Francisco.

Daerr, E.G. (1999) Park News. *National Parks* 73, 11.

Despain, D., Houston, D., Meagher, M. and Schullery, P. (1986) *Wildlife in Transition: Man and Nature on Yellowstone's Northern Range*. Roberts Rinehart, Boulder.

Glick, D., Carr, M. and Harting, B. (1991) *An Environmental Profile of the Greater Yellowstone Ecosystem*. Greater Yellowstone Coalition, Bozeman, Montana.

Greater Yellowstone Coalition (1996) Noise from snowmobiles can shatter the peaceful silence of a Yellowstone winter. *Greater Yellowstone Report* 13, 5–6.

Greider, T. and Garkovich, L. (1994) Landscapes: the social construction of nature and the environment. *Rural Sociology* 59, 1–24.

Houston, D.B. (1971) Ecosystems of national parks. *Science* 172, 648–651.

Hudson, B.J. (1999) Fall of beauty: the story of a Jamaican waterfall – a tragedy in three acts. *Tourism Geographies* 1, 343–357.

Kelsey, E. (1898) Letter to Sister 'G', 3 December 1898. Yellowstone Research Library, Mammoth Hot Springs, Wyoming.

Knopf, R.C. (1988) Human experience of wildlands: a review of needs and policy. *Western Wildlands* 14, 2–7.

Majoc, C.J. (1999) *Yellowstone: the Creation and Selling of an American Landscape, 1870–1903*. University of New Mexico Press, Albuquerque.

Meyer, J.L. (1996) *The Spirit of Yellowstone: the Cultural Evolution of a National Park*. Rowman and Littlefield Publishers, Lanham, Maryland.

Milstein, M. (2000) Park's advocates blast noise by snowmobiles. *Billings Gazette* http:www/billingsgazette.com/wyoming/2000310_ymain.htm

Oakes, T. (1997) Place and the paradox of modernity. *Annals of the Association of American Geographers* 87, 509–531.

Olwig, K.R. (1996) Recovering the substantive nature of landscape. *Annals of the Association of American Geographers* 86, 630–653.

Pomeroy, E. (1957) *In Search of the Golden West*. Alfred A. Knopf, New York.

Pritchard, P.A. (1999) *Preserving Yellowstone's Natural Conditions: Science and the Perception of Nature*. University of Nebraska Press, Lincoln.

Proctor, J.D. (1998) The social construction of nature: relativist accusations, pragmatist and critical realist responses. *Annals of the Association of American Geographers* 88, 352–376.

Schein, R.H. (1997) The place of landscape: a conceptual framework for an American scene. *Annals of the Association of American Geographers* 87, 660–680.

Schullery, P. (1980) *The Bears of Yellowstone*. Yellowstone Library and Museum Association, Yellowstone National Park, Wyoming.

Schullery, P. (1997) *Searching for Yellowstone: ecology and wonder in the last wilderness*. Houghton Mifflin Company, Boston.

Shamai, S. (1991) Sense of place: an empirical measurement. *Geoforum* 22, 347–358.

Stoddard, J.L. (1898) *John L. Stoddard's Lectures Volume 10*. Balch Brothers Company, Boston.

Tuan, Y.F. (1977) *Space and Place*. University of Minnesota Press, Minneapolis.

Tuan, Y.F. (1979) Space and place: humanistic perspective. In: Gale, S. and Olson, G. (eds) *Philosophy in Geography*. D. Reidel, Boston, pp. 387–427.

Vale, T.R. and Vale, G.R. (1989) *Western Images, Western Landscapes: Travels Along US89*. University of Arizona Press, Tucson.

Watkins, T.H. (1999) Call it silence. *National Parks* 73, 41.

Wuerthner, G. (1988) *Yellowstone and the Fires of Change*. Dream Garden Press, Salt Lake City.

Responsible Tourism With Great Apes in Uganda

7

Carla Litchfield

Department of Psychology, The University of Adelaide, Adelaide, Australia

Introduction

Globally, tourism is the fastest growing industry (Ceballos-Lascuráin, 1993). For developing countries, such as Uganda, 'ecotourism' is becoming the most significant section of the travel industry (Cater, 1995). After the turmoil of past decades, the 1990s brought political stability and economic growth to Uganda. The government is very supportive of both conservation and tourism. In the words of the Ugandan Minister of Tourism, Wildlife and Antiquities: 'Uganda has recently introduced policy, legislative and institutional reforms to ensure protection of its wildlife. It is regrettable that the rhinoceros disappeared forever from this country. But we are determined not to let any other species . . . become extinct' (Edroma *et al.*, 1997, p. 22).

Uganda is unique in terms of its biological and topographical diversity (Kigenyi, 1997). Located in east-central Africa, with altitudes ranging from 600 m at the bottom of the western rift valley to 5000 m in the Rwenzori mountains, the ecosystems vary from dry savannahs (typical of East Africa) to rainforests (typical of Central Africa). This convergence of East and Central African ecosystems has resulted in a particularly rich diversity of plant, bird, insect and animal species (Kigenyi, 1997). Since Uganda is home to mountain gorillas (*Gorilla gorilla beringei*) and the eastern subspecies of chimpanzee (*Pan troglodytes schweinfurthii*), these great apes and their spectacular habitats are the prime 'draw card' for tourists.

This chapter explores some of the paradoxes that occur in

developing *responsible tourism* programmes, using the endangered African great apes as 'flagship' species (Primack, 1993), focusing attention on conservation of the whole ecosystem in which they live (Goodall, 1994). Tourism is recognized as perhaps the most important conservation management tool to protect the great apes. Paradoxically, it also poses the greatest threat to their survival (Homsy, 1999). For the purposes of this report, the term 'responsible tourism' (which cares for the Earth, and means, simply, not exploitation, but sharing), rather than 'ecotourism', will be used.

The first part of this chapter examines the nature of tourism associated with the unique African great apes, regarded by some as a globally valued 'resource'. How much human-induced impact is acceptable for great ape tourism to remain ecologically and economically sustainable in the long term? In the second part, specific issues that impact on tourism in the great ape range countries are examined: political and economic instability, the crisis facing the great apes, unrealistic expectations and demands by tourists, and challenges to the implementation of conservation management strategies. The third part discusses the specific problems that have arisen at the chimpanzee and mountain-gorilla tourist sites in Uganda and subsequent management actions implemented by the appropriate authorities. Another paradox is examined in the fourth part: how do we encourage people to engage in appropriate behaviours during a leisure-time activity? With respect to great ape tourism, strict guidelines are in place, constraining tourist behaviour (no freedom of choice). If tourists are provided well in advance with the reasons for these restrictions, then they are able to make an informed choice about whether they feel able to engage in minimum-impact behaviours or not. In conclusion, global applications of principles and propositions derived from great ape tourism in Uganda are discussed, as well as the future of responsible tourism and the great apes.

Nature of tourism associated with the African great apes

Wildlife tourism in protected areas is beset with a number of problems and negative impacts (direct and indirect) that are well recognized in the literature (Ceballos-Lascuráin, 1996; Roe *et al.*, 1997; Lilieholm and Romney, 2000; Weaver, 2000). However, there is one overriding problem that is unique to great ape tourism, namely the susceptibility of the great apes to human diseases, as a result of our genetic closeness. Tourists who visit chimpanzees and gorillas in Uganda come from all over the world, and en route have passed through other countries, or even continents. 'This represents, from an epidemiological point of view, a very effective means of transport for an increased number of exotic germs due to the speed and diversity of modern transport systems' (Homsy, 1999, p. v).

The importance of responsible tourism as a means of protecting the great apes

In the 1970s, gorilla tourism was considered to be the 'only immediate option capable of galvanising sufficient and immediate support to save mountain gorillas from poaching, habitat encroachment and possible extinction' (Homsy, 1999, p. 1). It is still viewed by the majority of conservationists as the most 'lucrative' and effective way to protect the great apes and their natural habitats (Homsy, 1999). Without mountain-gorilla tourism in Uganda, it is unlikely that the tiny Mgahinga Gorilla National Park (< 40 km^2) would even exist today.

In Uganda, 'responsible tourism' means working for the benefit of local communities – of animals and of people. The income generated from tourism so far has been shared with local communities. Monies are used to help fund park management, to build and maintain trails, and to train and equip guides and rangers. Local communities receive 12.5% of the gorilla permit revenues at Bwindi Impenetrable National Park, and are able to determine for themselves which local projects these monies will fund (Schmitt, 1997). During the pilot phase (April 1993 to June 1994), local communities received approximately US$15,000 (Meder, 1996). At Mgahinga Gorilla National Park, 20% of entrance fees support local community projects, and the park rangers' salaries are covered by proceeds from tourism, resulting in considerable financial independence, security and confidence of local communities (Karlowski and Weiche, 1997). Money from tourism projects, as well as funding from the Mgahinga and Bwindi Impenetrable Forest Conservation Trust (MBIFCT), helps 'mitigate . . . loss of access to natural resources' for local communities (Meder, 1999d, p. 10).

Local communities also benefit financially by providing accommodation, food, drinks, guiding services, handicrafts, and cultural entertainment for tourists (Uganda Community Tourism Association, 2000). 'This positive development is changing the attitudes of the local people who now advocate for the protection of chimpanzees' (Edroma, 1997, p. 179). Profits from the Kaniyo Pabidi tourist site support 17 local communities (park guide, Uganda, 2000, personal communication). Ngamba Island Chimpanzee Sanctuary combines successfully tourism, education and community involvement (Ward and Nelving, 1999). Sustainable technologies, such as solar-powered compost toilets (already available for tourists) and better water and waste management strategies, are planned for the local communities living on neighbouring islands (D. Cox, Uganda, 2000, personal communication). Fuelefficient stoves are being constructed at the Amajambere Iwacu Community Campground in Mgahinga (Uganda Community Tourism Association, 2000). Thus, sharing technological advances, as well as profits, enhances the quality of life for local communities. Their help and cooperation, in turn, particularly in the elimination of poaching and snaring, is vital for the survival of gorillas, chimpanzees and the ecosystems that they are a part of (Edroma *et al.*, 1997).

Human-induced impacts on the great apes as a result of tourism

Some negative impacts upon the African great apes (disease transmission, behavioural disturbance and vulnerability to poachers as a result of habituation) have already been attributed to increased exposure to humans through tourism.

Transmission of human diseases
As gorillas and chimpanzees are genetically so similar to humans (just under 2% difference in DNA for chimpanzees), they are extremely vulnerable to human diseases (Diamond, 1991). Just a 'common cold' can be life threatening to 'wild' populations of great apes, who may have no natural immunity (Macfie, 1992; Uganda National Parks, 1995; Edroma *et al.*, 1997). Similarly, although the risk may be small, the potential exists for humans to be exposed to potentially deadly new viruses (Homsy, 1999).

Homsy (1999) points out that researchers have tended to focus on the risk of tourists passing on respiratory infections to the great apes. Such infections include measles, tuberculosis, pneumonia, influenza and respiratory syncytial virus. Disturbingly, measles microbes can travel great distances in the open (especially if it is windy), and polio microbes can survive in the soil for several months (Homsy, 1999). There are, however, many other diseases that can be contracted by gorillas and chimpanzees if they come in contact with human faeces or fomites. Hepatitis A and B viruses, shigellosis, trichuriasis, herpes simplex, scabies, polio and intestinal worms may pose an even greater threat to the ultimate survival of wild populations of great apes (Homsy, 1999).

Tourists are not the only humans that wild populations of great apes encounter. In Uganda, a number of gorilla groups and chimpanzee communities are also exposed to park staff, researchers and local communities that live in the surrounding areas. Wallis and Lee (1999) point out that researchers (and visitors) who work with laboratory apes in the US undergo stringent testing procedures for tuberculosis (TB) (at least annually) and usually wear gloves and masks if they come in contact with the apes. Yet, ironically, these same people can visit the great apes in the wild, without having to take similar precautionary measures. The mountain gorilla sites are located in some of the most densely populated areas in Africa (200–300 people per km^2), where many pathogens and infections exist in the human populations. The emergence of multi-drug-resistant TB strains and poor hygiene practices are just two of the problems that must be dealt with (Homsy, 1999).

Research following the baseline studies of intestinal parasite fauna of gorillas prior to tourism by Ashford and his co-workers (e.g. Ashford *et al.*, 1990, 1996) suggests that exposure to tourists (and other humans in the parks) has indeed introduced new parasites (e.g. *Entamoeba* sp., *Trichuris* sp., *Chilomastix* sp. and *Endolimax nana*) or altered the natural parasite fauna of the mountain gorillas (Homsy, 1999).

Behavioural disturbance and increased vulnerability to poachers
Although the risk of disease transmission is the human-induced impact of greatest concern at the moment, two other negative impacts should not be overlooked. The decline of the Katendegere group at Bwindi (from nine to three individuals) and change of home range by up to 10 km (east) may be attributed to stress, behavioural disturbance and disease (scabies) transmitted by contact with humans (Butynski and Kalina, 1998).

Wild apes have to become habituated to the presence of humans, which can take years. This process, which reduces the great ape's fear of humans, may increase the ape's vulnerability to poachers. In 1995, poachers killed eight habituated gorillas, which included three silverbacks (International Gorilla Conservation Programme, 1996). Last year, as a result of war, all seven habituated groups of gorillas in the Kahuzi-Biega National Park were decimated (Yamagiwa, 1999; Wrangham, 2000). Loss of fear can also make the great apes dangerous to tourists. Adult chimpanzees are about six times stronger than an adult male tourist and, if threatened, could attack (Goodall, 1994, p. 402).

Different types of great ape tourism in Uganda

Uganda offers tourists the opportunity to visit mountain gorillas or chimpanzees at a number of sites, located in a variety of habitat types.

Mountain-gorilla tourism
There are only about 600 mountain gorillas left (International Gorilla Conservation Programme, 1996). Approximately half of these are found in the Bwindi Impenetrable National Park (Uganda), designated

as an UNESCO World Heritage Site. This unique ecosystem is home to both mountain gorillas and chimpanzees (Goldsmith and Stanford, 1997). The rest of the mountain gorillas are found in the Virunga volcanoes region, which straddles three countries: Uganda (Mgahinga Gorilla National Park), Rwanda (Parc National des Volcans) and the Democratic Republic of Congo (Parc National des Virunga) (Werikhe *et al.*, 1998). The Uganda Wildlife Authority manages the two Ugandan mountain-gorilla sites (of approximately 370 km^2). With so few individuals left in just two small populations, every mountain gorilla is vital for the survival of this subspecies. Some researchers argue that the gorillas of the Bwindi Impenetrable National Park are in fact not mountain gorillas, but a separate subspecies (Butynski and Kalina, 1998). If this is the case, then there is only one small population of about 300 mountain gorillas left.

Mountain-gorilla tourism is designed to be 'high cost–low impact' tourism. Only a few visitors per day spend 1 h observing gorillas. In April 2000, the permit and park entrance cost at Bwindi was US$265 (personal observation). Six tourists per day can visit each habituated group of gorillas at Bwindi (Mubare and Habinyanja groups) and Mgahinga (Nyakagezi group), which are seen almost daily at both sites.

'Wild' chimpanzee tourism

In Uganda, ten major forest blocks ranging from altitudes of 750 m (Semliki Forest) to 2750 m (Rwenzori Mountains) provide 4394 km^2 of potential forest habitat for chimpanzees (Kigenyi, 1997). Since 1991, tourists have visited semi-habituated 'wild' chimpanzees at five sites (Kyambura/Chambura Gorge, Kaniyo Pabidi, Busingiro, Kanyanchu and Semuliki). In 1998 there was an 80% chance of viewing chimpanzees at Kanyanchu (L. Rothen, Uganda, 1998, personal communication), but there is no guaranteed viewing at any sites. In the future, it should be possible for tourists and tour companies to be informed as to which site is most likely to maximize the chance of viewing chimpanzees at a particular time of year (Wrangham and Goldberg, 1997). Unless awareness of the plight of chimpanzees, as well as their public profile, is marketed aggressively, the success of chimpanzee tourism remains dependent upon whether tourists enter the country to visit gorillas.

Orphaned chimpanzee tourism

There are almost 30 orphaned chimpanzees in Uganda that have been confiscated from poachers and dealers, and are cared for at the Uganda Wildlife Education Centre (Entebbe) and at the Ngamba Island Chimpanzee Sanctuary. The latter provides the chimpanzees with 40 ha of natural forest habitat, without the risks (e.g. transmission of disease and inappropriate behavioural patterns) associated with releasing captive chimpanzees into areas where wild chimpanzees live. Tourists can travel by boat to Ngamba Island, located in Lake Victoria. These sanctuaries give tourists, who are pressed for time, the chance to engage in a complementary form of chimpanzee tourism, and also give local communities the opportunity to view chimpanzees. Every year, up to 80,000 people (mostly Ugandans) visit the Uganda Wildlife Education Centre in Entebbe (Edroma *et al.*, 1997, p. 126).

How much impact is acceptable, given the need for local economics?

'Even the most environmentally conscientious tourist will have some degree of impact, however small' (Cater, 1995, p. 77). Since African great apes live in particularly complex and fragile 'island' ecosystems, and their numbers may, in some cases, be too low to be viable populations, no impact whatsoever is acceptable. Therefore, there should be no tourism. However, in Uganda at least, this view has been recognized as 'unrealistic and untenable' (Homsy, 1999, p. 15). The ever-increasing human population around the national parks (hungry for land and natural resources), the lack of financial resources in the region, and the need for positive publicity for the great apes are all reasons for implementing tourism programmes in Uganda.

Many conservationists do not believe that these few precious great apes should have to be the focus of tourism, thereby paying 'for their own conservation, their habitat protection and to community development' (Werikhe *et al.*, 1998, p. 130). There are concerns that viewing great ape conservation or tourism projects merely in terms of monetary gains, does not communicate the message that the great apes and their ecosystems (particularly forests) play a vital role in preventing soil erosion, protecting water catchment areas, stabilizing local climates and compensating for greenhouse gas emissions (Werikhe *et al.*, 1998). However, until the rest of the world is willing to pay for the survival of the great apes and education programmes address the other issues, they must continue to fund themselves through high-value–low-impact tourism.

Some studies have estimated the value of a specific animal to the economy of a country (e.g. a live and fully grown maned lion is worth over US\$500,000 to Kenya's economy), or the financial value (from tourism revenue) of a park per hectare in its protected state (Ceballos-Lascuráin, 1996). As yet, no such detailed financial analyses exist for Uganda's national parks or its great apes, although Kigenyi (1997) suggests that chimpanzee-focused tourism is likely to produce more money per hectare than timber in areas such as Budongo (despite this forest being Uganda's most important source of timber, having been exploited commercially for almost 90 years). In 1990, prior to the war in Rwanda and the Democratic Republic of Congo, tourists paid nearly US$2 million in entry fees to visit mountain and lowland gorillas, generating more than half of the money earned during the same period at Amboseli National Park in Kenya, but with 430% fewer tourists (Weber, 1993).

Statement of the problem or paradox

Tourism brings in money and protects the great apes, while exposing them to potentially life-threatening diseases and viruses. Therein lies the paradox. Research tends to focus on the benefits of successful tourism programmes on local communities. However, researchers should also examine the devastating effects on communities, who have come to depend upon profits, when a successful tourism programme suddenly collapses.

Examination of contextual material

As a result of military conflict, during the peak season in 1997 (June to September), the Ugandan mountain gorilla sites were the only ones in the region officially open to tourists (Macfie, 1997). Most permits for Mgahinga had been sold at least 3 months in advance, and at Bwindi, up to 60% had been sold a year in advance, the remaining 40% 3 months in advance (Macfie, 1997). Any unsold permits were made available to tourists on the stand-by list on the morning of the visit. Up to five overland trucks at a time (with perhaps 20 or more tourists in each) were arriving at Mgahinga and Bwindi. In 1998, the numbers of waiting overland trucks almost doubled (B. Tudor, Adelaide, 1998, personal communication). Since most overland truck tours had a fairly restricted timetable, serious breaches of the site rules occurred.

The completion of an airstrip at Kisoro a couple of years ago (near Mgahinga), as well as a wide range of accommodation (from luxury resort style to budget camping), made this area accessible to all kinds of tourists, aggravating the existing problems. At both sites, pushy tourists and tour leaders (guides/drivers) attempted to bribe park staff (with offers of more than £600) to take more of them illegally to look for gorillas, or allow double visits (Macfie, 1997). The excessively high visitor numbers at Mgahinga Gorilla National Park clearly disrupted the daily duties of the park rangers. In order to manage the day-to-day problems associated with the large number of tourists, rangers may have neglected duties such as anti-poaching and boundary patrols, as well as preventing wood cutting in the park (Karlowski and Weiche, 1997).

Clearly, Uganda alone was unable to meet the demands of the tourism industry. However, before the problem could be resolved, a catastrophic event took place at Bwindi that threatened the tourism programme in another way.

Political and economic instability in the region and its effect on tourism in Uganda

Recent political turmoil and civil unrest in Rwanda and the Democratic Republic of Congo have resulted in thousands of refugees accumulating in border areas, as well as armed rebels hiding in the parks. These encroach ever further into the national parks in the Virunga volcanoes region, thus increasing the risk of transmission of disease and parasite infections to the gorillas. The mountain gorillas' habitat is being deforested for firewood and building materials (Werikhe *et al.*, 1998). Increases in poaching and the setting of snares have resulted in gorilla disappearances or deaths (Meder, 1997). Rebel activity has also led to the disappearance or death of tourists.

On 15 August 1998, four tourists, two drivers, two rangers and three porters vanished while visiting mountain gorillas in the Democratic Republic of Congo, probably kidnapped by Interahamwe rebels (Meder, 1998). On 1 March 1999, 100 armed rebels attacked three tourist camps in Buhoma (Bwindi Impenetrable National Park). Seventeen people were kidnapped (by members of the Interahamwe, Hutu militia or Rwandan Liberation Army), taken into the forest and eventually eight tourists were hacked to death with machetes. A Ugandan community conservation officer was also shot and set on fire (Meder, 1999a). Although this event has kept many tourists away even a year later, the day after the massacre, a number of tourists asked to purchase permits at Bwindi. Workers at the site began to label such tourism as 'death-wish tourism' (N. Thompson-Handler, Uganda, 1998, personal communication).

Prior to the massacre, tourism was Uganda's second largest source of foreign currency (after export of coffee). Gorilla tourism represented about 75% of tourist money spent (Meder, 1999a). Following the massacre, the gorilla sites were closed for one month of mourning. After this time, many tours were cancelled, but tourism continued, with up to 60 soldiers working alongside park staff (Meder, 1999a). At Bwindi, when the site was reopened in April 1999, the number of visitors for that month was 85. Five months later, this figure increased to 193 (Meder, 1999c), which is still below the approximately 360 permits per month that are available at Bwindi (i.e. 12 people per day for the two habituated groups of gorillas).

The Ugandan government is desperate to keep tourists coming. A year after the massacre, the Ugandan President (Yoweri Museveni) himself trekked gorillas at Bwindi, to show the world that it was safe to do so (New Vision, 2000). Although the Interahamwe rebels travel across the borders of Uganda/Democratic Republic of Congo/Rwanda, they are probably more likely to be encountered on the other sides of the Ugandan border.

Despite the military conflict, there is a unity amongst the park officials of Rwanda/Uganda/Democratic Republic of Congo, who, often at great risk to themselves, protect the mountain gorillas. If these great apes are to survive, the three bordering reserves must work together, formulating similar goals, rules and guidelines, functioning as a single 'super-reserve' (Litchfield, 1997). It has been suggested that the Virunga Volcano Range could be managed as a Peace Park (a trans-frontier conservation area), which might offer gorillas and tourists greater protection, regardless of the political situation in the region (Werikhe *et al.*, 1998). Such international parks result in cross-border cooperation, promoting both conservation and peace (Timothy, 2000).

Great apes in crisis: finite scarcity of gorillas and chimpanzees

The African great apes are in crisis. War, deforestation and the bush-meat trade are resulting in our closest relatives being hunted towards extinction at an alarming rate. Their large size makes them an easy target on the ground or in the trees. Like humans, the great apes have a very long period of growth and development, which contributes to their vulnerability to extinction. Infants are usually born 4–6 years apart, and are completely dependent upon their mothers for the first 5–6 years. During this time they are suckled and carried, and taught vital social and survival skills. They continue to learn during their long childhood and adolescence, and spend at least 8 years with their mothers (Goodall *et al.*, 1993). Since female chimpanzees only begin to reproduce at about 12 years of age, and produce no more than five live births in a lifetime (with only two expected to survive until adulthood), the loss of even one female chimpanzee in a community can be devastating (Peterson and Goodall, 1993). So, 'Poaching impacts adult age classes most severely and the loss of adult females constitutes the most severe demographic threat to wild populations' (Edroma *et al.*, 1997, p. 73).

In just 1 year, as a result of war in the Democratic Republic of Congo, Yamagiwa (1999) estimates that more than half of the remaining 240 gorillas in the Kahuzi-Biega National Park may have been killed and their meat sold for half the price of beef (25 cents US per kg). Gorilla and chimpanzee meat, however, is not only eaten out of desperation or need during times of war, as these endangered species are found on the menu at middle-class restaurants throughout central Africa and form part of the diet of logging crews (Wrangham, 2000). Although Ugandans traditionally do not eat chimpanzees, other migrants (e.g. from Congo), who work as sawyers, may do so. Chimpanzees are also killed for other reasons in Uganda. Wrangham (2000) provides evidence that they may be killed for their body parts, which can be sold (as aphrodisiacs or traditional medicine), or farmers may kill them in defence of crops (and/or feed body parts to their dogs, so that they may gain the chimpanzee qualities of courage, strength and intelligence).

The bush-meat trade has led to a dramatic increase in the number of orphaned and confiscated chimpanzees (Cox *et al.*, 2000). Once the adult chimpanzees have been killed, the infants who cling to their dead mothers are forcefully removed (often by breaking or damaging their fingers) and kept alive by poachers in the hope of selling them as pets. Often the orphaned infants die as a result of trauma, malnutrition or dehydration. For every orphan that survives, the mother and up to ten or more chimpanzees may have been killed (Goodall, 1996). More than 400 chimpanzee orphans are cared for at 15 sanctuaries across Africa, and it is estimated that twice as many again are held illegally (Cox *et al.*, 2000). These figures do not include the many orphaned gorillas and bonobos that are often cared for in the same sanctuaries. Since chimpanzees live up to, or even over, 50 years, typically arriving at sanctuaries when they are only a few years old (or less), and most of the sanctuaries are full beyond carrying capacity, the situation is dire.

On average, one orphan a month arrives at the Uganda Wildlife Education Centre. Most of these chimpanzees are brought illegally across the border from the Democratic Republic of Congo, and then confiscated by Ugandan authorities (D. Cox, Uganda, 2000, personal communication). Although Ngamba Island Chimpanzee Sanctuary provides an excellent environment for such orphans, it too is fast approaching the limit of its carrying capacity.

The great apes are all in danger of extinction, and their numbers are declining at such a rate that any tourism programme involving wild ape populations faces more challenges and moral dilemmas than any other form of wildlife tourism.

Relatively high demand from tourists

More than half of all the remaining mountain gorillas are habituated to the presence of tourists or researchers. Tourists can visit approximately 200 gorillas per day, during times of political stability (see Table 7.1 for more specific details). Whereas approximately 25% of the total Bwindi population of gorillas is habituated for tourism and

Table 7.1. The number of mountain gorillas habituated for tourism or research (adapted from Homsy 1999, p. 17).

Park	Number of groups habituated for tourism	Number of gorillas habituated for tourism	Number of groups habituated for research	Number of gorillas habituated for research
Bwindi Impenetrable National Park (Uganda)	3 + 1[a]	41 + 22[a]	1	13
Mgahinga Gorilla National Park (Uganda)	1	8	–	–
Parc National des Volcans (Rwanda) + Parc National des Virungas (D.R. Congo)	11	150	3	82
Total	16	221	4	95

[a]The number of groups or individuals currently being habituated.

research (more than 20% for tourism alone), a staggering 75% of the total Virunga Volcanoes population of gorillas is habituated to human visitors (about 50% for tourism alone). Therefore, the risk of a disease epidemic is very real, and there is no 'reservoir' population of gorillas, since even those gorillas that are not habituated for tourism share their environment with those that are regularly exposed to visitors.

Each of the habituated groups of mountain gorillas is exposed to more than 2000 visitor-h per year, as well as 900 h of visits by the park guides accompanying the tourists on each trek (Homsy, 1999). These figures are based on a tourism occupancy rate of 80% (during politically stable periods) and adherence to the 1 h viewing rule. In 1 year, habituated gorillas are exposed to more visitors than 'an average person is likely to receive in his or her own house over a lifetime' (Homsy, 1999, p. v). Therefore, although six tourists per day, per group of habituated gorillas in Uganda does not seem a very high figure, the cumulative hours of potential disturbance over an average year are high.

Constraints to tourism management

Although a comprehensive set of rules and guidelines exists, it is often difficult, or even impossible, for park staff to enforce these rules. In addition, the rules are not yet standardized across all mountain-gorilla sites in the region, which may further undermine enforcement efforts in Uganda (which has the most stringent rules).

Current research suggests that the minimum distance of 5 m or 15 feet (the 'buffer distance' rule) in place at the tourist sites in Uganda is inadequate to protect the great apes from the risk of disease transmission. In the absence of wind, sneeze particles can travel 6 m (20 feet), influenza can be transmitted up to 20 m, and other airborne organisms may travel even further in favourable wind and ultraviolet light conditions (Homsy, 1999). To protect primates from human diseases in zoos, plexiglass structures are often built as a barrier (Homsy, 1999). The only protection that can be afforded to wild great apes is the strict enforcement of an adequate minimum distance. Unfortunately, it is the one rule that the guides and park staff report that they have the most difficulty enforcing (Homsy, 1999).

Sick tourists and staff are prohibited from tracking the great apes. However, this sickness rule cannot be monitored, since most people are only capable of recognizing obvious symptoms of illness (e.g. coughs, sneezes, rashes or stomach ailments). In addition, the self-report rule depends on the honesty of the individual tourist and staff member. Unfortunately, a tourist could be shedding viruses or bacteria before or after symptoms have appeared (Homsy, 1999).

Tourist problem behaviours and impacts, and responding management actions

Tourists may arrive at a great ape site with two main unrealistic expectations. Some documentaries and movies (e.g. *Gorillas in the Mist*) have shown researchers touching or interacting with wild apes. Some tourist brochures show photos of tourists sitting next to a wild ape, preferably a massive silverback, but this is in clear breach of the existing guidelines for gorilla tourism. Tourists who want to be photographed next to a gorilla sometimes pressure or attempt to bribe park staff into allowing them to approach the gorillas more closely than 5 m. In some cases, the tour operators themselves simply ignore the guide's instructions, and lead the tourists in the group closer (Schmitt, 1997).

Tourists also often expect to view great apes, and may heap abuse upon the park guides and rangers if they do not (personal observation). Yet, they are visiting 'wild' inhabitants of a 'wild' environment.

Furthermore, the 'fission–fusion' social structure and 'life style' of the chimpanzee makes them more elusive than gorillas, but tourists are often unaware of the behavioural differences between gorillas and chimpanzees (Litchfield, 1997).

Souvenirs and illegal poaching

Tourists can inadvertently encourage poaching. For example, in Uganda, souvenir drums are often made of duiker skin (rather than cow). These duikers (antelopes) are captured illegally in wire snares set up in forests and national parks. Gorillas and chimpanzees can be maimed, crippled or even killed by snares. Many souvenirs in Africa are made of animal products: bones, skulls and skins. This means that tourists must make a concerted effort to find out what they are buying (Friends of Conservation, 1996; Holing, 1996).

A well-meaning tourist may buy a tiny malnourished and suffering orphan chimpanzee, thus inadvertently supporting the trade in endangered wildlife. Money has been made on a sale, which only encourages unscrupulous dealers and poachers to illegally obtain another infant chimpanzee (Cox et al., 2000).

Responding management actions implemented by the appropriate authorities

Uganda Wildlife Authority, the International Gorilla Conservation Programme and park wardens are trying to eliminate corruption and prevent the problems that were prevalent before the massacre from reoccurring. They are mainly directing their efforts towards educating tourists and tour operators about rules and guidelines, as well as habituating more gorilla groups (Macfie, 1997).

Homsy's (1999) recent consultancy for the International Gorilla Conservation Programme has made a number of recommendations about changes to the rules and suggestions about strengthening enforcement of those rules. In order to limit the possible transmission of disease from visitors (and spread of disease throughout the gorilla population), it has been suggested that tourists only visit gorilla groups that have between 6 and 15 individuals and that the minimum distance is increased to 7.5 m (25 feet). It has also been recommended that tourists and park staff be immunized (for further recommendations, see Table 7.2, Appendix to this chapter).

Encouragement of appropriate behaviours

Many of the problems mentioned previously could have been avoided, if tourists had had access to specific information regarding great ape sites, as well as guidelines and rules at the time of booking or at least prior to their arrival at the sites. In 1997, this researcher was only able to obtain guidelines and rules in the form of loose pages at the sites in Uganda. An awareness of these rules (see Table 7.2, Appendix to this chapter), especially the reasons behind them, would hopefully eliminate corruption and inappropriate behaviour (Macfie, 1997).

Two recent publications have been developed to disseminate relevant information. In 1998, the *Berggorilla and Regenwald Direkthilfe* organization designed a leaflet with hints and rules for tourists visiting gorillas. *Treading Lightly: Responsible Tourism with the African Great Apes* is a booklet that has been designed specifically for those planning to visit the African great apes, and funds from the sale of the booklet will be used to support great ape projects in Uganda (Litchfield, 1997). It is being distributed as widely as possible, both within Uganda and overseas (Australia, USA and Europe).

It has been suggested that tourists should provide a financial deposit before their trek (which is only refunded if no rules are broken) or that tour operators are penalized or fined if tourists break the rules. However, as Homsy (1999) maintains:

> the best law is one which is not needed. In other words, the most powerful enforcement tool is self-limitation, or viewed more positively, self-motivation. For no matter how many sophisticated punitive or coercive schemes we can conceive, rules can – and will – always be broken . . . the best hope for a least damaging tourism programme resides in the widespread sensitisation, awareness and understanding of the catastrophic consequences of unconscious gorilla tourism . . . it is not the rules, but the attitude of the human community towards its non-human environment that will decide the fate of the gorillas, and indeed of many life forms on this planet, including our own. Awareness therefore, albeit a long and strenuous process, is the only sure investment.
>
> (Homsy, 1999, p. 57)

Conclusions

Uganda as a model for responsible tourism with endangered species

A population and habitat viability assessment (PHVA) should be the first and most vital step in formulating a practical conservation management programme for the survival and recovery of endangered species in their 'wild' habitats. Stochastic simulation modelling of populations is used to determine the risk of extinction. In 1997, Uganda hosted two such workshops for the eastern subspecies of chimpanzee (*Pan troglodytes schweinfurthii*) and the mountain gorilla (*Gorilla gorilla beringei*), and a chimpanzee sanctuary workshop was held in May 2000. Wildlife managers, researchers, veterinarians, biologists, and others participated and shared invaluable information (Edroma *et al.*, 1997). In all three cases, the importance of tourism as part of the overall conservation management strategy was stressed. The recommendations concerning tourism strategies made at the first two PHVAs are provided in the appendix (Tables 7.3 and 7.4, Appendix to this chapter).

The guidelines for mountain-gorilla tourism in Uganda are probably the most stringent and carefully thought out rules for any wildlife tourism in the world. Most of the programmes are community-based. All of the sites share profits with local communities, educating and involving them in decision-making processes.

Some lessons learned

'Take only photographs, leave only footprints' is a message that is promoted by researchers in the area of wildlife tourism (Roe *et al.*, 1997). However, in the case of the great apes, even that message is not enough to ensure their long-term survival. 'Take only photographs – without flash and from a distance of more than 5 m, leave only twelve footprints per day – preferably by boots that have been recently disinfected', would be a more appropriate message for prospective gorilla tourists. 'Treading lightly' is a phrase that has found favour in Uganda (Litchfield, 1997).

Other forms of wildlife tourism could no doubt benefit from a more stringent and restrictive set of guidelines, in line with those used for the great apes in Uganda. Limiting visitor numbers, only allowing tourists to enter a national park with a trained guide, and buffer distances of at least 5 m could help limit the negative impacts on other species. However, as Roe *et al.* (1997) point out, limitations of visitor numbers are not always enforced. Thus, again, tourists must be well informed and encouraged to control their behaviour.

The future of African great ape based tourism

It is too soon to determine whether responsible great ape tourism in Uganda (yet alone other African countries) is a sustainable option. If all the guidelines are followed, local communities are involved, rebel activity is contained and public interest (both local and global) in conserving great apes is aroused, tourism will become a sustainable option in Uganda. Certainly, the Ugandan government is very supportive of both conservation and tourism. It must be remembered, however, that for mountain gorillas the issue is more complicated, since their ultimate survival depends on the political and social situations prevalent in three countries (Uganda, Rwanda and the Democratic Republic of Congo).

In the short term, mountain-gorilla tourism has been affected adversely in Rwanda and the Democratic Republic of Congo. During the 1980s, gorilla tourism in Rwanda became the third highest source of foreign exchange (behind tea and coffee), with over 7000 tourists per year visiting the gorillas (Adams and McShane, 1996). In June 1999, the Parc National des Volcans (Rwanda) reopened its gorilla tourism site, after being closed for 2 years. A maximum of eight people (accompanied by soldiers) can visit each of the two gorilla groups per day. An additional gorilla group is in the process of being habituated. As in Uganda, visits are 1-h long, and permits cost US$250 (Meder, 1999b). It is too soon to determine whether the re-establishment of gorilla tourism in Rwanda will become a sustainable option in the long term.

Of course, the greatest threat to the sustainability of the mountain-gorilla tourism industry is the low number of mountain gorillas. Although the recent PHVA determined that the current population is biologically viable, researchers are still divided upon the issue. Poaching, war, habitat destruction and disease epidemics could push the mountain gorillas irreversibly towards the brink of extinction (Homsy, 1999). Although lowland gorilla, bonobo and chimpanzee numbers exceed those of the mountain gorilla, they too are endangered and face extinction in the very near future. Most populations are located in politically unstable areas, with a rampant bush-meat trade and rapid deforestation, and no responsible tourism programmes (for those very reasons).

Although this chapter has focused on great ape tourism in Uganda, many of the points covered are also applicable to other great ape sites throughout Africa. For economic and ecological sustainability to be achieved, an optimal number of visitors must visit the sites (a steady stream of low numbers). It is ironic that political stability in this part of Africa can result in too many tourists (ecological sustainability threatened), whereas instability can result in too few visitors (economic sustainability threatened)! Every tourist can make a difference to the ultimate survival or demise of the great apes. The interest and support of responsible tourists at responsible sites may help some populations of 'wild' great apes survive. Perhaps tourists can help promote the message and impassioned plea that biological anthropologist and conservationist, Richard Wrangham (2000), has recently put forth:

> We can relish the species that most closely share the dawning of our consciousness, or we can let them go. While we're pondering, the forests are falling and the apes are dying . . . Let us be bold. There's an international agreement not to hunt whales and dolphins. Why not an equivalent for the great apes? Can we persuade the United Nations to make the great apes the first World Heritage Species?

Acknowledgements

In Australia, I am especially grateful to Dr Heather Phillips and Dr Robert Kass (Travellers' Medical and Vaccination Centre). Special thanks to my mother, Anita O'Hair, for her help in editing this chapter, and to Professor Richard Wrangham for his invaluable comments. In Uganda, I am indebted to the Ugandan Government; in particular, the Uganda National Council for Science and Technology, Uganda Forest Department, and Uganda Wildlife Authority (previously Uganda National Parks), for allowing me to conduct research at Kibale National Park. Thanks also to Makerere University Biological Field Station (and its directors), the Zoology Department at Makerere University (especially Dr Gilbert Isabirye-Basuta and Dr John Kasenene), and to Professor Richard Wrangham and the Kibale Chimpanzee Project. In the field, special thanks to Joseph Basigara, Elisha Karwani, Christopher Katangole, Sam Mugume, Francis Mugurusi, Christopher Muruuli, Peter Tuhairwe (and Kato Innocent). I am also extremely grateful to Dr Jane Goodall, Linda and Oskar Rothen, Debby Cox, Angela Meder, Annabel Falcon and Helga Rainer (IGCP), Dr Norm Rosen, Drs Philip Miller and Ulysses Seal (CBSG), Dr Wayne Boardman and other friends and colleagues that are too numerous to mention.

References

Adams, J.S. and McShane, T.O. (1996) *The Myth of Wild Africa: Conservation Without Illusion.* University of California Press, Berkeley, California.

Ashford, R.W., Reid, G.D. and Butynski, T.M. (1990) The intestinal faunas of man and mountain gorillas in a shared habitat. *Annals of Tropical Medicine and Parasitology* 84, 337–340.

Ashford, R.W., Lawson, H., Butynski, T.M. and Reid, G.D.F. (1996) Patterns of intestinal parasitism in the mountain gorilla *Gorilla gorilla* in the Bwindi-Impenetrable Forest, Uganda. *Journal of the Zoological Society of London* 239, 507–514.

Butynski, T. and Kalina, J. (1998) Is gorilla tourism sustainable? *Gorilla Journal* 16, 15–19.

Cater, E. (1995) Ecotourism in the Third World – problems and prospects for sustainability. In: Cater, E. and Lowman, G. (eds) *Ecotourism: a Sustainable Option?* John Wiley & Sons, Chichester, pp. 69–86.

Ceballos-Lascuráin, H. (1993) Overview on ecotourism around the world: IUCN's ecotourism program. In: *Proceedings of the 1993 World Congress on Adventure Travel and Ecotourism.* The Adventure Travel Society, Englewood, Colorado, pp. 219–222.

Ceballos-Lascuráin, H. (1996) *Tourism, Ecotourism, and Protected Areas: the State of Nature-Based Tourism Around the World and Guidelines for its Development.* IUCN (The World Conservation Union), Gland, Switzerland.

Cox, D., Rosen, N. and Seal, U.S. (2000) *Chimpanzee Sanctuary Guidelines and Management Workshop: Report.* SSC/IUCN Conservation Breeding Specialist Group, Apple Valley, Minnesota.

Diamond, J. (1991) *The Rise and Fall of the Third Chimpanzee.* Vintage, London.

Edroma, E. (1997) Evaluation of management strategies for chimpanzees in protected areas of Uganda. In: Edroma, E., Rosen, N. and Miller, P. (eds) *Conserving the Chimpanzees of Uganda: Population and Habitat Viability Assessment for* Pan troglodytes schweinfurthii. SSC/IUCN Conservation Breeding Specialist Group, Apple Valley, Minnesota, pp. 177–180.

Edroma, E., Rosen, N. and Miller, P. (eds) (1997) *Conserving the Chimpanzees of Uganda: Population and Habitat Viability Assessment for* Pan troglodytes schweinfurthii. SSC/IUCN Conservation Breeding Specialist Group Apple Valley, Minnesota.

Friends of Conservation (1996) *Conservation Code.* Friends of Conservation, London.

Goldsmith, M.L. and Stanford, C.B. (1997) Comparative behavioural ecology of Bwindi gorillas and chimps. *Gorilla Journal* 15, 17–19.

Goodall, J. (1994) Postscript – conservation and the future of chimpanzee and bonobo research in Africa. In: Wrangham, R.W., McGrew, W.C., de Waal, F.B.M. and Heltne, P.G. (eds) *Chimpanzee Cultures.* Harvard University Press, Cambridge, Massachusetts, pp. 397–404.

Goodall, J. (1996) Foreword: conserving great apes. In: McGrew, W.C., Marchant, L.F. and Nishida, T. (eds) *Great Ape Societies.* Cambridge University Press, Cambridge, pp. xv–xx.

Goodall, J., Nichols, M., Schaller, G.B. and Smith, M.G. (1993) *The Great Apes: Between Two Worlds.* National Geographic Society, Book Division, Washington, D.C.

Holing, D. (1996) *World Travel: a Guide to International Ecojourneys.* Reader's Digest Press, Sydney.

Homsy, J. (1999) *Ape Tourism and Human Diseases: How Close Should We Get?* International Gorilla Conservation Programme, Kampala, Uganda.

International Gorilla Conservation Programme (1996) *IGCP Update*, Issue No.1, April. Nairobi, Kenya.

Karlowski, U. and Weiche, I. (1997) Mgahinga Gorilla National Park. *Gorilla Journal* 15, 15–16.

Kigenyi, F.W. (1997) Forest conservation in relation to chimpanzees. In:

Edroma, E., Rosen, N. and Miller, P. (eds) *Conserving the Chimpanzees of Uganda: Population and Habitat Viability Assessment for* Pan troglodytes schweinfurthii SSC/IUCN Conservation Breeding Specialist Group, Apple Valley, Minnesota, pp. 141–149.

Lilieholm, R.J. and Romney, L.R. (2000) Tourism, national parks and wildlife. In: Butler, R.W. and Boyd, S.W. (eds) *Tourism and National Parks: Issues and Implications.* John Wiley & Sons, Chichester, pp. 137–151.

Litchfield, C.A. (1997) *Treading Lightly: Responsible Tourism with the African Great Apes.* Travellers' Medical and Vaccination Centre, Adelaide, Australia.

Macfie, E.J. (1992) Appendix 1: Gorilla Tourism Programme for Uganda: veterinary recommendations. In: *Bwindi Impenetrable National Park Tourism Plan.* International Gorilla Conservation Programme Nairobi, Kenya, pp. 1–3.

Macfie, E.J. (1997) Gorilla tourism in Uganda. *Gorilla Journal* 15, 16–17.

Meder, A. (1996) Report from Uganda. *Gorilla Journal* 12, 8–9.

Meder, A. (1997) Appeal for Donations. *Gorilla Journal* 15, 6.

Meder, A. (1998) Tourists kidnapped in Congo. *Gorilla Journal* 17, 3–4.

Meder, A. (1999a) Tourist killings in Bwindi. *Gorilla Journal* 18, 3–4.

Meder, A. (1999b) Tourists can visit the gorillas again. *Gorilla Journal* 18, 9.

Meder, A. (1999c) Gorilla tourism in Uganda. *Gorilla Journal* 19, 10.

Meder, A. (1999d) A different conservation concept. *Gorilla Journal* 19, 10.

New Vision (2000) Museveni treks through Bwindi. *The New Vision* 15(45), 1–2.

Peterson, D. and Goodall, J. (1993) *Visions of Caliban: On Chimpanzees and People.* Houghton Mifflin, New York.

Primack, R.B. (1993) *Essentials of Conservation Biology.* Sinauer Associates, Sunderland, Massachusetts.

Roe, D., Leader-Williams, N. and Dalal-Clayton, B. (1997) *Take Only Photographs, Leave Only Footprints: the Environmental Impacts of Wildlife Tourism.* Wildlife and Development Series No.10, International Institute for Environment and Development, London.

Schmitt, T.M. (1997) Close encounter with gorillas at Bwindi. *Gorilla Journal* 14, 12–13.

Timothy, D.J. (2000) Tourism and international parks. In: Butler, R.W. and Boyd, S.W. (eds) *Tourism and National Parks: Issues and Implications.* John Wiley & Sons, Chichester, pp. 263–282.

Uganda Community Tourism Association (2000) *UCOTA News,* Issue No. 3, February. Kampala, Uganda.

Uganda National Parks (1995) *Tourist Rules.* International Gorilla Conservation Programme/Uganda National Parks (now Uganda Wildlife Authority), Kampala, Uganda.

Wallis, J. and Lee, D.R. (1999) Primate conservation: the prevention of disease transmission. *International Journal of Primatology* 20, 803–826.

Ward, M. and Nelving, A. (1999) Island home for orphaned chimps. *Sanctuary* 1, 56–61.

Weaver, D. (2000) Tourism and national parks in ecologically vulnerable areas. In: Butler, R.W. and Boyd, S.W. (eds) *Tourism and National Parks: Issues and Implications.* John Wiley & Sons, Chichester, pp. 107–124.

Weber, W. (1993) Primate conservation and ecotourism in Africa. In: Potter, C.S., Cohen, J.I. and Janczewski, D. (eds) *Perspectives on Biodiversity: Case Studies of Genetic Resource Conservation and Development.* AAAS Press (American Association for the Advancement of Science), Washington, DC, pp. 129–150.

Werikhe, S., Macfie, L., Rosen, N. and Miller, P. (eds) (1998) *Can the Mountain Gorilla Survive? Population and Habitat Viability Assessment for* Gorilla gorilla beringei. SSC/IUCN Conservation Breeding Specialist Group, Apple Valley, Minnesota.

Wrangham, R.W. (2000) The other apes: time for action. A view on the science: physical anthropology at the millennium. *American Journal of Physical Anthropology* 111, 59–63.

Wrangham, R.W. and Goldberg, T. (1997) An overview of chimpanzee conservation and management strategies. In: Edroma, E., Rosen, N. and Miller, P. (eds) *Conserving the Chimpanzees of Uganda: Population and Habitat Viability Assessment for* Pan troglodytes schweinfurthii. SSC/IUCN Conservation Breeding Specialist Group, Apple Valley, Minnesota, pp. 156–162.

Yamagiwa, J. (1999) Slaughter of gorillas in the Kahuzi-Biega Park. *Gorilla Journal* 19, 4–6.

Copies of *Treading Lightly: Responsible Tourism with the African Great Apes* can be obtained from: Travellers' Medical and Vaccination Centre Group, 29 Gilbert Place, Adelaide 5000, Australia. Tel.: 61–8–8212 7522; fax: 61–8–8212 7550; http://www.tmvc.com.au

Appendix

Table 7.2 lists the rules and guidelines in place in Uganda, which have been developed to try to protect the mountain gorillas' health and safety (Macfie, 1992; Uganda National Parks, 1995). Similar guidelines apply at chimpanzee tourist sites, but local variations may exist (Edroma *et al.*, 1997, p. 7). Homsy's (1999) recommended changes to the rules are also provided.

The 15 recommendations concerning tourism that were made by the Ecotourism and Education working group at the chimpanzee PHVA in Uganda are given in Table 7.3. The highest priority was given to recommendations 2, 5, 8 and 14, which are given in bold type in the table. These are followed in the table by the recommendations concerning tourism made by other working groups (part of the Executive Summary, taken from Edroma *et al.*, 1997, pp. 7–8).

The recommendations concerning tourism that were made by the working groups at the mountain gorilla PHVA in Uganda are given in Table 7.4 (part of the executive summary, taken from Werikhe *et al.*, 1998, pp. 5–11).

Table 7.2. Rules and guidelines in place in Uganda to try to protect mountain gorillas' health and safety.

	Rule	Reason
1	If a tourist is ill, the park staff have the right to refuse a visit to gorillas or chimpanzees	To protect the great apes from contracting an illness or disease
	Homsy's (1999) recommendations: Strengthen enforcement through: • active sensitization of tourists before booking a tour through direct information, IEC campaign and development/distribution of a pamphlet dedicated to this issue; • immunization of tourists and park staff against diseases of concern	
2	Only one visit is allowed per day, and the number of tourists is limited to 4 or 6 per group (or two visits per day at some chimpanzee sites where 'nature walks with the possibility of chimpanzee viewing' are offered)	To minimize behavioural disturbance, stress and possible risk of infection
	Homsy's (1999) recommendation: • only allow tourists to visit gorilla groups that have 6–15 individuals	
3	Visitors must be at least 15 years old (or 12 years old at some chimpanzee sites where 'nature walks with the possibility of chimpanzee viewing' are offered)	To minimize risk of exposing apes to childhood diseases (e.g. mumps, chickenpox, measles) and cold or flu viruses
4	The time spent with great apes is limited to 1 h (or perhaps a bit longer at some chimpanzee sites where 'nature walks with the possibility of chimpanzee viewing' are offered)	To minimize behavioural disturbance, stress and possible risk of infection
	Homsy's (1999) recommendation: • if gorillas are not visible at the initial encounter, allow up to 15 min waiting at 20 m or more from the gorillas before the clock is started	

Table 7.2. *continued*

	Rule	Reason
5	Flash photography is not permitted	It can upset or frighten apes and may provoke an aggressive reaction or charge
6	All visitors must remain at least 5 m away from great apes at all times. If the great apes approach to 2 or 3 m (as curious juveniles sometimes do), then visitors should slowly retreat back to 5 m. If this is not possible, then the visitors will be asked to remain where they are. The guide's instructions should be followed at all times. Keep your backpack and other items in places where young apes can't approach and investigate them. Homsy's (1999) recommendation: • increase minimum distance to 7.5 m or 25 feet in non-emergency situations to allow for inadvertent sneezes, coughs and movement of people and gorillas during the visit	To minimize disease transmission, stress and behavioural disturbance; to reduce the chance of possible future aggression towards tourists; and to prevent the apes becoming too habituated to humans
7	Tourists should remain in a tight group, without spreading out or surrounding the great apes	This allow the apes plenty of room to move where they want to, without feeling threatened (which may provoke a charge)
8	Where possible, visitors should sit or crouch while watching the apes	It can be very intimidating or threatening to apes if you stand, if you are taller than they are, and stare. Standing bipedally is part of the great apes' threat or aggressive displays
9	Body language is important, and visitors should not raise hands or arms, nor point, nor touch the apes, nor stare at them	To gorillas and chimpanzees these behaviours are signs of threats or aggression
10	Visitors should not clear vegetation to get a better view	This can disturb or frighten the apes. The guides will clear away vegetation, if it is possible

Table 7.2. *continued*

Rule	Reason
11 If a silverback gorilla beats his chest, displays or charges at you, do not run away. If a chimpanzee displays or charges do not run away either. Visitors are asked to stop other tourists from moving or running	Although a charge may be frightening, the safest thing to do is to remain quietly where you are
12 Eating, drinking and smoking are not permitted near the apes, nor within 200 m of them	These behaviours could distract them, cause problems if they approach out of curiosity, and food and other remains can be a source of infection
Homsy's (1999) recommendation: • a minimum 5-min walking distance from gorillas before eating can take place; • all food remains must be removed from the park	
13 Visitors should be as quiet as possible, and whisper. If bitten by safari ants, do not scream	To minimize behavioural disturbance and avoid frightening gorillas and chimpanzees. Newly habituated chimpanzees may be too afraid to come anywhere near noisy tourists, and if chimpanzees are already present, they may leave
14 If you, the tourist, need to sneeze or cough, turn away from the great apes and try to cover your nose and mouth.	To minimize the spread of airborne bacteria or viruses that you might unknowingly be carrying
Homsy's (1999) recommendation: • refrain from spitting or nose-blowing on the ground	
15 All faecal material must be buried. A machete may be borrowed from the guides, a 30 cm (10 inch) hole dug and then the hole filled	Faeces can be highly infectious to great apes and other animals
Homsy's (1999) recommendation: • promote and allow time for toilet use before the trek; • dig holes at least 0.5 m (2 feet) deep; • treat faeces with antiseptic solution before filling holes (150 ml of 2% chlorine)	

Table 7.2. *continued*

Rule	Reason
16 All rubbish must be removed from the park, and visitors are asked to be particularly careful not to drop small items, such as film boxes/canisters, tissues or handkerchiefs	Apart from being unsightly, rubbish can interest animals, can cause problems if swallowed and can be a source of germ or disease transmission
Strengthen enforcement through: • training and monitoring of staff; • ensuring and monitoring safe and adequate rubbish deposits and removal around parks; • prevent access of animals near rubbish disposal sites	

Table 7.3. Ecotourism recommendations. (The recommendations given the highest priority are set in bold type.)

1 Chimpanzee tourism is a beneficial and desirable management programme in Uganda and should be maintained as a viable conservation alternative

2 **Chimpanzee tourism should be managed under a standardized set of rules and regulations to be presented in pre-walk briefings, and widely distributed in advance to tourists, tour operators and travel agents to facilitate adherence**

3 Chimpanzee tourism management factors should also be standardized across tourism sites, but should also take account of local circumstances

4 Protocols must be developed that aim to reduce corruption among tourism staff through an awareness and belief in the rules and regulations that they are enforcing. In addition, these protocols must ensure a sense of motivation among the staff to ensure their adherence

5 **Chimpanzee tourism should be selective. The current number of sites marketing tourism is considered sufficient; no new sites should be opened or planned pending market review and the drafting of an Environmental Impact Assessment**

6 Wild chimpanzee tourism and captive-based tourism should have complementary roles as part of an overall conservation programme

7 Ideally, tourism and chimpanzee population research should be done in different groups

8 **Protected Area authorities should strive to view ALL chimpanzee populations in Uganda as important and in need of protection, not just those providing tourist income**

9 Local community participation must be stressed as part of any chimpanzee tourism project

10 Creative financing for chimpanzee conservation should emerge from tourism-based projects

11 Uganda should promote and/or market chimpanzee tourism at its current sites

Table 7.3. *continued*

12   Private-sector management of endangered species conservation (i.e.
     concessions) should be avoided
13   Standardization of chimpanzee tourism management between the two primary
     responsible authorities, Forest Department and UWA, should be encouraged
     and strongly linked
14   **Chimpanzee tourism development and management should be guided by
     management plans/tourism development plans and should be part of a
     nationwide strategy**
15   Education centres targeting Ugandans, schoolchildren in particular, should be
     developed, with transport facilities available for those visitors wanting to reach
     the centres. The opportunity to see wild chimpanzees will have a great impact
     on their attitudes towards conservation in Uganda
16   Tourism activities (one of the threats to chimpanzee populations): control of
     tourist activities and movements. Rules and regulations to come from
     Ecotourism and Education working group (Chimpanzee Population Threats
     working group)
17   Because of the great potential danger to chimpanzee populations posed by
     outbreaks of human-transmitted diseases, minimum distances should be
     maintained between fully habituated chimpanzees and either tourists or
     researchers, in order to minimize the potential for disease outbreaks. Where
     appropriate, a signpost giving minimum distances could be erected to inform
     those concerned (Population Biology and Modelling working group)
18   Sanctuaries: sanctuaries should be established outside the protected areas,
     away from wild populations and not immediately adjacent to human
     settlements. Accessibility for tourists must be considered before designating a
     site for a sanctuary (Captive Population Management working group)

Table 7.4. Tourism recommendations. (The recommendations given the highest
priority are set in bold type.)

1   Guarantee a consistent, reliable source of funds dedicated for sharing with local
    communities, ensuring: (i) transparency in decision-making; (ii) management of
    expectations; (iii) strong conservation linkage; (iv) substantial community
    investment and capacity to sustain; and (v) clear policy guidelines. **The most
    effective, practical mechanism would be to guarantee a proportion of total
    park revenue for this purpose. In the absence of this policy, it is recommended
    that an additional fee be charged for each gorilla permit**. However,
    investigation of means to diversify the source of funds to be shared should be
    undertaken
    (Human Population Issues working group)
2   We recommend that research focused on areas that are of critical importance
    for management be initiated and implemented. The following four key areas
    were identified:
    • poaching of plant and animal forest products
    • crop raiding by animals from the park
    • **impacts of tourism and habituation of gorillas**
    • impacts of resource sharing
    (Management and Research working group)

Table 7.4. *continued*

3 We recommend that continued support be given to protected area management authorities to increase the effectiveness of conservation
- by implementing planning both at strategic and operational level
- by researching options for sustainable funding for protected area authorities and to develop funding mechanisms
- by furthering the decentralization of the protected area authorities and building upon existing capacity within those institutions
- **by strengthening existing tourist programmes**

(Management and Research working group)

4 We recommend that sensitization programmes targeted at all levels be implemented
- to raise government awareness
- **by developing strategies and programmes for interpretation, for both national and international tourism**
- **to encourage national tourism**

(Management and Research working group)

5 **We recommend that a framework be developed for regional collaboration, such as a Peace Park. We also recommend that improved mechanisms for communication and collaboration between partners be developed. One of the objectives of this will be the development of regional tourism**

(Management and Research working group)

6 Legislation and policy:
- lead agencies to encourage Ministers of Range States (Uganda, Rwanda, Congo) to meet to discuss legal issues, IGCP/DFGF to help to facilitate;
- **lead agencies to encourage countries to give greater priority to nature conservation and related tourism by placing responsibility for the environment, nature conservation and tourism in a single Ministry**;
- lead agencies to have more contact with political leaders regarding legal issues, e.g. invitation to meetings; press conferences; to open and address meetings; to be supplied with more information;
- lead agencies to improve by action – discussion meetings, dinner debates. Use or form (e.g.) Park Management Advisory Committees at District level

(Governance working group)

7 Ownership;
- immediate action: to sensitize all stakeholders about importance of the correct interpretation of the word 'ownership' – to mean shared responsibility in the joint protection of the mountain gorilla
- longer term:
  1. to investigate the use of the Migratory Species Convention to strengthen joint protection measures, although it is recognized that gorillas are not considered migratory (in science);
  2. to investigate the possibility of a World Heritage Site for Uganda and Rwanda;
  3. to investigate management of Virunga Range as a Peace Park

(Governance working group)

Table 7.4. *continued*

8   Integration of mountain-gorilla tourism into national tourism: **there is a need to integrate gorilla tourism into the whole tourism sector at both national and regional level**
     (Finance, Revenue, and Economics working group).

9   Regional and institutional collaboration:
     • **the various stakeholder groups in gorilla conservation and tourism in each range state (government, non-government, private sector) should meet internationally to share information and to develop mechanisms for promoting a collaborative, regional perspective, with diversification of funding mechanisms and sources;**
     • donors also need to be informed of the long-term need for external funding to ensure the sustainable conservation of mountain gorillas;
     • the group recommends that these informal groupings should evolve progressively into a fully representative, formal body for regional gorilla and habitat conservation
     (Finance, Revenue, and Economics working group)

10   Enhancing values for conservation of mountain gorillas and their habitat:
     • **relevant authorities in each range state should be encouraged to promote the mountain gorilla as a symbol of ecotourism and good practice worldwide, and they should be supported in developing a full campaign in 1998–1999 to promote the gorilla as an emblem**
     • **existing Africa-based formal and informal education networks (some with international reach) should be used to launch a programme of deliberate education on the values of gorilla conservation to key target audiences, including funding bodies, corporate entities, tourists and the general public internationally, as well as government bodies, companies, expatriate communities and individuals – especially children – in each range state**
     (highest level of priority given by the Finance, Revenue, and Economics working group)

11   Should mountain gorillas be expected to pay for their own conservation and the associated development of the community?
     The mountain gorilla is a special case, and the group recommends that:
     1. gorilla conservation should **not** have to meet narrow interpretations of financial self-sufficiency (i.e. monetary);
     2. an analysis of costs and benefits to the community (financial and non-financial) of gorilla conservation, including the world's willingness to pay for their survival, be summarized and be made widely available;
     3. the mountain gorilla should be used as a special case study which is incorporated into formal and informal education in all range states at all levels to demonstrate the broadest values of species and habitat conservation
     (Finance, Revenue, and Economics working group)

Society, Recreation and Sustainable Tourism

Stephen F. McCool and R. Neil Moisey

School of Forestry, University of Montana, Missoula, Montana,
USA

The community, as a tourism product, plays a very influential role in the success or failure of the tourism industry. If resident perceptions and preferences do not support tourism development policies and programmes, then programmes are likely to fail or be ineffective in their implementation – ultimately failing to achieve sustainability. Therefore, the goals and strategies of both community and tourism development should reflect or incorporate the views of the local residents through active participation in the decision-making process.

This section builds upon the frameworks introduced in the previous section and provides the reader with a variety of situations in which tourism development is related to larger societal concerns. In this section, public participation in both tourism planning and marketing and incorporating sense of place are presented in terms of building more sustainable tourism systems. Tourism development holds many consequences for how residents and tourists assign and derive meanings from specific communities and tourism destinations. The call for wider public participation in tourism planning has many subscribers; such calls are based on a possible restructuring of political power to achieve more sustainable objectives.

To this end, Mitchell explores the notion that, to achieve sustainability, the existing patterns of power and unequal development must be breached through the involvement of local communities in tourism development. Mitchell argues that higher levels of integration within the planning process lead to enhanced socio-economic benefits for the community, thus increasing the potential for tourism sustainability. The level of community solidarity, in turn, determines not only support for tourism development but also the degree of citizen participation. Mitchell notes that a 'collective indifference' toward tourism results from lack of participation in the planning process and the subsequent uneven sharing of tourism benefits and costs.

Horochowski and Moisey further propose that to even initiate community involvement, underlying social and political structures that engender public participation must exist. Societal values and political systems dictate to a large degree the role of the citizenry to participate in governance. Obviously, for local participation to be possible, the political system must be based on participation. While national policies might embrace such participation, Horochowski and Moisey note that if such structures are either rudimentary or nonexistent at the local level, then meaningful participation and ultimately achieving sustainability become less likely.

Likewise, the likelihood of community self-determination depends upon the availability of social capital. Lewis reports on implementation of 'self-developed tourism' and its role in engendering community-level group processes. Lewis notes that with increased levels of self-determination, community members feel that in their community tourism is indeed sustainable. Self-determination is largely dependent upon the ability of the community to work together. In contrast, one might hypothesize that lacking a shared vision for tourism development and the inability to reach consensus would result in tourism developments that were not sustainable.

Up until this point, the discussion has focused more on achieving sustainability through the inclusion of community in the planning process. Once completed and plans implemented, the role of public participation to ensure sustainability must continue. To ensure social equity, stakeholder involvement throughout the development needs to be incorporated in the tourism product, market identification and in destination promotion. Walsh *et al.* argue adopting a 'societal marketing approach' that shifts from a consumer focus to one more in line with sustainability of the local residents. Central to this approach is the concept of understanding, protecting and marketing an area's 'sense of place'. Walsh *et al.* note that the inclusion of 'sense of place in a societal marketing approach may lead to more authentic tourism experiences for tourists and the host community, and ultimately a more sustainable form of tourism development'. Indeed, for many communities, it is their shared and individual 'sense of place' that defines residents' attachment to the community and the surrounding resources, and determines how tourism developments may or may not meet sustainability goals.

The type of tourism can ultimately affect the role of tourism development in achieving sustainability. Typically, the discussion of tourism and sustainability focuses more on nature-based tourism in less-developed or rural areas. However, issues of sustainability and the role that tourism should, and can, play are broader than those found in just these settings. Carmichael discusses the perceived community and regional impacts as well as objective assessment of changes induced by casino development. A more holistic framework that encompasses the goals of sustainability in evaluating developments such as casinos provides a more comprehensive assessment of the social and environmental consequences of such developments.

In the final chapter of this section, Wearing and Neil explore a type of tourism that has great promise in achieving goals of sustainability. Alternative types of tourism (e.g. ecotourism) have received much attention to this end. Wearing and Neil propose that by combining traditional ecotourism with volunteerism and serious leisure, a type of tourism is created that 'provides a potentiality for the cooperative exchange and interaction of other values beyond just economic value and that a significant part of this is reliant on the recognition of the host community's centrality in this experience'.

8

Community Perspectives in Sustainable Tourism: Lessons from Peru

Ross E. Mitchell

Department of Rural Economy, University of Alberta, Edmonton, Alberta, Canada

Introduction

Tourism is the fastest growing industry in the world, with receipts from international tourism having increased by an average of 9% annually for the past 16 years. By the year 2010, the World Tourism Organization predicts that there will be one billion international tourists and more than US$1500 billion generated in revenue (WTO, 1998). The tourism sector is also recognized as an important job creator, employing an estimated 100 million people worldwide and growing 150% faster than any other industrial sector (WTO, 1998). Latin America accounts for approximately 8% of the world visitor arrivals (Euromonitor, 1994, p. 6) and this is forecasted to grow yearly by 5% through 2000 (Húescar and Luhrman, 1995). However, Schülter (1991) notes that most Latin American countries have not sufficiently exploited their unique cultural and ecological products and have preferred instead to place emphasis on beach tourism. Since the mid-1980s, countries such as Costa Rica, Belize, Ecuador and Peru have been promoting 'sustainable' tourism to generate revenue and employment in rural areas, while striving to reduce or avoid negative impacts. Peru, in particular, has enormous opportunities in many 'new' forms of tourism, including nature watching, heritage and archaeology, trekking and mountain climbing, river trips and other activities. At the same time, many remote, rural areas of Peru, including the once relatively isolated islands of Lake Titicaca and mountain villages of the Andean region, are experiencing rapid, unplanned growth.

It is widely accepted that as tourism expands in rural regions, sociocultural and environmental impacts can also be expected to increase. Potential impacts may be reduced if adequate precautions have been taken to ensure that ecological, economic and sociocultural factors have been taken into account at all stages for a given community-based tourism project, although in reality this is often easier said than done. Godde (1999) states that the key to improving environmental conservation and community well-being is the direct involvement of local communities within a climate of supportive regional or national policy. Still, the current debate is not whether local communities should be involved, but just *how* they should be involved and whether such 'involvement' means 'control'. Furthermore, it is the *degree* of control that is generally perceived as a significant element of sustainability (Mowforth and Munt, 1998, p. 103).

Defining sustainable tourism

There is a growing literature on tourism and sustainability (for example Hunter and Green, 1995; France, 1997; Stabler, 1997; Middleton, 1998; Mowforth and Munt, 1998) which brings into discussion many of the difficulties both of defining sustainability and of applying its concepts to the tourism sector. As mentioned in Chapter 1, the lack of consensus on meanings is becoming a significant pitfall in the search for sustainability. Sustainable tourism generally implies a balanced mix of sustaining local economies, local cultures and local environments.

One definition in particular considers sustainable tourism as a type of development that 'connects tourists and providers of tourist facilities and services with advocates of environmental protection and community residents and their leaders who desire a better quality of life' (McIntyre, 1993, p. 16). McIntyre claims that to be truly beneficial, 'it must also be dedicated to improving the quality of life of the people who live and work there, and to protecting the environment . . . Tourism must be environmentally sustainable – in both the natural and cultural environments – to be economically sustainable' (McIntyre, 1993, p. 5). Sustainable tourism is often equated with 'ecotourism' which the Ecotourism Society defines as 'responsible travel to natural areas which conserves the environment and sustains the well-being of local people' (Epler Wood, 1998a, p. 10).

In reality it may be difficult to achieve such laudable outcomes, since local communities are often inappropriately exploited and do not receive adequate benefits from tourism (Epler Wood, 1998a). Going even further, Weaver (1999) argues that any insistence that ecotourism must not negatively affect the environment or host society is unrealistic, since it is impossible to ensure that a particular visit or resort will not result in any significant long-term negative consequences. Therefore, 'an emphasis on sustainability in intention is thus more realistic than an insistence on sustainability in outcome' (Weaver, 1999, p. 794). In their critical analysis of 'new' tourism and sustainability in the Third World, Mowforth and Munt (1998) contend that sustainability is a contested concept, one 'that is *socially constructed* and reflects the interests of those involved' (Mowforth and Munt, 1998, p. 24–25). They argue that First World interests are served by the promotion of sustainability and ask 'who decides what sustainability means and entails, and who dictates how it should be achieved and evaluated?' (Mowforth and Munt, 1998, p. 12).

There are other criticisms aside from defining sustainability and sustainable tourism. Not only do existing measurement practices of sustainable tourism rarely point out linkages between socio-economic and environmental factors, the wide variety of indicator sets and measurement techniques in use makes comparative evaluation difficult (IISD, 1999). Moreover, monitoring of tourism impacts is almost always absent or inadequately informal (Drumm, 1998). Recognizing, then, that sustainable tourism, ecotourism and other such classifications are normative concepts, this research determined that, for the communities in question, a certain type and degree of sustainable tourism exists in order to concentrate efforts on socio-cultural factors.

Finally, exactly what may constitute 'local involvement' or 'participation' is the subject of great debate. The type, amount, intensity and equability of community participation require closer examination if a potentially sustainable tourism project is to be qualified as having achieved a high degree of local involvement. It is important to know just how local participation may affect the people's means of livelihood and the equitable sharing of benefits. Is the level of local participation in decision-making merely of a consultative nature, or is the community largely in control of its tourism development and management? This research examines the assertion that the only forms of local participation likely to break existing patterns of power and unequal development are those that originate from local communities themselves (Mowforth and Munt, 1998, p. 240).

Community integration

The central question considered in this chapter is whether a relatively high degree of community involvement in tourism planning, management and ownership, hence local control, can help reduce negative sociocultural impacts while providing benefits to local residents. Is it possible that a highly integrated community may increase the likelihood of success for tourism sustainability? The extent of community integration in tourism can be distinguished by the following characteristics (Mitchell, 1998):

- the extent of a broad-based, equitable and efficient democratic process;
- the number of participating citizens;
- the degree of individual participation, i.e. influence, in decision making;
- the amount of local ownership in the community-based tourism sector;
- the degree of long-term involvement in planning and management by local communities, i.e. not a 'once-off' event.

True community integration would necessitate more than mere participation – the concept of 'equality' must be linked to fair, democratic and meaningful decision-making (Mitchell, 1998). An integrated community would demonstrate a mature social, psychological and political integration that may be measured partially by its perceived and actual social, cultural and economic benefits (Mitchell, 1998). However, other factors may complicate this assumedly desirable outcome, including property ownership, local elite domination, government policies and economic leakages.

Mitchell and Reid (2001) and Mitchell and Eagles (2001) have proposed a framework for community integration in tourism planning and management that outlines three integral components of a public participation triangle discussed throughout this chapter: awareness, unity and power. Arnstein (1969), Freire (1970), Chambers (1983), Cernea (1985) and others have elaborated at length on community participation as a complex process of awareness building, control and action, equating it with empowerment or the ability of a community to 'take charge' of its development goals on an equitable basis. That said, the general objectives in this chapter are as follows:

1. To examine the role of community integration, especially power structures and processes, in relation to sustainable tourism planning and management.
2. To determine if community integration in sustainable tourism may:

- increase the likelihood of social benefits;
- influence or cause negative impacts.

These objectives can be linked to the fifth pathway or pitfall elaborated in Chapter 1: *forms of knowledge and public participation*. In particular, this chapter examines the role and accessibility of knowledge in community-based tourism. For example, how is knowledge of tourism potential disseminated, what forms of knowledge are considered, who are the principal advocates and what are their motives, and to what extent do local residents collaborate with tourism policy-makers, managers and industry players? Is the public being equitably engaged to identify desirable futures and acceptable pathways to develop sustainable tourism? These questions are examined throughout this chapter by a comparative case-study approach of two communities in Peru.

Tourism in Peru

Peru is the third-largest country in South America and is bordered by five neighbours: Ecuador to the north-west, Columbia to the north-east, Brazil and Bolivia to the east, and Chile to the south (see Fig. 8.1). Its total population of 22.6 million people (1993 census) includes over 7 million that live in the capital, Lima, on the Pacific coast.

The combination of economic and political instability, widespread terrorist activities, and a serious cholera outbreak resulted in the virtual destruction of the country's tourism industry during the late 1980s and early 1990s. Peru was one of only three countries in the western hemisphere where tourist arrivals actually declined from 1980–1992 (Blackstone Corporation, 1995). With increased socioeconomic stability during the latter half of the 1990s, tourism became the fastest-growing sector in Peru's economy (Boza, 1997). In 1998, international arrivals to Peru increased 11.5%, exceeding by almost five times the world rate of 2.4% estimated by the World Tourism Organization for the same period (WTO, 1999). Among the principal reasons for the increased tourism demand is its incredible ecological, cultural and historical diversity. Peru is likely the most diverse country in the world in terms of bird species (over 1600) and third most diverse in mammals (Blackstone Corporation, 1995). It also possesses some of the most exciting heritage resources in the world, including the Inca ruins at Machu Picchu and the Nazca Lines.

Study area

The first community selected for this comparative study was Taquile Island (pronounced 'Tah-key-lay'), located on Lake Titicaca in southeastern Peru. The other community was Chiquian (pronounced 'Cheekey-an'), which lies just south of Huaraz in the central part of Peru.

Fig. 8.1. Map of Peru and location of study sites (adapted from
www.theodora.com/wfb/peru/peru_map.html, 19 July 1998).

Tourism in the Chiquian region is principally nature-based, while both
culturally and ecologically oriented for Taquile Island. Table 8.1
indicates some shared characteristics of the two study sites.

Taquile Island

Taquile Island lies on Lake Titicaca at the extreme south-east end of
Peru, about 25 km or 3–4 h by motorized boat from Puno (regional
capital with approximately 100,000 inhabitants). Total surface area is
754 ha with 65% of the area being cultivated (Valencia Blanco, 1989).
Taquile has an estimated population of 1850 primarily Quechua-
speaking people, who are highly industrious in agriculture, fishing and
weaving. The administration of Taquile Island is based on unique
socio-geographical divisions that combine traditional with modern
political systems (Healy and Zorn, 1983).

Foreign tourists began arriving on the dock at Puno in the mid-
1970s and local private boat owners soon added the island to their

Table 8.1. Research site comparison.

Key characteristics	Taquile Island	Chiquian
Altitude	3812 m	3374 m
Dominant languages	Primarily Quechua; minor Spanish	Spanish; minor Quechua
Location	Lake Titicaca; accessible by boat from Puno	Central Andes; accessible by road from Huaraz or Lima
Major economic activities	Subsistence agriculture, tourism services, weaving	Subsistence agriculture, guiding, weaving
Number of visitors	Est. 27,000 in 1996	Est. 1000 in 1996 to Huayhuash
Population	1850 (1997 estimate); 350 households	3801 (1993 census); 1204 households
Production of handicrafts	Very high; tourist-based and functional	Low to moderate; predominantly export-based
Tourism frequency	Year-round; high season from June to August	During high season only, from May to September
Tourism economic importance	Very high; basic services including lodging, food, transport	Low to moderate; basic services including lodging, food, transport
Tourism type	Cultural/nature	Nature/cultural

tourist run on the lake. Taquile Island sailboat cooperatives were formed in early 1978 by groups of 30–40 families (Healy and Zorn, 1983). By 1982, the number of boat cooperatives had expanded to 13, with 435 Taquile residents sharing boat ownership and management responsibilities (Healy and Zorn, 1983). The islanders proved to be competitive with boat owners from Puno and eventually displaced them by obtaining an officially sanctioned monopoly. Protection of islander-controlled tourist transport ended during the early 1990s with the advent of President Fujimori's privatization and anti-monopolization policies.

One of the principal attractions for many tourists to Taquile are the extraordinary textiles, skilfully woven from sheep and alpaca wool. Weavings are sold in two community-run artisan stores (Manco Capac Cooperative), and prices are based on workmanship quality and labour (Healy and Zorn, 1983). Prices are also fixed by all members to avoid harmful competition, with a small percentage (5%) retained for cooperative maintenance. Community law, in keeping with islander traditions of equality, prohibits private sales, although in reality they occur on a discreet basis. By 1990, Taquile had control over all stages of its textile manufacture and marketing, and controlled most tourism services (Prochaska, 1990).

When tourists arrive on Taquile, a reception committee greets and registers them by age, duration of stay and nationality. The new arrivals are assigned accommodation with a local family in an adobe hut. Several committees help to manage the daily tasks, such as housing, weaving, food and transportation. Each household approved by an accommodation committee as suitable for tourists directly receives the lodging fees (in 1997, about US$2 per night). Tourist income revenues have encouraged household improvements (such as simple bedding gear, extra rooms and kerosene lanterns). Island restaurants are owned and managed by groups of families.

Chiquian

Chiquian has an urban population of 3801 inhabitants and 1204 households (1993 census). It is 110 km south-east of Huaraz, 340 km north-east of Lima and situated at 3374 m. In many respects, Chiquian remains as isolated as Taquile Island since it is surrounded by mountains and is still a relatively arduous journey (about 4 h by bus), even considering the recent road improvements from Huaraz. There is a distinct preference for tourism in the immediate Huaraz area compared to the relatively isolated Cordillera Huayhuash area. An estimated 95% of foreign visitors to the Chavín Region (of which Chiquian belongs) visit cities in the Callejón de Huaylas (the mountain valley north of Huaraz, in which the national park of Huascarán is located), while only 1% visit Chiquian and the Cordillera Huayhuash (TMI, 1996).

People working in local mountain-based tourism in the Chiquian area may be hired as porters, mule drivers and cooks. Other local services that cater to tourists (although not exclusively) include restaurants, hostels, bus transportation, woollen clothing manufacturing and cheese making. Chiquian and its neighbouring towns offer other attractions, such as colonial churches, thermal springs and archaeological sites. Most foreign tourists that come to Chiquian prefer to trek or climb mountains in the nearby Cordillera Huayhuash, covering an area of 140,000 ha and 45 km long from north to south. The Huayhuash is 'virtually an undiscovered treasure' with its extensive 'hiking and trekking routes, climbing attractions, archaeological sites, alpine lakes and cultural uniqueness' (Kolff and Tohan, 1997, p. 29). It contains 46 alpine lakes and has six peaks higher than 6000 m, including the second highest mountain in Peru, Yerupaja (6634 m).

The flow of visitors to the Huayhuash started in the 1970s and reached its peak by the mid-1980s. From this point until approximately 1992, tourism virtually ceased in the Huayhuash due to terrorist activities of the Shining Path. With increased security as terrorism declined, tourism levels may now be superseding those of 10 years ago. One local expert estimated that approximately 1000 visitors came to the Huayhuash during 1996, staying an average of 10 days per person (Kolff and Tohan, 1997). However, it was found that local people of the Cordillera Huayhuash 'perceive tourism as only a means of economic benefits', and in general do not have a well-developed understanding of the industry (Kolff and Tohan, 1997, p. 61). In nearby mountain communities such as Llámac, the tourism sector has been dominated by just a few families (Kolff and Tohan, 1997, p. 61). In addition, there are many concerns about the future of the Cordillera Huayhuash, because of the interest of foreign mining companies and increased tourism. Since 1997, The Mountain Institute has been discussing a community-based ecotourism programme with local communities, with the eventual aim of designating the Huayhuash as a nationally recognized protected area.

Data collection

This research was carried out from December 1996 to September 1997. Recognizing that a given level of tourism dependence existed for each community, emphasis was placed on 'why' and 'how' individual and community participation may affect sociocultural parameters and reduce potential impacts. Individual and community well-being (i.e. personal satisfaction and democratic, equitable participation in local decision-making) were measured by individual and community perceptions toward the tourism sector, equity inherent in local decision-making power and participation factors.

A household survey was applied to adult family members considered as community residents (defined as any household member 16 years or older living in the community for at least 6 months of the year). The survey objective was to examine household perceptions of socio-economic benefits from local tourism activities by a combination of closed-ended (i.e. choices provided) and Likert scale questions (i.e. five-point scale ranging from 'strongly agree' to 'strongly disagree'). Other questions concerned local tourism history, community unity, tourism planning and development, decision-making power, and impacts. A total of 101 surveys for Taquile and 136 surveys for Chiquian were carried out, usually at the place of residence, with a sample frame that consisted of all occupied households. The minimum confidence interval was established at 90%, with a level of confidence of 10%.

Qualitative methodology was applied to 'key informants' to obtain a greater perspective of the historical development of tourism for each respective community. Nine residents of Taquile Island and eight residents of Chiquian were selected for their extensive knowledge of, or involvement with, the respective local tourism sector, including tourism founders and owners, travel agencies and guides, politicians and weavers. The interviews also examined decision-making processes and attitudinal responses of the socio-economic and environmental impacts of tourism in each community.

Results

Research findings have been grouped as follows: (i) growth and development; (ii) planning; (iii) solidarity and support; (iv) community participation; and (v) impacts. These themes are not intended to be definitive; several other factors beyond community control, such as destination attractiveness and government policies, may be critical to the ultimate success of a locally based tourism industry (whether measured by longevity, equitability or other parameters). Some key findings from the household surveys are indicated in Table 8.2. Principal factors recognized as responsible for sociocultural, economic and environmental changes for both communities are summarized in Table 8.3.

Growth and development

In 1970, Taquile Island and Chiquian were still relatively new destinations, although a limited amount of mountain-climbing activity and domestic tourism occurred in the latter community. In the first of six possible stages, exploration, unique natural and cultural features inherent to both areas initially attracted visitors. Numbers remained

Table 8.2. Selected household survey findings.

Question	Taquile Island (%)	Chiquian (%)
Hold administrative role of any kind in community	88	15
Hold tourism administration role	79	8
Have attended a tourism meeting	96	18
Feel authorities encourage participation in tourism	93	65
Feel there is high municipal support for tourism	79	30
Are employed in tourism (part-time or full-time)	98	10
Feel that tourism benefits household	89	40
Desire more tourism activities for community	93	93

Percentages are based on $n = 101$ for Taquile Island and $n = 136$ for Chiquian.

Table 8.3. Comparison of tourism growth and impacts by community.

Theme	Taquile Island	Chiquian
Tourism growth	Started mid-1970s; highest levels reached in 1990s; tourism has increased to near mass proportions	Started mid-1950s; highest levels reached by mid-1980s; tourism returning after years of terrorism
Tourism control	Formerly high control has decreased to moderate level partly due to privatization and ineffectual leadership	Low control with outside domination of local tourism industry
Community unity	Strong but declining unity linked to diminished control	Divided opinion over unity but marked pattern of disharmony and conflict
Sociocultural impacts	Modernization due to demands of tourism have affected traditional lifestyles; emergence of individualism and globalization; begging by children	Community feelings about tourism often negative; suspicion mixed with adverse intercommunity relationships, less openness
Economic impacts	Most residents benefiting; opportunism linked to high revenues for shrewdest islanders; high leakages; Puno agencies blamed	Some revenues and jobs from tourism, but most residents not benefiting; high leakages; potential for community-wide benefits; Huaraz agencies blamed
Environmental impacts	Increasing litter affecting consumer demand; neglect of agriculture due to handicraft production	Mining exploitation and roads in Cordillera Huayhuash; perceived need to protect natural and cultural environment
Future of local tourism	Highly optimistic, but concern to maintain traditional ways; regaining control, training youth as guides, educating tourists important	Guarded optimism; tourism in early stages of development; community awareness and outside support needed

relatively small, restricted by lack of accessibility, proper facilities and national or international awareness of their existence. As word spread during the latter part of the 1970s, both areas were visited by a growing number of tourists, and particularly so for Taquile Island due to its proximity to the so-called 'gringo trail' (combination of road, rail and boat) linking Lima, Cuzco and Puno with La Paz in Bolivia.

By 1988, violence from terrorism began to spread throughout Peru, but it affected the Huayhuash region near Chiquian much more dramatically and directly than Taquile. Tourism declined somewhat in Taquile and dropped to near zero levels in Chiquian. By 1994, tourism had started to pick up again in Chiquian but fell short of the numbers of tourists experienced in the early 1980s. Based on general observations with local people employed in the tourism industry, there were 800 trekkers and climbers in 1997, down slightly from 1000 in 1996 (Kolff and Tohan, 1997). Visitor numbers to the Huayhuash may have declined somewhat in 1997 due to the combined effects of El Niño and the December 1996 MRTA (Tupac Amaru Revolutionary Movement) takeover of the Japanese Embassy in Lima. According to Puno Coast Guard records, there were a total of 27,685 visitors to Taquile Island in 1996. By the end of the 1990s, tourism on Taquile appears to have risen to Butler's (1980) critical range in terms of negative social and environmental effects, as well as declining visitor satisfaction. Interestingly, when asked if tourism was responsible for any negative impacts (either social or environmental), 84% of Taquile and 90% of Chiquian respondents disagreed with the statement.

Still, many key informants claimed that tourism has caused certain problems for both communities, but especially so in Taquile, due to its higher visitation numbers and relatively fragile setting, e.g. limited space and resources, dependency on lake for transport and food. Some tourists and agencies interviewed prefer to visit other nearby islands, e.g. Amantaní, Islands of the Sun and Moon, or Suasi, due to the increasing amount of congestion and litter on Taquile. This would indicate that local tourism demand is relatively elastic, although many Taquileños feel that their island is so unique that it will continue to draw more visitors by reputation alone. Visitor numbers to the Chiquian area may also decline due to increasing litter, poorly marked trails, inadequate promotion and heightened mining activity in the Huayhuash. Likewise, there are other unique areas for hiking and climbing in the nearby Cordillera Blanca that may influence visitor preferences.

Planning

This research found that key individuals in both communities have played important roles in the early stages of tourism planning. On Taquile Island, initial reluctance changed to outright support when economic benefits from community-wide participation in handicraft sales and lodging provision became apparent. Many respondents suggested that the determination of ex-governor and expert weaver Francisco Huatta Huatta, Belgian priest Father Pepe Loits and US

Peace Corps worker Kevin Healy persuaded the islanders of tourism's economic advantages. It was made clear from the start that equitable participation could be obtained by providing tourism services locally without drastically changing traditional ways. For example:

> Father Loits . . . is one of the important factors of the island's development and was there when the first tourists came, [but the islanders] did not want to bring [them] . . . they felt tourism would change them. [Father Loits] explained that it would be OK and told them about [cultural] interchange, and how the monetary system worked . . . It seems to me that what he did was to conscientize the people that their island had value and richness, and that they had to maintain their identity . . . So when tourism increased, the [negative] effect was reduced and [Taquile] was able to maintain itself.

Chiquian, too, has had its tourism champions, although some interviewees felt that their motives may not have been entirely altruistic. Roberto Aldave, considered by many respondents and interviewees to have put Chiquian on the map for its excellent opportunities in adventure tourism, was personally involved in early documentary film-making of the Cordillera Huayhuash in the 1970s. He also initiated the 'Ecoventura' festival (Eco-Adventure) in May 1994. Ecoventura essentially reopened the Huayhuash to trekkers and climbers after years of terrorism activity had virtually decimated the local tourism industry. According to its founder, it was an ideal venue to promote the area for outdoor activities such as trekking, climbing, horseback riding and mountain biking:

> [Ecoventura] was an incentive for bringing visitors to Chiquian. The City of Huaraz has always had attention, like their Alpine Week . . . so we had to compete with them. [Ecoventura] was formed for cultural, adventure and ecotourism motives . . . We wanted to promote Chiquian so that money would be invested in it.

Chiquian and nearby communities were also given the opportunity to show their unique customs, historical sites and other tourism possibilities. Although the original Ecoventura enjoyed some degree of success both locally and nationally, a bitter dispute in 1996 between the Ecoventura founder and the new Chiquian Municipal Council resulted in the festival management takeover by the municipality.

Many respondents asserted that tourism planning by Chiquian residents has favoured those already involved in the local industry, such as established guides with connections to non-local agencies. Recently, some Chiquian residents working in the nature–adventure industry have attempted to organize themselves. In 1997, local guides, porters and donkey drivers joined together with the Municipality of Chiquian and its newly created Tourism Commission to form The Cordillera Huayhuash Mountain Climbing Provincial Association.

However, the association was established not only to 'improve tourism service quality', but to lend support to other initiatives as well. One interviewee noted that perhaps the local government felt its scope would be too limiting with tourism as the sole objective. Many felt that travel agencies from Huaraz, Lima and Europe have controlled local tourism development, and some stated that Chiquian residents with experience in trekking and climbing are often bypassed in favour of those from nearby mountain communities.

Solidarity and support

Both communities differ substantially in their respective level and intensity of community solidarity within the context of support for the local tourism industry. Taquile islanders have historically, and even passionately, defended their rights in a collective fashion. An example of their solidarity occurred during the 1990 fight on the Puno docks, when travel agencies tried to wrest control over the right to take passengers to the island. Although the tourist agencies sued in court, Taquile won transport rights to the island through a Ministry of Tourism directive (Stone, 1996). However, this victory for Taquile residents was later thwarted by Fujimori's anti-monopolization laws of the early 1990s, which effectively prohibited Taquile boat cooperatives from maintaining control over transport rights. In contrast, many Chiquian respondents were ambivalent towards not only tourism but community planning and administration in general. Several persons blamed this inherent disharmony on spillover effects of fear and suspicion of outsiders from the terrorism years, whereas others pointed fingers at the high emigration levels from surrounding villages or lack of financial incentives. Recent planning efforts with the town council and some local guides were 'to improve the quality of service to the client', rather than detailing how this organization could involve or benefit the entire community. Those lacking previous experience in adventure tourism tend to be excluded from membership in such organizations or from receiving specialized training. Still, one local guide felt there was less hostility and more willingness to help tourists than before:

> Tourists have always been well-received by the people of Chiquian, because tourism generates income for restaurants, business people . . . more than the farmers could make . . . That's why the mountain folk were happy.

Only those owners and employees of tourism-related businesses were deemed to be strong supporters of tourism. One key informant felt that the nearby communities of Llámac and Pocpa support tourism more since many guides, donkey drivers and porters originate from there. It was also suggested that trekkers have a more visible presence in these smaller villages on the Huayhuash circuit, whereas tourists may not be as noticeable in Chiquian. Local political support for tourism would seem to be relatively high, with new tourism committees and events, but many of those surveyed expressed discontentment with the municipality. The former mayor was considered very supportive of local tourism (some recognized that he had helped create and organize the first Ecoventura), but only 30% of survey respondents in Chiquian, compared to 79% in Taquile, felt that the local government supports tourism.

Community participation

According to the household surveys, Taquile residents participate to a great extent in tourism service administration (79%) and community tourism meetings (96%). Most respondents agreed (93%) that local authorities encourage participation in tourism meetings. Likewise, there is a strong tradition of consensual, democratic decision-making on Taquile, at least for men. Representatives of the various tourism committees and the local government are annually elected by all residents of legal voting age. Most posts cannot be held for more than a year, creating greater opportunities for participation as community leaders. Authorities are not only expected to lead but to participate in the very decisions they make, and any leader can be dismissed for incompetence or other factors. Tourism on Taquile has become such an important part of daily life that it has become interwoven with local politics. For example, most residents (77%) belong to the Manco Capac Cooperative, which requires a minimum of 3 weeks of administrative work from every member (although a close relative of a member can substitute).

In contrast, few Chiquian respondents hold any kind of adminis-trative role in the community (15%) or have attended tourism meetings (18%); only 8% are involved in some capacity in tourism administra-tion, and most of those employed in tourism (apart from local restaurant and hostel owner-operators) work for Huaraz or other agencies. Many felt that only those already working in tourism are invited to take part in meetings and event planning (only 65% of respondents agreed that local authorities encourage participation). Several respondents commented that only those working in tourism 'participate' in tourism service provision, since most people are either busy working on their farms or are simply not interested. At least one person attributed the lack of participation as a consequence of terrorism and its socio-psychological impacts on the community.

It is apparent, then, that there is a greater degree of participation in the overall administration of socio-political aspects of Taquile compared to Chiquian. Many Chiquian respondents indicated that tourism management is highly selective and geared toward those working in the industry, whereas many Taquileños have roles in local government or one of the several municipal or cooperative committees. Ecoventura (1994–1996) in Chiquian may have created a perception of high community participation when, in reality, only a select few have been involved in organizing the event. Training opportunities in trekking and climbing are not currently extended to those lacking experience. On the other hand, high participation levels for Taquile say little about the intensity of individual involvement or the type of participation. Public meetings on Taquile tend to be 'information sharing' by local leaders on recent achievements and upcoming projects, rather than actively soliciting public input.

In addition, gender appears to play an important role in the variety (or intensity) of tourism meetings attended for both communities. Interestingly, Taquile women are visibly present at most community meetings, but this was not the case observed in the male-dominated tourism committee meetings in Chiquian. Still, soft-spoken members of Taquile community, such as the generally shy women, are rarely encouraged to speak out except during 'special' sessions on domestic-related issues. This may be an indication that: (i) men have more spare time to attend such meetings; (ii) men are more interested in tourism meetings than women; and/or (iii) it may be a cultural role assigned to men. Differences attributable to gender are likely a combination of all three possibilities, but the last one, in particular, is a characteristic common to traditional Andean cultures.

Impacts

The survey and interview results indicate that tourism has brought many changes to the way of life and environs of both Taquile and Chiquian residents. Sociocultural impacts are considered primarily in this chapter, since the economic and environmental aspects have been described in other publications (see Mitchell, 1998; Mitchell and Eagles, 2001; Mitchell and Reid, 2001).

Taquile Island

CONSUMERISM. According to one interviewee, money was a relatively new commodity for most islanders when tourism began. Since the local economy was based on subsistence agriculture and fishing, and because they were so isolated from mainland Peru, money was of little use to most residents. Hard currency was needed only to purchase sugar or coca leaves (which are chewed), or to make house improvements. To obtain cash, Taquile men travelled to nearby towns to work as farm labourers, or sold their cattle and *colle* (a local shrub used for firewood). Tourism has made it possible to stay on the island and earn sufficient income for the family. In addition to handicraft sales, most respondents acknowledged that revenues collected from transport, entrance fees, stayovers and the community restaurant have contributed to both individual and community wealth. Today money is readily available for the import of televisions, radios, dry foods, fertilizers, pesticides, building materials and other so-called 'luxury' items previously unknown to most islanders.

INDIVIDUALISM. Traditionally, duty to one's family and to the community have been considered of equal importance on Taquile Island. However, the general perception is that, with the spread of free enterprise and consumerism, a growing number of residents are pursuing individual material wealth. Diminishing unity was seen by some as linked to economic interests, such as increasing individualism, external leakages to Puno agencies and businesses, and other socio-economic factors. Some felt that this trend of individualism is causing negative impacts on community cohesiveness:

> It's probably true that [unity] has diminished . . . With more solidarity, spirituality and sense of community [in the past], there used to be more concern for each other.

Many interviewees felt that individual ownership is adversely affecting the work-sharing ethic common to Taquileño society. Reciprocal work-sharing systems, such as the *ayni* and *minka*, are still practised by the majority of residents, but payment is now demanded for work on government-sponsored community projects. One key informant deplored the growing number of children that are begging for money or candy from unsuspecting tourists. Another felt that individualism was due directly to tourism and the national economic situation, e.g. recession, inflation and devaluation.

MODERNIZATION. Most respondents mentioned several changes that have occurred over the past two decades since tourism began. It was noted that the introduction of boat motors at the end of the 1970s significantly reduced travel time for tourists. Still, modern technology did not begin to affect islander lifestyles significantly until the early 1990s. Major improvements in keeping with modern trends have included a community telephone, solar lighting, television sets and the increased use of pesticides. Perhaps the greatest visual change has been the replacement on many houses of traditional straw thatching with corrugated tin roofs, since tin can be installed quickly and is low maintenance. In addition, synthetic wool is gradually replacing the traditional use of sheep and alpaca wool in islander handicrafts. Simpler patterns and techniques may earn greater revenues but many felt that the quality of workmanship has deteriorated compared to 20 years ago. Still, one key informant suggested that it is up to the Taquileños to decide for themselves what degree of change is acceptable:

> There was a period when the influence of tourism was so strong that everybody was weaving and nobody farmed. But they still had to eat. The good thing is that they maintain their cultural identity and their principles . . . [Still,] we shouldn't impede what they want. It would be a crime if we prevented contact from the rest of the world and turned Taquile into a living museum.

GLOBALIZATION. Non-local interviewees noted that globalization is negatively affecting Taquile and its traditions. It was observed that extensive media coverage of Taquile since the mid-1970s has revealed its unique culture once 'hidden' from the world, causing an annual influx of thousands of foreign tourists. A few Taquileños now travel frequently to Europe and North America on promotional tours, to dance at folklore festivals and sell weavings. This fast pace of change is worrisome to many interviewees, who believe that the island has become more cosmopolitan and risks losing its traditional sense of identity.

Chiquian

DISHARMONY. Chiquian appears to be divided about its own sense of unity. There is a sense of trying to self-organize for tourism but without achieving broad-based support within the community. Some believe that jealousy or laziness hinders the improvement of services, or that the mining issue causes division among neighbouring communities. Whatever the case, little evidence was demonstrated from key informants to indicate that community unity in Chiquian was anything other than low.

EMIGRATION. Some interviewees felt that a cultural factor influencing residential attitudes toward tourism was the high emigration from neighbouring towns and regions to Chiquian (only 54% of Chiquian respondents were native born compared to 99% of Taquile respondents). Lack of homogeneity among residents in terms of birthplace may be partly responsible for the general lack of overall support. There may be significant sociocultural differences in language, skin colour and/or level of education that make it difficult to achieve consensus on tourism-related issues. In addition, residents may spend only part of their time in Chiquian, or just long enough to provide an education for their children. These factors may contribute to feelings of indifference about the community.

TERRORISM. Several years of terrorism not only effectively eliminated tourism as an economic option for Chiquian and the Cordillera Huayhuash, it created difficulties for residents in openly welcoming strangers again. There was a sense of fear and suspicion from some key informants (and many questionnaire respondents), perhaps attributable to the aftermath of a very traumatic period. Therefore, although terrorism is not an impact that can be attributable to tourism, the image of safety may not only be important from a national or international perspective (i.e. tourists and travel agencies), but from a local one as well (i.e. residents).

Community perspectives: a comparative analysis

Finding new models of sustainability is a process that must have all stakeholders involved at the initiation of a project, including both the local community and the private sector (Epler Wood, 1998b). Reed (1997) feels that tourism development requires a slow process of community building, particularly when conventional stakeholders, including residents, entrepreneurs, politicians and tourism advocates, do not view it as a productive activity. Moreover, community building may not be an easy process to initiate and maintain, given the many pitfalls and pathways along the way, as illustrated throughout this book. On Taquile Island, it took several years until people became convinced of the economic advantages of tourism. Still, there was clearly greater individual involvement and influence compared to Chiquian, and apparently more widespread discussion among islander residents before allowing tourism to occur. Several individuals did more than promote the island and its unique culture to the outside world – they employed a deliberate process of awareness raising or *conscientization* (Freire, 1970). That is, Taquile directed its own tourism development through self-awareness and self-reliance. In contrast, the average resident in Chiquian has minimal awareness of the local tourism industry and few opportunities to participate in its management and potential benefits.

Since its beginnings in the 1970s, tourism planning on Taquile has been a participatory, albeit unstructured, process. As a process of empowerment, 'participation helps local people to identify problems and become involved in decision making and implementation, all of which contribute to sustainable development' (France, 1997, p. 149). Rocha (1997) delineates five types of 'empowerment' within planning, of which perhaps the most relevant to Taquile is 'socio-political' empowerment, defined as 'the development of a politicized link between individual circumstance and community conditions through collective social action, challenging oppressive institutional arrangements' (Rocha, 1997, p. 34). Given their traditional sense of duty to the community and their intrinsic participatory nature, a tourism 'dialogue' was conceived and established through public discussions and entrenched by community laws.

Local planning has not been confined to operational issues but to normative (value-based) planning as well. The islanders took the initiative and decided for themselves what type of services to offer tourists, who would be involved, how everyone could participate and to what extent benefits would be shared. This collective action for self-reliance concurs with Galjart's (1976) claim that an obvious common opponent (e.g. the Puno-based travel agencies) can lead to increased solidarity. Nevertheless, the Taquile-based results indicate that community solidarity has deteriorated in the past few years due to a trend towards individualism, consumerism and globalization, albeit not to the extent of that seen in Chiquian. Growth in individualism is often accompanied by a decline in traditional solidarity, or a transition from 'brotherhood to otherhood' (Chodak, 1972).

In Chiquian, there is a sense of 'collective indifference', rather than the 'increased hostilities' that Theophile (1995) mentions is a possible outcome if most residents are excluded from tourism revenues. Many residents recognize that local and non-local elites, including government officials, former residents and single families from smaller communities of the Huayhuash zone, have captured most of the benefits. Brandon (1996) states that non-cohesive communities have little decision-making input, and decisions made usually favour the needs of the tourist and the operator/owner of the site, rather than the needs of the community.

The situation is much more positive for tourism potential and support by local residents and the national government on Taquile Island. As Godde (1999) ascertains, supportive national and regional policies play a major role in stimulating sustainable mountain tourism activities. High public involvement in local decision-making regarding tourism, and the combined financial and promotional assistance provided by President Fujimori in recent years, have likely contributed to feelings of support for local tourism on Taquile Island. The results also concur with the findings of Prentice (1993) that beneficiaries of tourism revenues are more likely to support its development. If residents perceive themselves to benefit from tourism, they may feel a greater sense of ownership and need to ensure its continued growth (albeit, on a sustainable basis), particularly if their livelihood depends upon its survival.

Still, not all is positive concerning increased earning potential that tourism revenues have brought to Taquile Island. As Brandon (1996) illustrates in her description of how village elites in Nepal have captured benefits, ecotourism may exacerbate local levels of income inequality within communities, or among communities in a region. One Taquile resident commented that money is changing them, which alludes to socio-economic and political transformations that they have experienced with tourism. The concept of private ownership is relatively new to a society characterized by traditional sharing of benefits, and certain individuals were perceived as responsible for causing disharmony through materialistic wants. At this stage it is uncertain which direction tourism will take in either area – either rejuvenation or decline. From the perspective of local residents, both communities would prefer tourism to continue expanding (for example, 93% of respondents for both communities want more tourism). Still, it will require more than just an expressed wish on the part of residents for tourism to continue on a steady path of growth. Definitive steps or processes would have to be established to assure sustainable rejuvenation or continued growth, which would necessitate long-term, participatory planning.

Given the demand for more tourists by local residents, it may be difficult to control growth. This concurs with Butler's (1991) assertion that intervention in the form of limiting tourist numbers is politically difficult in a free market situation. The 'truly unique area' or a site categorized as having a 'timeless attractiveness' that Butler (1980, p. 9) claims as necessary to 'withstand the pressures of visitation' may not be sufficient for rejuvenation to occur. This is especially the case given the current context of competitive markets, unfavourable tourism policies, socio-economic instability, lack of community support or other internal and external factors. Nevertheless, it is possible that Taquile, with its higher perception of community support and benefits due to tourism, combined with past achievements largely based on community awareness, solidarity and sharing of power, may have a greater likelihood of rejuvenation in its tourism industry compared to other island communities of Lake Titicaca, or relatively neglected and isolated mountain communities such as Chiquian.

Conclusions and implications

This chapter has examined the pathway or pitfall considered as 'forms of knowledge and public participation', and made explicit reference to community-based or social integration within a sustainable tourism framework. The results indicate that the respective degree and nature of community integration can influence sustainable tourism to varying degrees of success, although it is doubtful that sustainability can ever be guaranteed. On the positive side, it was found that a community more highly integrated in its local tourism industry may at least reduce the potential for negative impacts in the provision of local tourism services and products. Likewise, a more equitable sharing of decision-making power, combined with a relatively unified citizenry, should result in a more balanced distribution of tourism benefits. Additionally, favourable municipal and national government support and polices may ensure that a greater proportion of residents ultimately gain from local tourism activities.

Although a participatory, democratic framework and mechanism should allow for greater local control of tourism management and ownership, it was shown that such control may be affected negatively by both internal and external forces or interests. The downside is that local tourism opportunities may attract outsiders who may not have the community's best interests at heart. Moreover, increased individualism and consumerism may erode community harmony and weaken local control. Tourism may be desired but not at the expense of forfeiting local traditions, since to weaken or destroy these could also undermine the very social and ecological environment upon which people depend.

It is hoped that this chapter has demonstrated that those rural communities more thoroughly involved, i.e. *integrated*, in their local tourism sector, from the early planning and development stages to the day-to-day administration, stand a much greater chance of enhancing overall tourism sustainability and reducing negative impacts. Factors such as social unrest and globalization in previously isolated communities may cause tensions and disharmony as opportunities for revenue generation are made increasingly available. This chapter has also shown the importance of encouraging community integration at the *onset* of tourism development, perhaps by the support of facilitators or local tourism champions. This may avoid an unpopular redistribution of wealth afterwards if a long implementation delay is anticipated in the integration process. In this scenario, integration potential may dissolve as local entrepreneurs and power holders solidify and augment their personal stakes.

Recommendations for sustainable tourism projects and research

In summary, facilitating community or social integration in sustainable tourism planning, development and management is crucial to the overall outcome of such projects. Community residents, planners, government agencies, non-government organizations and other stakeholders must work in conjunction on tourism planning efforts to allow for relatively accessible and equitable decision-making power. Political leaders, entrepreneurs and other power holders from within and outside the community are perhaps the pivotal link in the integration process. If their support is not obtained, any sustainable tourism initiative is likely to fall far short of its anticipated goals. There is a significant 'buy in' aspect that must be carefully addressed in a marketing strategy, especially considering the dominant influence often exercised by leaders of remote rural communities. Potential adversaries may become the most enthusiastic advocates of a given sustainable tourism project if their support is obtained at an early stage. However, care must be taken so that the process does not become circumvented and used to the advantage of those with significant decision-making control or influence, especially those that may not have the community's best interests at stake. For this reason, it is crucial that a sustainable tourism strategy is created and implemented not only *for* the community, but also *by* the community. As mentioned earlier in this chapter, local empowerment in the context of community development is as much part of the equation as adequate tourist demand and resources. Obviously, human capital is an invaluable resource that must be appropriately considered and utilized, including incorporating traditional or indigenous knowledge and concerns into tourism strategies.

Some suggestions for either evaluation or implementation of sustainable tourism projects from a community integration perspective are outlined here:

- Determine degree of cohesion and support for tourism among community residents and industry players.
- Assess local and external power relationships using key informants, focus groups, participatory or rapid rural appraisal, or other appropriate techniques.
- Encourage and incorporate indigenous and ad hoc forms of knowledge as much as possible, in conjunction with 'scientific' or mainstream strategic information gathering.
- Identify and encourage key individuals or agencies to assist in the dissemination of opportunities and drawbacks to implementing a sustainable tourism programme.
- Within a democratic and transparent process, create a sustainable tourism strategy with appropriate visions, goals, objectives, targets, activities and a marketing plan.
- Monitor and evaluate the tourism strategy with community input once implemented.

Finally, the lessons learned from this case study have left several questions that could be addressed in future research. There are at least three avenues that could be explored to provide a greater understanding of community integration in sustainable tourism. Firstly, what effect, if any, does community integration have on environmental parameters associated with sustainable tourism? Could greater community integration help protect a nearby tourism destination from potentially destructive forces such as excessive tourist numbers? Secondly, how can local, national and transnational policies be considered in an integrated tourism planning process, and would greater social integration facilitate their development and implementation to the benefit of local residents? Thirdly, how does community integration in sustainable tourism correlate to economic factors such as direct and indirect employment and revenues? Basic cost–benefit accounting or a more complex economic analysis of regional and local data with a detailed examination of leakages and economic multipliers could be considered in future research.

References

Arnstein, S.R. (1969) A ladder of citizen participation. *Journal of the American Institute of Planners* 3, 216–224.

Blackstone Corporation (1995) *Ecotourism and Environmental Linkages in Peru: a Framework for Action.* Prepared for the World Bank, Toronto.

Boza, B. (1997) *Peru El Dorado* No. 6, January–March.

Brandon, K. (1996) *Ecotourism and Conservation: a Review of Key issues.* Global Environment Division, The World Bank, Paper No. 033.

Butler, R.W. (1980) The concept of the tourist cycle of evolution: implications for management of resources. *Canadian Geographer* 24, 5–12.

Butler, R.W. (1991) Tourism, environment and sustainable development. *Environmental Conservation* 18(3), 201–209.

Cernea, M. (ed.) (1985) *Putting People First: Sociological Variables in Rural Development.* World Bank, Oxford University Press, Washington, DC.

Chambers, R. (1983) *Rural Development: Putting the Last First.* Longman, London.

Chodak, S. (1972) From brotherhood to otherhood: some aspects of social change in modernizing rural Africa. *Sociologia Ruralis* 12(3/4), 302–314.

Drumm, A. (1998) New approaches to community-based ecotourism management: learning from Ecuador. In: Lindberg, K., Epler Wood, M. and Engledrum, D. (eds) *Ecotourism: a Guide for Planners and Managers*, Vol. 2. The Ecotourism Society, North Bennington, Vermont, pp. 197–213.

Epler Wood, M. (1998a) *Meeting the Global Challenge of Community Participation in Ecotourism: Case Studies and Lessons from Ecuador.* America Verde Working Papers Number 2. The Nature Conservancy, Arlington, Virginia.

Epler Wood, M. (1998b) New directions in the ecotourism industry. In: Lindberg, K., Epler Wood, M. and Engledrum, D. (eds) *Ecotourism: a Guide for Planners and Managers*, Vol. 2. The Ecotourism Society, North Bennington, Vermont, pp. 45–61.

Euromonitor (1994) *Travel and Tourism in Latin America.* Euromonitor Publications, London.

France, L. (ed.) (1997) *The Earthscan Reader in Sustainable Tourism.* Earthscan Publications Limited, London.

Freire, P. (1970) *Pedagogy of the Oppressed.* Herder and Herder, New York.

Galjart, B.F. (1976) *Peasant Mobilization and Solidarity.* van Gorcum, Assen/ Amsterdam.

Godde, P. (ed.) (1999) *Community-Based Mountain Tourism: Practices for Linking Conservation with Enterprise: Synthesis of an Electronic Conference of the Mountain Forum, April 13–May 18, 1998.* Mountain Forum and The Mountain Institute, Franklin, West Virginia.

Healy, K. and Zorn, E. (1983) Lake Titicaca's campesino controlled tourism. *Grassroots Development* 6(2)/7(1), 5–10.

Húescar, A. and Luhrman, D. (1995) Globe trotting trends: Latin America shines on the world tourism stage. *Tourism in Latin America 1995; a Latin Finance Industry Supplement* May, 1995.

Hunter, C. and Green, H. (1995) *Tourism and the Environment. A Sustainable Relationship?* Routledge, London.

IISD (1999) International Institute for Sustainable Development. html://www.iisd.ca/measure/compindex.asp

Kolff, A. and Tohan, A. (1997) *Initial Field Study of the Cordillera Huayhuash, Peru: an Evaluation of the Ecotourism Potential in the Area.* The Mountain Institute, Huaraz, Peru.

McIntyre, G. (1993) *Sustainable Tourism Development: Guide for Local Planners.* World Tourism Organization, Madrid.

Middleton, V.T.C. (1998) *Sustainable Tourism: a Marketing Perspective.* Butterworth-Heinemann, Oxford

Mitchell, R.E. (1998) Community integration in ecotourism: a comparative case study of two communities in Peru. MSc thesis, The University of Guelph, Guelph, Ontario.

Mitchell, R.E. and Eagles, P.F.J. (2001) An integrative approach to tourism: lessons from the Andes of Peru. *Journal of Sustainable Tourism* (in press).

Mitchell, R.E. and Reid, D.G. (2001) Community integration: island tourism in Peru. *Annals of Tourism Research* 28(1), 113–139.

Mowforth, M. and Munt, I. (1998) *Tourism and Sustainability: New Tourism in the Third World.* Routledge, London.

Prentice, R.C. (1993) Community-driven tourism planning and residents' preferences. *Tourism Management* 14(3), 218–227.

Prochaska, R. (1990) *Taquile y Sus Tejidos.* ARIUS S.A., Lima, Peru.

Reed, M.G. (1997) Power relations and community-based tourism planning. *Annals of Tourism Research* 24(3), 566–591.

Rocha, E.M. (1997) A ladder of empowerment. *Journal of Planning Education and Research* 17, 31–44.

Schülter, R.G. (1991) Latin American tourism supply: facing the extra-regional market. *Tourism Management* 12(3), 221–228.

Stabler, M.J. (ed.) (1997) *Tourism and Sustainability: Principles to Practice.* CAB International, Wallingford, UK.

Stone, M.L. (1996) Indigenous culture brings development. *Aymara Qhichwa, Revista Intercultural* 3, 21–23.

Theophile, K. (1995) The forest as a business: is ecotourism the answer? *Journal of Forestry* 93(3), 25–27.

TMI (The Mountain Institute) (1996) *Plan de Uso Turistico Recreativo del Parque Nacional Huascarán*, Vol. 1. PRO-NATURALEZA, FPCN, Lima.

Valencia Blanco, D.S. (1989) La mujer en el proceso productivo en la comunidad de Taquile. Unpublished Bachelor of Anthropology thesis, Universidad Nacional de San Antonio Adad del Cuzco, Cuzco, Peru.

Weaver, D.B. (1999) Magnitude of ecotourism in Costa Rica and Kenya. *Annals of Tourism Research* 26(4), 792–816.

WTO (1998) World Tourism Organization. html://www.world-tourism.org/Offer.htm#Mission

WTO (1999) World Tourism Organization. Tips Press: news bits from Peru. Year 1, No. 7, February html://www.tips.org.uy/tips/eng/news/noti181.htm

Sustainable Tourism: the Effect of Local Participation in Honduran Ecotourism Development

9

Katerina Horochowski[1] and R. Neil Moisey[2]

[1]Department of Parks, Recreation and Tourism, University of Missouri, Columbia, Missouri, USA; [2]School of Forestry, University of Montana, Missoula, Montana, USA

Introduction

Ideally, sustainable tourism combines present benefit with the protection of future opportunities. Under the rubric of sustainable tourism lies the notion of 'ecotourism' which is tourism development that protects the ecological and cultural resources of a tourism site while providing local economic opportunity. It is theorized that through local participation and control in the decision-making process of tourism planning and development, long-term economic and ecological sustainability can be achieved while reinforcing cultural integrity.

Ecotourism refers to low-impact, nature-based tourism that produces less damaging effects on a destination's environmental, social and economic resources than conventional mass tourism. It is widely believed that by minimizing these negative impacts and maximizing benefits locally, ecotourism can be used as an effective sustainable development tool. As such, it is challenged with the goal of enriching and preserving the natural and cultural landscapes of host destinations for the common good and for future generations (Murphy, 1985; WCED, 1987; Barré and Jafari, 1997). Ecotourism strives to give travellers a greater awareness of environmental systems and to contribute positively to the economic, social and ecological conditions of the tourism site (Butler, 1989). Accordingly, ecotourism attracts visitors to relatively undisturbed and pristine natural locations with the objective of studying and enjoying the scenery and its wilderness, as well as the existing cultural manifestations found in these areas (Ceballos-Lascuráin, 1987; Cater, 1994).

As the fastest growing segment of the tourism industry, ecotourists have a special attraction to destinations in less-developed countries (LDCs), where the greatest variety and extent of unspoiled natural environments are often found. Consequently, ecotourism destinations in LDCs have become commonplace in the industry. However, the tourism market in LDCs has long been characterized and dominated by large, capital-intensive resorts, owned by and catering to the needs of consumptive foreign cultures while having little or no concern for, or interaction with, the local people.

Unlike many industries, tourism is intimately tied to location – the culture, ecology and economy of destination sites. The host community and the natural environment not only provide the goods and services for the tourism industry but also are the product of it (Haywood, 1988; Getz and Jamal, 1994; Joppe, 1996). As a commodity, the community's intensive interaction with visitors is of utmost importance in the long-term sustainability of the industry, since it is the culture and hospitality, along with the natural attraction, that create the image and experiences that attract visitors (Haywood, 1988). None the less, considerable development activity and income generated by tourism have not always been compatible with a location's social and economic objectives and can threaten the community's integrity.

The integration of local control and ownership, the meeting of individual needs and economic self-reliance are goals of a sustainable ecotourism development strategy (Redclift, 1987; Cronin, 1990; Berno, 1996; Wallace and Pierce, 1996; Schaller, 1997). Despite these idealistic goals, prevalent local social and cultural institutions and characteristics often limit the strategy's effective implementation. Nowhere are these challenges more apparent than in the rural sectors of LDCs, near national parks or protected areas, typically where ecotourism projects are being introduced. As a result, and despite the copious use of ecotourism as a marketing gimmick, very few examples can be found where the actual goals and essence of ecotourism are fully embraced.

The success of any rural development strategy, such as ecotourism, can be influenced by outside events (Honadle, 1990). While much of the economic health of a community is determined by national or regional economic conditions, the economic vitality of a community can be strongly influenced by local residents. Humphrey and Wilkinson (1993) note that economic growth is positively correlated with the degree of local participation in rural tourism development. Their results suggest that economic growth from tourism is most likely in areas endowed with scenic natural resources. Betz and Perdue (1989) concur with these findings by concluding that 'tourism development built on the foundation of amenity resources is the logical sensible strategy to ensure sustainable community economic development'.

The capacity with which a community may participate in successful economic development projects of any type depends, according to Flora *et al.* (1997), on its existing entrepreneurial social infrastructure and social and economic capital. Furthermore, it also relies on the community's ability and willingness to resolve internal and external issues concerning the inequitable distribution of wealth and power. In political ecology theory, Belsky (1999) suggests that a community is a 'political arena, grounded in a particular history and constituted through multiple scales and networks of social relations entailing contexts of unequal power'. Although often simplified as 'ecologically noble' or 'backward and nature plunderers', communities are often sophisticated conglomerations of various traditions, interests, relations and visions, and their dynamic constitution and evolution should be considered in the process of participatory planning.

The community, as an integral component of the tourism product, plays a significant role in the success or failure of the tourism industry. If resident perceptions and preferences do not support tourism development policies and programmes, they are likely to fail or be ineffective in their implementation (Pearce, 1980). Therefore, the goals and strategies of tourism development should reflect or incorporate the views of the local residents through participation in the decision-making process (Lankford, 1994).

Finally, it should be noted that most theories involving community participation in development assume that negotiations will be conducted under a democratic process, which would entitle all stakeholders to an equal voice in the negotiations; this is not always necessarily true. King and Stewart (1996) advise that 'local populations often need assistance from state, regional, national, and international levels in regard to "political power, organization skills, capital and technical know-how to manage protected areas and to develop ecotourism facilities" ' (Walsh, *et al.*, Chapter 11, this volume). Under such conditions, it would seem that tourism development initiatives would be tainted by biased external objectives and agendas; thus making such an endeavour alien to a community's organic self-development.

Whether the communities possess the skills, organization and resources required to negotiate effectively with forces within and outside their jurisdiction (e.g. local power struggles, resistance, competition, international tourism industry, regional and national governments, and non-government organizations (NGOs)) determines the potential for community-effective articulation in the strategic ecotourism planning process (Horochowski and Moisey, 1999). Of particular importance in such mobilization, especially among the rural poor, is broad support for, and participation of, large numbers of people in organizations, associations or structures for the realization of common goals (Rahman, 1993; Kahn, 1994). Development scholars believe that local organizations are an important and necessary component of social action in community development (Esman and Uphoff, 1984; Garkovich, 1989; Smith, 1997).

This chapter focuses on how existing social organizational frameworks may restrict or enhance the successful implementation of sustainable tourism development. More specifically, this chapter evaluates the perception of local political and ecotourism industry leaders, on one level, and the effectiveness of formal and informal community organizations, their support for changes in natural resource use, and the community awareness and support for ecotourism development, on another. The communities surrounding two natural areas are compared to determine whether the stage of tourism development affects the perceptions and opinions of local residents.

Research setting

Honduras, the second largest country in Central America – with a population of 6 million – is also the second poorest in the western hemisphere. Like most Central American countries, the population of Honduras is primarily rural in character. Nearly 80% of the country is mountainous, with only narrow lowlands along its coasts. Most of the arable land is used to produce export crops such as bananas and pineapple. Much of this land is owned by large international agri-businesses (Keller et al., 1997) (Fig. 9.1).

The Cuero y Salado and Guaimoreto Wildlife Reserves of northern Honduras are located in the Caribbean coastal region and protect mangrove forest estuaries. Cuero y Salado Wildlife Reserve has been managed since 1987 by an NGO – Fundación Cuero y Salado (FUCSA). Cuero y Salado Wildlife Reserve receives an increasing number of visitors departing from La Ceiba (population 105,000), a port town 37 km east of the reserve, which hosts many tourists also visiting the popular Bay Islands. Tourism in La Ceiba and the Bay Islands has been dominated by large-scale, capital-intensive projects that accommodate large numbers of foreign tourists.

The second site, Guaimoreto Wildlife Reserve, was assigned protected status in 1992 and has experienced low-scale tourism development. It is located only 3 km from the city of Trujillo and is being managed by an NGO – Fundación Capiro-Calentura y Laguna de

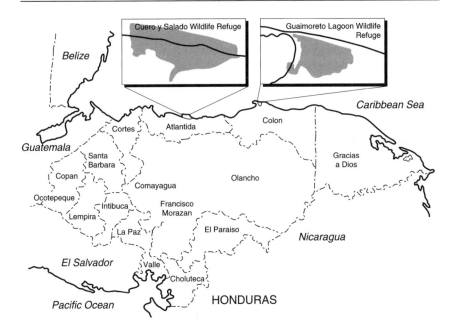

Fig. 9.1. Map of Honduras.

Guaimoreto (FUCAGUA). The city of Trujillo is also a popular tourist stop for beach goers and for its historical importance – Columbus landed near Trujillo on his fourth and final voyage to the New World and the city was the first Honduran national capital. It is a more colonial town than La Ceiba and is more accustomed to low-budget, adventurous travellers.

Methods

The present chapter reports on results from a larger study of sustainable ecotourism development in northern Honduras. These results are based on scheduled, personal structured interviews with community leaders, ecotourism operators and local residents. The key individuals were identified through snowball sampling techniques using their potential influential capacity as criteria. Local residents were randomly selected. During the months of August to December 1997, 32 key individuals and 208 local residents were interviewed. Key individuals included local government officials, the mayors of the regional centres, local ecotour operators, community leaders and the NGOs managing the reserves or working in the region. At all levels, respondents were asked to give their views on topics concerning protected areas and conservation, social institutions, the political processes, community participation and tourism development.

Findings

Community organization (formal and informal)

The formal organizational structures into which the communities of Cuero y Salado and Guaimoreto organize themselves are similar in both areas. Communities are consistently (although not entirely) associated into three core formal organizations which address basic needs. These groups are the 'patronato' (town council), 'junta de agua' (water commission) and 'sociedad de padres de familia' (local PTA). With very few exceptions, all northern Honduran communities possess at least one of these three groups.

The functions of the formal groups generally consist of recruiting support from their community for specific activities or projects. Most people said they joined these groups when they were solicited to do so, but otherwise they did not participate. A strong sense of moral obligation when called upon was evident but individual proactive initiative is very rare.

A common complaint among respondents is the lack of follow-up after community projects were completed. Ironically, the very people who complained generally admitted that they did not partake in any of the planning and/or organized activities since the completion of projects in their respective towns. Distrust in the (mis)allocation of funds is repeatedly cited as a reason for not being more supportive and active. One interviewer's response, which resonated with many others, was '. . . people in charge always do what they want and use public money for their own personal benefit. Why should I support them after I receive what I need?'.

In both study sites, informal groups are present, especially church groups and soccer players who met regularly to play the game. Of the few informal groups mentioned, the church groups (Catholic, Mormon and evangelical) are the most permanent. Other organized groups are addressed in the past tense, especially women's groups and cooperatives. Many such groups had generally been organized by an outside agency (i.e. Peace Corps, Ministry of Agriculture) and disbanded after the volunteer or programme left the area. Generally speaking, none of the informal groups cited by the respondents met to carry out community planning, activities or services. In the organization of informal groups, the two areas differ more from each other than in formal organization. This is primarily due to the ethnic make-up of the communities. In the vicinity of Cuero y Salado, the population is primarily Latino (98%) whereas in Guaimoreto, over a quarter of the population is Garífuna (Black Caribe). The Garífuna, unlike the Latino, rely more on community or neighbourhood support in their traditional and modern activities. The reasons for this appear to be influenced by tradition and culture as well as by political and social marginalization and racial discrimination. Accordingly, the Garífuna count heavily on mutual support. At the same time, their unique culture with a distinct language, music and dance, food, etc. creates a social bond not found equivalently in their Latino counterparts. As a result, the Garífunas tend to more frequently congregate informally to carry out their business activities, play music, dance, play soccer, etc. Generally, the Garífunas demonstrate greater solidarity than do the Latinos. None the less, the Garífunas do not consider these groups as organized per se, but as cultural tradition and, thus, do not consider them as either formal or informal organizations. One Garífuna teacher stated that 'we resent the imposed political structures of the whites because it dismantles our traditional system of elders based on respect. Now, anybody can buy or sell his position; it's corrupt'.

Perceptions of the functional efficiency of community structures

The perception on the efficiency of formal and informal community structures was a virtually unanimous response of distrust. Although the distrust was directed primarily toward the government, many people also expressed suspicion of other members of their community. The mistrust was usually generalized and was founded on past experiences or rumours of misallocation of funds, insidious land transactions and failed projects. 'Politicians make promises when they want your vote but once they reach office, they forget us (the poor) and steal from the projects intended to help our country', was one man's complaint. Many subjects claimed that whether or not a group could be trusted depended mostly on the leaders (organizers) of that group. Overall, people did not join or trust groups unless they felt an obligation to do so.

When asked if they trusted non-political leaders more than political ones in their community, most people pointed out that such leaders (people who mobilize the community without a personal political agenda) did not exist in their communities. In rare instances that non-political leaders where identified, people said they trusted them over politicians. Surprisingly, an overwhelming number of the respondents claimed they would rather trust a foreigner than someone from their own community. The reasoning behind this confidence toward foreigners is the belief that outsiders (usually associated with international development agencies such as CARE, Peace Corps, etc.) have no ulterior motives for uniting people into groups, whereas 'the Hondurans who organize other people are always looking to take advantage of them by having access to project money or by taking their land after it has been cleared'.

Level of community awareness of, and support for, tourism development

In both areas, the mass influx of beach-going vacationers during Holy Week, TV ads from Miami and international advertisements seem to guide people's expectations of what tourism is: sun, sea, sand and sex. Generally, people believe that tourism is accomplished through the building of large-scale resorts, requiring substantial investments and offering many services to a large number of visitors. Consistently, people considered the development of the industry in their area beyond their means and frequently stated that it was the responsibility of government to either build resorts or find investors for it.

Of all the respondents, only two had a general knowledge of the meaning of ecotourism and a few others had heard the term before but had no idea what it meant. Despite the lack of familiarity with the terminology, the respondents considered tourism a positive and worthwhile development for their area. A frequent view of tourists was defined as 'rich people who come to the beach for Holy Week; they are good for businesses'. Most felt it stimulated the economy, generated cultural exchange and brought positive changes. However, only a few had contemplated how these changes would affect their society or them personally. They tended to believe that 'others' benefit from tourism; that tourism is something that only the upper classes enjoyed and benefited from.

Level of support for changes affecting local natural resource use

Whether landowners or farm labourers, most of those living in proximity to the reserves have a close relationship with the natural resources that surround them. Most express a fondness for fishing and hunting but referred to these activities as something of the past, claiming that animals, such as tapirs, deer, turkeys and agouti, could no longer be found in their area. This is among some of the reasons mentioned for ideologically supporting conservation efforts. They express concern for the state of the ecology (in comparison to the past) and agree that measures are needed to prevent further deterioration. Environmental problems are often seen as an important issue but rarely in their own area of influence or as result of their own actions. Where local problems are admitted, external causes such as large corporations or immigrants are often blamed for them: 'Since the cooperatives were established during the land reform and people moved from other parts of the country, we started having problems with over fishing in the lagoon'.

Even though most favour conservation, many sympathize with migrant farmer activities (considered to be at the very bottom of the socio-economic scale) as every man's right to possess a piece of land with which to feed his family. That is, they do not find it irregular for someone to clear a parcel of forest for growing food. When asked if they would mind if that forest were on their own private property, most said they would. According to a Gallup poll conducted for USAID, a majority of Hondurans believes that there is a need to control migrant agriculture in order to save the forests. Thus, even though many sympathize with the needs of the poorest class, they also realize that their practices are detrimental to the preservation of the national forests and threaten the quality of water.

The controlled use of natural resources is supported by nearly all people, especially if such controls do not affect them directly. Surprisingly, most people claim that they are willing to accept changes in their customary use of resources (i.e. limit their extraction) if there is a valid reason for this, such as an improvement in the environment and alternative gains from the activity. Objections to regulations were raised, not as a result of subsequent sacrifices but, rather, in regard to the equitable implementation of such practices. Both FUCSA and FUCAGUA were accused of preferential treatment in the enforcement of established rules. People claim overwhelmingly that individuals with influential connections or money are allowed to continue destructive practices while the poor and powerless are punished for doing so. 'If a poor man gets caught, his equipment and catch is confiscated but if someone working for a powerful man is caught, everyone looks the other way; no one is punished.'

Conclusions

The Honduran Tourism Institute, along with other government offices and international agencies, is eager to capitalize on the thriving tourism business, particularly ecotourism. To attain this goal, many of those working with the park system are enthusiastically programming a participatory strategic planning process for the communities surrounding some of the country's protected areas. Their aspiration is that, through participation, the local needs and views will be addressed and accommodated while natural resources are protected and the tourism industry is developed. However, it is assumed that the affected populations will welcome this opportunity and participate fully. In this chapter, we argue that the social conditions, traditions and attitudes must be examined carefully before such assumptions can be made and before such endeavours are undertaken.

The communities neighbouring the Cuero y Salado and Guaimoreto wildlife reserves frequently organized themselves in similar ways. Family connections, ethnic heritage, basic infrastructure needs (i.e. potable water and electricity), religion and emergencies were all influential reasons for uniting individuals into organized groups, even if temporarily. In the rural sector of northern Honduras, the single most important institution was the family. People generally distrusted anyone outside of their immediate circle of relatives and intimate acquaintances.

Need was the greatest and most frequent motivator in the unification of these communities. Emergencies, such as floods or untimely deaths in poor families, constituted the reasons for which people united into common efforts. However, once an immediate need was met, the organization was disbanded. With very few exceptions, actions did not express community interest that contributed to the creation of development organizations (Humphrey and Wilkinson, 1993), leadership skills and roles (Beaulieu, 1990) and shared sentiments among local residents (Luloff, 1990). The overall perception of institutional frameworks, political or not, was of distrust and incompetence, but with theoretical potential. Thus, unifying associations and entrepreneurial social infrastructure, components deemed necessary for community development, were not apparent. A long and vivid history of political corruption and abuse of power, along with their daily preoccupation of seeking out a subsistence living, created an environment not of 'community', but rather of individual struggle and survival.

Only the Garífuna culture in Guaimoreto demonstrated more permanent solidarity and unity, bound by ethnicity and against perceived general social injustices. As a formal national group, they have taken some legal action to further their cause, but have failed to do so at the local level in this region. None the less, the Garífuna congregated much more in informal group activities, presented their culture as a tourist attraction, and seemed to maintain a strong community network of support and solidarity.

In other communities, it was surprising to find that many people trusted foreigners more than members of their own community. They believed that, unlike their own, others had more altruistic motives and were not as susceptible to the temptations of corruption prevalent in their society. With remnant attitudes of colonial and neo-colonial times, the poor still view the foreigner as a provider of aid, jobs and wealth.

Along similar lines, people expected outside investment to develop tourism – large resorts to accommodate large numbers of tourists. They were not familiar with the concept of ecotourism nor did they consider small-scale, low-impact tourism as adequate development. Having little or no capital for investment and viewing tourists as rich people with fancy expectations, they did not conceive the possibility of being a part in that industry.

Despite (or perhaps because of) a very limited understanding of the industry and its implications in developing destination sites, the support for tourism development was overwhelmingly positive at both locations. People perceive tourism as a favourable development in their community because they believe it creates jobs, pays better, stimulates development, and encourages cultural exchange. As a general rule, respondents viewed tourism as a possible and attractive source of employment and income and, hence, development, but expected government or outside investors to take the initiative. Support for its development was very strong and enthusiastic, even if foreign to them.

Although social structures, democratic principles and practice, education, information and communication were mediocre, people in both sites showed a surprisingly high level of support for conservation efforts, tourism development, and a willingness to learn and change, given the opportunity. Considering that the majority of the population depends on natural resources for their subsistence, the goals of the Foundations' working in the regions were strongly endorsed. In addition, dire poverty and high unemployment make the residents of these areas eager to try any alternative that might alleviate or improve their well-being.

Coupled with their generally agreeable view of tourism and tourists, the populations demonstrated, on the one hand, a willingness and preparedness to embrace tourism development, if this meant an improvement in their quality of life. On the other hand, their deficiencies in community cooperation and involvement would indicate that they do not possess the adequate resources or skills to participate successfully in a strategic planning process, at this time. Significant and long-term commitment to modification in institutional structures, functions and common objectives would be necessary on the part all stockholders for such development to take place.

References

Barré, H. and Jafari, J. (1997) Culture, tourism, development: crucial issues for the twenty-first century. *Annals of Tourism Research* 24(2), 474–477.

Beaulieu, L. (1990) Building partnerships for people: addressing the rural South's human capital needs. *Economic Development Review* 8(1), 13.

Belsky, J.M. (1999) Misrepresenting communities: the politics of community-based rural ecotourism in Gales Point Manatee, Belize. *Rural Sociology* 64(4), 641–666.

Berno, T. (1996) Cross-cultural research methods: content or context? A Cook Islands example. In: Butler, R. and Hinch, T. (eds) *Tourism and Indigenous Peoples*. International Thomson Business Press, New York.

Betz, C.J. and Perdue, R.R. (1989) The role of amenity resources in rural recreation and tourism development. *Journal of Park and Recreation Administration* 2(4), 15–29.

Butler, R. (1989) Alternative tourism: pious hope or Trojan Horse. *World Leisure and Recreation* 31(4), 9–17.

Cater, E. (1994) Ecotourism in the Third World – problems and prospects for sustainability. In: Cater, E. and Lowman, G. (eds) *Ecotourism: a Sustainable Option?* John Wiley & Sons Ltd, London.

Ceballos-Lascuráin, H. (1987) *Estudio de Prefactibilidad Socioeconómica del Turismo Ecológico y Anteproyecto Arquitectojico y Urbanístico del Centro de Turismo Ecológico de Sian Ka'an*. Quintan Roo, Suede, Mexico.

Cronin, L. (1990) A strategy for tourism and sustainable development. *World Leisure and Recreation* 32(3), 12–17.

Esman, M.J. and Uphoff, N.T. (1984) *Local organization: intermediaries in rural development*. Cornell University Press, Ithaca, New York.

Flora, J.L., Sharp, J., Flora, C. and Newlon, B. (1997) Entrepreneurial social infrastructure and locally initiated economic development in the nonmetropolitan United States. *Sociological Quarterly* 38, 623–645.

Garkovich, L.E. (1989) Local organizations and leadership in community development. In: Christenson, J.A. and Robinson, J.W. Jr (eds) *Community Development in Perspective*. Iowa State University Press, Ames, Iowa.

Getz, D. and Jamal, T.B. (1994) The environment–community symbiosis: a case for collaborative tourism planning. *Journal of Sustainable Tourism* 2(3), 152–173.

Haywood, K.M. (1988) Responsible and responsive tourism planning in the community. *Tourism Management* 9(22), 105–118.

Honadle, B.W. (1990) Extension and tourism development. *Journal of Extension* Summer, 8–10.

Horochowski, K. and Moisey, R.N. (1999) Environmental NGOs in Northern Honduras. *Tourism Recreation Research* 24(2), 19–29.

Humphrey, C.R. and Wilkinson, K.P. (1993) Growth promotion activities in rural areas: do they make a difference? *Rural Sociology* 58(2), 175–189.

Joppe, M. (1996) Sustainable community tourism development revisited. *Tourism Management* 17(7), 475–479.

Kahn, S. (1994) *How People Get Power*. NASW Press, Washington, DC.

Keller, N., Rachowiecki, R., Reioux, B., Hubbard, C. and Brosnahan T. (1997) *Central America on a Shoestring*. Lonely Planet Publications, Oakland, California.

King, D.A. and Stewart, W.P. (1996) Ecotourism and commodification: protecting people and places. *Biodiversity and Conservation* 5, 293–305.

Lankford, S.V. (1994) Attitudes and perceptions toward tourism and rural regional development. *Journal of Travel Research* 32(3), 35–43.

Luloff, A.E. (1990) Community and social change: how do small communities act? In: Luloff, A. and Swanson, L. (eds) *American Rural Communities.* Westview Press, Boulder, Colorado, pp. 214–227.

Murphy, P.E. (1985) *Tourism: a community approach.* Methuen, New York.

Pearce, J.A. (1980) Host community acceptance of foreign tourists: strategic considerations. *Annals of Tourism Research* 7(2), 224–233.

Rahman, A. (1993) *People's Self-development.* Zed Books, New Jersey.

Redclift, M. (1987) *Sustainable Development: Exploring the Contradictions.* Methuen, London.

Schaller, D.T. (1997) Indigenous ecotourism and sustainable development: the case of Río Blanco, Ecuador. Ecotourism Research Home Page. April 9, 1997: http://www.geog.umn.edu/~schaller.html

Smith, S.E. (1997) Deepening participatory action-research. In: *Nurtured by Knowledge: Learning to do Participatory Action-research.* The Apex Press, New York.

Wallace, G.N. and Pierce, S.M. (1996) An evaluation of ecotourism in Amazonas, Brazil. *Annals of Tourism Research* 23(4), 843–873.

WCED (World Commission on Environment and Development) (1987) Tokyo Declaration, 27 February. *Our Common Future* (the Brundtland Report). Oxford University Press, Oxford.

Self-developed Rural Tourism: a Method of Sustainable Tourism Development

10

James B. Lewis

Department of HPER, Western Michigan University, Kalamazoo, Michigan, USA

Introduction

In 1987, the Brundtland Report to the United Nations first suggested a definition for sustainable development. The report defined sustainable development as 'development that meets the needs of the present without compromising the ability of future generations to meet their own needs' (World Commission on Environment and Development, 1987, p. 43). According to Garrod and Fyall (1998, p. 200), the idea of sustainable development as cited in the Brundtland Report was to 'bring together the apparently disparate concepts of economic development and environmental conservation'. The report envisioned economic development and conservation as entities that could coexist. That is, economic development did not have to occur at the expense of the environment. Since 1987, there have been many different variations of the definition of sustainable development, many of which do not seem to agree with the definition in the Brundtland Report. In their 1998 article, Garrod and Fyall suggested that the definition of sustainable development is often twisted by researchers to fit their study. In fact, since the definition was put forth in the Brundtland Report in 1987, sustainable development has become the topic of a great deal of discussion and there has been an ongoing debate (especially among researchers) about the definition. Additionally, debate has continued over whether it is possible to achieve sustainable development and how (methods) it might be achieved.

As the argument for sustainable development became more

© CAB *International* 2001. *Tourism, Recreation and Sustainability* (eds S.F. McCool and R.N. Moisey)

prevalent, the idea that tourism development could not only be economically feasible, but also sustained, gave birth to the contention that it was possible to create sustainable tourism (Twining-Ward, 1999). Therefore, just as there was debate over the possibilities of sustainable development (Barbier, 1987; Butler, 1991; Garrod and Fyall, 1998), the possibility of sustainable tourism has generated controversy. Butler (1993, p. 28) said that 'while certain forms of tourism have been hailed as being sustainable, most notably those such as alternative tourism, or ecotourism, in reality, there is no empirical data to substantiate such claims'. Garrod and Fyall (1998) suggested that while it is laudable that tourism researchers have recognized the need for sustainable tourism, the concept has been defined in so many different ways that there does not seem to be a general consensus on its definition. In fact, these authors list at least eight different definitions of sustainable tourism found in research, and go on to suggest that while definitions seem to be abundant, it is debatable as to whether those definitions agree with the definitions set forth by the Brundtland Report. The authors go on to propose that it is now important to move 'with all due urgency from defining the concept to a more thorough consideration of how it may best be implemented in practice . . .' and 'to identify the conditions for its achievement' (Garrod and Fyall, 1998; p. 203).

As stated earlier, the development of tourism has become an important economic development tool, not only for states, regions and towns, but for rural communities throughout the US (Allen *et al.*, 1993; Hill, 1993; Burr, 1994; Crotts, 1994). The idea that development of tourism in a rural community could be sustained and thus lead to sustainable economic development is attractive to rural communities, but those communities often struggle to find a method for implementing and sustaining tourism as an economic development process. Recently, however, a method of community development, called 'self-development', has become popular and could present a strategy for implementing sustainable tourism development. For rural communities, sustainable tourism would be defined as a tool for economic development and a method to enhance and sustain economic opportunity within a community (see Chapter 1, this volume). Self-development is a process that utilizes and involves the residents of a community in the development process, and emphasizes building on the existing strengths and capacity of the community. Because self-development is supported by residents and utilizes community resources, it could be an important and achievable method of creating sustainable tourism within a rural community. Thus, self-developed tourism that is sustained in a rural community could provide a good method of economic development that utilizes an important component often left out of other methods of community development, the residents of a community.

Although it would appear that self-developed tourism in a rural community might be exactly what Garrod and Fyall (1998) call for, a method of implementing sustainable development, the linkage between self-developed tourism and sustainable tourism development has not been explored. This linkage is crucial to rural communities because as community leaders struggle to implement tourism for the promise it holds as an economic development tool, they need to understand and be assured that it will deliver economic development that can be sustained.

Self-developed community development for rural areas, first advocated and defined by Reid (1988), suggests that projects in rural communities be developed from within a community. This method of community development also suggests that development be controlled using local resources that will enable the community to sustain the project (in this case tourism) as a viable economic development tool over a long period of time. Therefore, while the concept of sustainable tourism seeks a viable method of economic development that can be sustained over a long period of time, self-development (of tourism in this case) seeks viable development from within a community that can be sustained over a long period of time. Thus, self-developed tourism might be a method of implementing sustainable tourism, which is a sustainable economic development tool.

This chapter will examine self-developed tourism as a method of development on the community level because it appears to meet many of the goals of sustainability and sustainable tourism. First, the concept of self-development within a rural community context is defined and discussed. Next, there is a discussion of a research study that investigated how the self-development process has been utilized to develop tourism in several case studies of rural communities. Following that section, the effects of tourism development on several important developmental variables, such as income, employment and community level group processes, are identified. Finally, the implications of the findings in terms of sustainable tourism are discussed.

Self-development

Self-development is a method of community development first advocated and discussed by Reid (1988). He suggested that self-development was a method of community development that focused on enhancing the internal strengths and capacities of a rural community. The author further advised that instead of concentrating development efforts on luring manufacturing plants and companies (buffalo chasing), rural leaders should focus on using local resources to develop their communities from within, that is, self-develop. The entire concept of self-development is based on the fact that a community can develop itself from within the community.

A self-development strategy 'fundamentally calls on communities to identify their comparative economic advantages and undervalued local resources and to initiate locally controlled ventures that increase the amount of value added to the local economy' (Reid, 1988, p. 333). Self-development requires a community to envision what the community can be by discussing various opportunities with its members. According to Flora et al. (1991, p. 20), 'Self-development has imbedded within it a realization that the local community is both responsible for economic well being of its citizens and empowered to act to help them generate it'.

As a method of community development, self-development has become very important to rural communities, because since the early 1980s rural communities have faced the prospect of less federal and state government assistance. Rural community leaders realized that economic development must come from within the community (Gale, 1990). At the same time, those leaders recognized that tourism was a clean, attractive development tool that could be developed by residents of the community (so it can be sustained).

In 1990, Green and co-workers investigated the concept of self-development by identifying and then surveying rural communities throughout the US that had initiated self-development projects. They defined self-development as:

> the implementation of a project or the creation or expansion of a firm that increases income to the community, and/or generates a net increase in jobs. In addition, a self-development project must include the following three characteristics: (1) involvement by a local organization (in most cases, a local government); (2) investment of substantial local resources (this does not preclude the use of outside resources); and (3) local control of the enterprise or activity.
>
> (Green et al., 1990, p. 56)

Later research by Flora et al. (1992) illustrated that self-development was a viable option for development of a rural community. It was a form of community development that stressed greater reliance on community and local resources. The authors found that self-development projects were successful in communities that had flexible and dispersed leadership, and where appropriate choices were made. That is, the leadership and residents of a community together decided what type of development was appropriate for the community and how much development was needed. Again, self-development is a process that not only encourages, but also requires community commitment and involvement. It requires that the residents of a rural community understand their community and the resources available, and make choices based on what the resources can bear. Imbedded in that decision is the type of development that will occur in the community.

Interestingly, the self-development research conducted by Green *et al.* (1990) found that the most prevalent and popular type of self-development project or activity was the creation of recreation, cultural events and tourism. According to the authors, the appropriate choice for many communities was the development of tourism because it tended to be a very local affair. Tourism was created because, as a resource, it was available to the community, and the local residents tended to understand tourism. Flora *et al.* (1992) pointed out that a community must choose a project based on appropriateness to a local resource, organizational structure, finances and linkages to the outside. Tourism development was an appropriate choice because: (i) the communities or individuals within the community possessed the resources and financing; (ii) there was an organizational structure in place; and (iii) tourism created a linkage to the outside of the community that non-local individuals desired. If self-developed tourism was a popular method for economic development in a rural community, then it could be a method of implementing sustainable economic development in a rural community. Thus, this study concentrated on self-development and tourism, and whether that development was sustainable.

Study methods

The concepts of tourism and self-development were studied in four rural Indiana US communities (Nashville, Nappanee, Centerville and Parke County), the results of which are reported here. In order to study both the development of tourism and the concept of self-development, a qualitative case study was constructed by interviewing tourism influentials (a name assigned to tourism leaders in each community) in each of the communities. Primary tourism influentials were defined as: (i) the president or executive director of the convention and visitors bureau (CVB); (ii) the president or executive director of the chamber of commerce; and (iii) an elected governmental official in each community. During an interview, each primary tourism influential was asked to identify further tourism influentials in their community, who were then interviewed for this study.

Respondents were asked for information on the development of tourism in their community. The questions were asked to determine whether or not the tourism development process that had occurred met the criteria as set forth by Green *et al.* (1990). Those criteria included involvement of local organizations and resources, local control of decisions, and the generation of income and employment. The primary tourism influentials (respondents) were identified using a directory provided by the State of Indiana Tourism Office. As previously stated, additional respondents were then identified utilizing a modified snowball sampling technique.

Since the communities in the study were rural and small (populations did not exceed 6000), the number of respondents varied from community to community. For example, in Nappanee (the largest case community with a population of approximately 5500) there were several tourism businesses and individuals involved in tourism organization. Thus, seven respondents were interviewed. However, in Parke County, where there are far fewer tourism businesses, and the largest tourist attraction is operated by the county CVB, only four respondents were interviewed. All respondent interviews were conducted using a discussion guide designed for the study. The discussion guide was designed by first obtaining a copy of an interview instrument used by Luloff *et al.* (1994) in a study of tourism efforts in the US, utilizing qualitative interviews with Cooperative Extension agents in 31 states. Utilizing that instrument as a guide, several individuals who were active in tourism within Indiana were asked to provide questions that could be used to elicit tourism information in Indiana rural communities. An Indiana Tourism Discussion Guide was finalized, and all respondents were asked the same questions in the study. All respondents were interviewed in their offices, or somewhere within their community (place of business, etc.) during a 2–3 day period of time. After all the interviews, a preliminary case study was written and read by two individuals independent of the study. After corrections, a final case study was constructed. As a final step, the cases were compared and a comparative case study was then used to construct a model of the tourism development process in the rural communities.

Nashville, Nappanee, Centerville and Parke County were selected as the case-study communities because they were non-metropolitan, had a population fewer than 6000 and, according to the Director of the Indiana Division of Tourism, were either developing tourism, or had developed tourism.

Nashville, Indiana because of its small shops, history of artisans and the presence of the largest state park in Indiana (Brown County State Park), is one of the most popular tourism destinations in the state. Nashville is a very small community (population 873) that attracts over 2 million tourists per year, the majority of whom come in the summer for shopping and crafts, and early autumn for views of the changing colours in Brown County State Park. Nashville was selected and studied as a case of well-developed tourism because the community began the development of tourism more than 50 years ago, and it has become one of Indiana's most well-developed tourism communities.

The community of Nappanee, Indiana is famous because of its large population of Amish residents, and the recreational vehicle manufacturing companies that are headquartered in the community. According to one Nappanee respondent, the Amish have always been renowned for the ability to build horse carriages (buggies). Many of the recreational vehicle manufacturers were started by, and are still owned by, the Amish, because recreational vehicles are, according to the same respondent, simply carriages with motors. Although several of the manufacturing companies are still owned by the Amish, they choose not to use modern amenities in their offices. Because of the recreational vehicle manufacturing, Nappanee has a strong industrial base, but among tourists it is known because one can visit a working Amish farm, dine in Amish restaurants and purchase Amish furniture, another skilled craft for which the Amish are known. Although the tourism development process is not quite as old as the one in Nashville (perhaps 25 years old), it was also studied as a case of well-developed tourism.

At one time Centerville, Indiana was the ultimate tourist destination in the state of Indiana. In fact, it was known throughout the country for its antiques and antique shops. Antiques, however, were not the only reason that Centerville was a tourism attraction. Because of a Quaker settlement within the county, Centerville was a stop along the Underground Railroad during the Civil War. In addition, the founders of the community constructed a series of unique arches within the community that, according to one Centerville respondent, have been studied by architects from all over the world. In addition, a community historian pointed out that in Centerville more historically significant homes are occupied and used (as a place of residence) than in Williamsburg, Virginia. (Williamsburg is one of the largest areas of reconstructed historically significant homes. Occupation is an important factor because the historic buildings in Centerville are original and have remained as residences, as opposed to Williamsburg where the buildings are not occupied by residents.) For 40 years, Centerville was at the centre of a tourism boom, but in the past 5 years, tourism has begun to stagnate in the community. Centerville was chosen as a case because it is both a case of developed tourism and developing tourism, as the community leaders are trying to re-start the tourism process.

The final case that was studied was Parke County, Indiana. Because the communities within the county are very small, Parke County has developed tourism and marketed itself as a county. Parke County is unique because there are more authentic covered bridges (32) in the county than in any other county or community in the US.

For years, several European master bridge builders lived within Parke County and designed and constructed the bridges. The primary tourist attraction for the past 25 years has been the Annual Covered Bridge Festival which, in a 10-day span each October, attracts more than 1 million tourists. In addition to the bridges, the county also has Billie Creek Village, where turn-of-the-century life is recreated; Turkey Run State Park, which is one of the more popular parks within the Indiana State Park System; and a large state recreation area called Raccoon State Recreation Area. Although the Covered Bridge Festival is over 25 years old, Parke County was included as a case of developing tourism because it is still seeking to develop and sustain its tourism system.

Results

As defined earlier, self-developed projects increase income and generate employment in a community by involving local organizations, investing local resources and using local control. This section will discuss how the four case communities utilized local organizations to control the tourism process locally, created income by developing tourism, how the communities gained employment through the process, and why tourism developed from within the community is sustainable.

Local organizations, resources and control

Community leaders fear that when tourism is created, it will become such a large process that it will eventually outgrow the community and will attract non-local businesses to manage tourist attractions. In fact, in his tourism life-cycle statement, Butler (1980) suggested that as tourism developed in a community, it tended to grow beyond the scope and control of the community and was eventually overtaken by non-local companies because local firms can no longer sustain the process.

Surprisingly, the results of this investigation clearly contradicted Butler's (1980) notion that the tourism process grows beyond the scope of the community. Rather, this study illustrated that tourism had not yet grown beyond the scope or management capabilities of any of the case communities. Many of the respondents were well aware of the possibility that tourism could grow beyond local management and had taken steps to make sure that it would not happen. Respondents in several of the communities pointed out that the tourism organizations and businesses were home-grown and would remain home-grown because it was vital that local (home-grown) organizations and businesses controlled the process. Nashville and Parke County respondents pointed out that almost all tourism businesses were locally owned and that out-of-town owners are often snubbed because they are seen as outsiders (especially in Parke County).

One reason the tourism process has not grown beyond control in the case communities is the involvement of local organizations that started the process and continue to sustain tourism. Evidently the involvement of local residents in tourism organizations and in the overall tourism process resulted in the successful development of tourism in three of the four communities. Unfortunately, in Centerville, while tourism began because of local involvement in the process, currently there is little or no local involvement in the tourism process. When local organizations and people maintain tourism, as is the case in Nappanee, Nashville and Parke County, and to some extent in Centerville, there exists a vested interest in sustaining the process. Nappanee, Nashville and Parke County have all established local tourism organizations with the sole purpose of maintaining and improving tourism in the community, and there is every indication to suggest that the local organizations are going to sustain tourism for quite a while.

In all of the communities the tourism development process was begun by local organizations, or individuals, utilizing local resources (in most cases, non-governmental resources). For example, in Parke County, Parke County Incorporated (PCI), a non-governmental, non-profit organization was responsible for tourism development. In Nashville and Nappanee, local entrepreneurs financed tourism development. For example, a tourism entrepreneur who was born and raised in Nashville funded the majority of development in the community, owns several of the attractions, owns and/or manages several restaurants and owns a hotel. Because of his resources (non-governmental) and efforts, the tourism process has been successful and Nashville has been able to sustain tourism.

In Nappanee, two individual tourism entrepreneurs financed tourism development. Originally both worked together, but have since split and have developed different attractions. Both were born and raised in Nappanee, and both are Amish. Interestingly, although they compete for tourist revenue, they also work together to assure that tourists enjoy a complete Amish experience in Nappanee. According to one Nappanee respondent (not affiliated with either entrepreneur), although it is unusual for an Amish business to open on Sunday, one attraction stays open on Sunday while the other does not. Thus, a tourist is encouraged to visit one attraction on Saturday and the other on Sunday to 'round out or complete' the Amish experience.

In both Nashville and Nappanee the tourism entrepreneurs were wealthy and the local resources (financing, land, capital) were, for the most part, provided by them. For example, in Nashville, the tourism entrepreneur donated large sums of money to establish tourism services in the community, such as the local CVB. He also donated land to the community government for infrastructure to support tourism. For example, he donated land to the community to build a new post office. In Nappanee, together the two tourism entrepreneurs created a non-profit community organization to revitalize the downtown of the community. According to one of the respondents in Nappanee (not one of the tourism entrepreneurs), the majority of the funding for the downtown revitalization was also donated by the entrepreneurs.

Unlike Nappane and Nashville, Parke County has not had the benefit of a wealthy local tourism entrepreneur. Tourism development first started in the mid- to late 1960s when the editor of the county newspaper encouraged several local leaders to join together, form a tourism organization, and raise revenue for tourism development. Instead of depending on one or two wealthy individuals, the community and tourism influentials worked as a team to create the Covered Bridge Association, the forerunner of PCI. As an association, they then created the Annual Covered Bridge Festival that is now the largest tourism festival/attraction in the county. As a result of their efforts, the Covered Bridge Festival successfully generated, and continues to generate, nearly all of the revenue needed to sustain smaller festivals and tourism organizations in each of the communities of the county.

There was also a wealthy tourism entrepreneur in the community of Centerville, but he took a different approach to tourism development. He owns a large antique mall, located on the outskirts of the community that has drawn business away from downtown Centerville. When this entrepreneur developed his antique mall on the outskirts of the community, tourists stopped coming into the middle (downtown) of Centerville. This tourism entrepreneur was also born and raised in Centerville, but has not assisted the community to develop and sustain tourism. In fact, his decision to locate the antique mall on the fringe of the community caused many of the other tourism leaders in the community to react in a negative manner. By establishing a business that draws tourists away from the rest of the community, the other tourism influentials feel that they have been excluded from the process. The respondents also feel that the exclusion has contributed to the stagnation of tourism. The respondents felt that because of his actions, tourism might not ever again be sustainable (or successful) in Centerville.

It is interesting that three of the four communities in this study have wealthy tourism influentials that have not only influenced the tourism process, but also influenced the sustainability of tourism in their communities. In Nappanee and Nashville the respondents (themselves tourism influentials) spoke very highly of the tourism entrepreneurs, while those in Centerville refer to the tourism entrepreneur with disgust. That seems to illustrate that members of a community have immense influence on the success not only of the process, but also on the sustainability of the process. Also of interest is the fact that in all of the communities, resources supplied by local individuals were used to develop tourism. With very few exceptions, in all four communities, local residents own the tourist amenity services (attractions, hotels, motels and restaurants). For example, in Parke County, one respondent suggested that local ownership and control was so prevalent that even the fast food establishments were owned by local franchisees (not very common in small rural communities).

There is little doubt that the control and ownership of tourism businesses and attractions by native residents is a factor not only to the development, but also to the sustainability of tourism. According to the respondents, local ownership contributes to local control of the process, which in turn means that the process is 'owned' and controlled by the community. One respondent in Parke County went as far as suggesting that non-local business owners could not be successful in the community because residents did not take kindly to out-of-town business owners (strangers – the respondent's words). In fact, that same respondent pointed out that although she had been born and raised in Parke County, she left for several years to pursue a job and, upon returning for her present position, was viewed for a while as a non-local interfering with local affairs. It seems easy to conclude that local control of tourism in a rural community is vital to the sustainability of tourism. In this investigation, the tourism influentials understood the importance of local ownership, felt ownership in the process, and knew how important it was to sustain that ownership.

While it is apparent that local ownership and control is an important factor to tourism and to sustainability of the tourism process, Centerville presented an interesting dilemma. Similar to the other case communities, tourism in Centerville was developed locally, the antique mall is owned locally, and tourism has always been controlled locally, yet tourism has reached a point where several respondents feel that it has stagnated. Centerville serves as a good lesson for the sustainability of tourism because it seems that the sustainability of tourism in a rural community relies not only on the community, but also on an individual's (in this case one tourism entrepreneur) willingness to buy into and support the process.

Increased income

At the time of this study, three of the four communities relied heavily
(if not solely) on revenue and income generated by tourism and the
taxes associated with tourism. In terms of income or revenue generated
for economic development and sustainability of the community, of the
four case communities, Nashville and Parke County rely almost
exclusively on tourism for income. In those two communities, very
few businesses (if any) exist that do not cater to tourists. Centerville
was heavily dependent on tourism until the early 1980s, when the
tourism process stagnated (although there are several tourism
influentials that hope to re-start the process). And finally, Nappanee,
which has a strong manufacturing foundation, has come to rely heavily
on income from tourism. (Interestingly, the recreational vehicle
manufacturing plants are not considered part of the tourism industry.
At the time of this study, there were no tours of the plants, nor could
one find a history of recreational vehicles at the plants. Although
Nappanee manufactures tools for the tourism trade, there is no tourism
based on that manufacturing process.)

The community of Nashville was founded by artisans and crafts-
men as a tranquil place in which to practise their trade and sell their
wares. Even today, Nashville remains a small rustic community of
shops and galleries. Millions of tourists are attracted by the artisans
(both woodcarving and painting) and Brown County State Park. Parke
County generates the majority of its tourism revenues from one large
tourism event, the Annual Covered Bridge Festival. Nappanee has
capitalized on its Amish heritage and community, and established
shops that sell Amish food and wares. One of the largest attractions in
Nappanee (the one open on Sunday) is a working Amish farm where
tourists are able to watch as work is done using traditional Amish
methods. Finally, Centerville was at one time the thriving centre of the
Midwest antique trade, tourism revenue poured in as the antique
businesses thrived and attracted enthusiasts from all over the country.
Unfortunately tourism, and the income generated by tourism, has
stagnated in Centerville.

This investigation involved qualitative case studies (data were
collected by respondent interview) not quantitative statistics that
would illustrate the income derived from tourism. In fact, economic
impacts and analysis for the case communities were not calculated for
this study. However, since the respondents were all people who had
been involved in the tourism process within their communities for a
long time, their opinions concerning income and employment present
a good picture of the economic impact of tourism on the community.
(Interestingly, when asked, one of the respondents from Nashville
suggested that it was very difficult to calculate income and revenue

gained by tourism because while tourism entrepreneurs enjoy sharing general information, they were loath to share any type of revenue or income information with anyone.) Additionally, except for those in Centerville, all respondents indicated that revenue due to tourism has increased almost every year in their community (remember, at least one respondent in each community was an elected official who would be very familiar with the revenue).

In order to understand the income gained from tourism, it is helpful to read the responses to questions concerning tourism revenue. For example, Nashville Respondent 1 suggested, 'Tourism produces so much revenue in Nashville that the budget of the Brown County CVB is more than twice as large as the county government budget' (the CVB budget is generated from tourism-dedicated taxes). Another respondent in Nashville (Respondent 4) said, 'Tourism has been pumping money into the economy [of Nashville] for at least 20–30 years and it will continue to do so for a long time'. Finally, another response by Nashville (Respondent 1) puts income derived from tourism into perspective. The respondent suggested that, 'It is almost impossible to find a store within the community that sells men's or women's underwear. Quite simply, those items are not what a tourist shops for, and the stores in town don't carry items that a tourist doesn't need'. Respondent 1 in Parke County suggested that 'The bank tellers constantly talk about deposits during the Covered Bridge Festival made by merchants who simply dump bills in garbage bags and bring them up to the desk for deposit'. Nappanee Respondent 1 suggested that although many people see the recreational vehicle industry as a boom for Nappanee, 'The first hotels, the first restaurants, and certainly the fast food establishments were established because of tourism, not because of the recreational vehicle manufacturers. In fact, until tourism was developed there were no hotels in this community'. Respondent 4 in Centerville said, 'I can remember back when the antique business was thriving. There were actually lines of people waiting to get into most of the antique shops, and the benches outside of the local restaurants were constantly full of people waiting for tables'.

In terms of being able to sustain the income and revenue from tourism, the respondents were very confident that the revenue would be sustained because the process was and is locally controlled. As reflected in the earlier statement by Nashville Respondent 4, there did not seem to be any worry among the respondents (except in Centerville) that the process would be sustained. In fact as of the end of this study (1995), in all four case communities, there were very few businesses (including the recreational vehicle businesses, although one was being purchased by a larger corporation) that were owned or operated by non-local people.

Employment

Employment produced by the tourism industry is often a topic of debate because it is perceived that the industry produces short-term, low-paying jobs. In this study, there is no question that tourism development created jobs, and further that many of the jobs, whether they were short or long term, were sorely needed. For example, in Nashville, tourism resulted in the creation of shops, hotels and restaurants that, in turn, provided jobs. While many of the jobs created by those tourism businesses might be low paying, several other positions, such as management positions at hotels, attractions and restaurants, pay quite well. More importantly, Respondent 4 in Nashville suggested that many of the tourism businesses offer jobs that serve as training for future tourism entrepreneurs. He suggested that people often take jobs that train them at one business and then leave to open their own tourism business. By doing that, the tourism business is not only sustaining jobs, it is creating opportunities and enabling the tourism trade to grow in the community.

Overall, approximately 90% of the respondents agreed that tourism development had created all types of jobs in the community. More importantly, the jobs that were created were home-grown and occupied by local residents. Therefore, the jobs were being sustained and the revenue stays in the community. In addition, several respondents suggested that tourism employment assists the community to sustain itself because the jobs help to keep young people from leaving the community to find employment.

Sustainability

As suggested earlier, the majority of respondents in this study felt that in their community tourism was sustainable. One factor that came out in the interviews, and is also discussed in the introduction to this text, is the planning for tourism. For the most part, in these communities, tourism was planned and was a project in which the residents participated. For example, the respondents in Nappanee suggested that the residents of the community were involved and took an active role in the tourism process. Nappanee Respondent 1 suggested that the revitalization of the downtown area was a community process where community input was actively sought and utilized. Parke County was also an illustration of a successful planning project because of the dispersed nature of the county. All of the communities within the county participate in tourism planning, and the tourism events, especially the Annual Covered Bridge Festival, affect all of the communities. If in fact, planning for the future is a factor in the sustainability of tourism, perhaps rural communities such as the ones in this study provide a good illustration of how a public planning process that involves local residents can lead to substantial and sustainable tourism.

There is one additional factor to note, however, when discussing the link between tourism planning and sustainability. In these case communities, tourism was created using a process that encouraged public participation. In fact, there continues to be a great deal of public participation in the process. However, there is also a negative aspect to the public participation, and one that should concern those interested in the sustainability of tourism. For example, in Nashville, several respondents suggested that as tourism developed and became a major economic force, many people started to think twice about tourism development. During the off season, Nashville is a very small, wooded, rustic community that is a haven for those that enjoy small town life, especially retirees. However, during peak tourist season the community is crowded, traffic is almost at a standstill (basically there is one road in the town) and the sidewalks are packed with tourists. Several respondents said that many community residents now have problems with tourism because of how popular the community has become as a tourist destination. One respondent pointed out that during off season, a trip to the post office might take at the most 10 min, while during peak tourist season that same trip can take 2 h. The beginning of resident resentment toward tourism may become quite an issue and a challenge to the sustainability of tourism, especially in Nashville.

Discussion

The case communities in this study developed tourism according to the criteria set forth for self-development. Tourism, developed from within the community, generated income and employment, was locally controlled and was established by local organizations using local resources. More importantly, because tourism was established and is controlled by the community residents, it appears (at least to the respondents) to be sustainable. The local residents control and sustain the process. Therefore, self-developed tourism seems to be a valid method of establishing not only viable tourism, but sustainable tourism (in this case sustained economic development through tourism). However, some further questions are generated by the data in this study.

The most obvious question is why has tourism been developed in all four communities, but has been sustained in only three? All four communities developed tourism in similar fashion, yet it has stagnated (in the respondents' opinions) in Centerville. That raises the concern of whether it is destined to stagnate in the other three? Perhaps the environment in Nappanee, Nashville and Parke County was more conducive to sustainable tourism development than that of Centerville. In a recent study of rural communities, Flora *et al.* (1997) suggested that communities that work together collectively and have a high degree of social capital tend to be more successful, especially when it comes to economic development. Applied to this study, perhaps Nashville, Nappanee and Parke County work together (collectively) better as a community than does Centerville. That was somewhat apparent in conversations concerning the tourism entrepreneurs in the communities. Perhaps the ability to work together as a community is a condition needed to develop a tourism industry that is sustainable.

Yet another question generated by this investigation is whether self-developed tourism is the best method of developing sustainable tourism? That is, can a rural community that has developed tourism from within sustain it better than tourism that is developed by a large company moving into the community? For example, what type of tourism might exist in any one of the communities if Disney moved into the community and set up a theme park? Would that form of tourism be as sustainable as self-developed tourism? This is a good question that may be very difficult to answer because there is very little indication that a large corporation would ever move into a rural community, and because of the reluctance of rural communities to accept outsiders and outside businesses. However, one of the respondents in Nashville did indicate that a large golf corporation had investigated the feasibility of establishing a course and resort in Nashville. Whether that would have been successful, and how it may have contributed to the sustainability of tourism would have been an interesting topic to follow up.

As stated in the introduction to this text, the view of sustainable tourism in this chapter is that of tourism as an economic development tool. When measured quantitatively, does tourism generate income and jobs in a rural community? Can that income and employment be sustained? These questions can only be answered by revisiting the communities many years after this study and asking the same questions, and utilizing quantitative methods to measure the effects of tourism on the communities.

Finally, there is quite a bit of community development research that not only advocates self-development as an approach to community development, but also advocates that communities use this self-development for strong community development. This study investigated self-development through tourism and suggested that in a rural community, self-developed tourism is a good method of developing sustainable tourism. Although many researchers advocate tourism and sustainable tourism as a good method of community development, is self-developed tourism a promising source of community development? There is not a great deal of research to support this belief because there is very little research that investigates the links between tourism and community development. Community developers often think of development as attracting manufacturing to a community, not developing tourism. Perhaps it is time to change the way we, as a society, think of development, especially in a rural community. In order to answer these questions, we must determine what are the indications of successful community development, what is successful and sustainable development, and does one lead to the other?

If sustainable tourism is, in fact, tourism that is developed and maintained in an area (community, environment) in such a manner, and to such a scale, that it remains viable over an indefinite period, and is a good economic development tool, then it would appear that self-developed tourism could be a viable method of sustainable tourism development. In this study, three of four communities developed tourism (using self-development) that was controlled by the community and has been sustained for a long period of time. Therefore, it seems reasonable that if a community is encouraged to self-develop tourism, this may lead to successful tourism development and, more importantly, sustainable tourism development.

Acknowledgements

The author would like to express his appreciation for the comments received on this manuscript by Stephen F. McCool, and invaluable assistance on the topic of self-development provided by Cornelia Flora.

References

Allen, L.R., Hafer, H.R., Long, P.T. and Perdue, R.R. (1993) Rural residents attitudes toward recreation and tourism development. *Journal of Travel Research* 31, 27–35.

Barbier, E.B. (1987) The concept of sustainable economic development. *Environmental Conservation* 14(2), 101–110.

Burr, S.W. (1994) The rural action class's perception of tourism and its potential for economic development – case studies from four rural Pennsylvania counties. Paper presented at the Leisure Research Symposium of the National Recreation and Parks Association, October.

Butler, R.W. (1980) The concept of a tourist area cycle of evolution: implications for management of resources. *Canadian Geographer* 29, 5–12.

Butler, R.W. (1991) Tourism, environment, and sustainable development. *Environmental Conservation* 18(3), 201–209.

Butler, R.W. (1993) Tourism – an evolutionary perspective. In: Nelson, J.G.,

Butler, R.W. and Wall, G. (eds) *Tourism and Sustainable Development: Monitoring, Planning and Managing.* Heritage Resources Center, University of Waterloo, pp. 27–43.

Crotts, J.C. (1994) Trends and issues in sustainable rural development: an introduction. *Trends* 31, 2–3.

Flora, C., Flora, J.L., Green, G.P. and Schmidt, F. (1991) Rural economic development through local self-development strategies. *Agriculture and Human Values* 8(3), 19–24.

Flora, J.L., Green, G.P., Gale, E.A., Schmidt, F.E. and Flora, C.B. (1992) Self development: a viable rural development option? *Policy Studies Journal* 20, 276–288.

Flora, J.L., Sharp, J., Flora, C. and Newlon, B. (1997) Entrepreneurial social infrastructure and locally initiated economic development in the non-metropolitan United States. *Sociological Quarterly* 38, 623–645.

Gale, E.A. (1990) Rural community self development: an analysis of community dynamics in a bootstrap approach to economic development. Unpublished Master's thesis, University of Vermont.

Garrod, B. and Fyall, A. (1998) Beyond the rhetoric of sustainable tourism? *Tourism Management* 19(3), 199–212.

Green, G.P., Flora, J.L., Flora, C. and Schmidt, F.E. (1990) Local self development strategies: national survey results. *Journal of the Community Development Society* 21, 55–73.

Hill, B. (1993) The future of rural tourism. *Parks and Recreation* September, 98–123.

Luloff, A.E., Bridger, J.C., Graefe, A.R., Saylor, M., Martin, K. and Gitelson, R. (1994) Assessing rural tourism efforts in the United States. *Annals of Tourism Research* 21, 46–64.

Reid, J.N. (1988) Entrepreneurship as a community development strategy for the rural south. In: Beaulieu, L.J. (ed.) *The Rural South in Crisis: Challenges for the Future.* Westview Press, Boulder, Colorado, pp. 325–343.

Twining-Ward, L. (1999) Towards sustainable tourism development: observations from a distance. *Tourism Management* 20, 187–188.

World Commission on Environment and Development (1987) *Our Common Future.* Oxford University Press, Oxford.

Sense of Place as a Component of Sustainable Tourism Marketing

11

Jeffrey A. Walsh[1], Ute Jamrozy[2] and Steven W. Burr[3]

[1]Lock Haven University, Lock Haven, Pennsylvania, USA;
[2]Department of Health, Leisure and Exercise Science,
Appalachian State University, Boone, North Carolina, USA;
[3]Institute of Outdoor Recreation and Tourism, Department of
Forest Resources, Utah State University, Logan, Utah, USA

> However attractive the notion of sustainable tourism as balanced
> development, difficult questions remain to be addressed.
>
> (Hunter, 1997, p. 856)

Introduction

For years, tourism has been viewed as a double-edged development
tool, one with tremendous potential to impact places and people both
positively and negatively. Greater awareness of the impacts specific to
the tourism industry triggered a demand for 'responsible' tourism
development; development that exploits the positive impacts of
tourism and minimizes its negative impacts (Butler, 1991). Sustainable
tourism, touted as a form of responsible tourism development, grew
out of pleas for the sustainable development of communities, and
entreaties to end the exploitation of natural resources (WCED, 1987).
This idea was anything but new, as sustainable development had
evolved from environmental concern about the allocation, utilization
and depletion of natural resources (Slocombe and Van Bers, 1991;
Potts and Harrill, 1997). Accordingly, tourism research studies began
to focus on the relationships between the conservation and protection

of ecosystems and tourism development, ultimately leading tourism product developers and marketers to advocate integrated planning, zoning and various forms of ecotourism (Orams, 1995; Wight, 1996).

While the economic and environmental impacts of tourism development remain major concerns for host populations and tourism practitioners, tourism development has also evolved to become much more mindful of the significance of the sociocultural benefits and costs associated with such development (Hunter, 1997; McMinn, 1997). A prevalent theme addressed implicitly and explicitly within contemporary sustainable tourism literature is the need for equitable allocations and distribution of the benefits and costs of tourism development (Goulet, 1995). For example, Swarbrooke (1999, p. 241) has described sustainable tourism as,

> tourism which is economically viable but does not destroy the resources on which the future of tourism will depend, notably the physical environment and social fabric of the host community.

This definition is fairly typical of those found in present-day sustainable tourism literature, and is more comprehensive than in the past. Traditional definitions have been expanded to include concern for cultural and community diversity, concern for social issues of justice and fairness, and a strong orientation towards stability rather than constant and erratic change (Dehart, 1991). The maturation of the tourism development paradigm can be attributed partially to a general consensus that any sustainable tourism development framework should reflect an ethical foundation or basis (Shearman, 1990; Gale and Cordray, 1994; Dovers *et al.*, 1996).

The tenet that the core principle of sustainability is one of ethical decision-making appears to have evolved since WCED's (1987) seminal publication of *Our Common Future* (Potts and Harrill, 1997). This Brundtland Report includes both inferential and specific references to the ethical implications of sustainable development, many of which have been further discussed in the sustainable development and sustainable tourism literature (Court, 1990; Butler, 1991; Hughes, 1995; Caalders, 1997; Zeiger and McDonald, 1997). Additionally, other researchers and scholars have examined the development, use and effectiveness of an increasing number of ethical codes of conduct related to sustainable tourism development (D'Amore, 1992; Orams, 1995; Walsh and Matthews, 1995; Ewert and Shultis, 1997). Advocates for the inclusion of local community participation in tourism planning and development have also utilized ethic-based frameworks (Hughes, 1995). For example, Pearce *et al.* (1996) assert that sustainable tourism development is a normative (value-based) process and, as such, should encompass local residents' active participation. Sautter and Leisen (1999) formulated a 'stakeholders' tourism planning model that is predicated on the belief that each stakeholder group 'has the *right* . . . regardless of the relative power or interest held by each' (p. 314) to be incorporated in the decision-making of tourism planning. It is from this perspective, that sustainable tourism must be developed within an ethical framework and that local residents must have the opportunity to participate actively in tourism planning and development, that this chapter is written.

As a response to the call for the development of a more theoretical paradigm of sustainable tourism development (Fennell and Malloy, 1995; Hultsman, 1995; Hunter, 1997; Potts and Harrill, 1997), this chapter provides an over-arching, theoretical paradigm for sustainable development founded on the percept of *social equity*. Social equity within development strategies and initiatives is called for implicitly in tourism literature: local residents, along with other stakeholders of tourism, must be included in the planning, development and implementation phases of the sustainable development process.

While local stakeholders' participation in decision-making is not a new idea, the significance of their contribution to sustainable marketing has often been ignored. The host community at a tourism destination is an integral component of the tourism system, it simultaneously impacts and is impacted by the tourism industry. For example, the host community is involved in producing the tourism product, which is a combination of *both* the local natural resources and the social and cultural characteristics of the host community. Local residents enhance, build and create tourism attractions and services for a total tourism product, the destination experience. Just as natural resources are unique to a specific place, so are the social and cultural resources of that place. Together, these resources represent the community's local identity and meaning; as a unique combination they are the *sense* of that place (Shamai, 1991; Stokowski, 1991). A sense of place is important to the tourists and tourism developers because it represents what is unique about a place and what is worth preserving. For these reasons, this chapter investigates the potential of including local stakeholders' sense of place in the societal marketing of sustainable tourism development. For, as Gartner (1997, p. 190) suggests, 'host communities must become directly involved in identifying the appropriate images to project'.

Community members, who live and work at tourism destinations, have the potential to both identify the nature of product elements, such as sense of place, and to design and produce tourism experiences. Social equity and stakeholder involvement need to be incorporated in tourism product and market identification and in destination promotion. With this in mind, the second portion of this chapter demonstrates how a shift from traditional consumer-oriented marketing to a societal marketing approach prescribes consumers' and society's well-being as necessary outcomes of the marketing process. Traditionally, the development and utilization of a destination image reflects a consumer-oriented marketing strategy, rarely relying on a local sense of place. Societal marketing, a modernistic perspective, demonstrates a concern for not only consumer needs and wants, 'but also the long term interests of the host society, before, during, and after planning, development, and marketing activities' (Go, 1989, p. 169). The third section of this chapter outlines how this shift in marketing philosophy can be implemented in specific marketing strategies. Such images, when created without local perspective, and thus often ignoring social issues and, in turn, social equity, can pose serious problems to the community. Unauthentic images often lead to unfilled expectations for tourists, leading to dissatisfying travel experiences. Conversely, striving for social equity through the utilization of sense of place in a societal marketing approach may lead to more authentic tourism experiences for tourists and the host community, and ultimately a more sustainable form of tourism development.

A sustainable tourism paradigm

An increased appreciation of the ethical underpinnings of sustainable tourism development has accompanied discussions of the need for a stronger theoretical foundation or paradigm from which to approach sustainable tourism development. Reviewing the tourism literature, one can find several models for sustainable tourism development emanating from ethical principles. For example, Wight (1993a, 1996) developed an ethical framework for ecotourism planning, development and operations that included ecological, social/cultural and economic sustainability. Fennell and Malloy (1995) introduced a slightly more complex 'model of ethical triangulation for ecotourism', utilizing teleology, deontology and existentialism theories of ethics to enable individuals to move closer to making 'good, right, and authentic' choices.

Finding no 'founding paradigm' for ethical practices in the tourism literature, Hultsman (1995) utilized a framework supporting Leopold's 'land ethic' (1949) as an ethical framework for the tourism industry. He viewed this framework as intuitively logical and based on a belief that those actions that are 'right' or beneficial to an entire system, are ethical actions. Hultsman's 'just' tourism, focused on both the tourist and the tourism industry, is intended to allow the tourist to 'find meaning in and derive benefits from activities in which [he or she] engages'. These activities would promote or produce 'more good than could have resulted from any other potential action available to the agent of the act' (Hultsman, 1995, p. 560).

Claiming that sustainable development lacks an ecological foundation and focus on community and is therefore short-sighted, Potts and Harrill (1997) called attention to the need for sustainable tourism development with a better delimited ethical foundation. They recommended a model of 'travel ecology' for 'sustainable development' because they believe that 'we [have] an ethical responsibility to think beyond sustainability, that we should make this a better place for all to live' (Potts and Harrill, 1997, p. 198). They claimed that 'travel ecology' differs from other forms of tourism in that it emphasizes an ecological bottom line, a focus on local community development, and realizes the 'inherent potential' of tourism to improve the quality of life for all.

Although different in their respective details, these frameworks or paradigms of sustainable tourism development share a commonality of addressing the ethical responsibilities associated with the concept of sustainable development. In general, these frameworks promote the importance of considering how sustainable tourism development should contribute to the general well-being of the environment and to those individuals who are, or will be, impacted by tourism development. The need for a holistic paradigm of sustainable tourism development, where resources and opportunities are fairly distributed throughout populations and across generations, sets the stage for discussion of the potential of social equity as an over-arching paradigm for sustainable tourism development.

Social equity: an ethical paradigm for sustainable tourism development

According to the Brundtland Commission's report, a core component of sustainable development is the belief that all development paths adhere to a sense of 'responsibility between generations' (Burr and Walsh, 1993). This responsibility is realized through development paths that 'meet the needs of the present [generation] without compromising the ability of future generations to meet their own needs' (WCED, 1987, p. 43). Thus, sustainable development must be designed to include social equity or 'the fair distribution of resources and opportunities' both within and across generations. This type of development can be characterized as:

> provid[ing] the basic necessities of life and secure living conditions for all people, promote equity, and avoid unequal exchange; must foster self-reliance, local control over resources, empowerment and participation by the underprivileged and marginalized, and opportunities for action people feel is fulfilling; and allow for mistakes without endangering the integrity of the immediate ecosystem and resource base.
>
> (Burr and Walsh, 1993, p. 2)

Within this chapter, social equity can be thought of as encompassing two concepts: 'fair share' and 'fair play' (Ryan, 1981). Fair share 'emphasizes the right of access to resources as a necessary condition for equal rights to life, liberty, and happiness, . . . a reasonable share of society's resources, sufficient to sustain life at a decent standard of humanity' (Ryan, 1981, p. 8). Fair play 'stresses the individual's right to pursue happiness and obtain resources' (Ryan, 1981, p. 8) or the right to pursue happiness and resources, but without a guarantee of attaining them. Thus, fair share precedes and leads to fair play.

These concepts of social equity, albeit not in these exact terms, can be found in the sustainable tourism literature in a variety of forms and configurations, most often under the guise of 'equality among and between generations' (WCED, 1987; Cronin, 1990; Fennell and Malloy, 1995), and focused on financial matters. For example, refuting the contention that sustainable development is an oxymoron (Disinger, 1990), Verburg and Wiegel (1997) claimed that the Brundtland Report was developed to present a conceptualization of sustainability that included not only equity between present generations and those generations to come, but also equity within each generation. They believed that sustainability demands an ethical framework, where an individual's freedoms to pursue economic wealth, particular standards of living and the consumption of resources is limited by that same individual's concern for humanistic solidarity or concern for equitable distribution of resources to the rest of humanity.

Others have expressed similar notions, which can be interpreted as forms of social equity. While Court (1990) discussed the need for equal distribution of both the costs and benefits of development, Cronin (1990) emphasized that social equity is necessary because it incorporates 'the contributions that people and communities, customs and lifestyles make to the tourism experience' (in Burr, 1994, p. 5). In their statement that it would be unethical to either hinder future generations' opportunities to prosper or to restrict the present generations' chances to prosper, Zeiger and McDonald (1997) promoted social equity. Davis (1991), on the other hand, addressed social equity advocating for an 'international community' within sustainable tourism development; and, finally, Caalders (1997) implies the role of social equity in tourism development in his call for 'democracy and social bases for policy-making' for sustainability (p. 129). Finally, according to Middleton and Hawkins (1998), equity in a tourism context means balancing the needs of the host community with those of the visitors. They stated that 'setting targets locally is the essential first step in moving towards sustainable goals' (Middleton and Hawkins, 1998, p. 121).

In summary, while social equity, conceptualized here as being comprised of equal access and distribution, has not appeared or been identified explicitly in the sustainable tourism literature by name, it has been discussed implicitly. One approach towards increased social equity can be operationalized and conceptualized in the process of sustainable tourism development as 'stakeholder involvement'.

Stakeholder involvement as a form of social equity in sustainable tourism

A practical implementation of the social equity concept within sustainable tourism development occurs when those who are impacted by decisions are involved in the making of those decisions. Thus increasing their chances of getting their respective *fair share* of both the costs and benefits associated with tourism. In the tourism literature, these individuals are often referred to as *stakeholders*. Many of the models previously discussed in this chapter assert the importance of stakeholder involvement, in other words, adhering to a local focus, while also considering other individuals, organizations and/or institutions at extra-local levels who are involved in the establishment of sustainable tourism development (Burr and Walsh, 1993).

King and Stewart (1996) support the involvement of local stakeholders within the development of tourism, arguing that local residents should have (at least theoretically) control over the resources base because they know the resource, have property rights to it, and have few alternative sources of livelihood. They did warn, however, that local populations often need assistance from state, regional, national and international levels with regard to 'political power, organization skills, capital and technical know-how to manage protected areas and to develop the ecotourism facilities' (King and Stewart, 1996, p. 300). In a similar manner, Fennell and Malloy (1995) claimed that when personal freedom is held in balance with social equity, stakeholders are encouraged '[to] be aware of their own freedom to act and the accompanying responsibility for these actions upon the local and global environment' (p. 179). Dovers, *et. al.* (1996) contend that sustainability efforts can account for future generations by implementing 'contingency planning' that includes both proactive measures and reactive responses, as well as 'buffers against cata-strophe' and 'spare capacity' (pp. 1160–1161). Addressing the same problem, McMinn (1997) warned that while sustainable tourism, by its very nature, implies ambiguity with regard to definitional components and measurement criteria, it must be viewed from a local focus, as well as from a regional or global perspective.

The need for stakeholder involvement in this tourism development process is so important to Hunter (1997) that he stated it would be difficult to imagine 'any approach to sustainable tourism without a strong local (including regional) authority planning and development control, and without the involvement of local communities in the planning process to some degree' (Hunter, 1997, p. 864).

For Hunter, sustainable tourism is a malleable concept that 'can be shaped to fit a spectrum of world views' (p. 852), allowing specific destination areas to implement a sustainable tourism development approach dependent upon their respective needs. He suggested that such an 'adaptive paradigm' would allow for location – or destination-specific 'world views encompass[ing] different ethical stances and management strategies' (p. 853). He envisioned an over-arching paradigm of sustainable tourism that allows for self-determined courses of development, thus allowing each tourism destination to satisfy the demand for tourism (tourists), meet the needs of tourism industry operators and the local host community, and protect the resource base for tourism.

A social equity paradigm of sustainable tourism development would allow those individuals affected by decisions and policies related to tourism development, the 'stakeholders', a more active involvement in the process itself. This is especially crucial for local communities being marketed as travel destinations. Lea (1993) has suggested that attention be drawn to ethical decisions regarding 'local ownership and control, the use of local resources, the extent to which local amenities are alienated, and marketing strategies' (p. 711). In addition, Wheeler (1994) specifically identified destination marketing as one of several areas within the tourism industry where ethical challenges exist and need greater investigation. The social equity paradigm can be utilized to address these types of ethical challenges often associated with destination marketing.

Marketing tourism destinations

The marketing of tourism destination has long played a major role in tourism development and growth. Marketing strategies, historically associated with extensive growth in supply and a push for higher sales, have evolved into sophisticated practices focusing on a consumer orientation. The major responsibilities of a tourism marketer are to identify the market's needs and wants and a destination's tourism resources. The destination marketer will then identify target markets best served by the destination. These practices follow the widely used 'consumer orientation' of marketing (Go, 1989) or, in the words of Kolter and Armstrong (1990, p. 13): 'The marketing management philosophy holds that achieving organizational goals depends on determining the needs and wants of target markets and delivering the desired satisfactions more effectively and efficiently than competitors'.

A consumer orientation consists of 'listening to the customers', determining their needs and wants, responding to those needs and, at the same time, assuring a competitive edge for the organization/ destination. A marketing strategy would also include designing the appropriate product, price, place/distribution and promotion of the destination. The development of special-interest tourism (e.g. island tourism, mountain tourism, adventure travel and tours for women) has evolved from a focus on a special need of an identifiable target market. However, tourism marketing, even consumer-oriented marketing, is not nearly this straightforward. It involves ethical dilemmas in management and social responsibility. Horner and Swarbrooke (1996) pointed out the complex ethical issues of tourism, indicating that destinations and tour operators 'face dilemmas on how they should present their product to potential consumers' (p. 442). For example, in terms of marketing places to potential tourists, the destination marketers or tour operators must, among other things, decide:

- to what extent should those who do not gain financially from tourism subsidize the tourism industry;
- the degree to which public money is spent on tourism rather than other sectors of the economy and society;
- the tension between short-term and long-term perspectives in the development of destinations;
- how honest tour operators/marketers should be in their promotional activities;
- how much adequate advice should be given to tourists about potential hazards and inconveniences;
- whether to add to the problems of already overcrowded destinations.

Although many of these dilemmas deal with an *equitable distribution* of resources and financial benefits, traditionally in many cases these decisions are made implicitly and focused on the financial implications of tourism. For instance, ecotourism had been touted as a form of tourism with potential to lead to a more equitable distribution of both the costs and benefits associated with tourism, but often it has been utilized solely to target special-interest markets (Wight, 1993b).

Ecotourism: a consumer-oriented approach or more?

In recent years various forms of 'ecotourism' have developed as a result of changing corporate policies and the development of ethical codes. Ecotourism practices range from complete marketing gimmicks related to the recent trends of the 'greening of marketing', to serious attempts to face environmental and cultural challenges affiliated with tourism. Wight (1993b) demonstrated in her segmentation model that 'eco-sell' focuses on profit, has low local involvement and high negative impacts, while a more ethical form of ecotourism calls for high local involvement and has few negative impacts. Ryel and Grasse (1991) described how a marketing process for ecotourism could be designed. Their marketing strategy was based on four components of an ecotourism conservation ethic:

- to increase awareness of nature;
- to maximize economic benefits for local people;
- to encourage cultural sensitivity;
- to minimize negative impacts on the environment.

Knowing that ecotourism has great marketability in today's society, the authors outlined the following marketing steps: finding the target market (small groups of 'elusive' ecotourists) and getting a well-crafted message out to the targeted segments in 'special-interest' magazines or publications. Once the 'elusive ecotourists' were aware of the product, they would request more information and eventually be placed on a mailing list for direct mail pieces from the tour operator, organization or destination marketer, which would include detailed brochures and other information about the product/tour. If there is a good match between the product and the target market, the target market is ready for purchase, and the ecotour will be booked. In the best event, the destination will reap the environmental, economic and cultural benefits, minimizing negative impacts. However, while implementing these strategies, destination marketers should address the varied interests of tourism business suppliers, outside stakeholders and residents of the communities. Wight (1993b, p. 7) feels that 'the term "ecotourism" must be viewed with caution until a majority of stakeholders agree upon the definition'. In a similar fashion, Horner and Swarbrooke (1996, p. 442) emphasized the inclusion of 'all participating parties' with regard to addressing social responsibility and business ethics.

Societal marketing in sustainable tourism

Beginning in the 1970s, organizations started to recognize some ethical responsibilities beyond their customers' satisfaction and beyond a profit orientation, thus leading to the development of *societal marketing*. The 'societal marketing' concept recognizes: 'the idea that the organization should determine the needs, wants, and interests of target markets and deliver desired satisfactions more effectively and efficiently than competitors in a way that maintains or improves the consumer's and society's well-being' (Kolter and Armstrong, 1990, p. 14). According to this definition, societal marketing not only considers consumer wants, but also the long-term interests of the host society, before, during, and after planning, development, and marketing activities. Go (1989, p. 169) asserted that societal marketing 'provid[es] the host-society with the opportunity to participate . . . to assist in satisfying particular needs of the destination area'. Middleton and Hawkins (1998) adopt this 'modern' approach of marketing and state that 'a marketing perspective provides the optimum process for achieving sustainability at tourism destinations into the next century' (p. 118). They also feel that marketing needs to consider what they refer to as the three '*Es*': Economy, Ecology and Equity. Middleton and Hawkins state that equity means a shift towards a fairer distribution of resources and that in the 'tourism context equity also means recognition and response to the needs and interests of residents of visited destinations balanced against those of visitors' (p. 121). Similarly, Hunter (1997) argued that in sustainable tourism development, 'equity implies attempting to meet all basic human needs and the satisfaction of human wants, both now (intra-generational equity) and in the future (inter-generational equity)' (p. 851). He also noted that, 'across several generations, it may be appropriate to abandon any notion of balance in favor of a skewed distribution of priorities. What is crucial, is that tourism development decision making should be both informed and transparent' (Hunter, 1997, p. 859).

These principles could also be applied to a market strategy development which is in accord with sustainable tourism development. All members of the tourism system should participate in an informed and transparent decision-making process, including the marketing process. For example, Morrison (1989 see Pearce *et al.*, 1996) stressed the need for marketers to be responsible to the community they are promoting, a form of societal marketing which allows 'effectively the vetoing of promotional material by the community to ensure that an acceptable image has been crafted' (in Pearce *et al.*, 1996, p. 89).

Destination image: a traditional component of marketing marketing

Destination marketers often include 'image development and management' as their primary strategy. Gartner (1997, p. 180) emphasized the relationship between destination image and sustainable tourism development by stating:

> Destination images, regardless of how they are formed, play an important

and powerful role in an individual or group's travel decision process. Since sustainable development is a function of use and destination images can be used to increase use, there appears to be a direct link between how images are formed and the concept of sustainable tourism systems.

Destination image can be used to instil beliefs, ideas and impressions of a place. Such an image can lead to a new product-positioning strategy or determine where the tourists perceive the destination to be versus other competitive destinations (Ahmed, 1991). From the local community's perspective this becomes critical, because as Gartner (1997, p. 190) has stated 'images build experience expectations and different touristic experiences will tax local systems in different ways' Therefore, 'without proactive planning, the chances for achieving a sustainable system diminish[es]' (Gartner, 1997, p. 190). However, images can arise without any significant planning or promotion.

A place's 'image' formulated in the absence of any planned tourism advertising or promotion campaign it is referred to as *organic* image (Gunn, 1972, 1988). An organic image is akin to a sense of place (described earlier in the chapter); both arise from direct, personal interaction with a place. On the other hand, those images developed predominantly through planned promotion efforts are referred to as *induced* images (Gartner, 1986, 1993; Fridgen, 1991). The primary difference between an organic and an induced image is often the amount of control locals have over the presentation of the image (Gartner, 1997). Induced images are developed and presented by destination promoters, while organic images usually lie outside their control. Although both types of images are dynamic in nature, induced images are often more easily modified than organic images, since these are formulated on very little corporeal knowledge of the destination. While organic images are more liable to remain stable, they may be altered through visitation to the destination or setting, when the traveller experiences first-hand what the setting is actually like. The additional information one gains from actually visiting a destination increases that person's ability to better identify the attributes of that setting and to better differentiate between destinations (Chon, 1990; Fakeye and Crompton, 1991) – to begin to develop a sense of that place.

Destination marketers create and influence a tourist's image of a place through marketing communications. For example, Thurot and Thurot (1983) argued that tourism advertisements reflect what people perceive as real and desirable within a given society or culture. Uzzell (1984) argued that 'tourists are not motivated by the specific qualities of the destination, but rather the matching of the destination's major attributes to the tourist's psychological needs' (p. 80). This reflects a consumer-oriented marketing approach, creating an image that promises to fulfil the tourist's needs. The promotion and advertising create expectations about what is to be found at a place. Hummon (1988) explained that tourism advertising becomes a cultural text that symbolically transforms ordinary places and times into extraordinary tourist worlds. This type of marketing strategy may cause problems if an inauthentic image is created. Tourists often try to verify the induced image with her or his interpretation of a destination. In situations where the advertised information cannot be verified, tourists' expectations are not met and they can become dissatisfied, thus never returning to the site. Hummon (1988) documented a similar phenomenon from the local residents' perspective, at times residents witness advertisements that often do not seem to depict 'their' community, as they know it, yet advertisers claim to tell the prospective consumer 'what a place is like'. If societal marketing considers the long-term benefits of society and wants to be socially responsible in terms of cultural sustainability, the local community should determine how the culture is represented and how the tourists can·derive meanings and set expectations from the residents' sense of place.

Lew (1989) discussed this matching of images, expectations and the needs of the visitors with the proper arrangements of the destination's resources. He suggested that efforts to reduce the amount of conflict arising from tourism development should include a strategy of incorporating 'constituencies', or those having potential interest in tourism development (previously referred to in this chapter as stakeholders), at all levels in any developmental process. This perspective was based on the belief that conflicts often result from clashes between constituencies and their respective relationships and identity with a place (their 'sense of place'). A similar situation often results when the manipulation of a traditional product, through marketing for tourism development, 'undercut[s] a peoples' sense of identity and self-worth even while providing extra income' (Lew, 1989, p. 16). Discussing Gunn's (1972) distinction between organic and induced image, Lew (1989) characterized 'mass images' (those arising from forms of mass media, induced images) as 'hav[ing] little or no relationship to the unique character of any specific place. Thus, they cater to outside values rather than those of resident insiders' (p. 16). On the other hand, he described organic images as 'locally oriented images, the opposite of mass images, are those that express the uniqueness of a place . . . to which many in the community feel a strong attachment' (p. 16), in other words a local sense of place. According to Lew, a stronger visitor-orientation of development often leads to a stronger tendency to develop non-local images of a place or attraction. This can occur because although visitors often travel to a destination to interact more intimately with residents and their life styles, these visitors often 'bring with them different images of what the experience should be' (p. 16), based on these non-local images.

According to Go (1989), all too often this disparity between advertised image and 'reality' occurs in tourism because 'this kind of information is not simply harmless propaganda, but adversely affects the visitor's quality of travel experience, and the host society in terms of social impact' (p. 175). He proclaims that, 'the time may have come that the international travel industry must proceed on a new assumption, namely that it will become welcome only when it is willing to respect what the [host] community is, i.e. "to fit the fabric" of the host community' (Go, 1989, p. 168). His recommendation is that tourism marketing needs to 'capitalize on the unique features of the host community in order to make maximum use of local resources and to ensure a product with a differential, competitive edge' (p. 177). Perhaps by marketing a local 'sense of place' – where people can get a feel for and truly experience what the destination really is like; where market segments that fit the community's needs are targeted; and when tourism products are designed with resident's participation – the unique natural and cultural resources of that destination will be sustained.

Social influences on image formation

Social factors can influence not only the information individuals collect and often implement in their formation of images, but they can also influence image development through broader cultural factors, such as the symbolic meaning places might represent (Um and Crompton, 1990). Lee (1972) examined outdoor recreational places and concluded, 'settings might best be understood in terms of the meanings assigned to them by particular sociocultural groups' (p. 68), partially because '[they] serve[s] as a repository of meanings for symbolizing relationships' (p. 69). In a similar manner, Rapoport (1976) pointed out that while one might be able to list the attributes of a particular place, the elements of that environment that are noticed and accepted as being important or relevant to a particular person are culturally variable. Therefore, the sense or meaning of a place, setting or destination has been conceived as subjective, and dependent in a large part upon the sociocultural perspectives the individual brings to that interpretation.

Stokols and Shumaker (1981) referred to this 'social aspect' of the images as 'social imageability', and identified several distinctions of 'social images of place', which led to their typology of places. They pointed out that there appears to be a distinction between geographical and generic places, the former relates to specific places whereas the latter to a category of similar places. They also contended that 'first-time users' and 'non-users' were more likely to have indirect information (that gathered from others) of generic rather than specific places, and therefore would probably not have the same place meanings as active users.

This same phenomenon led Greider and Garkovich (1994) to conclude that 'landscapes', or natural settings, are symbolically transformed via self-definitions and that these symbolic meanings are sociocultural phenomena. That is, while individuals are able to assign personal meaning to places, the influences of their respective cultures are so natural and subconscious that they are often indistinguishable from the individual's self-definitions. In the end then, the meanings associated with a given landscape 'are socially and culturally constructed through social processes and become land-scapes through social interaction and negotiation' (p. 10).

Although 'tourism studies which have focused on locational perceptions have been principally concerned with the image of destinations' (Brown, 1990, p. 3), often at the individual level, there is also evidence that places may have a 'social imageability' or a 'commonality' of place associated with them. Therefore, while an individual's perception of a tourism setting may be one's own individualized perspective, the creation or formulation of that particular perception is not done in a vacuum, it is more of an interactional process. This cultural 'sense of place', arising from the interactional process, can be held collectively by individuals, aggregates of individuals and/or groups of people who have been influenced through socialization by their respective 'personal communities' (i.e. friends, family and associates), their cultural or society and the tourism industry. This same phenomenon occurs within the local community, where individual residents, through daily social interaction, construct a local sense of their community and locale.

A sense of place

> Sense of place, is ultimately a social idea, created and magnified in social discourse and action. The meanings people collectively hold about communities and place are developed and confirmed in a social context through social interaction, and these meanings are transmitted and sustained through social relationship in extended networks of people.
> (Stokowski, 1991, p. 3)

The 'sense of place' concept also has been interpreted as being an individualized phenomenon or personal value (Tuan, 1974; Williams and Roggenbuck, 1990; Bricker *et al.*, 1996), a social construct (Pred, 1983; Eyles, 1985; Stokowski, 1991; Greider and Garkovich, 1994) and both (Stokols and Shumaker, 1981). It has only received marginal attention in tourism research, most likely due to a general feeling that 'sense of place' is a concept too complex to investigate (Relph, 1976; Shamai, 1991; Burr, 1995a, b). Stokowski (1991) postulated that the underlying problem of the 'sense of place' concept is that there is 'no single definition of what people mean by the term . . . and no way to verify that people who use the term are talking about the same things', however, she also acknowledged that, 'people seem to have some positive, affective, sentiments for certain places . . . and these sentiments are elevated into communal meaning, and sometimes behavioral decisions based on the strength of those sentiments are enacted' (Stokowski, 1991, p. 2).

Stokowski and Antholine (1995) found evidence that sense of place becomes more obvious at the local level during times of conflict. They observed that it emerges through 'an exercise in community power, positioning, and suppression', and is often 'negotiated in a politically-charged environment where rhetoric is used to advance goals particular to the desired outcomes of particular local and extra-local groups' (p. 79). This is precisely why Norton and Hannon (1997) emphasized the importance a locally derived sense of place can have in environmental policy development and implementation. They believe that a local 'sense of place' should be reflected in the sustainable planning in communities because such a perspective 'identifies and protects the distinctive character of a place and the culture–nature dialectic that emanates from that place' (Norton and Hannon, 1997, p. 231).

A similar situation exists within tourism development because power and conflict are central to the planning process, it 'is a cultural arena in which hegemonic ideas of superiority and inferiority are continuously played out' (Morgan and Pritchard, 1998, p. 15). In such an arena, it seems intuitive and reasonable to assume that local 'senses of place' would become more evident and tangible, as local stakeholders attempt to preserve and promote their respective sense of place in the context of tourism development. Is this not the essence of sustainable tourism development, sustaining the unique character-istics and qualities of the place, while meeting tourist demand? If tourism development is to be socially equitable, who better than the local host community to determine what should be marketed and 'how' it should be marketed; what should be protected or preserved; what should be changed or remain unaltered? If a developing tourism destination must define its comparative advantage and distinction from its competitor destinations, who better to identify the uniqueness of a place than the local stakeholders? If as, Ashworth and Voogd (1990, p. 8) suggest, there are times when places are marketed by agencies 'without any clear idea of the nature of the product being consumed', who better than the locals to determine the nature of the product. If, within marketing, the credibility of market medium is as important as 'the character of the information itself' (Ashworth and Voogd, 1994, p. 50), who is more credible than the residents of the host community? Perhaps, in an attempt to incorporate more social equity in tourism development, the use of a locally derived sense of place in the societal marketing strategies of travel destinations could change the entire structure of traditional tourism development. Ultimately reversing the traditional 'top-down' initiatives (generated from the *macro* analysis of economic, social and cultural impacts) to a 'bottom-up' approach of grassroots promotion, planning and development policies more suited to addressing the destination-specific impacts of tourism development, and leading to a more sustainable form of tourism (Middleton and Hawkins, 1998).

Conclusions

The intent of this chapter was to explore the potential of incorporating 'sense of place' as a component of sustainable tourism development. Towards that end, the literature reviewed within this chapter indicated that:

- There is consensus that sustainable tourism should be founded on an ethical framework, and that a social equity concept may provide such a framework.
- Stakeholder involvement is critical to the process of sustainable tourism development.
- Societal marketing addresses the needs and wants of the customers, while also addressing the well-being of the host society, and therefore, can be a more socially equitable form of marketing.
- At times, tourists' expectations of a destination prior to visitation are incongruent with their actual experiences of that place.
- An authentic representation of the destination leads to the emphasizing of the uniqueness of a place, because it helps tourists 'match themselves to the destination that will be of most value to them' (Go, 1989, p. 175).
- One of the processes that partnerships, formed to share the management of tourism, need to be involved in is the development of 'jointly agreed images reflecting and respecting the characteristics of the destination' (Middleton and Hawkins, 1998, p. 129).
- Tourism marketing strategies can place traditional people in a position of inequity, where they pay higher costs for tourism development than other groups (through loss of personal identification, culture identification and tradition) (Walle, 1993).
- Tourism development can be a stressful time for the host community, given the diversity of local stakeholders' perspectives about the

values, benefits and costs of tourism; and local senses of place may become more evident during these times of conflict.

Based on this information, it would appear that 'local sense of place' should be an integral component of the societal marketing of travel destinations for several reasons. The inclusion of local stakeholders' 'sense of place' in the marketing of a destination not only promotes greater local involvement in tourism development, but can also lead to more social equity within such development, as diverse groups discuss the 'meaning of a place' and then structure tourism development within that meaning. Allowing local stakeholders to develop cooperatively the marketing image of the destination encourages the host community to determine how to utilize, conserve and preserve the resources of that community. The entire process could result in a more realistic or authentic image of the destination and, in turn, limit the incongruity between the image tourists have prior to arriving at a travel destination and their sense of the place once they have experienced it.

References

Ahmed, Z.U. (1991) The influence of the components of a state's tourism image on product positioning strategy. *Tourism Management* 12(4), 331–340.

Ashworth, G.J. and Voogd, H. (1990) Can places be sold for tourism? In: Ashworth, G.J. and Goodall, B. (eds) *Marketing Tourism Places*. Routledge, London, pp. 1–16.

Ashworth, G.J. and Voogd, H. (1994) Marketing and place promotion. In: Gold, J.R. and Ward, S.V. (eds) *Place Promotion*. John Wiley & Sons, New York, pp. 39–52.

Bricker, K., Kerstetter, D. and Walsh, J. (1996) An exploratory analysis of place-identity and its relationship to socio-demographic and tourism behavior variables. *Book of Abstracts for The Sixth International Symposium on Society and Resource Management: Social Behavior, Natural Resources, and the Environment*, 18–23 May. The Pennsylvania State University, University Park, Pennsylvania, p. 196.

Brown, G.P. (1990) Tourism and place-identity. Unpublished dissertation, Texas A&M University, College Station, Texas.

Burr, S.W. (1994) Sustainable tourism development and use: follies, foibles and feasible approaches. *Papers and Presentations at the 1994 Leisure Research Symposium*. National Park and Recreation Association, Minneapolis, Minnesota.

Burr, S.W. (1995a) What research says about sustainable tourism development. *Parks and Recreation* 30(9), 12–14, 21–26.

Burr, S.W. (1995b) The rural action class's perceptions of rural tourism in relation to their sense of place: an exploratory study. *Proceedings of the 1995 Northeastern Recreation Research Symposium*. State Parks Management and Research Institute, Saratoga Springs, New York, pp. 167–172.

Burr, S.W. and Walsh, J.A. (1993) An interactional approach – sustainable tourism in rural community development. In: Riddrick, C.C. and Watson, A. (eds) *Abstracts from the 1993 NRPA Leisure Research Symposium*. Gallaudet University Leopold Institute, and National Recreation and Park Association Resource Development Division, p. 90.

Butler, R.W. (1991) Tourism, environment, and sustainable development. *Environmental Conservation* 18(3), 201–207.

Caalders, J. (1997) Managing the transition from agriculture to tourism: analysis of tourism networks in Auvergne. *Managing Leisure* 2, 127–142.

Chon, K.S. (1990) The role of destination image in tourism. *The Tourist Review* 45(2), 2–9.

Court, T. (1990) *Beyond Brundtland: Green Development in the 1990s*. Zed Books, London.

Cronin, L. (1990) A strategy for tourism and sustainable development. *World Leisure and Recreation Journal* 32(3), 12–18.

D'Amore, L.J. (1992) Promoting sustainable tourism – the Canadian approach. *Tourism Management* 13(3), 258–262.

Davis, D.E. (1991) Uncommon futures: the rhetoric and reality of sustainable development. *Environment, Technology, and Society* 63, 27–34.

Dehart, H.G. (1991) The future of the preservation movement. *Historic Preservation Forum* 5(5), 6–21.

Disinger, J.F. (1990) Environmental education for sustainable development. *Journal of Environmental Education* 21(4), 3–6.

Dovers, S.R., Norton, T.W. and Handmer, J.W. (1996) Uncertainty, ecology, sustainability, and policy. *Biodiversity and Conservation* 5, 1143–1167.

Ewert, A. and Shultis, J. (1997) Resource-based tourism: an emerging trend in tourism experiences. *Parks and Recreation* 32(9), 94–105.

Eyles, J. (1985) *Senses of Place*. Silverbrook Press, Cheshire, UK.

Fakeye, P.C. and Crompton, J.L. (1991) Image differences between prospective, first-time, and repeat visitors to the Lower Rio Grande Valley. *Journal of Travel Research* 30(2), 10–16.

Fennell, D.A. and Malloy, D.C. (1995) Ethics and ecotourism: a comprehensive ethical model. *Journal of Applied Recreation Research* 20(3), 163–183.

Fridgen, J.D. (1991) *Dimensions of Tourism*. Educational Institute of the American Hotel and Motel Association, East Lansing, Michigan.

Gale, R.P. and Cordray, S.M. (1994) Making sense of sustainability: nine answers to 'what should be sustained?'. *Rural Sociology* 59(2), 311–332.

Gartner, W. (1986) Temporal influences on image change. *Annals of Tourism Research* 13, 635–644.

Gartner, W. (1993) Image formation process. *Journal of Travel and Tourism Marketing* 2(2/3), 191–215.

Gartner, W. (1997) Image and sustainable tourism systems. In: Wahab, S. and Pigram, J.J. (eds) *Tourism Development and Growth: the Challenge of Sustainability*. Routledge, New York, pp. 179–196.

Go, F.M. (1989) Appropriate marketing for travel destinations in developing nations. In: Singh, T.V., Theuns, H.L. and Go, F.M. (eds) *Towards Appropriate Tourism: the Case of Developing Countries*. Peter Lang, New York.

Goulet, D. (1995) Authentic development: is it sustainable? In: Trzyna, T.C.

(ed.) *A Sustainable World: Defining and Measuring Sustainable Development*. International Center for the Environment and Public Policy, Sacramento, California, pp. 45–59.

Greider, T. and Garkovich, L. (1994) Landscapes: the social construction of nature and the environment. *Rural Sociology* 59, 1–24.

Gunn, C. (1972) *Vacationscape: Designing Tourist Regions*. Bureau of Business Research, University of Texas, Austin, Texas.

Gunn, C.A. (1988) *Tourism Planning*, 2nd. edn. Taylor and Francis, New York.

Horner, S. and Swarbrooke, J. (1996) *Marketing Tourism, Hospitality and Leisure in Europe*. International Thomson Business, London.

Hughes, G. (1995) The cultural construction of sustainable tourism. *Tourism Management* 16(1), 49–59.

Hultsman, J. (1995) Just tourism: an ethical framework. *Annals of Tourism Research* 22(3), 553–567.

Hummon, D.H. (1988) Tourist worlds: tourist advertising, ritual, and American culture. *The Sociological Quarterly* 29(2), 179–202.

Hunter, C. (1997) Sustainable tourism as an adaptive paradigm. *Annals of Tourism Research* 24(2), 850–867.

King, D.A. and Stewart, W.P. (1996) Ecotourism and commodification: protecting people and places. *Biodiversity and Conservation* 5, 293–305.

Kolter, P. and Armstrong, G. (1990) *Marketing: an Introduction*, 2nd edn. Prentice-Hall, Englewood Cliffs, New Jersey.

Lea, J.P. (1993) Tourism development ethics in the third world. *Annals of Tourism Research* 20, 701–715.

Lee, R.G. (1972) The social definition of outdoor recreation places. In: Burch, W.R., Cheek, N.H. and Taylor, L. (eds) *Social Behavior, Natural Resources and the Environment*. Harper and Row, New York, pp. 68–84.

Leopold, A. (1949) *A Sand County Almanac*. Oxford University Press, New York.

Lew, A.A. (1989) Authenticity and sense of place in the tourism development experience of older retail districts. *Journal of Travel Research* 27(4), 15–22.

McMinn, S. (1997) The challenge of sustainable tourism. *The Environmentalist* 17, 135–141.

Middleton, V.T.C. and Hawkins, R. (1998) The marketing process for sustainable tourism at destinations. *Sustainable Tourism: a Marketing Perspective*. Butterworth-Heinemann, Oxford, pp. 118–130.

Morgan, N. and Pritchard, A. (1998) *Tourism, Promotion, and Power: Creating Images, Creating Identities*. Wiley, West Sussex, England, p. 266.

Norton, B.G. and Hannon, B. (1997) Environmental values: a place-based approach. *Environmental Ethics* 19(3), 227–246.

Orams, M.B. (1995) Towards a more desirable form of ecotourism. *Tourism Management* 16(1), 3–8.

Pearce, P.L., Moscardo, G. and Ross, G.F. (1996) *Tourism Community Relationships*. Pergamon Press, Oxford, UK, pp. 181–209.

Potts, T.D. and Harrill, R. (1997) In search of a travel ecology paradigm. *The Evolution of Tourism: Adapting to Change*. Proceedings of the 28th Annual Conference. Travel and Tourism Research Association Norfolk, Virginia, pp. 186–208.

Pred, A. (1983) Structuration and place: on the beginning of a sense of place and structure of feeling. *Journal of the Theory of Social Behavior* 13(1), 45–68.

Rapoport, A. (1976) Environmental cognition in cross-cultural perspective. In: Moore, G.T. and Golledge, R.G. (eds) *Environmental Knowing*. Dowden, Hutchinson and Ross, Stroudsburg, pp. 220–234.

Relph, E. (1976) *Place and Placelessness*. Pion Limited, London.

Ryan, W. (1981) *Equality*. Pantheon, New York.

Ryel, R. and Grasse, T. (1991) Marketing ecotourism: attracting the elusive ecotourist. In: Whelen, T. (ed.) *Nature Tourism: Managing for the Environment*. Island Press, Washington, DC.

Sautter, E.T. and Leisen, B. (1999) Managing stakeholders: a tourism planning model. *Annals of Tourism Research* 26(2), 312–328.

Shamai, S. (1991) Sense of place: an empirical measurement. *Geoforum* 22(3), 347–358.

Shearman, R. (1990) The meaning and ethics of sustainability. *Environmental Management* 14(1), 1–8.

Slocombe, D.S. and Van Bers, C. (1991) Seeking substance in sustainable development. *The Journal of Environmental Education* 23(1), 11–18.

Stokols, D. and Shumaker, S.A. (1981) People in places: a transactional view of settings. In: Harvey, J.H. (ed.) *Cognition, Social Behavior, and the Environment*. Lawrence Erlbaum Associates, Hillsdale, New Jersey, pp. 441–488.

Stokowski, P.A. (1991) '*Sense of place*' as a social construct. Paper presented at the 1991 National Recreation and Parks Association Research Symposium, Baltimore, Maryland.

Stokowski, P.A. and Antholine, W. (1995) Applications of a sociological approach to 'sense of place'. In: Freysinger, V.J., Stowokski, P. and Hendricks, W. (eds) *Abstracts of the Papers and Presentations at the 1995 Leisure Research Symposium*. Texas A&M University and National Recreation and Park Association Resource Development Division, San Antonio, Texas, p. 79.

Swarbrooke, J. (1999) *Sustainable Tourism Management*. CAB International, Wallingford, UK.

Thurot, J.M. and Thurot, G. (1983) The ideology of class and tourism: confronting the discourse of advertising. *Annals of Tourism Research* 10, 173–189.

Tuan, Y.F. (1974) *Topophilia: a Study of Environmental Perception, Attitudes, and Values*. Prentice-Hall, Englewood Cliffs, New Jersey.

Um, S. and Crompton, J.L. (1990) Attitude determinants in tourism destination choice. *Annals of Tourism Research* 17, 432–448.

Uzzell, D. (1984) An alternative structuralist approach to the psychology of tourism marketing. *Annals of Tourism Research* 11, 79–99.

Verburg, R.M. and Wiegel, V. (1997) On the compatibility of sustainability and economic growth. *Environmental Ethics* 19(3), 247–265.

Walle, A.H. (1993) Tourism and traditional people: forging equitable strategies. *Journal of Travel Research* 31(3), 14–19.

Walsh, J.A. and Matthews, B.E. (1995) The interplay between ethics and sustainable rural tourism. *Proceedings of the 1995 Northeastern Recrea-*

tion Research Symposium. State Parks Management and Research Institute, Saratoga Springs, New York, pp. 125–130.

WCED (World Commission on Environment and Development) (1987) *Our Common Future*. Oxford University Press, New York.

Wheeler, B. (1994) Egotourism, sustainable tourism and the environment – a symbiotic, symbolic, or shambolic relationship. In: Seaton, A.V. (ed.) *Tourism: the State of the Art*. John Wiley & Sons, Toronto, pp. 647–654.

Wight, P.A. (1993a) Sustainable ecotourism: balancing economic, environmental and social goals within an ethical framework. *Journal of Tourism Studies* 4(2), 54–66.

Wight, P.A. (1993b) Ecotourism: ethics or eco-sell. *Journal of Travel Research* 31(3), 3–9.

Wight, P.A. (1996) North American ecotourists: market profile and trip characteristics. *Journal of Travel Research* 34(2), 2–10.

Williams, D.R. and Roggenbuck, J.W. (1990) A framework for examining the meaning of recreation places: place attachment, mode of experience, and environmental disposition. *The 3rd Symposium on Social Science in Resource Management Proceedings*, Texas, pp. 71–72.

Zeiger, J.B. and McDonald, D. (1997) Ecotourism: wave of the future. *Parks and and Recreation* 32(9), 84–92.

Casinos, Communities and Sustainable Economic Development

12

Barbara Carmichael

Department of Geography and Environmental Studies, Wilfrid Laurier University, Waterloo, Ontario, Canada

Casinos, like theme parks, resorts, golf courses or any other tourism attraction, bring with them benefits and costs. In considering tourism growth, communities are faced with a situation in which they want to stimulate the economy but are nervous about the appropriateness of such development. Furthermore, different groups within communities hold different perceptions of, and attitudes toward, casino tourism impacts. This is particularly true for a controversial attraction such as a casino, where attitudes are likely to be more polarized, and in the situation of gaming on First Nation land, where the community is further divided on an ethnic basis.

Casino gambling and its recent rapid diffusion across North America represents an exciting wave of tourism dynamism. However, it is debatable whether this growth can be maintained, and to what extent casinos are either viable economic business entities or are appropriate tools for sustainable economic development. For example, in Ontario, the casino developments of the Ontario Casino Corporation are very recent (Casino Windsor 1994, Northern Belle River boat Casino 1996, Casino Rama, Orillia 1996, and Niagara Casino/Gateway Project 1996). Consequently, little is known about the long-term sustainability of these Canadian initiatives. Evidence from the US in longer-established casino areas is contradictory. While Las Vegas has been a casino boom town, in Atlantic City, despite the 30 million visitors a year and nearly 50,000 jobs in the industry's 12 casinos, the casino industry has not alleviated the urban blight and poverty that had plagued the city (Eadington, 1995). Goodman (1994) in an extensive study of legalized gambling as a strategy for economic development found that 'there is a critical lack of objective knowledge and research about the economic and social costs and benefits of legalized gambling' (p. 16).

The purpose of this chapter is to present a conceptual framework for the evaluation of the consequences of the introduction of a casino within an existing tourism destination area. The proposed research will focus on the perceptions and attitudes of different community stakeholders and assess the role of casinos as appropriate tools for sustainable economic development. This framework is not meant to be static. The changing power relations within the community in terms of wealth and authority provide an important secondary theme underlying the framework, especially in the context of Indian gaming, because of the dual nature of the host community. For example, in the case of Casino Rama, Ontario, the host community consists of the Chippewas of Mnjikaning First Nation, and the residents of several rural townships and the small town of Orillia. While this community may be defined on a geographical basis, it is composed of diverse groups with changing and emerging relationships, through which the community is constantly being redefined. The introduction of an external agent of change in the form of a casino may be perceived as an opportunity or a threat, and provides a focus for public opinion. Furthermore, community mechanisms in the form of task forces and social groups which are spawned as a response to the new casino development are underlying components of the framework and are agents that facilitate sustainability.

In this chapter, as an introduction, previous research on casino impacts is discussed; secondly, the concept of sustainability is explored as it applies to casinos, and casinos as sustainable economic development tools; and finally a conceptual framework is suggested for assessing casinos according to five functions of sustainability: environmental, socio-economic, productionist/experiential, budgetary and political. These five functions have applicability at the attraction, host community and regional levels, and examples from the casino industry are used to illustrate their relevance to sustainability.

Casino impacts

While there are important studies that have examined the impacts of tourism (Mathiesen and Wall, 1982) and resident attitudes towards these impacts (Pizam, 1978; Perdue *et al.*, 1990; Getz, 1994), there are fewer studies on the perceived impact of gaming on communities (Pizam and Pokela, 1985; Caneday and Zeiger, 1991; Long *et al.*, 1994). Previous studies reveal some of the major concerns of residents in connection with casino development. Pizam and Pokela (1985) found that residents of two Massachusetts towns considering casino development were concerned that their towns would change, that traffic conditions would worsen, and that crime would increase, while they predicted that there would be more jobs and recreational opportunities in their communities. Similar findings were obtained by the present author in Connecticut. Residents of three small towns near the Indian gaming resort at Foxwoods perceived mainly negative social effects on their communities while acknowledging that there were economic benefits (Carmichael *et al.*, 1996; Carmichael and Peppard, 1998).

Factors influencing resident attitudes towards casino development include personal factors, such as employment in the tourism industry or at the casino, distance of residence from the casino and socio-demographic factors. These factors will influence perceptions of casino impacts based on the assertion by Eadington (1986, p. 280) that 'one's attitude towards the casino project will depend largely on whether those changes are going to improve or deteriorate one's present quality of life in that community'.

The hidden costs of community expenditures on criminal justice, problem gambling and public infrastructure are often overlooked by decision makers when the approval of casinos is being considered by states. More often, impact reports tend to stress economic benefits while ignoring social costs (Goodman, 1994) and news reporting is biased towards positive benefits (Nickerson, 1995). Sometimes there are undesirable lag effects connected with casino development. Evidence from Atlantic City (Rubenstein, 1984), Deadwood (Stubbles, 1990) and Central City and Black Hawk, Colorado (Stokowski, 1993, 1996) suggests that anticipated social benefits have been slow to occur. Indeed, some researchers have questioned the appropriateness of gambling as an economic development strategy (Ravitz, 1988).

There is a need for studies that assess whether casinos attract new spending to an area or merely siphon off money from other tourism-related businesses or from other enterprises (Dimanche and Spreyer, 1996). This is important within the context of sustainability of casino gaming and its political support. As Rose (1995) so bluntly states, 'A casino acts like a black hole sucking money out of a local economy. No one cares if you suck money out of tourists but large scale casinos that do not bring in more tourist dollars than they take away from the local players and local businesses soon find themselves outlawed' (p. 29). Therefore, one question underlying the present research framework and discussed previously by the present author is: are casinos 'sink holes' draining economies or 'growth poles' which act as catalysts for economic activity? (Carmichael, 1994, 1998).

Casinos and sustainable development

According to the Bruntland Report, sustainable development is 'economic activity which meets the needs of the present without compromising the ability of future generations to meet their needs' (WCED, 1987). Since this introduction of the concept of sustainable development, most economic activities, including tourism, have been considered and discussed in the context of the idea (Nelson *et al.*, 1993). Butler (1993, p. 29) gives a working definition of sustainable development in the context of tourism as:

> tourism which is developed and maintained in an area (community, environment) in such a manner and at such a scale that it remains viable over an indefinite period and does not degrade or alter the environment (human and physical) in which it exists to such a degree that it prohibits the successful development and well being of other activities and processes.

Sustainable development in this context may be likened to the symbiotic relationship between tourism and conservation as discussed by Budowski (1976) in which both tourism and conservation are organized in such a way that they both benefit from the relationship in that a better quality of life is achieved.

Sustainable development concepts raise a number of questions: how do we protect the values, biophysical conditions and social meanings that are important to people? Whose values? Which people? Whose future? What about trade-offs in the sense of how many negative impacts are allowable if compensated by certain economic or quality of life benefits? Sustainability is a word that is defined, interpreted and imagined differently between individuals, organizations and social groups (Mowforth and Munt, 1998). Recently, the sustainable development debate is widening, and future discussions will likely draw on the wider debates in the social sciences, such as globalization, postmodernism, flexible production, power relationships and governance (Bramwell and Lane, 1999). In any tourism analysis, there is a need to examine the questions of who is stating the principles, priorities and policies, who will benefit from related action and who will lose.

Sustainable development is not the same as sustainable tourism (or sustainable profits), which is tourism that is economically viable in an area in so far as it is maintained because it is marketable and profitable. Sustainable development within the context of tourism in communities should not damage the environmental or social integrity, so the impacts of tourism need to be assessed carefully. In addition, in promoting tourism in the context of symbiotic development, the full range of needs as perceived by current tourists or people at leisure must be considered (Butler, 1991). Both tourists and hosts will represent and imagine sustainability, but often in different ways (Mowforth and Munt, 1998). Tourists interpret and represent their experiences in ways that may be fundamentally opposed to the experience of those being visited: and these interpretations and representations will differ between different types of tourists and different types of hosts.

Much of the current research on sustainability focuses on the physical rather than the human environment. According to Garrod and Fyall (1998, p. 202), 'The wider literature of sustainability tends to concentrate more on the use of natural resources, but it can be argued that human-made and socio-cultural resources are just as important in the context of tourism, if not more so'. Within the context of casinos, the physical environmental impact is only one part of the sustainability issue. In this chapter, a more holistic framework is suggested, which focuses on perceived community and regional impacts as well as objective assessment of changes induced by casino development.

While there is no doubt that casino development is the bandwagon of the 1990s in both the US and Canada, it is debatable to what extent casinos are either viable economic entities as sustaining in business, or are appropriate tools for sustainable economic development. Therefore, within the context of casinos and sustainability, two separate approaches may be taken. First, are casinos sustainable, and, secondly, are casinos sustainable economic development tools?

Are casinos sustainable?

The recent rapid diffusion of casino gambling across North America represents an exciting example of tourism growth. During the 1990s casino gambling operations were concentrated in a number of different types of locations: urban areas ranging from large cities like Chicago to small towns like Deadwood; riverboat and dockside locations as in Iowa, Mississippi, Louisiana and Illinois; and in rural communities in Indian reservations in the Midwest and in Connecticut. At present, demand for casino gaming outstrips supply, and very high revenues are generated by many establishments. While this reflects present economic viability, as the numbers of casinos proliferate, increasing competition will constitute intervening opportunities and shrink the draw areas or gambler hinterlands of longer-established casinos (Stansfield, 1996, p. 138). Indeed, in some areas of Indian gaming, for example in the Dakotas, this process of attrition is already happening (Berg, 1998). As Roehl states, a number of alternative destinations are now available to consumers who wish to gamble. Mere availability, which may have served success in the past, is no longer a sufficient lure (Roehl, 1996, p. 61). It is likely that most casinos in the future will be very local in market orientation (Eadington, 1995). To be competitive to a wider market, lavish destination resorts will emerge as the newly diffused casino product market matures and develops into a hierarchical spatial system. Even Nevada, with its well-established and successful casino industry, is vulnerable to the threat of casino gaming in California, its major market area. Thus, as with any business, casinos are likely to exhibit product life cycles, changing competitive environments and responses. Viability is dependent on profitability.

Are casinos sustainable economic development tools?

Apart from the economic viability of the tourism enterprise, which may make a casino sustainable, a more holistic framework is needed to understand a casino as a tool for sustainable development. Casino developments, like any other form of economic activity, need to fulfil a number of functions if they are to bring lasting improvements to local economies. While casinos draw on the local market, they also have the ability to attract considerable numbers of tourists from outside the region. Their role as tourist attractions depends on market access and competition, their social acceptability and the political climate in which they are allowed to operate, as well as the nature of the experience that they offer. Local resident endorsement of casino operations and their perceptions of casino impacts on their community, quality of life and environment are important considerations in understanding sustainability. Furthermore, backward linkages and job creation in local tourism and non-tourism enterprises are key factors in economic development, which may or may not result from the casino's entry into the local economies.

A conceptual framework is suggested for assessing casino sustainability according to five functions: environmental, socio-economic, productionist/experiential, budgetary and political. While a similar scheme was originally suggested for agricultural systems (Bowler, 1992), it has also been applied to tourism by the present author (Rickard and Carmichael, 1995). The five functions are summarized in Fig. 12.1 and have applicability at either the attraction level, within the host community or within the context of a wider region. While it is intended in future research to apply this framework in depth within the context of casino attractions, some preliminary findings and considerations are presented below.

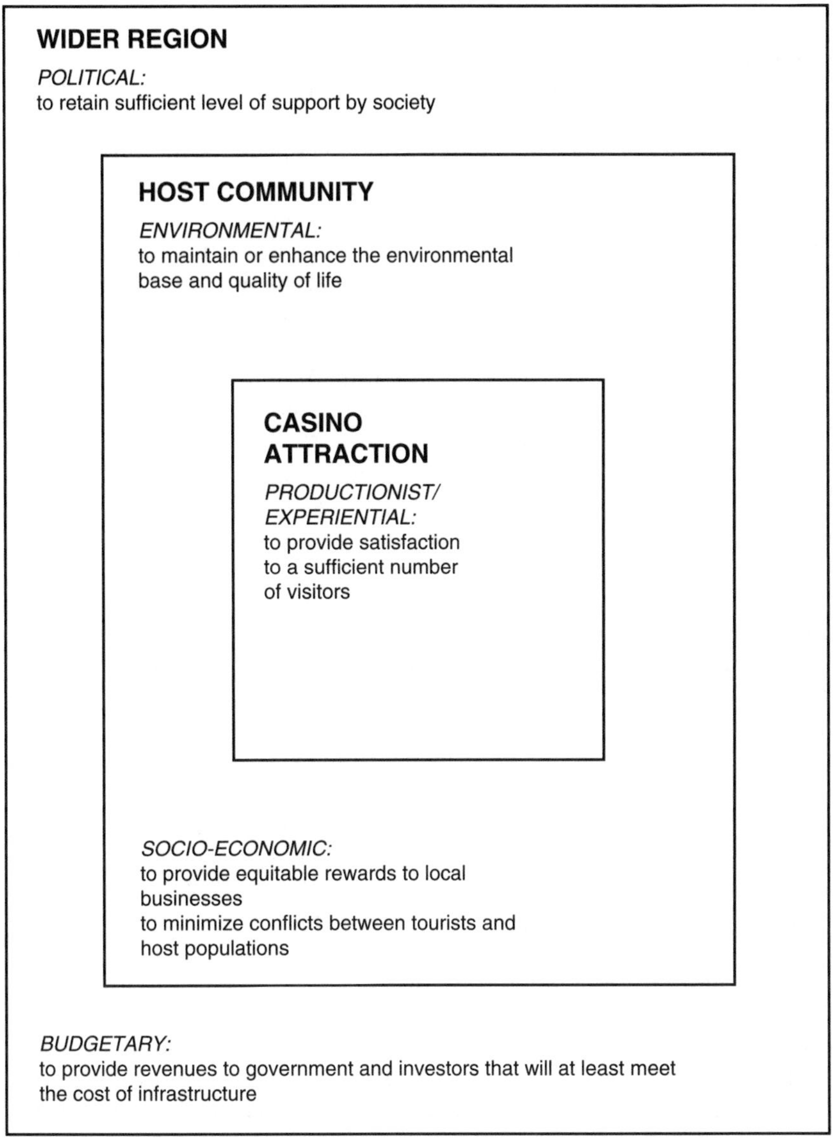

WIDER REGION

POLITICAL:
to retain sufficient level of support by society

HOST COMMUNITY

ENVIRONMENTAL:
to maintain or enhance the environmental
base and quality of life

**CASINO
ATTRACTION**

*PRODUCTIONIST/
EXPERIENTIAL:*
to provide satisfaction
to a sufficient number
of visitors

SOCIO-ECONOMIC:
to provide equitable rewards to local
businesses
to minimize conflicts between tourists and
host populations

BUDGETARY:
to provide revenues to government and investors that will at least meet
the cost of infrastructure

Fig. 12.1. A conceptual framework for assessing a casino's role in sustainable economic development.

Environmental function

Objective: to maintain or enhance the environmental base and quality of life
Casinos are located in a variety of different environments. They may

function as part of a tourism attraction mix within attractive physical and cultural environments. However, 'the location of new casino developments is dictated more and more by the existence of legislative and political support, the availability of capital and proximity to market than by the distribution of natural resources' (Smith and Hinch, 1996, p. 39). As part of the built environment, tourism planners need to be concerned about appropriate building design, scale of development and environmental impact assessment. Developments in rural areas may be more sensitive than those in urban areas that have already lost green space. Indeed, some urban areas in decline have used casino investment to refurbish historic downtowns, as in Colorado mining settlements (Stokowski, 1993). Several Canadian casinos fit the historic or refurbished structures designation: an old saloon, – Diamond Tooth Games in Dawson City; a railroad hotel, – Winnipeg's Crystal Casino; an Expo 67 pavilion, Casino de Montreal; a renovated railway station, – Regina Casino. Sometimes, urban industrial land becomes landscaped for the casino site, as in Hull/Ottawa which occupies an attractive quarry lakeside site.

With the emergence of mega resort casinos, especially if they are sited in sensitive rural areas, as in the case of Foxwoods, Connecticut, issues of the appropriateness of the scale and pace of development are raised. The Mashentucket Pequot Reservation, where Foxwood buildings dominate the skyline, is located within a quiet rural district of south-east Connecticut, described in the Connecticut Conservation and Development plan as either rural land, preservation area or conservation area. The tribe has limited amounts of land suitable for building since much of the reservation is swamp. Much of the water supply is from underground aquifer. As with any development there are likely to be pollution effects from de-icing agents on parking areas and nutrients from fertilizers on gardens (Casino Impact Study, 1991). However, the tribe, guided by the National Tribal Environmental Council, has taken a proactive rather than reactive response to environmental problems. They have put in a new sewage plant, using the latest technology, and spent US$1 million on purifying drinking-water at the nearby lake of Isles (Bush *et al.*, 1994). In fact, it is ironic that the tribe manages and monitors the environment much more carefully than the surrounding rural area of Connecticut, where the predominant form of sewage disposal is septic tanks. Here is an example of a large-scale tourism attraction being more sustainable environmentally than local small-scale infrastructure developments, which are outdated and ineffective. Of course, individual casino developments will vary in the extent to which they provide for the sustainable environment function. However, in any context, rural or urban, environmental resource integrity is one of the five functions that needs to be monitored carefully, planned for and managed.

Socio-economic function

There are two objectives to be discussed within this context: (i) to provide equitable rewards to individual entrepreneurs and resort communities; and (ii) to minimize conflicts between tourists and local people.

Objective: to provide equitable economic rewards to individual entrepreneurs and resort communities
As already discussed, most casinos have proved to be highly profitable business enterprises. Economic impact studies reveal their direct, indirect and induced effects. The establishments are labour intensive and multiplier effects are created as workers spend their wages within the employee catchment region. As such, we may argue that casinos are growth poles or catalysts for economic development, especially if they draw in basic money. However, we may take a different perspective and argue that casinos may be sink holes not growth poles.

The extent to which casinos cannibalize the product of local businesses is a key research question in assessing the socio-economic function of sustainability. For example, in Niagara Falls, a major existing tourism destination in Ontario, to what extent will the recent casino improve the economic viability of the tourism sector or cannibalize its business? In the case of Windsor, Ontario, although the accommodation sector benefited, the businesses in downtown Windsor were not as positive about the effects on themselves (Assessment of Casino Windsor Final Report, 1994). The substitution effect is defined as the power of one good to replace another good with no change in the utility or satisfaction of a customer. The extent to which other forms of gaming activity (horse racing, dog tracks, lotteries) suffer from the introduction of casino gaming suggests that the substitution effect exists despite the growth in real personal incomes and growth in spending on leisure and recreation. However, recent research by Marfels (1997) suggests that video lottery terminal (VLT) gaming is a distinct market segment which produces a 'supplementation' rather than a substitution effect by enhancing gaming expenditures.

Objective: to minimize conflicts between tourists and local people
Previous research shows that where the pace of development is rapid, resident attitudes become markedly more positive or more negative. Resident attitudes are affected by perceived positive or negative effects that are related to perception of how the development affects them personally and affects their town and their region. While residents often acknowledge positive economic impacts, they are also aware of social and environmental costs (Carmichael *et al.*, 1996). For tourism

development to be sustainable, local endorsement of the nature of the development is important. In the case of casinos, where the core tourism product is the gambling experience, perhaps there are limited opportunities for tourist and host interaction. Therefore, this function may be less important for casino development than for other types of tourist development. An important research question in this context is to what extent are casino visitors also visitors to other attractions in the area? And to what extent are casino visitors locals?

Productionist/experiential function

Objective: to provide satisfaction to a sufficient number of tourists
As well as safeguarding the natural and built environment and meeting the needs of the host community, the development should satisfy the needs of the tourists and visitors. In the case of casino gambling, there is no doubt about the activity's popularity and, for some, even popularity to the point of addiction. The proliferation of gaming venues and VLTs is increasing the popularity of gaming as a leisure activity, as well as tapping into latent demand. Gaming is offered at destination resorts, on riverboats, in urban areas and on Indian lands, and, depending on the jurisdiction, VLTs are increasingly available at convenient locations in service functions. While most players do not develop a compulsive gambling problem, approximately 4–6% of the population is likely to suffer from this addiction.

Budgetary function

Objective: to provide revenues to provincial and local governments that will at least meet the costs of infrastructure
Part of the reason for the rapid growth in the number of casinos is that they are regarded by states and provinces as lucrative sources of income as an alternative to raising taxes. In hard economic times, cities, states/provinces and countries need money, but raising taxes in a recession is faulty economics and bad politics. For example, in the early 1980s, more than 75% of US states had to cut their budgets to prevent deficit spending and in the past decade these problems have persisted (Cabot, 1996). The success of casino gaming in Nevada and on Native American land demonstrated a quick and easy way to raise money, provided the means was socially acceptable to the majority of voters.

Even where state taxes are not required, as in the case of casinos on

Native reservation land, deals are sometimes struck by tribes to maintain their monopoly positions. For example, the Mashentucket Pequot tribe of Foxwoods casino negotiated to provide 25% of their slot revenue to the State of Connecticut, provided that they remained the only location permitted to operate slot machines (this payment was substantial and amounted to US$113 million in 1994). Recently, with the opening of a second Indian casino in Connecticut by the Mohegan tribe, the tax-sharing deal was also agreed upon with this second group.

Political function

Objective: to retain a sufficient level of support by society
By the 1990s, in North America, Europe, Australia and New Zealand, as well as in various developing countries, there has emerged a substantial increase in the legal and social acceptance of gaming. It has changed from being perceived as a vice, available in very restricted locations, to being more of a mainstream participatory activity (Eadington, 1995). Despite this, legalizing casino gaming usually proves difficult to implement. A veto model suggests that a campaign to legalize casinos will be successful only if all major campaign factors are favourable (Dombrink and Thompson, 1990). These major campaign factors include: support by the political elite, support by the economic elite, dominance of economic issues in the campaign (the need for jobs and tax revenues), non-emergence of crime issues, lack of opposition from a rival gambling enterprise (particularly horse tracks) and financial advantages for proponents. Power relations are integral to this process and to the outcome.

However, as more jurisdictions accept casino gaming, the public are increasingly realizing the negative effects of casinos, i.e. compulsive gambling. Casinos are contentious attractions that create strong reactions among some groups in society. There will always be people who contend that gambling is immoral and that it is inappropriate as an economic development tool. In the past, it was a highly restricted activity and today it is still highly controlled in location. As Eadington states, 'historically, legal commercial gaming has seldom existed in a stable environment . . . If the image of commercial gaming moved strongly towards the negative pole, there is a real possibility that legislation prohibiting such gambling could again emerge' (Eadington, 1990, pp. 157–158). For example, the recent window of opportunity for casino gaming, especially in the US with the Indian Gaming Regulatory Act in 1988, could be reversed very easily. The NIMBY (not in my back yard) syndrome is clearly present with reference to casinos (Carmichael *et al.*, 1996), and was a factor in the June 1998 decision of the Ontario government not to implement their proposal to open 44 charity gaming establishments until after the pending elections. As of 2000, only four charity gaming establishments have been opened in Ontario and only in municipalities which voted in favour of their developments.

Conclusions

In this chapter, a framework was presented for assessing casinos as sustainable economic development tools. While it is proposed in future research to apply this framework to casino contexts, the framework could be applied within other tourism contexts. Tourism researchers need to model the elements of sustainability in different settings and contexts, develop indicators and monitor changes over time. The relationship of the proposed framework with existing frameworks in terms of natural and economic cycles may also be explored (seasonality, changing market conditions, capacity levels, resort cycle). This is important because any model development is naive if no attention is given to change. It may be that in the quest for sustainable development, planners and managers are shooting for a 'target', but fail to realize that their 'target' is moving. Researchers recognize that nothing remains economically viable forever, cultures do not remain constant, tourism markets change, natural environments experience cycles, political climate and social acceptability of developments change.

The proposed framework employs a number of levels of analysis, moving wider than the establishment level to a consideration of communities and resident perceived impacts, and outward to the surrounding region and political environment. The application is timely since casino gaming in North America has recently been adopted mainly as a tool perceived to bring economic development. This research is relevant to First Nation decision-makers, politicians and community stakeholders, in their assessment of the potential role and impacts of casino developments. In addition, this research will contribute to the growing body of literature on resident attitudes towards tourism and, more specifically, to the emerging literature on resident attitudes toward casinos and casino gaming. In an analysis of sustainability, community interests need to be considered in the widest sense. There is a need to balance the needs of the environment, the tourists and the hosts within the context of the wider political arena. This is not an easy task, especially when the many pathways and pitfalls associated with sustainability are considered. As this discussion shows, there are many players in the five functions of sustainability. However, if their needs are balanced within the casino context, it is debatable whether the result will actually be sustainable economic development.

In this book, a variety of themes and goals for sustainability have been developed, including sustainability as ecosystem maintenance, preservation of natural capital, provision of intergenerational equity, sustainable development, redistribution of political power and maintenance or restoration of human–environment systems' resiliency. While these are laudable themes and goals, it is highly unlikely that all will be perfectly achieved or measurable. Indeed, sustainability is a socially constructed concept with many different meanings and interpretations. According to Mowforth and Munt, (1998, p. 324), 'sustainability and sustainable tourism reflects a discourse that is contested and through which power circulates'.

References

Assessments of Casino Windsor Final Report (1994) *Ontario Casino Corporation*. Ernst and Young, Toronto.

Berg, D.J. (1998) The new buffalo: tribal casino expansion in the Dakotas. In: *Casino Gambling in America: Origins, Trends and Impacts*. Cognizant Communications, Elmsford, New York, pp. 76–90.

Bowler, I.R. (1992) Sustainable agriculture as an alternative part of the business development. In: Bowler, I.R., Bryant, C.R. and Nellis, M.D. (eds) *Contemporary Rural Systems in Transition*. Vol. 1: *Agriculture and Environment*. CAB International, Wallingford, UK, pp. 237–253.

Bramwell, B. and Lane, B. (1999) Sustaining tourism, contributing to the debates. *Journal of Sustainable Tourism* 7(1), 1–5.

Budowski, G. (1976) Tourism and environmental conservation. *Environmental Conservation* 3(1), 27–31.

Bush, S., Devitt, M., Krasnoff, S. and Tyrrell, T. (1994) The local impacts of Foxwoods 1992–1995: economic benefits and social costs. *New England Journal of Travel and Tourism* 5, 11–23.

Butler, R.W. (1991) Tourism, environment and sustainable development. *Environmental Conservation* 18(3), 201–209.

Butler, R.W. (1993) Tourism – an evolutionary perspective. In: *Tourism and Sustainable Development: Monitoring, Planning, Managing*. Department of Geography Publications Series Number 37, Waterloo University of Waterloo, pp. 27–44.

Cabot, A.N. (1996) *Casino Gaming. Policy, Economics and Regulation*. UNLV International Gaming Institute, Las Vegas, Nevada.

Caneday, L. and Zeiger, J. (1991) The social economic and environmental costs of tourism to a gaming community as perceived by its residents. *Journal of Travel Research* 30, 45–49.

Carmichael, B.A. (1994) Casino gambling and tourism in urban and rural communities. In: Murphy, P.E. (ed.) *Quality Management in Urban Tourism Conference: Balancing Business and the Environment*. School of Business, University of Victoria, Victoria, British Columbia, pp. 348–354.

Carmichael, B.A. (1998) Foxwood Resort Casino: who wants it, who benefits? In: Meyer-Arendt, K. and Hartmann, R. (eds) *Casino Gambling in North America*. Cognizant Communications, Elmsford, New York, pp. 63–71.

Carmichael, B.A. and Peppard, D. Jr. (1998) The Impact of Foxwoods Resort Casino on its dual host community: southeastern Connecticut and the Mashentucket Pequot Tribe. In: Lew, A. and Van Otten, G.A. (eds) *Tourism on American Indian Lands*. Cognizant Communications, Elmsford, New York, pp. 128–144.

Carmichael, B.A., Peppard, D. Jr. and Boudreau, F. (1996) Mega resort on my doorstep: local resident attitudes towards Foxwoods Casino and casino gambling on nearby Indian reservation land. *Journal of Travel Research* 34(3), 9–16.

Casino Impact Study (1991) An analysis of the impacts of the Mashentucket Pequct tribes proposed economic enterprises in Ledyard, Connecticut on the land use and traffic in the South East Connecticut Planning Region. South East Connecticut Regional Planning Agency.

Dimanche, F. and Spreyer, J.F. (1996) Report on a comprehensive five year gambling impact research plan in New Orleans. *Journal of Travel Research* 34(3), 97–100.

Dombrink, J. and Thompson, W.N. (1990) *The Last Resort: Success and Failure in Campaigns for Casinos*. University of Nevada Press, Reno.

Eadington, W.R. (1986) Impact of casino gambling on the community: comment on Pizam and Pokela (sic.). *Annals of Tourism Research* 13, 279–285.

Eadington, W.R. (1990) *Indian Gaming and the Law*. University of Nevada Press, Reno.

Eadington, W.R. (1995) The emergence of casino gaming as a major factor in tourism. In: Butler, R. and Pearce, D. (eds) *Change in Tourism People, Places and Processes*. Routledge, London, pp. 159–186.

Garrod, B. and Fyall, A. (1998) Beyond the rhetoric of sustainable tourism. *Tourism Management* 19(3), 199–212.

Getz, D. (1994) Resident attitudes toward tourism: a longitudinal study of the Spey Valley, Scotland. *Tourism Management* 15(4), 247–258.

Goodman, R. (1994) *Legalised Gambling as a Strategy for Economic Development*. United States Gambling Study, Northampton, Massachusetts.

Long, P., Clarke, J. and Liston, D. (1994) *Win, Lose or Draw? Gambing with America's Small Towns*. The Aspen Institute Rural Economic Policy Program, Washington, DC.

Marfels, C. (1997) Casino gaming and the substitution effect: a phenomenon in search of evidence. Paper presented at the 10th International Conference on Gambling and Risktaking, Montreal, Quebec.

Mathieson, A. and Wall, G. (1982) *Tourism: Economic, Physical and Social Impacts*. John Wiley & Sons, New York.

Mowforth, M. and Munt, I. (1998) *Tourism and Sustainability. New Tourism in the Third World*. Routledge, London.

Nelson, J.G., Butler, R. and Wall, G. (1993) *Tourism and Sustainable*

Development: Monitoring, Planning, Managing. Department of Geography Publications Series Number 37, University of Waterloo, Waterloo.

Nickerson, N. (1995) Tourism and gambling content analysis. *Annals of Tourism Research* 22(1), 53–66.

Perdue, R.R., Long, P.T. and Allen, L. (1990) Resident support for tourism development. *Annals of Tourism Research* 17, 586–599.

Pizam, A. (1978) Tourism's impacts: the social cost to the destination community as perceived by US residents. *Journal of Travel Research* 16, 8–12.

Pizam, A. and Pokela, J. (1985) The perceived impacts of casino gambling on a community. *Annals of Tourism Research* 12, 147–165.

Ravitz, M. (1988) Community development: salvation or suicide. *Social Policy* 19(2), 17–21.

Rickard, T. and Carmichael, B.A. (1995) Linkages between the agricultural and tourism systems in sustaining rural development in Jamaica. In: Bryant, C. and Marois, C. (eds) *The Sustainability of Rural Systems.* University of Montreal, Montreal, pp. 316–330.

Roehl, W.S. (1996) Competition, casino spending and the use of casino amenities. *Journal of Travel Research* 34(3), 57–62.

Rose, I.N. (1995) Gambling and the law: endless fields of dreams. *Journal of Gambling Studies* 11(1), 15–33.

Rubenstein, J. (1984) Casino gambling in Atlantic City: issues of development and redevelopment. *Annals of the American Academy of Political and Social Sciences* 477, 61–71.

Smith, G.J. and Hinch, T.D. (1996) Canadian casinos as tourist attractions: chasing the pot of gold. *Journal of Travel Research* 34(3), 37–45.

Stansfield, C. (1996) Reservations and gambling: native Americans and the diffusion of gaming. In: Butler, D. and Hinch, T.D. (eds) *Tourism and Indigenous Peoples.* International Thomson Business Press, London.

Stokowski, P.A. (1993) Undesirable lag effects in tourism destination development: a Colorado case study. *Journal of Travel Research* 32, 35–41.

Stokowski, P.A. (1996) *Riches and Regrets: Betting on Gambling in Two Colorado Mountain Towns Niwot, Colorado.* University of Colorado Press, Colorado.

Stubbles, R. (1990) The deadwood tradition: putting gambling before South Dakota. *Small Town* November–December, 20–27.

WCED (World Commission on Environment and Development) (1987) *Our Common Future.* Oxford University Press, New York.

13

Expanding Sustainable Tourism's Conceptualization: Ecotourism, Volunteerism and Serious Leisure

Stephen Wearing and John Neil

School of Leisure, Sport and Tourism, Faculty of Business, University of Technology, Lindfield, Sydney, Australia

Tourism is a complex experience, often involving subtle interactions among the tourist, the site and the host community. As research has moved beyond conceptualizations of the tourist as 'wanderer', 'gazer' or 'escaper', the focus has shifted to the character of the experience itself. This shift in focus, while maintaining the sociological context of a tourist experience, allows for the active construction of the role of the tourist in the 'tourist experience'. The idea of experience can be informed by a number of different elements in respect to the individual, the individual's social groups, their travel experience and the interrelating elements that sustain the experience. Here we desire to differentiate alternative forms of tourism – specifically here, ecotourism – through the placing of experience as a nodal point, this then allows for the elaboration of the conceptual, theoretical and practical differences and overlaps between specific tourism forms. This provides the basis for the introduction of other ideas that can inform us of these experiences, thus contributing to the movement towards an understanding and elaboration of the potential benefits of particular tourism experiences as an holistic interchange rather than chiefly evaluated through economic analyses.

In accounting for tourism as a global phenomenon, much of the initial sociological and social psychological work was concerned with the individual tourist and the part that holidays play in establishing identity and a sense of self. This self was predominantly posited as a universal, and tourism, like leisure, was seen in a dialectical relationship with the 'workaday world'. Cohen and Taylor (1976), for example, drew on Goffman's concern with the presentation of self in everyday life to argue that holidays are culturally sanctioned escape routes for Western travellers. One of the problems for the modern traveller, in this view, is to establish identity and a sense of personal individuality in the face of the anomic forces of a technological world. Tourism serves to provide a free area, a mental and physical escape from the immediacy of the multiplicity of impinging pressures in technological society and, as such, holiday experiences provide a scope for the nurturance and cultivation of human identity. As Cohen and Taylor argue, overseas holidays are structurally similar to leisure because one of their functions is identity establishment and the cultivation of one's self-consciousness. The tourist, they claim, uses all aspects of the holiday for the manipulation of well-being. However, in the tourist literature, these arguments became diverted into a debate about the authenticity of this experience (MacCannell, 1976; Cohen, 1988), serving to focus attention on the attractions of the tourist destination. Such a shift objectified the destination as place – a specific geographical site that was presented to tourists for their gaze (Urry, 1990). Thus the manner of presentation became all important – architecture, spatial layout, aesthetic appeal, landscape features – with 'authenticity' becoming the primary determinant of analysis amongst a proliferation of binarized categories: 'I categorised objects of the gaze in terms of romantic/collective, historical/modern, and authentic/ unauthentic', says Urry (1990, p. 135). The tourists themselves became synonymous with the *flâneur*, 'the strolling *flâneur* was a forerunner of the twentieth century tourist' (Urry, 1990, p. 138) who travelled as a passive observer, and this *flâneur* was generally perceived as escaping from the workaday world for an 'ephemeral', 'fugitive' and 'contingent' leisure experience (Rojek, 1993, p. 216).

In such an analysis, tourism essentially becomes a mass phenomenon, predicated on ontological universal categories with sharply dichotomous conceptions – authentic/inauthentic, for example – utilized to account for the dynamic processes, interrelations and the inherent divergences of tourism experiences. However, as Cohen acknowledges, authenticity does not have an 'objective quality', but is attributed by 'moderns' to the world 'out there', and thus is a socially constructed concept with a connotation that is not given but 'negotiable' (Cohen, 1988).

The theorization of tourism therefore, like that of leisure[1], not only needs to recognize the interrelation of time, the site and the activities provided for at the tourist destination. It also requires a fundamental

---

1 See, for example, Wearing and Wearing (1988) for a definition of leisure as experience. The term is used here to encompass tourist experiences which are considered to be a subgroup of leisure experience, leisure theory being the underlying theoretical contributor to the sociological analysis of tourism (Cohen, 1995).

focus on subjective experience itself in providing for the significance of the tourist experience that, while not being divorced from its sociological contextualization, allows for the elaboration upon the role of individual tourists themselves in the active construction of the 'tourist experience'. Thereby, identifying the relational complex of the individual, the individual's social groups, their travel experience and the interrelating elements that sustain the experience.

Tourism as experience, involving complex and often subtle interactions between the tourist, the site and the host community, questions analyses predicated on the conceptualization of the tourist as 'wander', 'gazer' and 'escaper' as is common in the tourism literature. As the tour group, the host community and the natural environment, to varying degrees, are interdependent components of any tourist experience, there is a need to move beyond these typologies towards a more analytically flexible conceptualization that allows for the exploration of the assumptions implicit in the 'tourist gaze', the tourist 'destination', the marketing 'image', the 'visit', in suggesting other modes of analysis that may better account for the significant range and diversity of tourist experiences. However, this needs to be achieved through conceptual frameworks that provide links to existing research. In short, this chapter, in positing experience as a nodal point, attempts to open a space for the elaboration of the conceptual, theoretical and practical differences and conjunctions between specific tourism forms, thus contributing to the movement towards an understanding and elaboration of the potential benefits of particular tourism experiences. The goals of ecotourism are to provide ecologically sound travel experiences that contribute to the natural, economic, social and cultural environments.

The provision of certain forms of alternative tourism services are beginning to play an important role in local communities, particularly in the shift away from a dependence on extractive industries. A more complete understanding of the nexus of relations between the individual tourist, including motivations and expectations surrounding and following an experience, and the interaction with the local destination community places us in a position to meet diversified needs and expectations, which may further enhance our ability to understand cross-cultural interaction.

Alternative forms of tourism – such as ecotourism – are now being considered seriously as a significant area of tourism experience (Holden, 1984; Cohen, 1987, 1995; Vir Singh *et al.*, 1989; Pleumarom, 1990; Smith and Eadington, 1992; Weiler and Hall, 1992). However, a number of authors (Butler, 1992; Cohen, 1995) have attempted to incorporate it into the analysis of 'mass tourism' thus subordinating it to mainstream tourism research. Questions thus arise as to the value of analysing alternative tourism in terms of a separate construct, independent variable or different paradigm. A major obstacle in specifying an alternative form of tourism, and the experiences that may be aligned to it, is the surrounding ambiguity in the perceptions and conceptualization of what defines it (Smith and Eadington, 1992). A significant and often raised question in this respect is to what extent has the specificity of alternative tourism types been disavowed through the inclusion of a range of experiences that may not relate to the initial conceptualization and the ethos that underpins it. In response, Butler (1992) – in relation to ecotourism – stated that a general understanding must be arrived at, suggesting that ecotourism is not just an activity but a philosophy, and that this philosophy must be modelled on a sustainable approach to the environment if the specificity of the experience is also to be sustained. This chapter attempts to contribute to the movement towards a more comprehensive theoretical under-standing, and hence provision of, these types of experience. It does so by positing a conjunction of interrelating elements that often contribute to alternative tourism experiences – ecotourism, volunteer-ism and serious leisure – which provide a wider explanation of the tourism experience (Fig. 13.1).

It is not the purpose of this chapter to focus on the relative dualism of positive or negative impacts of various tourism forms. Its focus is, instead, on developing an approach that recognizes the interdepen-dence of the tourism experience, culture and ecology, and explores ways of enhancing the understanding of the experience, and seeking means of researching that will provide a better understanding of tourist experiences by introducing additional conceptual ideas. In differen-tiating the specificity of alternative forms of tourism – specifically here, ecotourism – it will be argued that the conceptual basis underlying the analysis of tourism must significantly include experience, particularly as demonstrated in the social science literature (Wearing and Wearing, 1988).

Ecotourism

Ceballos-Lascuráin is widely acknowledged as having first coined the term ecotourism in 1981. He used the word in 1983 in discussions as president of PRONATURA, a conservation non-government organiza-tion and as director general of SEDUE, the Mexican Ministry of Urban Development and Ecology. At the time, he was lobbying for the conservation of rainforest areas in the Mexican state of Chiapas. One of the arguments he used for maintaining the integrity of the forests was the promotion of ecological tourism in the region, emphasizing that ecotourism could become a very important tool for conservation.

The first appearance of the word in the written form was in the

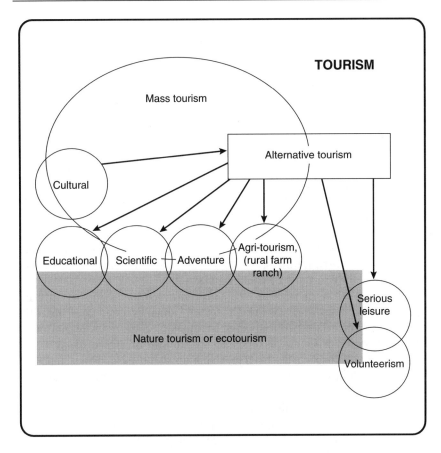

Fig. 13.1. A conceptual schema of alternative tourism and its relationship to ecotourism, serious leisure and volunteering.

March–April 1984 edition of *American Birds,* in an advertisement for a tourist operation initiated by Ceballos-Lascuráin. His definition first appeared in the literature in 1987 in a paper entitled 'The future of ecotourismo' which was reprinted in the *Mexico Journal* of 27 January 1988 (Ceballos-Lascuráin, personal communication) and this initial definition was expanded upon by Boo:

> We may define ecological tourism or ecotourism as that tourism that involves travelling to relatively undisturbed or uncontaminated natural areas with the specific object of studying, admiring and enjoying the scenery and its wild plants and animals, as well as any existing cultural aspects (both past and present) found in these areas. Ecological tourism implies a scientific, aesthetic or philosophical approach, although the ecological tourist is not required to be a professional scientist, artist or philosopher. The main point is that the person that practices ecotourism

has the opportunity of immersing him or herself in nature in a way that
most people cannot enjoy in their routine, urban existences.

(Boo, 1990, p. 10).

A number of important basic ecotourism concepts have emerged in
recent years. The notion of movement or travel from one location to
another is obviously a fundamental component. This travel should be
restricted to relatively undisturbed or protected natural areas, as
ecotourism focuses on the promotion of nature (O'Neill, 1991). Such
natural areas offer the 'best guarantee for encountering sustained
natural features and attractions' (Ceballos-Lascuráin, 1990, p. 2). Thus
in 'travel[ing] to unspoilt natural environments . . . the travel has to be
for the specific purpose of experiencing the natural environment'
(Jenner and Smith, 1991, p. 2). Ecotourism would thus seem to exclude
such activities as business travel, travel to cities, conventional beach
holidays and sporting holidays, where the experience is not focused on
the natural environment of the area visited.

The definition of ecotourism, after much discussion at international conferences and in the literature[2], has evolved significantly,
with conservationists and responsible tourism operators now believing
that conservation is an essential component of ecotourism. As a
segment of the tourism industry, it has emerged as a direct result of
'increasing global concern for disappearing cultures and ecosystems'
(Kutay, 1990, p. 34), with The Ecotourism Society in the US describing
ecotourism as 'responsible travel that conserves natural environments
and sustains the well-being of local people' (The Ecotourism Society,
1992, p. 1). Fundamentally, the central concept revolves around
people experiencing natural areas and their respective local communities first-hand, thus the potential exists that they will more likely be
concerned with preserving them (O'Neill, 1991). Mass tourism, on the
other hand, historically errs towards 'inappropriate tourism development . . . and can degrade a protected area and have unanticipated
economic, social or environmental effects on the surrounding lands'
(Ceballos-Lascuráin, 1990, p. 1).

Ceballos-Lascuráin (1990, p. 1) suggests that 'the pressures of
urban living encourage people to seek solitude with nature' and
therefore, 'the numbers of visitors to national parks and other protected
areas continue to rise'. Ecotourism is considered to be nature
dependent and some argue it should involve active nature appreciation, education or interpretation (for a general overview of definitions
see Mieczkowski, 1995). This educational role refers not only to the
tourists themselves but also to industry operators and local commu-

2 Hvenegaard (1994); The United Nations Conference of Environment and Development, Earth
  Summit; The International Union for Conservation of Nature and Natural Resources; IV
  World Congress on National Parks and Protected Areas.

nities. As Swanson (1992, p. 3) recognizes: 'Most ecotourists expect discovery and enlightenment from their ecotourism experience' and this is brought about by such factors as communication, culture, knowledge and information, which have to be conveyed effectively to become educative. Significantly, the last sentence of Ceballos-Lascuráin's definition was omitted by Boo and by others who have since quoted him. It reads:

> This person will eventually acquire a consciousness and knowledge of the natural environment together with its cultural aspects, that will convert him [sic] into somebody keenly involved in conservation issues.
>
> (Ceballos-Lascuráin, personal communication)

By their active participation in the experience, ecotourists may be able to be educated to appreciate the importance of natural and cultural conservation. 'The need to disseminate information to tourists on appropriate behaviour in fragile social and ecological settings' is being recognized increasingly as the responsibility of industry operators (Blangy and Epler-Wood, 1992, p. 1); ecotourism can also provide local people with the opportunity to learn about and use the area and its attractions (Wallace, 1992). It may also stimulate renewed appreciation of the 'unique value of their own cultural traditions' as a result of the interest shown by tourists (Kutay, 1990, p. 40).

Other activities occurring in natural environments, such as hunting and white water rafting, are more difficult to locate within this context and require further evaluation before consideration. Ecotourists generally express a strong desire to learn about nature on their trips (Eagles *et al.*, 1992) hence some authors put greater emphasis on nature appreciation, education and interpretation, and the explanation of 'concepts, meanings and inter-relationships of natural phenomena' (McNeely and Thorsell, 1989, p. 37). Ecotourism also seeks to generate revenue while, at the same time, protecting vulnerable natural resources (O'Neill, 1991, p. 25; Wheeler, 1992).

Additionally, it is believed that ecotourism will 'contribute to a sustainable future' (O'Neill, 1991, p. 25) in the form of equitable economic returns. It is intended that the ecotourist who is affected by the experience will want to ensure that the environments visited are sufficiently maintained for the benefit of others. In this way 'ecotourism has the potential to foster conservation of natural resources by increasing the awareness in people of the importance of the natural resources' (Swanson, 1992, p. 2), and for this reason the notion of conservation must be included in a definition of ecotourism. Ecotourism therefore 'promotes a greater understanding and respect of cultures, heritage and the natural environment – and people usually protect what they respect' (Richardson, 1991, p. 244).

The profile of an ecotourist is said to differ in matters of degree and purpose from the profile of an average conventional tourist. Ecotourists are 'relatively affluent, well educated, mature and environmentally-focused' (Williams, 1990, p. 85). Also, according to Eagles *et al.*, 'Ecotourists are interested in seeing as much of their money spent on conservation as possible' and they will pay a little extra for a more acceptable product (Eagles *et al.*, 1992, p. 1). Some common characteristics in the varying definitions of ecotourists do exist, such as higher income levels, tertiary education, environmental concern and awareness, the desire to travel in small groups and the desire to learn about nature (Kerr, 1991; Eagles *et al.*, 1992). Generally, the scale of ecotourism differs from that of conventional tourism, with most ecotourism operators averaging fewer than 300 clients per year (Ingram and Durst, 1989), rather than an equivalent number per day, or per week, which is the case for some larger conventional tour operators. Additionally, Palacio and McCool (1997), using a benefit segmentation approach based on multivariate analysis, found that ecotourists differed from other tourist segments in terms of socio-demographic and trip characteristics, but still had similar levels of activity participation.

This demonstrates that specific nature-based experiences within the Western market economy may be delicately balanced and difficult to differentiate. For example, the intrinsic pleasure that comes from being closer to nature, focusing on the education/interpretation elements rather then equipment-based activities such as rafting, and contributing in some way to conservation, does not necessarily equate with ecotourism (Williams, 1990; Butler, 1992; Pigram 1992; Mieczkowski, 1995). Boo (1990) uses the term 'nature tourism' synonymously with ecotourism. However, it is argued here that the terminology is not so easily transposable, because not all nature tourism endeavours to preserve natural ecosystems, whereas a fundamental defining principle of ecotourism is this very issue. In addition to this, some forms of volunteering can be considered ecotourism, but the focus of volunteering is not necessarily on the natural environment. The establishment of a conceptual framework that explores these interrelations may help clarify the commonalities between the two and their relationship with mass tourism (see Fig. 13.1).

The natural environment is central to ecotourism, which has a focus on biological and physical features. The conservation of natural areas and sustainable resource management is therefore essential to the planning, development and management of ecotourism. Valentine (1991a) draws attention to the 'two-way interaction' between ecotourism and the environment upon which it depends, by suggesting that one characteristic of ecotourism is that it is both contributory to conservation as well as enjoyment of nature, thus merging these two dimensions. Add to this the ideas inherent to the volunteer tourist, that is, a primary motivation for travel related to engagement and involvement with activities that contribute to the social, economic and physical environments while furthering knowledge and awareness of these. Therefore an essential feature of ecotourism, and by association volunteer tourism, is sustainability. The Bruntland Report introduced the concept of sustainable development, defining it as: 'development that meets the needs of the present without compromising the ability of future generations to meet their own needs' (Mieczkowski, 1995, p. 457). Similarly, the World Tourism Organization guidelines concluded that:

> Sustainable tourism can only take place if carrying capacities for key tourism sites are conducted and then rigorously implemented through a system of effective planning and operating controls. These studies and regulations will constitute the cornerstones of long term, local tourism management strategies and plans . . . it also requires acceptance of the concepts of validity and cooperation in its implementation from the tourism private sector, as well as the participation of local communities and tourists themselves.
>
> (World Tourism Organization, 1990, p. 47)

Volunteer tourism appears to fit into the general construction of sustainability and ecotourism, having minimal impacts, being small scale and requiring little specialized infrastructure and therefore not contributing to damaging the environment on which ecotourism (and all forms of tourism) depends.

Volunteering for serious leisure

The development of organizational volunteering, and specifically international volunteering, has occurred without it having been considered as a form of tourism. The modern phenomenon of travelling overseas as a volunteer appears to have begun in about 1915 (Gillette, 1968; Clark, 1978; Australian Volunteers Abroad, 1989; Beigbeder, 1991, pp. 109–110; Darby, 1994) and has involved a variety of organizations and groups throughout the world, with Australian Volunteers Abroad operating in Australia and similar types of organizations (such as the Peace Corps USA, Voluntary Service Abroad NZ) operating in other countries.

The Organization for Economic Cooperation and Development (OECD, 1994) estimated that in 1990 over 33,000 overseas volunteers were involved with projects, primarily in developing countries. The investment in over 18,000 volunteers for 1986 was US$389 million, a growth of 400% since 1976, according to OECD figures (Beigbeder, 1991, p. 103).

International volunteerism generally involves some form of travel and, as this brief outline will demonstrate, the underlying concepts comprising specific forms of alternative tourism and organizational volunteering overlap to a substantial degree, thus providing for a more specific form of ecotourism which falls outside the context of mass tourism and within a conceptualization that involves altruistically motivated travel. Significantly, there are a number of studies (Dickson, 1976; Clark, 1978; Darby, 1994) that focus on the range of volunteer programmes for the 17–25-year-old age group, which provides a perspective that allows for elaboration on the specificity of the conjunction between volunteer and ecotourist experiences (for a detailed account of volunteerism, see Darby, 1994).

It is generally agreed that the volunteer is one who offers service, time and skills to benefit others (Beigbeder, 1991, p. 109), provides voluntary personal aid while living in developing communities (Clark, 1978), and gains mutual learning, friendship and adventurousness (Gillette, 1968). Definitions of volunteers necessarily include the recognition that they are those who provide assistance, or unpaid service, usually for the benefit of the community (Australian Bureau of Statistics, 1986). This may be through formal involvement as a volunteer in an organization, or independently as an individual. For the purposes of this chapter, the concept of volunteering is defined as an action perceived as freely chosen, without financial gain, and generally aimed at helping others (Van Til, 1979; Stebbins, 1982, 1992). There have been suggestions that there are enough developed nations already working in developing countries (Chavalier, 1993) and increasing this level through alternative tourist activity is not going to help resolve local problems. One fundamental danger is that volunteers can reiterate the ethos of the 'expert', thus promoting deference in the local community to outside knowledge, therefore contributing to the curtailment of self-sufficiency.

A tourist experience that allows for the opportunity to live and work with people of other cultures may provide a type of alternative tourism that is able to meet effectively some of the concerns raised by destination communities about the impacts of tourism. Younger tourists are possibly more likely to use the knowledge gained from their volunteer tourism experiences to influence other areas of their lives, such as the choice and development of career paths, particularly if these experiences allow for inclusiveness of issues and impacts that relate to natural environments and destination communities.

Research in the area of volunteerism has shown that people working and living together on jobs of social significance often result in facilitating understanding and friendships that are more important to the participants than the physical construction itself (Clark, 1978, p. 13). Whatever the genesis of the programme, it is the personal encounter between the volunteer and the community that is essential (Clark, 1978, p. 4). Additionally, research on international volunteer organizations has demonstrated an orientation towards reviewing the issues around personal development. The links between volunteering and ecotourism can possibly be made more apparent when viewed as leisure experience, and the research on personal development and international development volunteer programmes initially provides some background for positing such a conjunction in alternative tourism experiences.

In reviewing the international volunteering literature[3], there is a focus on personal development and the role of learning in changing or influencing the self, which introduces to the alternative tourism experience issues relating to self-identity and change. It is proposed that the concept of international volunteering, as an element within the context of alternative tourism experience, highlights learning as a central element of the interaction with the destination culture and environment.

The research of Weinmann (1983, p. 16) and Carlson (1991), in considering exposure to a new culture, found personal development related to: greater tolerance, a more compassionate understanding of other people and their individual differences and the gaining of a more global perspective and insight into new values, beliefs and ways of life. Learning components within this exchange included academic learning, the development of personal knowledge, self-confidence, independence, cultural awareness and social abilities.

Stitsworth (1987) similarly indicated that participants, as part of a group for 6 weeks, contributed to their own personal growth and development while gaining a better understanding of the role of developed countries, particularly the issues surrounding development in experiencing another culture. 'The AFS Impact Study: 1986' (American Field Service, 1986) of over 1000 high-school students found that participants' greatest amount of positive change was in

---

3 The initial studies considered the more widely researched area of personal development and the university student, or college experience (Terenzini and Wright, 1987; Kuh *et al.*, 1988; Karen, 1990), as well as personal development through culture shock (Weinmann, 1983). These studies were followed by research on university student study abroad (Kauffmann and Kuh, 1984; Carlson, 1991), youth programmes and national service (Thomas, 1971; United Nations Department of Economic and Social Affairs, 1975), and international youth exchange (Stitsworth, 1987). Studies of international development experience include, specifically, youth-based Canadian Crossroads International and Operation Raleigh USA, as well as government-based volunteer programmes – US Peace Corps (Winslow, 1977; United States Peace Corps, 1980, 1989) and Volunteer Service Overseas (Clark, 1978).

awareness and appreciation of the host country and its culture. In this way, the studies of volunteering provide an added dimension to the examination of alternative tourism experiences.

Volunteering and serious leisure

The time contributed to participation in international volunteering can be considered serious leisure (Stebbins, 1982, 1992; Henderson, 1984) and many organizations rely on this 'free' time in order to operate (Bishop and Hogett, 1986). It is evident that the travel component of volunteerism in these alternative tourism experiences is an essential component of the appeal of organizations operating in developing countries. Rather than travelling simply as a 'tourist' the volunteer may regard travel as an activity for the stimulation and development of character. The appeal of travelling with a purpose, working with communities in developing countries and spending time to assist in saving natural environments, provides a strong platform for expanding the conceptualization of tourist experience.

Stebbins (1992), in defining 'serious leisure', uses the fields of amateurism, hobbyist and volunteering to encompass the range of specific characteristics. Similarly, Parker (1992) links 'serious leisure' to a range of activities such as volunteering, suggesting that these activities fundamentally affect individual values. Two distinguishing features of volunteering identified by Stebbins that may contribute to our understanding of alternative tourism experiences – particularly in relation to ecotourism – are that volunteers are usually motivated by a sense of altruism, and that they are often delegated tasks to perform, making them a 'special class of helper in someone else's occupational world' (Floro, 1978 in Stebbins, 1982).

Similarly, Stebbins (1982, p. 257, 1992, p. 18) in identifying a number of components that contribute to volunteerism (including demonstrated perseverance; significant personal effort based on special knowledge, training or skill; durable benefits relating to self-actualization, self-enrichment, recreation or renewal of self, feelings of accomplishment, enhancement of self-image, self-expression, social interaction and belongingness; lasting physical products of the activity; and a unique ethos demonstrating a subculture with intrinsic beliefs, values and norms) provides significant overlapping qualities between some alternative tourists and volunteerism.

Significantly, research indicates that some volunteers do not perceive themselves as being 'at leisure', but rather involved in a sense of 'good citizenship concern for the community' (Stebbins, 1982, 1992; Parker, 1992). The addition of volunteering to the analysis of an alternative tourism experience enables us to differentiate it from forms of mass tourism that are inclined towards a specific focus on relaxation and excitement. This is not to deny that relaxation and excitement are components of alternative tourism experiences, but allows for volunteering as a significant differentiating component.

The examination of motivation is significant in linking volunteer experience, serious leisure and ecotourism forms. Neulinger (1982, p. 30) and Henderson (1984) both note that volunteerism and leisure fulfil higher-level needs, such as self-esteem, belonging and self-actualization. In addition Stebbins (1982, 1992), in examining 'serious leisure', sees 'career volunteering' as a specific example. In his consideration of 'serious leisure', Stebbins points out that it is an important part of people's lives in its relation to personal fulfilment, identity enhancement and self-expression (1982, p. 253).

The research on volunteerism which focuses on individual motivation (Phillips, 1982; Allen and Rushton, 1983; Rohs, 1986; Independent Sector, 1990; Luks and Payne, 1991; Darby, 1994) acknowledges that volunteers seek to gain considerable personal benefits from their endeavours, including self-satisfaction and social and personal well-being (Henderson, 1981, 1984; Stebbins, 1982, 1992; Frank, 1992). Motivations, such as being useful (Independent Sector, 1990), altruism and being needed (Beigbeder, 1991, p. 106), personal satisfaction and being cared for by the organization (Tihanyi, 1991) are all considered important by the volunteers. Alternative tourist experiences could be studied within this rubric, as a fundamental motivating element for the participant is the desire to assist communities in developing countries.

The consideration of serious leisure with its component of volunteering thus becomes an element that provides a significant broadening of the analysis of alternative tourism experiences[4]. The early literature that attempted to clarify the concept of leisure (Wearing and Wearing, 1988) does so without adequately considering the relationship between leisure and natural environments, focusing instead on the ideas of non-work time and individual activity. It is this limitation that serves to obscure elements of leisure, such as volunteerism. A more inclusive approach beyond the simple paradigm of work/non-work serves to question the theoretical construction of leisure as individually conceived, arguing instead that it should be built around the micro-social dynamic exchanges that are a part of the participant's experiences. Such an approach allows incorporating the

4 The leisure profession and the consideration of available time for travel (Bishop and Hogett, 1986); serving communities through leisure (Neulinger, 1982; Henderson, 1984); the provision of purpose for leisure (Roberts, 1981, p. 61; Stebbins, 1992, p. 19); the high correlation between individual description of their volunteer efforts and their perception of leisure (Henderson, 1981); the degree of involvement and its correlation to commitment and more satisfying and rewarding experiences (McIntyre, 1994).

interaction of cultural or social influences, such as those between the host community, the participant and the site. Budowski (in Valentine, 1991b) draws attention to the two-way interaction between ecotourists and the environment upon which their experience depends, in that the environment consists, in part, of the dynamic social exchange, which establishes much of the experience of the natural environment. What is at issue here is, fundamentally, the dynamic social exchange between and within social groups (the host-community and the tour group) which forms the basis of the participants' experience and the way they construct their ideas of the experience.

The ideas developed here may be applied to a range of areas of tourism research, for example the characteristics that differentiate ecotourists, through an analysis of tourist motivation. In examining demographic and psychographic characteristics, the needs of ecotourists, the images and attitudes ecotourists ascribe to a destination, and the influence of social, cultural and physical environments may be determined. With a wider frame of reference informed by the areas of serious leisure and volunteering, we may be able to address the managerial implications for ecotourism operators. By understanding the nature of the target market, ecotourism operators can alter marketing mix components according to the needs of an environmentally conscious consumer. One way we can identify particular forms and styles of tourism is through an examination of the factors that motivate tourists. Motivation is aroused when individuals think of certain activities that are potentially satisfaction producing. Since people act to satisfy their needs, motivation is thought to be the ultimate driving force that governs travel behaviour.

Therefore, tourists' motivation could be informed by the literature on serious leisure and volunteering. Motivational research in tourism is based on the early works of Dann (1981) who identified that 'push' and 'pull' factors are central in motivating tourists. Push motives are internal to the individual, while pull motives are aroused by the destination. Push factors establish the desire for travel, and pull factors explain actual destination choice (Bello and Etzel, 1985). Crompton (1979) modified the push/pull model in identifying the tourist's desire for pleasure and the desire for a break from routine. He identified nine motives in determining causal factors resulting in a tourist's departure: push factors are motives concerned with the social and psychological status of the individual, while pull factors, on the other hand, are 'motives aroused by the destination rather than emerging exclusively from the traveller himself' (Crompton, 1979, p. 410).

Crompton (1979) conceptualized motives as being located along a disequilibrium continuum. When disequilibrium arises due to a feeling of dissatisfaction in relation to one or more push factors, it can be rectified by a break in routine, thus restoring homeostasis (equilibrium) – that is, through travel (Uysal and Hagan, 1993). For Crompton (1979) the destination site is merely a medium through which motives are satisfied. Significantly, Iso-Ahola (1983) found that the individual possessed an inclination to travel primarily for intrinsic rewards. Intrinsically motivated activities are engaged in for their own sake, rather than any external remuneration. The connection between intrinsic motivations and push and pull factors was made by McGehee *et al.* (1996), who recognized that most of the push factors are intrinsic motivators. It is important here to note that satisfaction for the ecotourist may come not only from the experience itself but from the external reward of having promoted environmentally sound travel and having made a contribution to the destination region in this way. Serious leisure which provides sound information on intrinsic motivation is able to better inform us about motivation.

A tourist motivation framework developed by Pearce (Pearce, 1988; Moscardo and Pearce, 1986 in Pearce, 1993) and based on Maslow's hierarchy of needs, provides an expansive framework to identify the needs that a tourist is fulfilling when travelling. A mainstream tourist is more concerned with fulfilling lower-level needs of relationship, stimulation and relaxation, whereas the ecotourist is more concerned with development and fulfilment, which includes self-education. If the focus of ecotourism is nature-based activity, often intrinsically aroused, with a degree of education and interpretation of the natural environment, it stands to reason that ecotourists are more focused on the self-actualization and higher-level needs than those identified at the base of Maslow's hierarchy. As Mayo and Jarvis (1981) note, intellectual needs can, in some instances, take precedence over some lower-order needs. For example 'curiosity, exploration, the desire to learn, the desire to understand – these are some times pursued even at great cost to the individual's safety' (p. 155).

A study conducted by Kretchman and Eagles (1990) also found that the motivations of an ecotourist and those of the general tourist differed in relation to intrinsic versus extrinsic motivations for travel. The study found that the general tourist, in most cases, liked to feel at home when away from home. The results from this study align strongly with the 'push' and 'pull' factors that influence tourist motivation. This is not to say that 'pull' factors alone provide enough stimulation for a trip departure, because despite the fact that 'pull' factors are paramount for ecotourists, push factors still do (to varying degrees) influence the departure decision. The application of Cromp-ton's (1979) theory illustrates that 'pull' factors are necessarily ranked higher for ecotourists than for mainstream tourists, based on their psychographic characteristics.

However, accurately gauging the motivations of ecotourists is difficult. To begin with, defining a tourist's motivations using the push and pull model is more complex when applied to a specific market niche such as ecotourists, rather than mainstream travellers. The internal push motives of discovery, enlightenment and personal growth are important to ecotourists, but features of a natural destination are more than simply pull motives to this group, for ecotourists see physical locations as motivation in themselves. To describe this as a 'pull' phenomenon is to overlook the importance of the natural environment as a motivator (Eagles, 1991).

The goals of ecotourism are to provide ecologically sound travel experiences that contribute to the natural, economic, social and cultural environments. The provision of tourism services is becoming central to local communities, particularly in a shift away from the dependence on extractive industries. A combination of ecotourist needs and the image they have of the destination pre-departure, creates expectations that an ecotourist assumes will be satisfied. By understanding ecotourist motivations, the local community will be in a better position to meet these needs and expectations.

The tailoring of products using motivational research is important in any sector of tourism. Recognizing that motives of ecotourists differ is essential for tourism managers. Due to reduced numbers of tourists, the likelihood of reduced impacts and interest in an educative component, roles and rules for ecotourists may be redefined and shaped about the needs this market niche possesses, resulting in higher rates of satisfaction.

Research on visitor expectations was used in the ecologically sustainable management of whale shark tourism in Queensland. Swayed respondents felt that regulations allowed divers to swim too near to whale sharks. Management used this research to modify guidelines, increasing the distance, which enhanced protection of the species, while still offering a satisfying experience for ecotourists (Birtles *et al.*, 1995). This demonstrates a differing managerial response to the market, based on its unique needs and characteristics.

Motivation alone exemplifies differences between ecotourists and mainstream tourists and the way the ideas of serious leisure and volunteering can help to expand this area; other areas of tourism research could also be explored to expand our understanding of tourism behaviour.

Time out for serious fun

Alternative tourism experiences, when contextualized in relation to the differential elements of volunteerism, serious leisure and ecotourism, illustrate the centrality of the interactions that take place within the destination area in conjunction with the exploration of personal identity and development through enabling the tourist to contribute to the community development of local area, often in specific relation to protected areas. This has significant implications in relation to tourism research and future policy, as it enables researchers to be able to examine protected areas, local communities and (eco)tourism as socially constructed institutions, and to draw on wider social constructs within theory, such as 'serious leisure', rather than simplifying and overgeneralizing the experience. This will provide policies with a more specific understanding of the differing types of tourist experiences, which may redirect resources in terms of funds being provided for tourist development in a more diverse way than just looking at economic return.

If we are able to better understand alternative tourism experiences, such as ecotourism, and are able to come to more specific understandings of these experiences (by, for example, better analysis of what motivates the tourists), then both tourism operator and local community will be better able to understand tourists and the experiences that they seek.

Kenny (1994) notes that the dominant characteristics of community development are participation in decision-making, acceptance of individual differences and the transference of skills that are held, but not controlled, by professionals. Community development involves multisector and multi-issue approaches to the whole and sees the interrelations between the parts. In this way it is a systemic (looking at the operations of the overall social system as a whole) rather than systematic (looking at parts sequentially and separately) approach, involving the breaking down of the barriers to cooperation, understanding the wider implications of issues, linking people together on issue-based actions, adopting a task orientation, exchanging knowledge and skill, and the constant renewal and consolidation of the relationship whereby support is maintained, trust continued, realistic tasks set and achieved and those involved rewarded. The perspective encapsulated and understood through serious leisure and volunteering is quite different from that of the tourism industry as a whole, which is predominantly focused on a profit ethos. Instead, these concepts place far more importance on accessing the information networks of people and, in particular, groups forming around particular issues. Alternative tourism experiences, such as ecotourism, when differentially analysed in terms of their volunteering and serious leisure components, actively facilitate the type of interaction and exchange identified here, thus significantly shifting the analysis of tourism research, and the provision of tourist experiences, into a realm that enables the elaboration of the specificity of component elements that sustain particular touristic experiences.

References

Allen, N.J. and Rushton, J. (1983) Personality characteristics of community health volunteers: a review. *Journal of Voluntary Action Research* 12(1), 36–49.

American Field Service (1986) *The AFS Impact Study: Final Report*. American Field Service, Washington, DC.

Australian Bureau of Statistics (1986) *Volunteering in NSW*. Australian Government Publishing Service, Canberra.

Australian Volunteers Abroad (1989) *Australian Volunteers Abroad: 25 Years Working for the World*. Australian Government Publishing Service, Canberra.

Beigbeder, Y. (1991) *The Role and Status of International Humanitarian Volunteers and Organizations*. Martinus Nijhoff, London.

Bello, D.C. and Etzel, M.J. (1985) The role of novelty in the pleasure travel experience. *Journal of Travel Research* 24(1), 20–26.

Birtles, A., Cahill, M., Valentine, P. and Davis, D. (1995) Incorporating research on visitor experiences into ecologically sustainable management of whale shark tourism. In: Richins, H., Richardson, J. and Crabtree, A. (eds) *Ecotourism and Nature-Based Tourism: Taking the Next Steps*. Proceedings of The Ecotourism Association of Australia National Conference, Alice Springs.

Bishop, J. and Hogett, P. (1986) *Organising Around Enthusiasms – Mutual Aid in Leisure*. Comedia, London.

Blangy, S. and Epler-Wood, M. (1992) *Developing and Implementing Ecotourism Guidelines for Wild Lands and Neighbouring Communities*. The Ecotourism Society, Vermont, USA.

Boo, E. (1990) *Ecotourism: the Potentials and Pitfalls*. World Wide Fund For Nature, Washington, DC.

Butler, J.R. (1992) Ecotourism: its changing face and evolving philosophy. Paper presented at the International Union for Conservation of Nature and Natural Resources (IUCN), IVth World Congress on National Parks and Protected Areas, Caracas, Venezuela, 10–12 February.

Carlson, J.S. (1991) *Study Abroad: the Experience of American Undergraduates in Western Europe and the United States*. Council of International Educational Exchange, New York.

Ceballos-Lascuráin, H. (1990) Tourism, ecotourism and protected areas. Paper presented at the 34th Working Session of the Commission of National Parks and Protected Areas, Perth, Australia, 26–27 November.

Chavalier, C. (1993) Letter to the Editor, *The Times* 7th December.

Clark, K. (1978) *The Two-way Street – a Survey of Volunteer Service Abroad*. New Zealand Council for Educational Research, Wellington.

Cohen, E. (1987) Alternative tourism – a critique. *Tourism Recreation Research* 12(2), 13–18.

Cohen, E. (1988) Authenticity and commoditization in tourism. *Annals of Tourism Research* 15, 371–386.

Cohen, E. (1995) Contemporary tourism – trends and challenges: sustainable authenticity or contrived post-modernity? In: Butler, R.W. and Pearce, D.

(eds) *Change in Tourism: People, Places and Processes*. Routledge, London, pp. 12–29.

Cohen, S. and Taylor, L. (1976) *Escape Attempts*. Penguin, Harmondsworth.

Crompton, J.L. (1979) Motivations for pleasure vacations. *Annals of Tourism Research* 3(1), 408–424.

Dann, G. (1981) Tourist motivation: an appraisal. *Annals of Tourism Research* 8, 187–219.

Darby, M. (1994) International development and youth challenge: personal development through a volunteer experience. Master of Arts (Leisure Studies) Thesis, School of Leisure and Tourism Studies, University of Technology, Sydney.

Dickson, A. (1976) *A Chance to Serve*. Dennis Dobson, London.

Eagles, P.F. (1991) The motivation of Canadian ecotourists. In: Weller, B. (ed.) *Ecotourism Incorporating the Global Classroom*. Bureau of Tourism Research, Canberra, pp. 12–17.

Eagles, P.F.J., Ballantine, J.L. and Fennell, D.A. (1992) Marketing to the ecotourist: case studies from Kenya and Costa Rica. Paper presented at International Union for Conservation of Nature and Natural Resources (IUCN) IVth World Congress on National Parks and Protected Areas, Caracas, Venezuela, 10–12 February.

Frank, D. (1992) Volunteers . . . a force to be reckoned with! *Australian Journal of Leisure and Recreation* 2(3), 33–39.

Gillette, A. (1968) *One Million Volunteers*. Pelican (Penguin), Ringwood, Victoria.

Henderson, K.A. (1981) Motivations and perceptions of volunteerism as a leisure activity. *Journal of Leisure Research* 13(3), 260–274.

Henderson, K.A. (1984) Volunteerism as leisure. *Journal of Voluntary Action Research* 13(1), 55–63.

Holden, P. (ed.) (1984) *Alternative Tourism: Report on the Workshop on Alternative Tourism with a Focus on Asia*. Ecumenical Coalition on Third World Tourism, Bangkok.

Hvenegaard, G. (1994) Ecotourism: a status report and conceptual framework. *The Journal of Tourism Studies* 5(2).

Independent Sector (1990) *Giving and Volunteering in the United States*. Independent Sector, Washington.

Ingram, D. and Durst, P. (1989) Nature-oriented tour operators: travel to developing countries. *Journal of Travel Research* Fall, 11–15.

Iso-Ahola, S.E. (1983) *Towards a Social Psychology of Leisure and Recreation*. Wm. C. Brown Company, Dubuque, Iowa.

Jenner, P. and Smith, C. (1991) *The Tourism Industry and the Environment*. Condor, The Economist Intelligence Unit Special Report No. 2453, London.

Karen, C.S. (1990) Personal development and the pursuit of higher education. Paper presented at Annual Meeting of American Educational Research Association, Boston, 16–20 April.

Kauffmann, N.L. and Kuh, G.D. (1984) The impact of study abroad on personal development of college students. Paper presented at the American Educational Research Association, New Orleans, 4–7 April.

Kenny, S. (1994) *Developing Communities for the Future: Community Development in Australia*. Thomas Nelson, Australia.

Kerr, J. (1991) Making dollars and sense out of ecotourism/nature tourism. In: Weiler, B. (ed.) *Ecotourism Incorporating the Global Classroom*. Bureau of Tourism Research, Canberra.

Kretchman, J. and Eagles, P. (1990) An analysis of the motives of ecotourists in comparison to the general Canadian population. *Society and Leisure* 13(2), 499–508.

Kuh, G.D., Krehbiel, L.E. and MacKay, K. (1988) *Personal Development and the College Student Experience: a Review of the Literature*. New Jersey Department of Higher Education, New Jersey.

Kutay, K. (1990) Ecotourism: travel's new wave. *Vis a Vis* July, 4–80.

Luks, A. and Payne, P. (1991) *The Healing Power of Doing Good*. Fawcett Columbine, New York.

MacCannell, D. (1976) *The Tourist: a New Theory of the Leisure Class*. Macmillan, London.

Mayo, E. and Jarvis, L. (1981) *The Psychology of Leisure Travel*. CBI, Boston.

McGehee, N.G., Loker-Murphy, L. and Uysat, M. (1996) The Australian international travel market: motivations from a gendered perspective. *Journal of Tourism Studies* 7(1), 45–57.

McIntyre, N. (1994) The concept of 'involvement' in recreation research. In: Mercer, D. (ed.) *New Viewpoints in Australian Outdoor Recreation Research and Planning*. Hepper Marriot, Melbourne.

McNeely, J.A. and Thorsell, J. (1989) *Jungles, Mountains and Islands: How Tourism can Help Conserve Natural Heritage*. International Union For Conservation of Nature and Natural Resources (IUCN), Switzerland.

Mieczkowski, Z. (1995) *Environmental Issues of Tourism and Recreation*. University Press of America, New York.

Neulinger, J. (1982) *To Leisure: an Introduction*. Allyn and Bacon, Boston.

OECD (1994) *OECD Societies in Transition: the Future of Work and Leisure*. OECD, France.

O'Neill, M. (1991) Naturally attractive. *Pacific Monthly*, September, 25.

Palacio, V. and McCool, S.F. (1997) Identifying ecotourists in Belize through benefit segmentation: a preliminary analysis. *Journal of Sustainable Tourism* 5(2), 234–243.

Parker, S. (1992) Volunteering as serious leisure. *Journal of Applied Recreation Research* 17(1), 1–11.

Pearce, P. (1988) *The Ulysses Factor: Evaluating Visitors in Tourist Settings*. Springer-Verlag, New York.

Pearce, P. (1993) Fundamentals of tourist motivation. In: Pearce, D. and Butler, R. (eds) *Tourism Research: Critiques and Challenges*. Routledge, London, pp. 113–134.

Phillips, M. (1982) Motivation and expectation in successful voluntarism. *Journal of Voluntary Action Research* 11(2–3), 118–125.

Pigram, J.J. (1992) *Human–Nature Relationships: Leisure Environments and Natural Settings*. University of New England, Armidale.

Pleumarom, A. (1990) Alternative tourism: a viable solution? *Contours* 4(8), 12–15.

Richardson, J. (1991) The case for an ecotourism association. In: Weiler, B. (ed.)

Ecotourism Incorporating the Global Classroom. Bureau of Tourism Research, Canberra.

Roberts, H. (ed.) (1981) *Doing Feminist Research.* Routledge and Kegan Paul, London.

Rohs, F.R. (1986) Social background, personality, and attitudinal factors influencing the decision to volunteer and level of involvement among adult 4-H leaders. *Journal of Voluntary Action Research* 15(1), 85–99.

Rojek, C. (1993) *Ways of Escape: Modern Transformations in Leisure and Travel.* Macmillan, London.

Smith, V.L. and Eadington, W.R. (1992) *Tourism Alternatives.* University of Pennsylvannia Press, Philadelphia.

Stebbins, R.A. (1982) Serious leisure: a conceptual statement. *Pacific Sociological Review* 25(2), 251–272.

Stebbins, R.A. (1992) *Amateurs, Professionals, and Serious Leisure.* McGill-Queen's University Press, Montreal.

Stitsworth, M. (1987) Third world development through youth exchange. Paper presented at the Annual Third World Conference, Chicago 9–11 April.

Swanson, M.A. (1992) Ecotourism: embracing the new environmental paradigm. Paper presented at the International Union for Conservation of Nature and Natural Resources (IUCN) IVth World Congress on National Parks and Protected Areas, Caracas, Venezuela, 10–12 February.

Terenzini, P.T. and Wright, T.M. (1987) Student's personal growth during the first two years of college. Paper presented at the Annual Meeting of the Association for the Study of Higher Education, 14–17 February.

The Ecotourism Society (1992) *Membership Brochure.* The Ecotourism Society, Washington, DC.

Thomas, M. (1971) *Work Camps and Volunteers.* PEP, London.

Tihanyi, P. (1991) *Volunteers, Why they Come and Why they Stay.* Centre for Voluntary Organisations, London School of Economics, London.

United Nations Department of Economic and Social Affairs (1975) *Service by Youth.* United Nations, New York.

United States Peace Corps Evaluation Division (1980) *A Survey of Former Peace Corps and VISTA Volunteers.* United States Peace Corps, Washington, DC.

United States Peace Corps (1989) *Final Report from the Returned Peace Corps Volunteer Pretest (RPCV) Survey.* United States Peace Corps, Washington, DC.

Urry, J. (1990) *The Tourist Gaze.* Sage, London.

Uysal, M. and Hagan, L.A.R. (1993) Motivation of pleasure travel and tourism. In: Kham, M.A., Olsen, M.D. and Turgut, V. (eds) *VNR's Encyclopaedia of Hospitality and Tourism.* Van Nostrand Reinhold, New York, pp. 798–821.

Valentine, P.S. (1991a) Nature-based tourism: a review of prospects and problems. In: Miller, M.L. and Auyong, J. (eds) *Proceedings of the 1990 Congress on Coastal and Marine Tourism – a Symposium and Workshop on Balancing Conservation and Economic Development.* National Coastal Resources Research and Development Institute, Newport, Oregon.

Valentine, P.S. (1991b) Ecotourism and nature conservation: a definition with some recent developments in Micronesia. In: Weiler, B. (ed.) *Ecotourism*

Incorporating the Global Classroom. Bureau of Tourism Research, Canberra.

Van Til, J. (1979) In search of volunteerism. *Volunteer Administration* 12, 8–20.

Vir Singh, T., Theuns, H.L. and Go, F.M. (eds) (1989) *Towards Appropriate Tourism: the Case of Developing Countries.* Peter Lang, Frankfurt.

Wallace, G. (1992) Real ecotourism: assisting protected area managers and getting benefits to local people. Paper presented at the International Union for Conservation of Nature and Natural Resources, IVth World Congress on National Parks and Protected Areas, Caracas, Venezuela, 10–12 February.

Wearing, B.M. and Wearing, S.L. (1988) All in a days leisure: gender and the concept of leisure. *Leisure Studies* 7, 111–123.

Weiler, B. and Hall, C. (eds) (1992) *Special Interest Tourism.* Belhaven Press, London.

Weinmann, S. (1983) *Cultural Encounters of the Stimulating Kind: Personal Development Through Culture Shock.* Department of Humanities, Michigan Technological University, Michigan.

Wheeler, B. (1992) Is progressive tourism appropriate? *Tourism Management* 13(1), 104–105.

Williams, P. (1990) Ecotourism management challenges. In: *Fifth Annual Travel Review Conference Procedings 1990: a Year of Transition.* Travel Review, Washington, DC.

Winslow, E.A. (1977) *A Survey of Returned Peace Corps Volunteers.* Office of Special Services, United States Peace Corps, Washington, DC.

World Tourism Organization (WTO) (1990) *Tourism to the Year 2000.* WTO, Madrid.

Sustainable Tourism Development: Some Applications

Stephen F. McCool and R. Neil Moisey

School of Forestry, University of Montana, Missoula, Montana, USA

This section presents some case-study examples of places that have attempted to develop sustainable tourism, with varying degrees of success. These places range from highly urbanized and rural settings in Europe to relatively empty or 'undeveloped' areas in the Arctic and Asia. What these chapters tell us is that the pathway to a more sustainable world embraces developed and undeveloped locations, although the specific parameters, actions and developments may vary significantly: in a sense, the search for sustainability forgoes 'cookie-cutter' solutions.

Johnston and Twynam report on a sustainable tourism project initiated in the Arctic in response to concerns about conservation of the environment and the mitigation of the negative impacts of tourism. Codes of conduct and ten principles of environmentally and culturally appropriate tourism for the region were established by local tourism operators, community representatives, non-government organizations, researchers and government representatives. Johnston and Twynam then discuss the complexities of initiating these principles of sustainable tourism and monitoring compliance and success in achieving goals. They note that widespread participation ensures not only that sustainable goals are appropriate for the region, but that there is real ownership in the final product.

Ross and Wall evaluate the potential for ecotourism in North Sulawesi, Indonesia, with a proposed framework that 'explicates synergistic relationships between local communities, biodiversity and tourism'. They outline the current status of tourism development in the region and the challenges that will need to be met. Ross and Wall note that many factors influence the degree to which tourism can impact communities, such as the type of tourism to be introduced, host–tourist relations, resident attitudes toward tourism and tourists, and other general community characteristics. These factors are generally positive in the community, although they note that villagers were concerned with conflicting social values and low tourist spending patterns, mainly due to a lack of tourist services. Ross and Wall note that in North Sulawesi, many of the linkages within their framework are underdeveloped or non-existent, and, unless developed, tourism will fall far short of fulfilling many of the goals of sustainable tourism.

In an interesting approach to assessing the likelihood of achieving sustainable tourism, Kaae compares residents' and tourists' interest in sustainable tourism and environmental issues in the Haderslev-Vojens valley in Denmark. Comparisons between the two groups' ratings of the importance of sustainable tourism indicators demonstrated surprising similarity. Indeed, Kaae notes that the high level of support for these issues is related strongly to awareness rather than a response to actual problems – which Kaae labels a 'mind over matter issue'. Kaae then concludes that education will be an effective tool to broaden support for sustainability.

In the final chapter in this section, Payne *et al.* compare residents' views of tourism with accepted criteria for social sustainability. As has been shown in many of the chapters in this book, they note that residents feel very strongly that they should have a role in defining the types of tourism developments planned in their area. In addition, residents on Lake Superior's north shore felt that they should exercise control over proposed developments, and such developments should be small and restricted to certain areas, environmentally sensitive, and take into consideration their way of life. Indeed, if local residents everywhere demonstrated this level of awareness, involvement and resolve, sustainable tourism might be a more universally attainable goal.

Evaluating Achievement of Sustainable Tourism Principles: the WWF Arctic Tourism Guidelines Initiative

14

Margaret E. Johnston[1] and G. David Twynam[2]

[1]*School of Outdoor Recreation, Parks and Tourism, Lakehead University, Thunder Bay, Ontario, Canada; [2]School of Tourism, University College of the Cariboo, Kamloops, British Columbia, Canada*

Introduction: principles, guidelines and codes of conduct in sustainable tourism

The past decade has seen tremendous efforts by individuals, organizations and governments to implement sustainable tourism ideals and to evaluate them in practice. Payne *et al.* (1999) identify three approaches to these attempts to define, implement and monitor sustainability in tourism. These are categorized as principle-based, managerial and scientific. The latter category involves developing indicators based on a scientific understanding of ecosystems and responses to stress, assessing baseline conditions and monitoring impacts (Payne *et al.*, 1999). This approach, state Payne *et al.* (1999), is strengthened when it includes customary or traditional knowledge of local people. Managerial approaches are those in which the individual organization manages its environmental impacts throughout its entire operations (Payne *et al.*, 1999). These efforts include 'greening' of companies, best practices, standards and environmental management systems. The principle-based approach is the one represented by the case study in this chapter.

The principle-based approach tackles the need for improved environmental and social outcomes of tourism by setting up a framework believed to be appropriate to those concerns and then developing various means for participants to follow its precepts.

Principles, or guidelines, are often linked with specific codes of conduct. Such codes provide a mechanism for the principles to be implemented by indicating expected behaviour in particular situations. Codes exist at a variety of levels, commonly the level of the individual tourist, the operator and the destination community or region (United Nations Environmental Program, 1995; Mason and Mowforth, 1996).

While identified as distinct, the scientific, managerial and principle-based approaches may well overlap in application. This is likely desirable if a comprehensive approach to sustainability in tourism is pursued in any region. At the least, these three approaches clearly are complementary and provide a variety of tools and mechanisms for moving toward tourism that offers the environmental and cultural advantages sought in sustainable tourism movements.

This chapter explores a principle-based project initiated to encourage a greater integration of conservation concerns in Arctic tourism. The chapter outlines the initiative through five stages of evolution: initiation, development, implementation, establishment and monitoring. It focuses upon the options in this initiative for evaluating operator achievement of the programme principles and uses a study of operator awareness and activities in Nunavut, Canada in order to identify challenges related to monitoring sustainable tourism guidelines. The chapter concludes by examining the relevance of this case study for the wider context of sustainable tourism initiatives.

The Arctic tourism project: initiation and development

Since 1995 the World Wide Fund For Nature (WWF) Arctic Programme, based in Oslo, has facilitated the process of establishing appropriate guidelines and codes of conduct for Arctic tourism. These are the tools of a sustainable tourism programme through which WWF hopes to encourage responsible and sensitive tourism, an effort seen as necessary given continuing increases in Arctic tourism numbers and the potential for negative impacts (see Johnston and Viken, 1997; Viken and Jørgenson, 1998). This section describes the initiation and development of the project and the particular approaches to sustainable tourism that it takes.

The project to develop and implement guidelines for Arctic tourism stems from a suggestion at the 1994 St Petersburg Arctic tourism conference that a mechanism for encouraging responsible tourism in the Arctic be pursued (Johnston and Mason, 1997). Discussion about the apparent effectiveness of the codes of conduct used in Antarctic tourism and the cooperation between Antarctic tour operators prompted a comparison with the situation in the Arctic. The recommendation that something similar be attempted in the Arctic was taken up by the WWF Arctic Programme, headed by Dr P. Prokosch, who was in attendance at the St Petersburg meeting (Prokosch, 1998). While the focus of the project was on tourism, the goals of the WWF project clearly reflect a primary concern with enhancing support for conservation in the Arctic and with recognizing the needs and rights of local people (see Pedersen, 1998). Though not framed initially as a project in sustainable tourism, these philosophical emphases and the practical approaches used place this effort firmly within the sustainable tourism movement.

Following a networking and information-seeking stage, WWF held a conference in Longyearbyen, Norway in January 1996 to identify ways in which guidelines for Arctic tourism could be established. Participants included tour operators, government representatives, tourism researchers, residents of Arctic communities, members of indigenous peoples' organizations and other interest groups (Johnston and Mason, 1997). At this initial meeting, participants drafted a memorandum of understanding that outlined key principles for Arctic tourism guidelines, and proposed a process for putting these into operation. This work was continued in August as a smaller group refined the principles and began developing codes of conduct. The project was described in a document entitled *Common Ground*. The document discussed the nature of conservation concerns regarding Arctic tourism, identified ten principles for environmentally and culturally appropriate tourism in the Arctic, and outlined codes of conduct for operators, tourists and communities (Johnston and Mason, 1997).

The initiative to this point focused on elaborating the principles for Arctic tourism that reflect a commitment to sustainable tourism ideals. For example, a strong emphasis within the ten principles is the idea that tourism and conservation should be compatible; another emphasis is that tourism should recognize and respect local culture (Johnston and Mason, 1997). The codes of conduct were intended to provide rules of behaviour for operators and for tourists regarding their interaction with the environment, wildlife and the people of the Arctic. The codes identify specific actions that should or should not take place within the context of the ten principles. For example, the first principle stated that tourism and conservation should be compatible. The code of conduct for tour operators states in relation to this principle that operators should: support conservation; plan tourism activities so they do not conflict with conservation efforts; ensure that clients understand the laws and regulations as they apply to import and export of products made from wildlife; develop an environmental management plan for daily operations; and do post-trip evaluations to confirm that activities were conducted in an environmentally sound manner (WWF, 1997). The code for tourists advised that tourists should: support reputable, conservation-minded operators and suppliers; get the necessary permits before visiting protected areas; not disturb the wildlife and leave areas as they found them; follow the laws and regulations that protect wildlife; provide feedback to operators on their environmental practice; and support and join in Arctic conservation projects and organizations (WWF, 1997). Each point in the codes of conduct is directly linked to a principle, providing a strong context and internal coherence.

Principles into practice: implementation and establishment

The implementation stage involves constructing the mechanisms and tools that will enable the sustainable tourism project to be put into operation. Establishment refers to the acceptance of the mechanisms and tools in the target user groups. This moves the effort from the concept, here identified in the principles and codes, into the realm of practice.

With a strong degree of commitment among participants to the principles and codes as developed through these consultations, WWF began to organize the implementation stage of the process. A workshop in Longyearbyen, Svalbard in March 1997 examined questions of how best to implement the programme. Broad participation was achieved and included individuals from conservation interests, the research sector, the tourism industry, Arctic communities and governments. These participants came from Canada, Denmark, Finland, Germany, Iceland, The Netherlands, New Zealand, Norway, Russia, Sweden, the UK and the US.

Implementation was to include a series of pilot projects to evaluate components of the project and an interim steering committee to oversee the development of the programme over a 12-month period. This committee, reflecting the constituents of the Arctic, comprised representatives of indigenous and other Arctic peoples, local tourism non-governments organizations (NGOs), destination tour operators, international operators, conservation NGOs and the research community.

Various tasks were identified for the interim committee to undertake in the following 12 months. The committee was to:

- support responsible tourism and promote the goals of the initiative;
- develop a consultation process for the involvement of communities and local people in the project;
- establish a membership organization with several categories of membership;

- establish criteria for membership in the organization;
- promote wide dissemination of the guidelines;
- maintain a web site/home page on the World Wide Web;
- coordinate the translation of the guidelines into appropriate languages;
- develop a name for the programme, a logo and a labelling system;
- promote communication among all parties concerned;
- provide information to communities, tour operators and tourists regarding the Arctic tourism guidelines;
- address and organize monitoring of the programme;
- establish an Arctic tourism database;
- promote national initiatives to implement the programme; and
- undertake fundraising on behalf of the organization.

In order to assist the interim committee achieve its objectives, staff resources were provided by the WWF Arctic Programme for an interim secretariat. It was intended that the permanent office of the secretariat would be located in the Arctic, but initially this function was housed in the Oslo office. These steps can be seen as an attempt by WWF to distance itself from the organizing function of the Arctic tourism project. An interim steering committee and eventually an ongoing, self-perpetuating committee heading a membership organization would be able to undertake the role of facilitating the programme. The reason for WWF involvement in the project was to initiate a sustainable tourism commitment among tour operators and in communities; once the principles had been set and a plan for implementation developed, the need for WWF involvement was diminished. It was clear that WWF had never intended to be the sole implementing body.

These tasks were quite ambitious for a diverse committee; it was most successful in disseminating the principles and codes. Five thousand copies of the principles and codes were published by WWF in December 1997, making them widely available to communities, tourists, tour operators and the general public (Pedersen, 1998). The original document, *Linking Tourism and Conservation in the Arctic*, was published in English and later translated into German, Norwegian, Inuktitut, and other languages used by residents of and visitors to the Arctic (Mason *et al.*, 2000).

Pilot project development was examined again at a February 1998 meeting in Iceland which brought together the interim steering committee and other interested parties. Objectives of the meeting included developing ways of evaluating the implementation of the codes, examining potential funding sources, and identifying pilot projects that would evaluate the implementation and usefulness of the principles and codes. The primary purpose of the pilot projects was to measure the relevance and applicability of the principles and codes. In addition, the projects would provide an opportunity to present the principles and codes to a broader audience of tourists, operators and communities. The principles and codes and their form of presentation were seen by WWF as subject to revision at this stage, with the expectation that ongoing consultation and recommendations from pilot projects would lead to improvements. Over the following months operators and researchers began to conduct pilot projects using a framework provided by the secretariat.

In March 1999 another meeting was convened, this one in Husum, Germany. The meeting was intended to provide an opportunity for participants to discuss the lessons learned from pilot projects, to enable participants to learn about issues such as certification and sustainable tourism, and to bring together interested parties in order to move the programme forward. Written reports for some pilot projects were prepared in advance, and oral reports occurred at the workshop. The presentations, for the most part, provided a more detailed explanation of the pilot projects and outlined further contextual information that had a bearing on the success and the findings of the projects. Most presentations gave details about the participants' ideas concerning the challenges and barriers in implementing the pilot projects. These presentations were helpful in determining how the overall programme might best be implemented in various circumstances and places.

Pilot projects varied widely in scope, method and results. The experiences of those who participated in Arctic tourism pilot projects raise points and themes that may well be common in other sustainable tourism initiatives. It was apparent at the Husum meeting that a major benefit of the projects was that companies reflected on their activities, assessed them and made changes. Related to this are the efforts the operators took to draw others into the programme. This is likely to continue to be of importance in generating wide operator acceptance throughout the Arctic. For this initiative to be successful, it is necessary to expand beyond the group of operators who already know about the programme and who are already committed to the principles.

Community interest and involvement was contentious in some projects and in others it was the key to their success. Implementing bodies must continue to focus on making this relationship work, perhaps by emphasizing the great potential that exists with strong interaction of operators and particular communities. Points raised in an unpublished evaluation document (Johnston and Twynam, 1999) presented to WWF after the Husum meeting included the following, again, which may have broader relevance:

- Tourist surveys (in pilot projects) show a high level of interest in conservation-oriented activities. This might reflect the particular nature of this segment of tourists, rather than being representative of all Arctic tourists. It cannot be assumed that since these tourists were supportive of the initiative that all tourists across the Arctic and in all activities will likewise be supportive. Decisions cannot be made on the results of these pilot projects alone. We need to know more about tourists and determine how they fit into the programme in order to establish what should happen with tourist codes.

- When asked, tourists provided recommendations for improvements to operations within the context of the codes. Clients are an important source of practical advice for operators and could act as an excellent evaluation source if needed by an implementing body.
- Some operators identified difficulties in developing a framework for actions and evaluating operational changes. It is likely that many of the small operators will require guidance and support in key areas in order to integrate the programme into their operations.

Johnston and Twynam (1999) also made specific recommendations about the principles and codes of conduct. They recommended that the implementing bodies:

- change the order of the principles and code items so that conservation issues and requests for money do not come first;
- prepare national codes that incorporate specific legislation and regulations to accompany the Arctic-wide code;
- prepare a sub-Arctic code that reflects differences in the scale of tourism, activities and the environmental and cultural situations in the sub-Arctic;
- prepare material that reflects and incorporates the views and needs of local and indigenous peoples; and
- reduce the content of the tourist code so that it can be read and absorbed more easily by visitors.

Johnston and Twynam (1999) provided some general recommendations for WWF and other implementing bodies. These recommended that such bodies:

- support the development of planning, evaluation and monitoring protocols for use by operators in the programme, including operator self-assessment and client assessment;
- evaluate and disseminate information about new technologies and management systems applicable to Arctic tourism and identify those that reduce impacts;
- provide information to assist operators in identifying conservation and protection issues in their areas of operation;
- provide information to assist operators in identifying education and training needs of local populations;
- assist operators in the development of Arctic interpretation

programmes, printed material and internationally recognized signage to support the programme; and
- support the organization of conferences and seminars for member operators.

Although it is impossible to say how well established the programme is at this stage, it is clear that the process used by WWF to develop and implement this sustainable tourism initiative was successful in introducing operators and other interested parties to the project. Each meeting, including a regional one in Arkhangelsk, Russia brought new individuals, many of whom attempted to incorporate the principles and codes into their operations. Broad establishment of the programme will reflect operator, community and tourist acceptance of the principles and codes and the degree of this acceptance should be measured across the various parts of the Arctic.

Monitoring: evaluation of effectiveness

At this point, participants in the project have not been successful in developing a membership organization which would be responsible for the programme. In part, this reflects a lack of agreement on what such a body should do, particularly in terms of evaluating operator achievement of the principles and codes of conduct. Should this be an accreditation body? Should this be a marketing body? Should the organization focus on providing information? The other component of implementation and establishment that remains unresolved is that of evaluation. One initiative – an annual award for operators – exists. The brochure for this award states: 'The Arctic Award for Linking Tourism and Conservation has been established to reward best practices in Arctic tourism by highlighting those operations with an outstanding commitment to linking tourism with conservation of the Arctic environment' (WWF, 1999). WWF continues to administer the award.

Other options discussed at various points included operator self-assessment, client assessment and a panel review (see Johnston and Twynam, 1998). For a variety of reasons, external evaluation of compliance with codes should accompany self-assessment (Mason and Mowforth, 1996; Enzenbacher, 1998). Drawing on research on the compliance of Antarctic tour operators with visitor guidelines, Enzenbacher (1998) recommends the creation of a new monitoring body to evaluate operator behaviour, to coordinate the collection of data and to provide information and advice. Operators would be able to become members of this organization, although it would monitor all operators in the Arctic. Enzenbacher (1998) recommends a number of specific mechanisms in this system, including a voluntary reporting form, ship-borne observers for cruise tourism and public recognition or other rewards for good practice. Johnston and Twynam (1998) recommend a variety of complementary approaches to assessment, including operator checklists, site visits, client surveys and the use of community or broad-level indicators. They recommend that awards be developed to recognize good practice and implementation of the programme.

The proposal by Johnston and Twynam identifies the ten principles and subcategories as key expectations about the attributes of sustainable Arctic tourism operations, stating that these can be considered the indicators of achievement. These indicators can be measured on the basis of required actions. A discussion of the use of managerial indicators for planning and managing sustainable tourism is available in a report by Consulting and Audit Canada (1995). The Johnston and Twynam (1998) proposal is directed at operational indicators, i.e. those attributes of the experience that can be controlled individually by operators. These indicators can be evaluated using specific measures outlined as actions to be taken during tourism operations or as components of an operator's environmental plan.

The form that monitoring will take in this initiative remains unclear. A comprehensive system that encourages operator participation is vital, as is one that allows for the tremendous variety and distinction within the Arctic region and Arctic tourism. The following section examines some of the issues related to implementing this sustainable tourism initiative, including introducing operators to the programme, establishing baseline information about operators and developing appropriate questionnaires.

Nunavut case study: baseline data

As sustainable tourism principles become more refined and more widely practised in various parts of the world, assessment of their use in different settings is vital. Evaluating the principles and practice is important in two ways: first, such evaluation can provide baseline behaviour data in advance of the implementation of a principle-based programme; second, it can indicate the effectiveness of the programme after implementation. The purpose of the Nunavut study was to gather baseline data prior to the intended introduction of the Arctic tourism principles.

In order to assess the need for the initiative and its potential effectiveness, it is necessary to understand current behaviour, awareness and motivation of operators who not only enable tourism, but also provide the opportunities and situations for tourist behaviour, with its resulting impacts. This study examined tourism operators' awareness, views and behaviour related to the principles of sustainable tourism outlined in the WWF (1997) *Linking Tourism and Conservation in the Arctic* initiative.

In conjunction with Nunavut Tourism, a survey was administered in 1998 to tour operators in the eastern Canadian Arctic. The principles were adapted for the survey in order to gather operator opinions on their present use of the ideas. The survey was translated into Inuktitut for the non-English speakers. Potential respondents were identified using Nunavut Tourism operator lists: this resulted in 53 operators being contacted and included only those who had telephone or fax numbers. Fifty-two telephone interviews were conducted as one operator chose not to participate in the survey. The survey asked the operator to identify the category that the business fell into, number of years in the business and number of clients in the previous year. These questions were used to provide detail of the scale and nature of the business. The main focus of the questions was on the behaviour of the operators specifically related to the ten principles for Arctic tourism (WWF, 1997).

Operators were first asked whether they had ever heard of responsible tourism. Twenty-nine of the 52 operators had heard of responsible tourism. The number of years in operation ranged from 8 months to 38 years, with an average of 11.7 years in business. The number of clients in the previous year ranged from 0 to 800, with a mean per year of 113 clients. Nunavut operators provided their clients with a variety and combination of tourism activities, such as hunting (19%), fishing (32%), adventure activities (79%), nature viewing (79%) and cultural appreciation (56%).

Operators' opinions of their present application of the principles are identified in Table 14.1. Of the 52 operators contacted, 50% knew of local and regional conservation plans. A majority of operators (77%) promote nature conservation through client education (73%) and 31% provide financial support for nature conservation. Operators said that they use resources in a sustainable way (96%) by not disturbing wildlife (83%), using existing trails and campsites (64%) and taking care in fragile areas (56%). All of the operators contacted follow local laws. Ninety per cent of operators contacted pay attention to Inuit rights by informing and coordinating with the local communities concerning their activities with clients. Many (48%) coordinate these activities with local individuals.

Most (96%) minimize the consumption of fossil fuels, minimize waste and pollution by limiting garbage (85%), cleaning up polluted areas (81%) and using recyclable products (62%). Client education assists operators in the protection of historic, cultural and scientific sites. The majority of operators (92%) felt that their operations provide benefits to the local communities by hiring local guides, purchasing

Table 14.1. Nunavut survey results.

	Principle	Frequency	Percentage
1	Do you know of any local and regional conservation plans?	26	50
	Do you use these plans in your operation?	18	34.6
2	Operation promotes nature conservation	40	76.9
	Financial support	16	30.8
	Client education	38	73.1
	Writing letters to government	10	19.2
3	Does your operation use resources in a sustainable way?	50	96.2
	Follow hunting and fishing rules	21	40.4
	Avoid disturbing wildlife	43	82.7
	Use existing trials and campsites	33	63.5
	Take care in fragile areas	29	55.8
4a	Does your operation follow local laws?	52	100
4b	Does your operation pay attention to Inuit rights?	47	90.4
	Coordinate with community	39	75
	Coordinate with individuals	25	48.1
5	Does your operation minimize the consumption of fossil fuels, and minimize waste and pollution?	50	96.2
	Use recyclable products	32	61.5
	Transportation	28	53.8
	Accommodation	10	19.2
	Limiting garbage	44	84.6
	Clean-up of polluted areas	42	80.8
6	Does your operation protect historic and cultural sites?	48	92.3
	Client education	42	80.8
	Being careful at scientific sites	38	73.1
7	Does your operation provide benefits to the local community?	50	96.2
	Employment	39	75
	Business partnerships	14	26.9
	Buying local supplies	40	76.9
	Supporting local business	32	61.5
8	Has your operation trained staff to follow local environmental, cultural, social and legal rules?	40	76.9
9	Does your operation give clients information about how to behave properly in Nunavut?	44	84.6
	The environment	33	63.5
	The people	22	42.3
	How to behave	44	84.6
	How to respect local customs	20	38.5
	When do you provide this info to your clients?		
	First contact with clients	9	17.3
	Information package	25	48.1
	When they arrive	25	48.1
	During the trip when needed	14	26.9
10	Does your operation follow safety rules for the Arctic environment?	47	90.4

supplies locally and supporting local businesses. In addition, most operators (77%) train staff to follow local environmental, cultural, social and legal rules. Eighty-five per cent of the operators provide their clients with information on how to behave in Nunavut, and the majority (90%) follow safety rules for the Arctic environment.

The findings of the telephone survey demonstrate a general understanding of, and commitment to, the kinds of ideals that are outlined in *Linking Tourism and Conservation in the Arctic* (WWF, 1997). This degree of operator acceptance of the general principles and specific activities suggests that this international initiative may be well received and ultimately effective in providing Arctic tourism operators with a template to sustain their operations within this challenging environment.

In the future, with local and regional implementation, and the establishment of the programme as a vital component in sustainable tourism in the Arctic, a system of evaluation will be required to monitor not only effectiveness of and compliance with the principles, but also emerging needs in the industry and new issues that arise. This system should measure the level of implementation and identify the particular initiatives taken in response to participation in the programme. The inclusion of a mechanism to provide feedback to operators is also important, in order to help them improve practice and to recognize achievement. Experiences with the pilot projects across the Arctic suggest that operators are in need of support as they attempt to promote sustainable ideals and improve their operations; how well this need is met by the Arctic tourism programme will be a key in its success.

Conclusions

Sustainable tourism initiatives have taken a variety of forms in numerous settings. This chapter has examined a project to develop and implement tourism guidelines and codes for the Arctic region. While the details of the codes and of the implementation reflect very clearly the particular requirements of the Arctic, the general themes and issues point to the connections between this project and other sustainable tourism efforts.

This project provides a good example of the challenges involved in attempting to implement a comprehensive principle-based programme. Several key points can be identified through this review of the initiation, development, implementation, establishment and monitoring. One is that initiation and development of principles and codes must take place within a wide community of interested parties. Input from communities, operators, researchers and others is needed to ensure not only that the sustainable tourism initiative makes sense for the intended region of use, but also that there is real ownership by these groups in the final product. The success of implementation may well depend on a high level of ownership.

In addition to ensuring involvement of all appropriate parties, initiators of such projects must be prepared to address issues related to implementation at the time of principle and code development. The best-outlined and most well-intentioned codes will not succeed if operators, tourists and communities are unable to implement them. The need for support in implementation was raised throughout this project and was particularly evident in the pilot projects. Operators, especially the small businesses, required assistance to be able to put the principles into practice.

It is also advisable that methods of evaluation are considered early on in the process. This would provide some structure for the users, which may assist in implementation, and it also gives direction for monitoring. Without adequate and appropriate monitoring mechanisms, it will not be clear how effective the initiative has been. The case study provides a simple method of obtaining baseline data that will aid in assessing the effectiveness of the guidelines for an Arctic tourism programme.

It seems likely that the principle-based approach to sustainable tourism will continue to be popular in many parts of the world. This chapter has outlined the evolution of the WWF initiative and demonstrated some of the experiences and concerns in the process that may have relevance for other sustainable tourism efforts. The issues raised here about development and evaluation of efforts extend beyond tourism into the wider context of sustainable development generally.

References

Consulting and Audit Canada (1995) *What Tourism Managers Need to Know. A Practical Guide to the Development and the Use of Indicators of Sustainable Tourism.* Consulting and Audit Canada, Ottawa, Canada.

Enzenbacher, D. (1998) Mechanisms for promoting and monitoring compliance with Arctic tourism guidelines. In: Humphreys, B., Pedersen, A.O., Prokosch, P., Smith, S. and Stonehouse, B. (eds) *Linking Tourism and Conservation in the Arctic,* Bulletin No. 159. Norwegian Polar Institute, Tromso, pp. 38–48.

Johnston, M. and Mason, P. (1997) The WWF initiative to develop guidelines and codes of conduct for Arctic tourism. *Polar Record* 25(2), 351–353.

Johnston, M.E. and Twynam, G.D. (1998) Implementation of the operator programme: evaluating effectiveness through principles, indicators and measures. In: Humphreys, B., Pedersen, A.O., Prokosch, P., Smith, S. and

Stonehouse, B., (eds) *Linking Tourism and Conservation in the Arctic*, Meddelelser No. 159. Norwegian Polar Institute, Tromso, pp. 6–12.

Johnston, M.E. and Twynam, G.D. (1999) Evaluation of 1998 pilot projects: linking tourism and conservation. Unpublished report submitted to WWF International.

Johnston, M.E. and Viken, A. (1997) Tourism development in Greenland. *Annals of Tourism Research* 24(4), 978–982.

Mason, P., Johnston, M.E. and Twynam, D. (2000) The World Wide Fund for Nature Arctic tourism project. In: Bramwell, B. and Lane, B. (eds) *Tourism Collaboration and Partnerships: Politics, Practice and Sustainability*. Channel View Publications, Clevedon, pp. 98–116.

Mason, P. and Mowforth, M. (1996) Codes of conduct in tourism. *Progress in Tourism and Hospitality Research* 2(2), 12–13.

Payne, R.J., Twynam, G.D. and Johnston, M.E. (1999) Tourism and sustainability in Northern Ontario. In: Nelson, J.G., Butler, R. and Wall, G. (eds) *Tourism and Sustainable Development: Monitoring, Planning, Managing, Decision Making: a Civic Approach*. Department of Geography, University of Waterloo, Waterloo, Ontario, pp. 237–266.

Pedersen, A.O. (1998) *Linking Tourism and Conservation in the Arctic. WWF International Arctic Programme, Internal Report – Project Description, WWF, Oslo*.

Prokosch, P. (1998) Introduction. In: Humphreys, B., Pedersen, A.O., Prokosch, P., Smith, S. and Stonehouse, B. (eds) *Linking Tourism and Conservation in the Arctic, Bulletin No. 159. Norwegian Polar Institute, Tromso, pp. 2–5*.

UNEP (1995) *Environmental Codes of Conduct*. Technical Report No. 29, United Nations Environment Programme, Paris.

Viken, A. and Jørgenson, F. (1998) Tourism on Svalbard. *Polar Record* 34(189), 123–128.

WWF (1997) *Linking Tourism and Conservation in the Arctic (Supplement)*. WWF-Arctic Bulletin, No. 4, Oslo, Norway.

WWF (1999) *The Award for Linking Tourism and Conservation*. WWF Arctic Programme, Oslo.

Ecotourism: a Theoretical Framework and an Indonesian Application

15

Sheryl Ross[1] and Geoffrey Wall[2]

[1]Pointe Claire, Quebec, Canada, [2]Faculty of Environmental Studies, University of Waterloo, Waterloo, Ontario, Canada

Ecotourism has been widely recognized as a form of nature tourism that is expected to contribute to both conservation and development. Yet, for a variety of reasons, ecotourism sites often fall short of these objectives and there is a need to design effective means to assess their accomplishments, shortcomings and potentials. Fundamental to ecotourism are the protection of natural areas, the provision of high-quality tourism experiences and the stimulation of local economies. These objectives can be achieved through such means as the provision of resources for conservation, environmental education and local empowerment. The degree to which such variables are functioning, or have the potential to function, essentially represents the effectiveness of an ecotourism site. Existing relationships between natural resources, tourism and local human populations can be used to assess the status of ecotourism and assist in the deployment of effective management strategies.

Although the literature on ecotourism is growing rapidly, a standardized means for site-level assessment of ecotourism has yet to be proposed. This presentation proposes a framework for the development and evaluation of ecotourism. It has been argued (Ross and Wall, 1999a) that ecotourism has the potential to contribute to both conservation and development (Fig. 15.1). As a minimum, it involves the creation of positive synergistic relationships between tourism, biodiversity and local people through the application of appropriate management strategies (Fig. 15.2). The framework provides both a means of describing relationships among key aspects of ecotourism as well as a pictorial means of indicating the status of ecotourism at particular sites. The framework has been described in great detail elsewhere (Ross and Wall, 1999a) and, therefore, is only introduced briefly here.

The purpose of this chapter is to demonstrate the utility of the framework as a tool for the evaluation of ecotourism through its application to a protected area and an adjacent community in North Sulawesi, Indonesia. A brief discussion of the Indonesian context is provided. Research methods and the nature of the evidence used are then discussed. The chapter concludes with a reflection on the general utility of the framework, as well as the challenges and opportunities for the development of ecotourism as revealed by the case study.

The Indonesian context

Following the global decline in oil prices which occurred in the 1970s, Indonesia was forced to seek alternative means of acquiring foreign

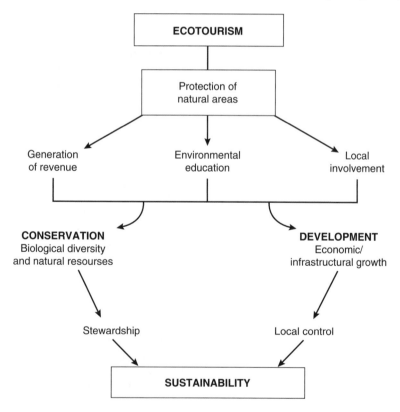

Fig. 15.1. Ecotourism as a means of conservation and development.

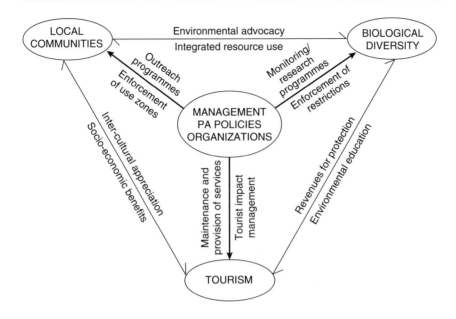

Fig. 15.2. An analytical framework for ecotourism.

exchange to fuel economic development. Blessed with great cultural and biological diversity, and located in the East Asia–Pacific region, which is the part of the world that has experienced some of the most rapid rates of growth in tourism in the 1990s (WTO, 1998), Indonesia turned increasingly to tourism to enhance its foreign currency earnings. International tourism received increased emphasis in each successive *Repelita* (5-year national development plans) and the growth in numbers of tourists and their associated expenditures have been among the highest of any country of substantial size.

Both international and domestic tourism in Indonesia grew steadily for approximately two decades prior to the Asian economic crisis of 1997 and the associated political unrest which resulted in the resignation of the president in 1998. These events have greatly reduced tourism activity, at least temporarily. However, even in more prosperous times, as with economic growth generally in Indonesia, tourism has also been highly concentrated. Jakarta is the recipient of a large number of international visitors, but this is due in part to the convergence of international airlines on the national capital, where most business activity is also located. Bali possesses approximately one-quarter of the country's star-rated accommodation and a similar proportion of international visitor activity. Growing numbers of short-stay arrivals are being attracted by the ferry connection from Singapore to Batam and the emerging resorts in Bintan. However, most tourism in

Indonesia is concentrated in the most prosperous parts of the country and has been slow to develop in peripheral regions, particularly the eastern islands.

In an attempt to address the challenge of regional imbalance in both economic and tourism development, a primary component of Indonesian tourism development strategies has been the establishment of tourism development corporations in selected locations scattered throughout the country (Wall and Nuryanti, 1997). These have been designed as integrated resorts following the model of the Nusa Dua resort enclave in Bali. They are funded through a combination of public and private capital, and are expected to act as catalysts of further growth. Less government support has been given to encouraging the establishment of small-scale tourism developments. This is unfortunate, for they might contribute to the diversification of the tourism product, make use of undeveloped tourism resources with great potential, and be more in harmony with the fragile ecosystems and small, unsophisticated, communities typical of rural and remote areas in Indonesia.

The province of North Sulawesi is a peripheral location which is relatively poor when compared with parts of Java but blessed with great biological diversity associated with a long and complex geological history (Fig. 15.3). The location of Sulawesi astride the contact zone of the Asian and Australasian geological plates, and the associated wildlife, attracted the attention of Alfred Wallace, a contemporary – some would even say the precursor – of Darwin (Severin, 1997), making Sulawesi the Asian Galapagos. Tourism has been recognized in the provincial development plans, along with fisheries, mining and agriculture, as one of its main economic opportunities. The coral reefs, the endemic and endangered species of the tropical forests, and the volcanic landscapes are attracting tourists in increasing numbers. This is introducing strangers and new forms of economic activity to residents of these communities, who have not generally had the chance to be tourists themselves and who have little experience with tourism. Local people are often unprepared to take advantage of the opportunities that tourism might bring, or for the changes that it may engender in their lifestyles. Thus, while tourism has the potential to strengthen and diversify local economies, it also has the potential to modify the lifestyles of long-time residents in ways that it is difficult for them to anticipate.

The degree to which a community is impacted by tourism depends greatly on, among other things, the characteristics of the community and attitudes towards tourism and development, the types of tourism being introduced and the nature of host–visitor interactions (Wall, 1996). The Minahasan village of Batuputih, bordering Tangkoko Duasudara Nature Reserve in North Sulawesi Indonesia, presents an

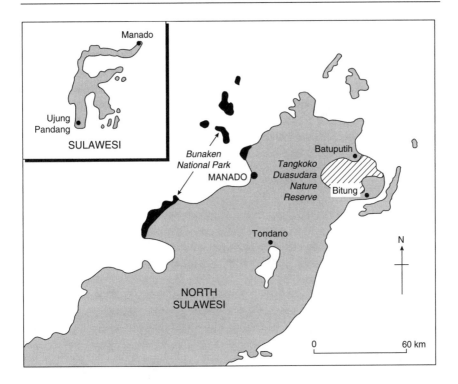

Fig. 15.3. Natural areas in North Sulawesi.

interesting opportunity to investigate these aspects of change (Fig. 15.4). As tourist numbers in the province of North Sulawesi continue to rise, the number of visitors to protected areas such as Tangkoko Duasudara Nature Reserve is rising accordingly. Prior to the recent economic and political crises, the province of North Sulawesi was receiving close to 330,000 tourists annually (30,285 of which were international). This is a threefold increase in total vistors and four times the number of international visitors received by the province in 1990 (Dinas Pariwisata 1996). The annual number of international tourists visiting Tangkoko has grown from 50 tourists in 1978 to over 2500 in 1994 (Kinnaird and O'Brien, 1995). Consequently, residents of Batuputih, a village located adjacent to the reserve, are encountering more and more foreigners in their village. Change, from economic, physical and perhaps even social standpoints, is happening quickly. To what degree will these changes affect the residents of Batuputih? And to what degree will change be welcomed or rejected?

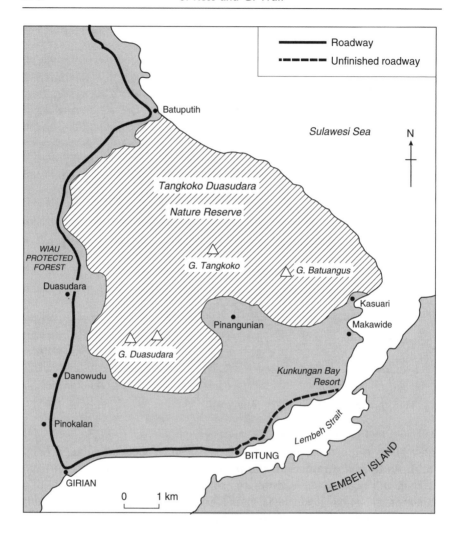

Fig. 15.4. The locations of Batuputih and Duasudara Nature Reserve.

Methods

This research is one of a number of ongoing studies into the
implications of different types of tourism for host communities in
general and, more specifically, in Indonesia (Ross and Wall, 1999b).
Following a brief visit to North Sulawesi in May 1995, approximately 1
month was spent in July and August 1995 collecting background
materials on ecotourism in North Sulawesi. During this period, an
exploratory visit was made to Tangkoko Duasudara Nature Reserve and
to Batuputih. Following a brief return visit to North Sulawesi in

December 1995, more extensive fieldwork was undertaken in a number of ecotourism sites in the province between June and August 1996. Several visits were made to Tangkoko and the village of Batuputih. Village information was gathered through:

1. consulting with the *Kepala Desa* (village head);
2. informal discussions with villagers and homestay (bed and breakfast) owners;
3. consultation with the reserve headquarters and their tourism records;
4. gathering existing reports on Batuputih and Tangkoko;
5. mapping the village; and
6. participant observation in tourist activities in the reserve.

In addition, a small survey consisting of 30 interviews was conducted with a convenience sample of residents aged between 18 and 60 years. The survey consisted of ten questions designed to ascertain the attitudes of residents of Batuputih towards tourism and the stewardship of reserve resources. It was administered orally in Indonesian by assistants from the village, and responses were recorded on prepared sheets.

The reserve

Tangkoko Duasudara Nature Reserve (TDS) encompasses 8867 ha bordering the Sulawesi Sea on the north-eastern side of the peninsula (Fig. 15.4). Recognized for its rich endemic biodiversity, the area was initially set aside as a nature reserve by the Dutch in 1919 and, after independence, retained its strict nature reserve status. The reserve contains three volcanoes and seven major habitat types, including lowland, submontane and elfin cloud forest (Kinnaird and O'Brien, 1995). Off the coast of volcanic sand, the waters are fringed with coral reefs. Tangkoko boasts high densities of some of Sulawesi's unique endemic rainforest wildlife, including spectral tarsiers (*Tarsius spectrum*) (one of the world's smallest primates), crested black macaques (*Macaca nigra*), primitive bear cuscus (*Phalanger ursinus*) and red-knobbed hornbills which are easily accessible and thus popular for wildlife viewing.

The area surrounding Tangkoko is in the municipality of Bitung Utara (North Bitung). The livelihoods of more than two-thirds of people residing in close proximity to the park are agriculturally based, including crops, plantations and livestock. According to 1990 statistics, close to 60% of the land of Bitung Utara has already been converted for agriculture, primarily plantations (Karwur *et al.*, 1994).

Despite relatively high densities of species in the reserve, the ecosystems of Tangkoko's are not free from threats (O'Brien and Kinnaird, 1996). Tangkoko has become more and more isolated because of encroachment in the form of agriculture and livestock grazing, and overharvesting of forest flora such as the palm, *Livistona rotundifolia*, which is used for thatching roofs. However, recently agricultural encroachment has slowed down considerably. According to Kinnaird and O'Brien (1995), the most serious problem within Tangkoko's boundaries is the pressure being put on wildlife by poachers. Bushmeat, (including the anoa, black macaque, tarsius, cuscus and hornbill) is traditional food for Christian Minahasans. Already, the babirusa (*Babyrousa babirussa*) and, most likely, rusa deer (*Cervus timorensis*) have been poached to extinction. Anoa, black macaques and bear cuscus all have a low reproductive capacity and, therefore, may be subject to overharvesting by Minahasans. Over-exploitation of maleo eggs has driven this remarkable bird to near-extinction with only an estimated seven breeding pairs remaining. In short, the local communities may be jeopardizing the future of very important rainforest resources.

In light of these threats, residents of villages such as Batuputih might be in the position to welcome alternatives, such as ecotourism, to curb unsustainable resource use. If managed appropriately, the economic and infrastructural benefits brought about by tourism might contribute not only to improved reserve protection, but also to positive local development, which can improve living standards and promote environmental stewardship. However, in order to benefit from tourism in the reserve, adjacent villages must be able and prepared to participate in tourism.

The village of Batuputih

The Minahasan fishing village of Batuputih was established in 1913 by islanders from Sangihe Talaud (Kinnaird and O'Brien, 1995). Batupu-tih, which means white rock, is situated on the shoreline of the Sulawesi Sea adjacent to the northern boundary of Tangkoko Duasudara Nature Reserve (Fig. 15.5). Access to the village is either by boat, or by vehicle on a poorly paved and badly maintained road which is accessed from the more substantial road that connects Bitung, a port, to Manado, the major city of the province. The village is approximately 2 km in length and consists primarily of one main street which runs parallel to the shoreline (Fig. 15.5). In 1996, the district had a population of 2611 residents, consisting of 1281 females and 1330 males, living in 585 families. However, a walk down the main street makes it hard to believe that the population is that large and suggests that some of the population live elsewhere in the district.

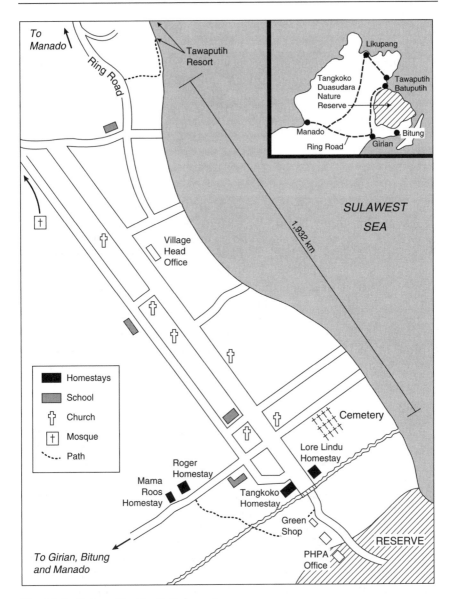

Fig. 15.5. Batuputih, North Sulawesi.

Reflecting the Minahasan context, the residents are predominantly Christian: 2105 are Christians and 145 are Muslims. There are six churches, one mosque, four schools, one market, one graveyard and over a dozen small stands selling either simple clothing, sweets or fruits. One small shop, located near the entrance of the reserve, is run by a local non-government organization (NGO). This is the only place for visitors to buy souvenirs in the village, but the stock is limited and the selection is poor.

Batuputih is a poor village. Livelihoods are derived mainly from subsistence fishing, some gardens and plantation crops, and a few livestock such as goats, pigs and chickens. It appears that the most basic needs of the majority of families are being met but standards of living are generally low.

Tourism context

The number of visitors registered at the Batuputih entrance to Tangkoko Duasudara Nature Reserve in 1995 was 5900. However, the majority of these tourists came and went within hours, mostly entering the reserve at dusk or dawn to view wildlife. Tangkoko attracts two main types of tourists: package tours and independent travellers. Those that arrive in groups on package tours spend an average of 2 h in the reserve and their main objective is to see *Tarsius spectrum*. Their origins are diverse and they include many international visitors. However, their immediate place of origin is usually the provincial capital, Manado. They are driven right up to and sometimes beyond the park entrance, and are driven back to Manado after their forest walk. Some package tourists do stay overnight, or have a meal at one of the homestays before returning to Manado, but generally they have very little contact with Batuputih villagers.

Independent travellers are 'backpackers' who arrive by local transport, usually crammed into the back of a truck with locals carrying goods back from the towns of Girian or Bitung. These visitors usually make use of the cheap, basic accommodation and make a quiet one- or two-night sojourn in the area. Both types of tourists travel to this fairly remote community primarily for the opportunity to view wildlife and to undertake short hikes in the forest.

For those who choose to stay overnight, there is a choice of four homestay accommodation establishments within the village of Batuputih, which together provide 32 rooms. However, since the village is not connected to the outside world by telephone, it is not possible to reserve accommodation. All of the homestays are owned by reserve staff (wardens) and are situated close to the park entrance, which minimizes the amount of vehicular and pedestrian tourist traffic entering the village. Since *Tarsius spectrum* is nocturnal, most visits to the reserve occur at dusk or dawn and, since tourists are not allowed to enter the reserve without a guide (and thus do not usually enter more than once or twice each day), many find themselves with free time during the day. The majority of overnight visitors will most likely stroll down the main street of Batuputih at some point during their stay.

There is pleasant beach for swimming inside the boundaries of the park as well as some good snorkelling opportunities. Tourists also have the option of swimming along the shore near the village, where they may interact with local fishermen. However, there are essentially no facilities for tourists outside of the rudimentary accommodation, and the interactions between tourists and residents are minimal at present. Communications between them are generally limited to 'Hello Mister, Hello Miss', especially from children, as the occasional tourist walks down the main street. The extent of interaction really depends on the degree to which tourists pursue communication opportunities, but few international visitors speak Indonesian or Minahasa.

Few residents currently benefit economically from tourism. Tourist expenditures are limited by the lack of items available for purchase. Only a few small stands, which cater primarily to local needs, attract occasional purchases by tourists. Locals are being encouraged verbally by outsiders, such as government officials and NGO members, to develop their own small tourist enterprises (such as shops, homestays and restaurants). Still, even if the desire exists, financial resources and knowledge of tourism are limited and there is no tangible evidence that such local initiatives have been taken. Perhaps this will change as the village receives a greater influx of visitors.

Although there is at present little evidence of tourism in the village, tourism is likely to be the catalyst of substantial changes in Batuputih. As of early July 1995, the wardens charged with protecting the reserve were the only people responding actively to the growing tourist numbers by building accommodation establishments. However, in the span of less than 1 month, two new homestay facilities were opened *inside* the reserve in time for the peak visitor season. This was done by transforming unused research stations along the beach into attractive tourist facilities. This may have consequences for wildlife conservation as it will increase vehicle and pedestrian activity in places that are currently part of the territory of black macaques. However, because these facilities are owned by the reserve, there is a possibility that a portion of any profits could go to PHPA (Department of Forestry and Conservation) which has responsibility for the reserve. Furthermore, the tourist use of these facilities will be discontinued if new researchers enter the area.

Incremental change: cumulative impacts?

The village of Batuputih has already witnessed dramatic change in the past two decades. A few years ago the village was only accessible by boat, or by foot through the forest. The first road into the village from

Girian (the main town visited for supplies) was a very rough path which was only traversable by four-wheel drive vehicles in the dry season. In 1996, the road, although still bumpy and tortuous, was passable throughout the year with cars, trucks, taxis, microlets (small public service vehicles) and vans transporting locals and tourists to and from Batuputih. The needs of tourism have been a stimulus for the improvement of the road network and it is likely that, in the future, tourism will influence the introduction of other types of infrastructure, such as electricity and telephone communication.

Less than 1 km to the north of Batuputih is a small, picturesque bay known to the locals as Tawaputih. It has white sand in contrast to the black volcanic sand which is characteristic of the region. Discovered by investors from elsewhere in Sulawesi, Tawaputih has become the site for a tourist resort development. Construction was under way throughout 1996, and 20 Minahasan-style cottages were being built approximately 250 m back from the beach. Eventually, the plan is to build up to 50 or 60 cottages. It is rumoured that the resort will have salt- and freshwater pools, a playing field and a disco. A large boat has been constructed to carry tourists, including divers, to Bunaken National Park, Linkungan, Lembeh Island and Bitung. This resort is only 30 km south-east of the five-star Paradise Resort, which opened for business in February 1996 (Simpson and Wall, 1999a, b). The road that rims the peninsula will be upgraded (in both directions) to facilitate transportation along the coast.

In addition to the evident growth in nature tourism at Tangkoko, the effects of the new resort development could be far-reaching. Batuputih will no doubt receive greater traffic (motorized, pedestrian and sea-borne), greater exposure to different cultures and, in all likelihood, more diverse types of tourists, greater opportunities to develop economically feasible tourist enterprises and, of course, increased employment opportunities. The developers of the new resort have hired local people to assist with construction and, apparently, they intend to train local people as staff once the resort is in operation.

It is difficult to separate the effects of an individual resort from the broader changes of which it is a part. It is likely that any given innovation will lead to a variety of impacts and a sequence of changes will have cumulative effects. Residents of Batuputih will be impacted by these changes but it is not clear how they will respond to these evolving circumstances, that is, whether they will resist, accept or embrace the changes that are occurring in their community (Dogan, 1981). The issues will be discussed in more detail below.

Attitudes of villagers towards tourism and change

In the absence of an intimate knowledge of the views of the people of Batuputih, it is difficult to discern the degree to which they recognize the changes that are occurring, what degree of importance they ascribe to them, or even if they are aware of the consequences, both good and bad, that a growing tourist industry can imply. Batuputih has, in fact, been the target of some creative tourism and conservation promotion efforts by the regional tourism department of Bitung. Tourism is being introduced to the residents of Batuputih as something they should take pride in and welcome. Hence, due to educational programmes and organized discussions, the people of Batuputih appear to be familiar with some of the potential benefits of being recognized as a tourist destination.

The survey of residents of Batuputih revealed that all of those interviewed would like to see more tourists visiting the village. The main reasons for wanting more tourists were to increase income in the village and to have the village become well-regarded. Furthermore, if given the opportunity to participate in a tourism enterprise, such as cultural performances, restaurant, homestay or guiding, all respondents indicated that they would like to be involved. Villagers expressed a desire for greater income yet, in spite of outside encouragement and internal enthusiasm, they have not yet actively sought ways to obtain it.

The residents' main concerns with respect to increased tourism, as revealed in a village meeting, were the possible negative effects of exposure to varied social and cultural situations, particularly the possible involvement of the younger generation in 'parties' or 'discos', and the increased exposure to tourists walking around the village or swimming in immodest beachware. There was also some resentment concerning the current low spending by tourists in the village. It was believed that tourists possessing the ability to pay large sums for transportation from their homelands should be able to spend more money in the community. However, there was a lack of recognition that there was very little for tourists to purchase and that most visitors who stay for any length of time are backpackers who may be interested in saving rather than spending money.

Discussion

North Sulawesi has outstanding resources for ecotourism, based upon its marine and forest environments, its volcanic landscapes and its biodiversity, and the emerging tourism industry is growing rapidly. Tangkoko Duasudara Nature Reserve is one site that is experiencing such growth. Batuputih is not the primary target of the tourist industry in this area but its location adjacent to the reserve seemingly means inevitable involvement in tourism. Although it is located in an attractive setting, it is an unexceptional village which does not at present possess the marketable qualities of a cultural tourism destination, such as a visible, rich heritage or traditional arts and crafts which can be shared and sold. While Batuputih has a rich natural heritage at its doorstep, it is a poor community which currently has a limited ability to service tourists and, consequently, a limited potential to benefit from tourism. However, although the natural resource is fragile and the capacity is small, the need for additional sources of income is great and even a small injection of revenues into the community would be very welcome.

It appears that rapid development is occurring and will continue whether the community of Batuputih invites it or not. At present, although there is a desire for greater income, residents may not have the resources, the knowledge, the initiative or even the confidence to become entrepreneurs. Given the low economic status of the majority of Batuputih villagers and their belief that tourism growth implies enhanced standards of living, tourism may be welcomed regardless of the possibility of some social changes. Increased employment and entrepreneurship opportunities may provide better housing, more material goods (including televisions and stereos which are becoming desired possessions), and greater access to education for children (students must be sent outside of the village to the city of Bitung or Manado for education beyond junior high school). The goals of young people are changing: some have already expressed an interest in becoming trained guides for the nature reserve. Are there acceptable compromises for villagers who desire change but fear its consequences?

Until now, Batuputih has only encountered a certain type of tourist, namely nature tourists, as the nature reserve has been the primary attractor to this area. However, certain aspects of this form of tourism, such as the hot climate of the dry, peak, tourism season; the nocturnal behaviour of one of the major attractions, *Tarsius spectrum*, and the requirement to hire a guide, discourage visitors from entering or hiking in the park during the day. Tourism entrepreneurs are aware that additional activities or attractions may be needed to develop and diversify the product. Residents are being encouraged to develop 'traditional' crafts or dances to redress the perceived problem of a narrow attraction base. However, the construction of the beach resort at Tawaputih at the opposite side of the village from the nature reserve may increase traffic along Batuputih's main street and along its shores. Furthermore, residents of Batuputih may encounter a new type of tourist – those interested in sea and sand. One can speculate that beach and nature tourists may have different characteristics that may affect their interaction with local people and, in turn, the latter's attitudes towards tourists. What will be the implications of these two types of tourists meeting in the village? Will it be advantageous to keep tourists with different motivations and behaviours apart, thus avoiding visitor conflicts and directing development pressures away from the nature reserve?

Application of the framework

Rather than dwelling upon the possible conflicts between tourism, biodiversity and community interests, the framework presented in Fig. 15.6 encourages the identification of positive, synergistic relationships and permits the visual presentation of the status of tourism through the presentation of weak and missing links. This figure shows that, in the case of Tangkoko, none of the links are developed adequately and some are missing entirely. From a positive perspective, tourism is managed through guides at the reserve and there has been some limited input of NGO resources and skills. Conversely, except for reserve wardens, essentially no revenues are captured through tourism, interpretation is limited, and there is little local involvement in conservation or tourism, limited patrolling and enforcement of regulations, and no ongoing ecological monitoring. However, the weak and missing links in Fig. 15.6 point to as yet unrealized potentials, such as opportunities for environmental education for visitors and residents, the use of indigenous knowledge in interpretation, and the potential for locals to protect and benefit from the maintenance of biodiversity.

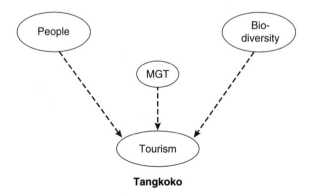

Fig. 15.6. The status of ecotourism in Tangkoko. MGT, management.

Conclusions

While Tangkoko is an example of nature tourism, it is not a good example of ecotourism as strictly defined. The latter requires that tourism stimulates conservation but, in this case, tourists currently contribute little directly to the maintenance of the reserve. Ecotourism should also contribute to education and understanding, but inter-pretation and interpretive materials in Tangkoko are rudimentary or non-existent. True ecotourism should enhance the livelihoods of local people, but there is little evidence that many residents of Batuputih benefit economically from ecotourism. Thus, as revealed by the missing links in Fig. 15.6, there is a gap between the ecotourism potential and the reality. Nevertheless, it is possible that the gap can be narrowed and the potential realized through actions that will complete and strengthen the links in the diagram.

The situation clearly illustrates that the mere attraction of tourists is insufficient to generate local economic impacts. Careful thought has to be given to means of encouraging visitor spending at the destination. It should not be assumed that this occurs automatically. In Batuputih, there is little to buy and, in consequence, little money is spent and limited income is gained by local residents.

The case study also indicates the difference between a tourism resource and a tourism product that can be marketed and sold. While the wildlife are highly visible and wildlife encounters can be almost guaranteed, the supporting infrastructure is poor and the communica-tion system so rudimentary that accommodation cannot be booked in advance.

Neither the residents of Batuputih nor the *Tarsius spectrum* are in control of their futures, yet the future of tourism is highly dependent upon both. It is important for the long-term existence of the reserve and its creatures that local people receive some benefit from its existence. It is difficult for people who may be uncertain where their next meal is coming from to be conservationists. Positive attitudes towards tourism could easily be replaced by a backlash of negative feelings if local people are unable to benefit from the resources just beyond their doorstep.

Tangkoko Duasudara Nature Reserve is an example of the rich but fragile resources for ecotourism which are found in threatened abundance in many parts of Indonesia. Batuputih is on the threshold of change. It is a poor village of people who have a need and desire to strengthen and diversify their economic base. Batuputih has much to offer tourists, and many villagers wish to attract and benefit from tourism but lack the means or experience to do so. This is a situation common to many potential tourism locations in eastern Indonesia and, indeed, in many peripheral areas in the developing world. The framework confirms this situation but also draws attention to unrealized potentials through the visual portrayal of weak and missing links which, if strengthened and completed, would move the system in the direction of sustainability, enhancing conservation, enriching tourists' experiences and stimulating the local economy.

Postscript

As part of a course on ecotourism being conducted in Manado, G. Wall planned to take a group of Indonesian colleagues to Batuputih and Tangkoko in August 1997. Unfortunately, this proved to be impossible for Tangkoko was engulfed in flames – a victim of the forest fires plaguing Indonesia – providing further evidence of the fragility of this protected area and ecotourism activities that might be based upon it, at least in the short term. A 1999 visit to North Sulawesi confirmed that the forest is regenerating, the tourists are visiting again, and the new resort is in operation, but management of the reserve and the local economy are largely unchanged. However, new threats are emerging as proposed new roads may impinge upon the reserve and, in the broader region, gold mining on land and intensive commercial fishing offshore may provide economic opportunities, particularly in the former case, but at the cost of environmental degradation.

Acknowledgements

The research reported in this paper was funded in part by a grant from the Social Sciences and Humanities Research Council of Canada to G. Wall and a Canada-ASEAN Travel Grant to S. Ross. Research was facilitated by Dr Louise Waworunto and Mr Denny Karwur of Universitas Sam Ratulangi, Manado and by the Environmental Studies Centres Development in Indonesia project.

References

Dinas Pariwisata (1996) Laporan: Kegiatan Tim Promosi Pariwisata Dan Kesenian Sulawesi Ubara. Komplex Perkantoran, Manado, Indonesia.

Dogan, H. (1981) Forms of adjustment: sociocultural impacts of tourism. *Annals of Tourism Research* 8, 216–236.

Karwur, D., Tampanguma, M. and Katuuk, D. (1994). *Aspek terhadap perusakan lingkungan hidup dan pelestarian alam di kawasan konservasi Cagar Alam Tangkoko Duasudara.* Falkultas Hukum, Univeritas Sam Ratulangi.

Kinnaird, M. and O'Brien, T. (1995) *Tangkoko Duasudara Nature Reserve,*

North Sulawesi Draft Managament Plan, 1996–2000. WCS and PHPA, Indonesia.

O'Brien, T. and Kinnaird, M. (1996) Changing populations of birds and mammals in North Sulawesi. *Oryx* 30(2), 150–156.

Ross, S. and Wall, G. (1999a) Ecotourism: towards congruence between theory and practice. *Tourism Management* 20(1), 123–132.

Ross, S. and Wall, G. (1999b) Evaluating ecotourism: the case of North Sulawesi, Indonesia. *Tourism Management* 20(6), 673–682.

Severin, T. (1997) *The Spice Island Voyage: in Search of Wallace.* Little Brown and Co., London.

Simpson, P. and Wall, G. (1999a) Environmental impact assessments for tourism: a discussion and an Indonesian example. In Pearce, D., Butler, R. and Din, K. (eds) *Contemporary Issues in Tourism Development.* Routledge, London, pp. 232–256.

Simpson, P. and Wall, G. (1999b) Consequences of resort development. *Tourism Management* 20(3), 283–296.

Wall, G. (1996) Rethinking impacts of tourism. *Progress in Tourism and Hospitality Research* 2(3/4), 207–215.

Wall, G. and Nuryanti, W. (1997) Marketing challenges and opportunities facing Indonesian Tourism. *Journal of Travel and Tourism Marketing* 6(1), 69–84.

World Tourism Organization (WTO) (1998) *Tourism Highlights 1997.* WTO, Madrid.

The Perceptions of Tourists and Residents of Sustainable Tourism Principles and Environmental Initiatives

16

Berit C. Kaae

Danish Forest and Landscape Research Institute, Hoersholm, Denmark

Introduction

Adding the perceptions of tourists and local residents toward sustainability and environmental initiatives to the ongoing academic and industry-related debate on sustainable tourism is highly relevant. Changes in tourism toward more sustainable practices need the support of not only tourists but also the local community, as several sustainability criteria involve changes in the destination beyond the individual tourism facility. Consequently, from a destination perspective, it is relevant for planners and managers both inside and outside the tourism industry to evaluate the level of support and priorities among tourists and residents of changing the current tourism towards more sustainable practices.

While interest in environmental initiatives and certification programmes is increasing within the tourism industry, many businesses do not participate. The uncertainty of tourist and local community support of these initiatives may be one of the barriers to adopting environmental programmes. Also, not all tourists and local residents may be equally supportive of these initiatives. Therefore, it is relevant to explore whether interest in sustainable tourism and environmental initiatives is related to background characteristics of both tourists and residents or to conditions in the destination such as the experience of impacts.

The purpose of this study was to assess and compare the interest in sustainable tourism and environmental initiatives among tourists and residents in a Danish tourist destination. Secondly, to analyse whether differences in interest in sustainability principles and environmental initiatives are related to background characteristics of the tourists and local residents. Thirdly, to analyse whether interest is related to destination factors, including the attraction to the area by certain destination attributes or to the experience of impacts. Within this discussion it is also important to determine whether the perceived importance of sustainability principles is related to local residents' satisfaction with the current environmental efforts in the area, use of coping strategies to adjust daily life to tourism, or to residents' interest in involvement in tourism planning.

Sustainability

Sustainable tourism has gained popularity since the concept of sustainability was introduced by the Brundtland Report (WCED, 1987) and reinforced at the Rio Summit in 1992. The environmental, sociocultural and economic impacts of tourism on local communities are well documented (reviewed by Mathieson and Wall, 1982; Murphy, 1985) and sustainable tourism may provide a viable approach to reduce these impacts by increasing the environmental and social performance of the tourism industry. In the tourism literature, the concept of sustainable tourism is widely discussed (Slater, 1991; De Kadt, 1992; Bramwell and Lane, 1993; MacGregor, 1993; Nelson *et al.*, 1993; McCool and Watson, 1994; Murphy, 1994; Coccossis and Nijkamp, 1995; Briguglio *et al.*, 1996; Priestly *et al.*, 1996; Clarke, 1997; France, 1997; Hall and Lew, 1998; Mowforth and Munt, 1998). A wide range of definitions is found in relation to various types of tourism and types of natural and urban settings. However, the potentially unique or different perspectives of tourists and local residents seem to have received limited attention in this discussion.

There are three principal levels for which shared or differing definitions of attitudes are important in this study. First, the degree to which tourists and residents share perceptions of the importance of the fundamental principles of sustainability and sustainable tourism suggests the extent to which there is general agreement about goals. Secondly, action in the form of planning is a significant issue and, thirdly, since action in society requires multiple actors, we need to see whether tourists and residents share in perceptions of the desirability for various measures taken to protect the environment. When assessing attitudes towards sustainable tourism principles, a definition from British studies (Eber, 1992) may be most applicable to tourism in relatively urbanized landscapes. Sustainable tourism is, in this study, defined as:

tourism and associated infrastructure that, both now and in the future operate within natural capacities for the regeneration and future productivity of natural resources, recognize the contribution that people and communities, customs and lifestyles make to the tourism experience, accept that these people must have an equitable share in the economic benefits of tourism, and are guided by the wishes of local people and communities in the local area.

(Eber, 1992, p. 3).

Sustainability criteria often used in tourism include environmental, social, cultural, economic, educational and local participatory aspects (Mowforth and Munt, 1998). The environmental, social, economic, experiential and planning issues included in this definition have been operationalized into 12 principles of sustainable tourism (Table 16.1), based on Eber (1992) combined with two principles from ecotourism (WWF, 1995).

Table 16.1 indicates to which of these criteria each sustainability principle is primarily related. Given the high cultural similarity of tourists and residents and the mostly self-catering type of tourism in the case area discussed in this chapter, the role of cultural and social sustainability was given less attention while criteria on local participation and educational aspects were upgraded and planning was added.

The sustainable approach to tourism is relevant to the industry, which needs to ensure its long-term viability; to resource managers, who need to secure the natural and cultural resource base; to local residents, to ensure that their quality of life is maintained; and to the tourists, who prefer to maintain quality experiences in the destination

Table 16.1. Sustainability principles included in the study and their primary focus.

Sustainability principle	Primary focus
Sensible use of nature resources	Environmental
Reduction of consumption and waste products	Environmental
Maintain diversity of plants and animals	Environmental
Studies of environmental and social impacts	Environmental and social
Responsible marketing of tourism	Environmental and social
Support of local economy	Economic
Tourism supports improvements in the area	Economic
Cooperation with local residents	Local participation
Consultation of interest groups including stakeholders	Local participation
Integration of tourism into local, regional and national planning	Planning
Information and nature interpretation for tourists	Educational
Training of staff	Educational

that match their intrinsic motivation and recreational needs. Consequently, sustainable tourism has to address environmental, sociocultural, economic, experiential and quality-of-life issues as well as
the planning and management practices of the industry.

Tools for achieving sustainability

A number of tourism-related initiatives have been taken, both within
and outside the tourism sector, which encourage a redirection of
tourism towards more sustainable practices. The initiatives are
diverse, including integration of sustainability in *policies*, such as
the national ecotourism policy in Australia (Commonwealth of
Australia, 1994), and in *planning*, including the integration of tourism
with Local Agenda 21 initiatives (WTTC, WTO and the EC, 1997). In
Denmark, tourism is gradually becoming an issue in national
environmental reports (Holten-Andersen *et al.*, 1998). Page and Thorn
(1997) find the lack of a national vision and an integrated long-term
plan to be constraints for achieving sustainable tourism development.
    Integration of sustainability principles in actual tourism develop-
ment projects is also needed (Ellul, 1997). This includes approaches
such as environmentally friendly *site planning* and *design* of tourism
facilities and areas. Examples include the sustainable design initiative
for national parks (US National Park Service, 1993) and development
of new types of tourism overnight facilities such as the eco-lodge
(Hawkins *et al.*, 1995). Landscape design and urban planning in
relation to tourist facilities have been reviewed and discussed by
Grenier *et al.* (1993).
    Another way of reducing impacts is by changing the behaviour of
tour operators and tourists through the use of *codes of conduct* (The
Ecotourism Society, 1993, 1995; UNEP, 1994; Tourist Industry
Association of Canada and National Round Table on the Environment
and the Economy, no date).
    Changing the environmental performance of the tourism industry
by *environmental management*, *environmental auditing* and *certification programmes* is one of the more common approaches. This
includes environmental management of hotels and resorts (Checkley,
1992; Minger, 1992; Henry and Jackson, 1996) and ski areas (Todd and
Williams, 1996) as well as environmental auditing (Goodall, 1992;
Westlake and Diamantis, 1998). Internationally, numerous environmental certification programmes exist in the overnight sector. In
Denmark, these include the Danish *Green Key* (*Grønne Nøgle*)
certification programme for hotels and hostels established in 1994
and now being expanded to holiday houses and camping, the
international *Green Globe 21* programme (Green Globe Global, 2000),

and the emerging *European Flower* and *Nordic Swan* labels (Gullestrup, 1997; Kaas, 1998). In addition, several hotel chains have established separate environmental programmes. In fact, the multitude of programmes is becoming confusing for both the industry and tourists. Another Danish initiative is the *Destination 21 certification programme* which is a certification of an entire tourist destination (Destination 21 Sekretariatet, 1999). Criteria for the certification programme have been established and will be tested during 2000. The programme is expected to start during year 2000. As the present study was conducted before Destination 21 criteria were established, tourist and resident perceptions of environmental initiatives from the Green Key programme were assessed.

To measure the status and progress of implementation of sustainable tourism, a number of *indicators of sustainable tourism* have been developed (Manning, 1993; Hart, 1995; WTO, 1996; Dymond, 1997), and a number of studies of tourism indicators have been carried out (Cammarrota *et al.*, 1997). The proposed indicators focus on environmental and economic aspects, while social aspects play a more limited role. Some of the obstacles in the indicator work include limited data availability, data comparability and limited availability on the regional and local scale. The few cross-national tourism indicators currently used in Europe focus on economics, employment and visitor numbers (Stanners and Bourdeau, 1995).

Resident and tourist support is a key prerequisite for successful implementation of sustainable tourism. Attitudes to environmental issues have been included in a few previous studies. About half of the tourists in Denmark are Germans and several studies suggest that German tourists have a stronger environmental orientation than other nationalities (Hjalager, 1995; Danmarks Turistråd, 1998b). Among German tourists environmental considerations in the choice of vacation destination increased from 22% in 1985 to 54% in 1991 (Hopfenbeck and Zimmer, 1993) and 32 million of the 52 million Germans travelling abroad are now interested in a 'green' vacation (Danmarks Turistråd, 1997). Also, differences in environmental orientation by accommodation type have been identified (Hjalager, 1995; Danmarks Turistråd, 1998a) while subgroups of environmentally oriented tourists could not be differentiated by socio-demographic criteria or specific accommodation types as the green attitudes transcended these categories (Njor, 1997).

Interest in environmental issues among local residents has been studied in Denmark. A survey of local residents in a Danish housing development indicates a very positive attitude towards implementation of urban ecological ideas (Guldager *et al.*, 1998). In particular, water saving and handling of garbage had a high priority. The survey, however, revealed a gap between a positive interest and actual behaviour among residents. In addition, few were willing to accept increased expenses or spending much extra time on environmental improvements (Guldager and Nuppenau, 1998). According to Mayer (1998) changes toward more environmental practices will only take place if they are not in conflict with peoples' deeply rooted hopes and values and when changes are seen as not only necessary but also desirable by the majority.

Case-study area

The case-study area was the 170 km² Haderslev-Vojens valley, located on the east coast of the Jutland peninsula and inhabited by 36,000 local residents (Fig. 16.1).

The valley begins with a series of springs and historical millponds in the inner, western part near the town of Vojens. This area is hilly and forested and the water flows into a lake and then into a 15 km long, narrow fjord. The city of Haderslev is located between the lake and the fjord. It has a restored medieval city centre with a cathedral from the 13th century, pedestrian streets, shopping areas, various accommodation facilities and museums presenting the rich history of the area,

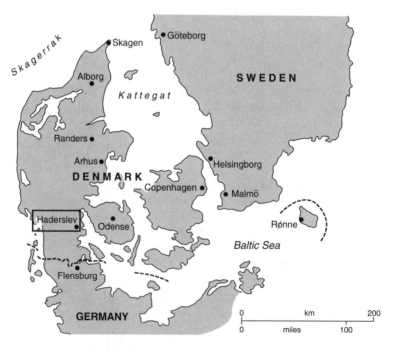

Fig. 16.1. The Haderslev-Vojens valley in Denmark.

with remains dating back to the Erteboelle culture (5200 BC). Further east of the city the landscape becomes flatter and the winding fjord flows into the Lillebælt narrows near the island of Årø. Along Lillebælt are sandy beaches and several holiday house areas, campsites, marinas and other forms of tourist accommodation.

The visitors are mainly Danish and German. They registered 0.5 million tourist overnight stays per year, primarily based on campsites and hotels/motels, but rented holiday houses, hostels, marinas, farm holidays, and bed and breakfast are also popular. Based on the World Tourism Organization definition (WTO, 1995) people staying in non-commercial overnight facilities, such as their own holiday houses and vacationing with family and friends, were also included as tourists, but the numbers are unregistered. In the present study, the definition was extended to also include one-day visitors as tourists. The tourism overnight 'bed capacity' is 4000 beds within the valley itself. But one-day tourists from the 16,000 tourist beds located within a 10 km radius also visit the area. The Haderslev-Vojens valley is a relatively low-intensity tourism destination with an increase of 10% in the summer population due to tourism. The summer population density is 235 persons (tourists and residents) per square kilometer.

Methods

The comparative study involved questionnaire-based surveys of tourists and residents undertaken in the Haderslev-Vojens valley.

The survey of tourists visiting the Haderslev-Vojens valley was conducted in the summer of 1997. The questionnaire was reviewed by a local-background group of authorities, managers and planners, tourist industry and non-government organizations, and pre-tested by 10 tourists in the area. Five local students personally contacted tourists at 24 locations throughout the area during the 7-week survey period. Contact points reflected the geographical distribution and a variety of natural and cultural settings. This sampling was chosen to include tourists outside commercial overnight facilities, such as one-day tourists and tourists visiting family and friends. Tourists received a verbal introduction and a questionnaire to be filled out on site or returned by mail in a pre-stamped addressed envelope. Of the 782 persons approached, seven were excluded because of language problems, previous participation or by not being tourists. Of the remaining 775 tourists, 733 agreed to participate and 602 returned the questionnaire, resulting in a response rate of 78% (including the 5% refusal rate). Given the high response rate and representation of many different accommodation categories, the sample was considered to be representative of tourists in the area.

The survey of local residents in the Haderslev-Vojens valley was conducted in the summer of 1998. A statistically random sample of the adult population aged between 15 and 79 years was drawn from the Civil Registration System in Denmark. The questionnaire was reviewed by the local-background group and pre-tested by five local residents. Questionnaires were mailed with a personal letter and a pre-stamped addressed envelope. Of the 910 respondents, 10 were removed from the sample as they had moved or were deceased. A total of 649 questionnaires were returned after two reminders, resulting in a 72% response rate. Based on t-tests for independence, no significant differences were found by age or gender between the response group in comparison to the subsample of valley residents drawn from the Civil Registration System or when comparing to the general population of the Haderslev municipality. Consequently, resident responses were considered to be representative.

Due to the categorical nature of most of the data, relations were tested by cross-tabulation of variables. The level of significance was tested with the t-test for independence using the Statistical Package for Social Sciences software version 9.0. In descriptions, only relations with a high level of significance of $P < 0.001$ are included.

Interest in the principles of sustainable tourism

Both samples were asked about how important (on a three-position scale) they felt the principles of sustainable tourism were. In addition, respondents were asked to rate the overall importance of the work on developing sustainable tourism in the area. As seen in Fig. 16.2, tourists found the overall work on sustainability of significantly higher importance than did local residents.

While 67% of tourists viewed the work as being of high importance and 29% of some importance, 40% of local residents found the sustainability work of high importance and 52% of some importance ($P < 0.001$). Few in both groups (5–7%) found the work of no importance.

Respondents were also asked to rate the importance of each of the 12 principles of sustainable tourism. As seen in Fig. 16.3, the majority of tourists and local residents found the principles of sustainable tourism to be of high or some importance.

The environmental principles were found to be of the highest importance among both tourists and residents. These include the maintenance of the diversity of plant and animal life (89–92%), sensible use of natural resources (82–89%), and reduction of garbage, energy consumption, water consumption and wastewater production (81–87%). Principles related to environmental and social aspects, such

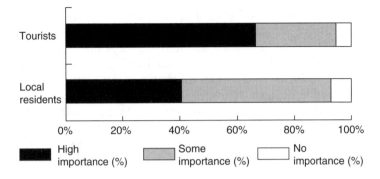

Fig. 16.2. Tourists' and local residents' perceptions of the overall importance of the work towards establishing sustainable tourism principles in the destination (*n* = 1146; *P* < 0.001).

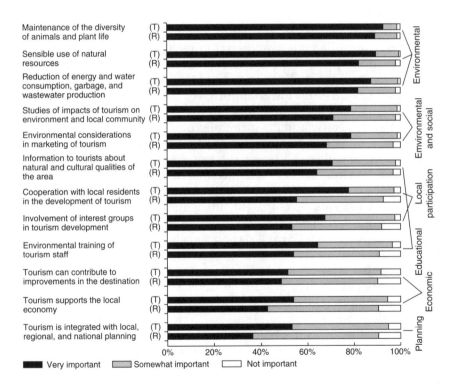

Fig. 16.3. Interest in the principles of sustainable tourism among tourists (T) and local residents (R). *n* = 1147–1181. Differences were significant at *P* < 0.001 for all factors except for sensible use of nature areas (*P* = 0.001), studies of tourism impacts (*P* = 0.011) and reduction of waste, energy and water consumption and wastewater production (*P* = 0.025). No significant difference was found in interest in maintaining the diversity of animals and plants, information to tourists about the area and contributions by tourists to improvements in the area.

as frequent studies of the impacts of tourism on the environment and local community (71–79%) and environmental considerations in the marketing of tourism (67–78%) also had a high priority in both groups.

Sustainability principles related to local participation, such as involvement of local residents in tourism development (54–78%) and consulting different interest groups in the development of tourism (53–65%) were of relatively high importance, in particular to tourists. Interest in educational aspects, such as providing information to tourists about the natural and cultural qualities of the area (64–70%) and environmental education of personnel in tourist areas (53–64%) was also fairly high. Economic principles, such as economic benefits to the local economy from tourism (42–55%) and contributions by tourists to improvements in the area (49–52%) tended to have a lower priority. Planning aspects by integration of tourism into local, regional and national planning (36–53%) had a rather low priority, in particular among local residents.

While tourists and local residents had a similar ranking of the top priorities, some differences are found in relation to the economic and planning principles. Tourists found their own contributions to improvements of the destination to be of the lowest importance, while local residents give the lowest priority to the integration of tourism into local, regional and national planning.

Tourists generally find the principles more important than do local residents. Tourists were significantly more interested than local residents in consulting different interest groups in the development of tourism, environmentally friendly marketing of tourism, environmental education of personnel in tourist areas, involvement of local residents in tourism development, integration of tourism into local, regional and national planning, economic benefits to the local economy from tourism ($P < 0.001$) and sensible use of nature resources ($P = 0.001$).

The higher interest among tourists was less significant in relation to conducting of studies of tourism impact on the environment and local communities ($P = 0.011$), and reduction of waste, energy consumption, water consumption and wastewater ($P = 0.025$). No significant differences were found in tourists' and local residents' interest in maintaining the diversity of animals and plants, information to tourists about the natural and cultural qualities of the area, or contributions by tourist to improvements in the area.

The most differing opinions were found in relation to cooperation with local residents in the development of tourism, which 78% of tourists find of high importance compared to only 55% of the local residents. The integration of tourism into local, regional and national planning was of high importance to 53% of the tourists and 36% of local residents.

Interest in environmental initiatives

The tourists' and residents' interest in a number of more specific environmental initiatives were also measured in the study. The criteria were primarily from the Green Key certification programme. Tourists were asked in relation to their overnight facilities, while local residents were asked in relation to similar initiatives in the community. Consequently, not all measures are directly comparable.

As seen in Fig. 16.4, 70% of tourists were highly interested in outdoor areas being maintained without the use of pesticides, 70% in environmentally friendly cleaning detergents and 67% in sorting of garbage, compared to 63%, 54% and 59% of the local residents. The use of environmentally friendly building materials was of high interest

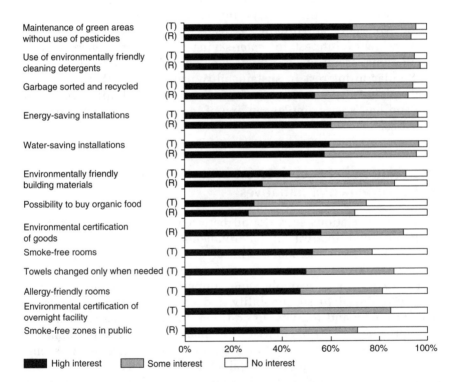

Fig. 16.4. Interest in environmental initiatives among tourists (T) and local residents (R). n = 1106–1129. Differences were significant (P < 0.001) for cleaning detergent, recycling and environmentally friendly building materials; and there was a slight difference (P = 0.030) for outdoor areas maintained without use of pesticides. No significant differences were found between tourists' and local residents' interest in water-saving installations, energy-saving installations or options to purchase organically grown food.

to 44% of the tourists and 32% of local residents. The lowest priority in both groups was the possibility to buy organically grown food, which 28% of tourists and 26% of local residents were very interested in. While 56% of the local residents were very interested in environmental certification of goods, the interest among tourists in certification of the overnight facility was relatively low (40%). Tourist-specific measures such as non-smoking rooms, allergy-friendly rooms and change of towels only when needed were of high interest to 47–52% of the tourists. Non-smoking zones in public were of high interest to 39% of the local residents.

Four of the seven comparable initiatives were of higher importance to tourists than to local residents. Tourists were significantly more interested in sorting and recycling of garbage, use of environmentally friendly cleaning products, environmentally friendly construction materials ($P < 0.001$), and slightly more interested in outdoor areas maintained without the use of pesticides than were local residents ($P = 0.030$). No significant differences were found between tourists' and local residents' interest in water-saving installations, energy-saving installations, or options to purchase organically grown food.

Similar to interest in sustainability principles, both tourists and local residents were very interested in environmental initiatives in the area and had a very similar ranking of importance of the comparable measures.

Interrelation between interest in sustainability principles and environmental initiatives

Very strong relations were found between interest in sustainability principles and interest in environmental initiatives, both among tourists and local residents. Almost all showed highly significant links ($P < 0.001$ or $P = 0.001$). Exceptions include non-smoking rooms, non-smoking zones in public, and support of local economy, which were less linked to sustainability and environmental issues among both residents and tourists. In addition, tourists perceived a limited link of integration of tourism in planning with environmental initiatives. Also, the change of towels only when needed was only partially linked to support of sustainability principles. The greater the support for sustainability principles, the higher the interest in environmental initiatives and vice versa. This is to be expected as the two types of initiatives are partially overlapping – the environmental initiatives may be seen as a more detailed description of some of the environmentally oriented sustainability principles.

Role of background characteristics of local residents and tourists

Sustainable tourism principles in relation to background characteristics of local residents and tourists

The role of age, gender, education level, family life cycle and environmental household behaviour was analysed in both groups, as well as nationality, accommodation type and previous visits of tourists, and length of residence and household dependence on tourism income among residents.

Environmentally responsible household behaviour was strongly related to several sustainability principles among both residents and tourists. The nationality of tourists was also related to interest in sustainability, while a couple of relations to accommodation type were found. In contrast, interest in sustainability was largely unrelated to other background characteristics of both local residents and tourists.

Both residents and tourists with more environmentally oriented household behaviour were significantly more supportive of sustainable tourism. This included higher support of maintaining the diversity of animals and plants, environmentally friendly marketing of tourism, of the overall importance of working towards establishing the sustainability principles in the destination ($P < 0.001$), and in sensible use of nature resources ($P < 0.001$). In addition, residents living in environmentally oriented households were more supportive of reduction of waste, energy consumption, water consumption and wastewater, studies of tourism impacts on the environment and local communities ($P < 0.001$), and in contributions by tourists to improvements in the area ($P = 0.001$).

German tourists were generally more interested in the sustainability principles than were other international tourists or domestic Danish tourists. German tourists had a higher interest in the overall work towards establishing sustainability in the vacation area, in environmental education of personnel in tourist areas ($P < 0.001$), in environmentally friendly marketing of tourism, and in involvement of local residents in tourism development ($P = 0.001$). International visitors had a lower interest than both German and Danish tourists in sensible use of nature resources ($P < 0.001$).

Accommodation type was related to a few sustainability principles. The interest in maintaining the diversity of plants and animals was lower among tourists sailing, camping, and on one-day visits, than among tourists in other types of accommodation ($P = 0.001$). The overall importance of working towards establishing the sustainability principles in the vacation area was found to be the highest among tourists renting holiday homes and the lowest among one-day tourists ($P < 0.001$).

Interest in environmental initiatives in relation to background characteristics of local residents and tourists

Environmental household behaviour of both local residents and tourists and the nationality of tourists influenced interest in environmental initiatives, while a few relations to gender and age of residents were identified. Interest in environmental initiatives was largely unrelated to other background variables.

The more environmentally oriented local residents and tourists were in their households, the more supportive were they of all environmental initiatives ($P < 0.001$). German tourists were found to be more supportive of sorting and recycling of garbage, energy-saving installations, use of environmentally friendly construction materials, options to purchase organically grown food ($P < 0.001$) and in environmentally friendly cleaning products ($P = 0.001$) than both other international and Danish tourists. Among residents, a higher percentage of women than men found sorting and recycling of garbage ($P = 0.001$) and non-smoking zones in public important ($P < 0.001$). Residents below 50 years old were more supportive of water-saving installations and energy-saving installations than older age groups ($P < 0.001$).

Role of destination factors

With the exception of environmental household behaviour and nationality, the socio-demographic characteristics of both residents and tourists were found to have limited relations to interest in sustainability and environmental initiatives. Consequently, the role of other factors was explored, including residents' and tourists' attraction to the area by different destination attributes and their experience of impacts. Among residents, the role of satisfaction with current environmental efforts in the area, use of coping strategies to adjust to tourism impacts, and residents' interest in involvement in tourism planning were explored. An overview of the linkages among the factors is found in Fig. 16.5 for local residents and Fig. 16.6 for tourists.

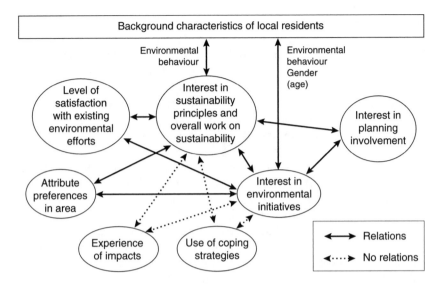

Fig. 16.5. Interrelationships between interest in sustainability and environmental initiatives and a number a variables among local residents in the Haderslev-Vojens area.

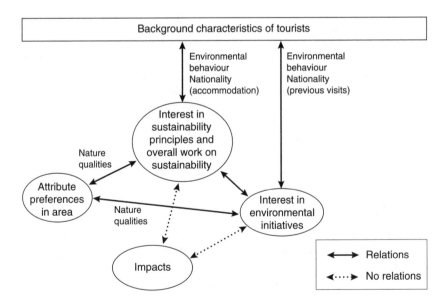

Fig. 16.6. Interrelationships between interest in sustainability and environmental initiatives and a number of variables among tourists in the Haderslev-Vojens area.

Role of attraction by destination qualities

Tourists and local residents were both strongly attracted to visit or live in the area by nature and nature-related qualities, and participated in similar outdoor recreational activities (Kaae, 1999). As sustainable tourism attempts to secure and improve many of these destination qualities, it was investigated whether the interest in sustainability principles and environmental initiatives was related to specific preferences.

Results indicate that local residents (Fig. 16.5) attracted to live in the area by the quality of nature, peace and quiet, clean environment, bicycling and walking trails, community bonds, activity options and friendliness of the area to children were more supportive of sustainable tourism ($P \leq 0.001$). Beaches and town atmosphere played a more limited role, while support for sustainability was largely unrelated to attraction to the area by job opportunities, family ties, cost of living, and sailing and fishing opportunities.

A less complex pattern was found among tourists (Fig. 16.6). Tourists attracted to the destination by the clean environment, nature, and peace and quiet were more supportive of most sustainability principles, with the exception of tourist support to the local area, economic benefits to the community and planning. Attraction by the friendliness of the area to children, town atmosphere, bicycling and walking trails, beaches and accommodation facilities played a more limited role, while interest in sustainability was largely unrelated to attraction to the area by price or fishing and sailing opportunities.

The interest in environmental initiatives was found to be related to attraction by several destination qualities. Local residents (Fig. 16.5) attracted to the area by clean environment, nature, bicycling and walking trails, activity options and the friendliness of the area to children were more supportive of environmental initiatives. Some increase in support was found among residents attracted by community bonds, peace and quiet, and cost of living, while attraction by job opportunities, family ties and town atmosphere played a more limited role. Interest in environmental initiatives was largely unrelated to attraction to beaches, fishing and sailing opportunities.

Again, a less complex pattern was found among tourists (Fig. 16.6). Tourists attracted by clean environment and nature were more interested in environmental initiatives. Some less significant relations were found between supporting environmental initiatives and attraction by bicycling and walking trails, peace and quiet, and beaches.

Role of impacts

Local residents experienced significantly higher impacts from tourism than did tourists (Kaae, 1999). Generally, the experience of tourism impacts was found to be unrelated to both local residents' and tourists' support of sustainable tourism principles (Figs 16.5 and 16.6). Of the 11 types of impacts surveyed, only residents who experience impacts from trampling of nature were significantly more interested in environmentally friendly marketing of tourism and in the overall importance of working towards establishing the sustainability principles in the destination area ($P < 0.001$). Tourists who experienced trampling of nature were significantly less supportive of economic benefits to the local economy from tourism ($P < 0.001$). Also, local residents irritated by the disturbance of wildlife found the overall importance of working towards establishing the sustainability principles in the destination area of higher importance ($P < 0.001$). Tourists irritated by parking problems found the overall importance of working towards establishing the sustainability principles in the destination area significantly less important ($P < 0.001$).

The experience of tourism impacts was also found to be generally unrelated to both residents' and tourists' support of environmental initiatives. Only local residents irritated by the disturbance of wildlife were significantly more supportive of outdoor areas being maintained without use of pesticides ($P = 0.001$).

Role of coping strategies

Interests in sustainability principles and environmental initiatives were generally unrelated to the use of seven different coping strategies among local residents in the Haderslev-Vojens valley (Fig. 16.5). Only residents who cope by using other beach and nature areas than those used by tourists were more supportive of cooperation with local residents in tourism developments and of the overall work on establishing tourism in the destination ($P < 0.001$). Residents who avoided areas with many tourists were less supportive of economic benefits to the local community ($P = 0.001$).

Role of interest in tourism planning

Interest in sustainability principles and environmental initiatives was found to differ significantly with residents' interest in involvement in tourism planning (Fig. 16.5). As tourists do not live in the area, they were not asked about planning involvement. Local residents interested in participating in tourism planning had a significantly higher interest in several sustainability principles. These included maintaining the diversity of animals and plants, reduction of waste, energy consumption, water consumption and wastewater, consulting different interest groups in the development of tourism, and in the overall importance of working towards establishing the sustainability principles in the destination area ($P < 0.001$) as well as information to tourists about the natural and cultural qualities of the area ($P = 0.001$). Of the environmental initiatives, local residents interested in tourism planning were significantly more interested in organically grown food, environmentally friendly building materials, outdoor areas being maintained without use of pesticides, water-saving installations and energy-saving installations ($P < 0.001$).

Role of satisfaction with current environmental efforts

Residents' satisfaction with the current environmental efforts in the area was related to a couple of sustainability principles (Fig. 16.5). Particularly those residents dissatisfied, but also those satisfied, with the current environmental efforts in the area, were more interested in environmental education of personnel and in the overall importance of working towards establishing the sustainability principles in the destination than residents with a neutral perception of the current environmental efforts ($P < 0.001$).

Similarly, they were more interested than the neutral group in environmental initiatives such as sorting and recycling of garbage, environmentally friendly building materials, outdoor areas maintained without use of pesticides and options to purchase organically grown food ($P < 0.001$) but also in use of environmentally friendly cleaning products, energy-saving installations and water-saving installations ($P = 0.001$).

Results indicate that residents with a higher awareness of current environmental efforts – whether perceived to be satisfactory or not – had a higher interest in sustainability principles and new environmental initiatives in tourism than residents with a neutral perception of the current environmental efforts.

Discussion

The results of the study add a consumer and community perspective to the ongoing debate on sustainable tourism and environmental certification. The high interest and fairly similar ranking of issues suggest that tourists and local residents largely share the definition of sustainability and priorities of environmental initiatives. This may be unique for the case area, and perceptions of tourists and residents in other regions and countries need to be added to the debate.

The higher support among tourists, especially for the overall work on sustainability, may be because tourists who visit the destination represent a more environmentally oriented segment than the general population. Secondly, these initiatives would not be as directly linked to changes of daily behaviour or with any costs of the tourists.

Local residents' high interest in sustainability principles and environmental initiatives support findings by Guldager *et al.* (1998) of a very positive attitude among residents towards implementation of urban ecological ideas. A high priority of water saving and handling of garbage was also found in the Haderslev-Vojens study. The high interest in environmental issues among tourists support findings by Hopfenbeck and Zimmer (1993), Hjalager (1995), Danmarks Turistråd (1997, 1998a) and Njor (1997).

Somewhat surprisingly, tourists find the involvement of local residents in tourism development and integration of tourism into local, regional and national planning more important than do local residents themselves. A possible explanation may be that the local residents generally find that there is a good balance in the existing tourism planning between tourists' and local residents' interests (Kaae, 1999) and are also fairly satisfied with the current level of environmental efforts in the local area. Tourists, on the other hand, may know little about the current initiatives in the area and want to ensure the involvement of residents and integration with planning.

The strong relations between environmentally oriented household behaviour and support of sustainability and environmental initiatives indicate that general environmental awareness in the household is also reflected in attitudes toward tourism. The stronger support of sustainability and environmental initiatives among German tourists supports findings by Hjalager (1995) and Danmarks Turistråd (1998b). The higher environmental orientation of German tourists questions the self-perception of many Danes of being very environmentally oriented.

The higher support for some environmental initiatives among female than male residents is interesting. Traditional division of labour within the household may offer an explanation for the identified gender differences, as the environmental initiatives involve more direct changes in households than do sustainability principles. The lower support of water- and energy-saving installations among older residents may possibly be due to increasing focus on personal comfort as one gets older, and from growing up and forming habits in times of less environmental concern. The otherwise limited role of socio-demographic variables in relation to environmental issues supports findings by Danmarks Turistråd (1997) and Njor (1997).

Somewhat surprisingly, the interest in sustainability principles and environmental initiatives among both tourists and residents was generally unrelated to the experience of impacts from tourism, and to local residents' use of coping strategies. This indicates that support for sustainability and environmental initiatives is not a direct reaction to negative experiences in the destination. This may be because the level of tourism development and associated impacts in the Haderslev-Vojens Valley are relatively low compared to many other destinations. Additional studies in more tourism-intense destinations are needed to further explore these relations.

In contrast, destination quality preferences play a role. Tourists and residents who are attracted to visit or live in the destination by nature-related qualities were more supportive of sustainability principles and environmental initiatives. This is not surprising as many of these principles and initiatives focus on improving the environmental and nature-related qualities of the area.

Interestingly, the support of sustainability and environmental initiatives was not linked directly to the level of satisfaction with environmental efforts in the area, but rather to the level of awareness of the current environmental efforts. The awareness of existing efforts increased residents' support for sustainability and environmental initiatives.

Residents who find it important to be involved in tourism planning (see Kaae, 1999 for a further description) were more interested in sustainability principles and environmental initiatives than those uninterested in involvement in tourism. This may be because many of the sustainability principles and some of the environmental initiatives would involve planning to be implemented in the community. It may reflect a higher level of awareness of community issues, including issues of sustainability, environmental initiatives and planning involvement, in this group.

Results suggest that the interest in sustainability and environmental initiatives is related primarily to attraction by nature-related qualities, environmentally oriented household behaviour, awareness of current environmental efforts and interest in planning, rather than being a response to the experience of tourism impacts or linked to personal characteristics of respondents. In the Haderslev-Vojens case, sustainability and environmental initiatives are largely a 'mind over matter issue' and this highlights the role of including educational and information aspects in sustainability principles and implementation strategies.

It is important to bear in mind that the study reflects resident and tourist attitudes and interests in sustainability and environmental initiatives. Transformation of these attitudes into action is difficult (Guldager and Nuppenau, 1998) and will only take place if benefits are gained by changing behaviour (Mayer, 1998).

Conclusions

In conclusion, results indicate that both tourists and residents are very supportive of sustainable tourism principles and environmental initiatives in the destination. The groups generally agree on priorities in sustainability and environmental initiatives. However, tourists find the issues and overall work on developing sustainable tourism of higher importance than do residents.

Support of sustainability and environmental initiatives is found to be related significantly to environmental household behaviour of both residents and tourists, nationality of tourists and gender of residents, but unrelated to other socio-demographic characteristics.

The experience of tourism impacts and the use of coping strategies do not influence the level of support of sustainability and environmental initiatives. In contrast, local residents and tourists attracted to live or visit the area by the nature-related destination qualities, residents interested in involvement in tourism planning and residents with a higher awareness of the current environmental efforts in the area are more supportive of sustainability principles and environmental initiatives.

This suggests that support of sustainability and environmental initiatives is related to awareness and interest in nature and environmental issues, rather than being a response to actual problems. It is largely a 'mind over matter issue'.

Implications of the findings

The high interest of both tourists and residents encourages the tourism industry, destination managers and local planners to take initiatives to increase sustainability and environmental performance in the destination. This includes integration of sustainability principles, improving environmental standards and participation in certification programmes for facilities and destinations.

The finding that interest in sustainability principles and environmental initiatives is primarily a 'mind over matter' issue has several implications. Efforts to implement sustainability and environmental initiatives must include a significant educational component to raise the level of awareness among both residents and tourists. Cooperation with other, more well-known, environmental initiatives (such as Local

Agenda 21) may strengthen the knowledge and awareness of initiatives in tourism. Highlighting the benefits from tourism initiatives may also facilitate the transformation of these attitudes into action.

The destination is fortunate to have environmentally oriented residents and tourists who, in addition to the destination itself, largely share preferences, activities and attitudes. This facilitates the implementing of initiatives to benefit both groups. As many of the international tourists are from Germany, the implementation of sustainability and environmental initiatives is likely to be received positively. But the number of German tourists has started to decline in the past few years and efforts to maintain this tourist market segment are important. An increase in environmentally friendly vacation opportunities may provide an innovative approach and competitive edge that can retrieve some of these tourists.

The positive attitude toward sustainability and environmental initiatives in tourism can only be transformed into action if attractive vacation opportunities are available. The provision of environmentally friendly tourism facilities is rapidly growing in Denmark. New and expanded certification programmes appear, and seven destinations are currently undergoing certification to become 'Destination 21' sustainable tourism destinations. These environmental initiatives provide a new competitive edge in Danish tourism, based on providing tourists with an environmentally friendly vacation causing fewer impacts. This provides a win–win situation for both tourists and local residents as well as the local tourism industry, nature managers and community planners. Future studies may report on the progress of this implementation process.

References

Bramwell, B. and Lane, B. (1993) Sustainable tourism: an evolving global approach. *Journal of Sustainable Tourism* 1, 1–5.

Briguglio, L., Archer, B., Jafari, J. and Wall, G. (eds) (1996) *Sustainable Tourism in Islands and Small States – Issues and Policies.* Pinter, London.

Cammarrota, M., Costantino, C. and Fängström, I. (1997) *Joint Final Report of the SIP Tourism Project.* Istat of Statistics Sweden, Stockholm.

Checkley, A. (1992) The greening of Canadian Pacific Hotels and Resorts: the Chateau Whistler case. In: Hawkes, S. and Williams, P.W. (eds) *The Greening of Tourism: from Principles to Practice: a Casebook of Best Environmental Practice in Tourism.* Centre for Tourism Policy and Research, Simon Fraser University, Burnaby, British Columbia, Canada, pp. 9–14.

Clarke, J. (1997) A framework of approaches to sustainable tourism. *Journal of Sustainable Tourism* 5, 224–243.

Coccossis, H. and Nijkamp, P. (eds) (1995) *Sustainable Tourism Development.* Ashgate Publishing Ltd., UK.

Commonwealth of Australia (1994) *National Ecotourism Strategy.* Commonwealth Department of Tourism.

Danmarks Turistråd (1997) *Resultater af turistundersøgelse på det tyske marked.* Data presented 12.08.97 by GfK Danmark a/s, Copenhagen, Denmark.

Danmarks Turistråd (1998a) *Danmark som destination for ferierejser and erhvervsturisme – en overordnet marketingrapport på tværs af indkvarteringsformer.* Danmarks Turistråd, Copenhagen.

Danmarks Turistråd, (1998b) *Grundene til at man har valgt Danmark fordelt på nationalitet – særudtræk af TØBBE-analyse om Turismensøkonomiske og Beskæftigelsesmæssige betydning, 1998.* Danmarks Turistråd, Copenhagen.

De Kadt, E. (1992) Making the alternative sustainable: lessons from development for tourism. In: Smith, V. and Eadington, W.R. (eds) *Tourism Alternatives: Potentials and Problems in the Development of Tourism.* University of Pennsylvania Press, Philadelphia, pp. 47–75.

Destination 21 Sekretariatet (1999) *Working Outline for Pilot Project Destination 21.* Destination 21 Sekretariatet, Copenhagen.

Dymond, S.J. (1997) Indicators of sustainable tourism in New Zealand: a local government perspective. *Journal of Sustainable Tourism* 5, 279–293.

Eber, S. (ed.) (1992) *Beyond the Green Horizon. Principles of Sustainable Tourism: a Discussion Paper.* World Tourism Concern and Wide Fund for Nature, London.

Ellul, A. (1997) Integrating sustainable principles in the development of tourism projects. *Naturopa* 84, 5–6.

France, L. (ed.) (1997) *The Earthscan Reader in Sustainable Tourism.* Earthscan Publications, London.

Goodall, B. (1992) Environmental auditing for tourism. *Progress in Tourism and Hospitality Management* 4, 60–73.

Green Globe Global (2000) Green Globe 21 Sustainable 21st Century Tourism. www.greenglobe21.com

Grenier, D., Kaae, B.C., Miller, M.L. and Mobley, R.W. (1993) Ecotourism, landscape architecture and urban planning. *Landscape and Urban Planning* 25, 1–16.

Guldager, S. and Nuppenau, C. (1998) Inhabitants' response to ecological issues affecting their daily lifestyle. In: Breuste, J., Feldmann, H. and Uhlmann, O. (eds) *Urban Ecology.* Springer Verlag, Berlin, pp. 384–386.

Guldager, S., Reeh, U., Persson, B., Attwell, K. and Nuppenau, C. (1998) *Grøn Struktur i byøkologisk perspektiv: proces og metoder i Egebjerggård og Skotteparken.* Park og Landskabsserien nr. 22, Forskningscentret for Skov & Landskab, Hoersholm, Denmark.

Gullestrup, A. (1997) Svaner og blomster – det gælder miljøet. *Hotel, Restaurant og Turisme* 115, 22.

Hall, M.C. and Lew, A.A. (eds) (1998) *Sustainable Tourism: a Geographical Perspective.* Longman, Harlow.

Hart, M. (1995) *Guide to Sustainable Community Indicators.* QLF/Atlantic Center for the Environment, Ipswich, Massachusetts.

Hawkins, D.E., Wood, M.E. and Bittman, S. (eds) (1995) *The Ecolodge Sourcebook for Planners and Developers.* The Ecotourism Society, Vermont.

Henry, I.P. and Jackson, G.A.M. (1996) Sustainability of management processes and tourism products and contexts. *Journal of Sustainable Tourism* 4, 17–28.

Hjalager, A.M. (1995) *Turister ved Blåvand. Karakteristika, besøgsmønstre og holdninger.* Miljøministeriets Eksempelprojekt nr. 9. Copenhagen, Denmark.

Holten-Andersen, J., Christensen, N., Kristiansen, L.W., Kristensen, P. and Emborg, L. (eds) (1998) *Natur og Miljø 1997: Påvirkninger og tilstand.* Miljø- og Energiministeriet, Danmarks Miljøundersøgelser, Copenhagen, Denmark.

Hopfenbeck, W. and Zimmer, P. (1993) *Umveltsorientiertes Tourismusmanagement. Strategien, Checklisten, Fallstudien.* Verlag Moderne Industrie, Landsberg/Lech.

Kaae, B.C. (1999) Living with tourism – exploration of destination sharing and strategies of adjustment to tourism. Unpublished PhD dissertation, The Royal Veterinary and Agricultural University, Copenhagen, Denmark.

Kaas, T. (1998) Svanemærket for overnatningsfaciliteter er på vej. *Hotel, Restaurant og Turisme* 116, 18.

MacGregor, J.R. (1993) Sustainable tourism development. In: Khan, M.A., Olsen, M.D. and Var, T. (eds) *Encyclopedia of Hospitality and Tourism.* Van Nostrand Reinhold, New York, pp. 781–789.

Manning, E.W. (1993) Managing sustainable tourism: indicators for better decisions. In: Hawkes, S. and Williams, P.W. (eds) *The Greening of Tourism: from Principles to Practice: a Casebook of Best Environmental Practice in Tourism.* Centre for Tourism Policy and Research, Simon Fraser University, Burnaby, British Columbia, Canada, pp. 97–104.

Mathieson, A. and Wall, G. (1982) *Tourism – Economic, Physical and Social Impacts.* Longman, New York.

Mayer, H.N. (1998) The social dimension of urban ecology. In: Breuste, J., Feldmann, H. and Uhlmann, O. (eds) *Urban Ecology.* Springer Verlag, Berlin, pp. 203–209.

McCool, S.F. and Watson, A.E. (eds) (1994) *Linking Tourism, the Environment, and Sustainability.* USDAFS Intermountain Research Station, Ogden, Utah, General Technical Report INT-GTR–323.

Minger, T. (1992) The green resort: environmental stewardship and the resort community. In: Gill, A. and Hartman, R. (eds) *Mountain Resort Development.* Proceedings of the Vail Conference 18–21 April 1991. Centre for Tourism Policy and Research, Simon Fraser University, Burnaby, British Columbia, Canada, pp. 66–69.

Mowforth, M. and Munt, I. (1998) *Tourism and Sustainability: New Tourism in the Third World.* Routledge, UK.

Murphy, P. (1985) *Tourism: a Community Approach.* Routledge, London.

Murphy, P.E. (1994) Tourism and sustainable development. In: Theobald, W. (ed.) *Global Tourism: the next decade.* Butterworth-Heinemann, Oxford, pp. 274–290.

Nelson, J.G., Butler, R. and Wall, G. (1993) *Tourism and Sustainable*

Development: Monitoring, Planning, Managing. University of Waterloo, Canada.

Njor, L. (1997) Hvem, Hvad, Hvor om de 'grønne' tyske turister. *Hotel, Restaurant og Turisme* 115, 20–21.

Page, S.J. and Thorn, K.J. (1997) Towards sustainable tourism planning in New Zealand: public sector planning responses. *Journal of Sustainable Tourism* 5, 59–77.

Priestly, G.K., Edwards, J.A. and Coccossis, H. (eds) (1996) *Sustainable Tourism? European Experiences.* CAB International, Wallingford, UK.

Slater, R.W. (1991) Understanding the relationship between tourism, environment and sustainable development. In: Reid, L.J. (ed.) *Tourism – Environment – Sustainable Development: an Agenda for Research.* Conference Proceedings of the Travel and Tourism Research Association, Canada, pp. 10–13.

Stanners, D. and Bourdeau, P. (1995) *Europe's Environment. The Dobriss Assessment.* European Environmental Agency, Copenhagen, pp. 172–201.

The Ecotourism Society (1993) *Ecotourism Guidelines for Nature Tour Operators.*

The Ecotourism Society (1995) *A Collection of Responsible Travel Guidelines.*

Todd, S.E. and Williams, P.W. (1996) From white to green: a proposed environmental management system framework for ski areas. *Journal of Sustainable Tourism* 4, 147–173.

Tourist Industry Association of Canada and National Round Table on the Environment and the Economy (no date) *Code of Ethics and Guidelines for Sustainable Tourism.*

United Nations Environmental Programme (1994) *Environmental Codes of Conduct for Tourism.* UNEP, Industry and Environment, Paris.

US National Park Service (1993) *Guiding Principles of Sustainable Design.* United States Department of the Interior, National Park Service, Denver, Colorado.

Westlake, J. and Diamantis, D. (1998) The application of environmental auditing to the management of sustainability within tourism. *Tourism Recreation Research* 23, 69–71.

World Commission on Environment and Development (1987) *Our Common Future.* Oxford University Press, Oxford.

World Tourism Organization (1995) *Concepts, Definitions and Classifications for Tourist Statistics.* WTO, Madrid, Spain.

World Tourism Organization (1996) *What Managers Need to Know: a Practical Guide to the Development and Use of Indicators of Sustainable Tourism.* WTO, Madrid, Spain.

World Travel and Tourism Council (WTTC), World Tourism Organization (WTO) and Earth Council (EC) (1997) *Agenda 21 for the Travel and Tourism Industry: Towards Environmentally Sustainable Development.* WTTC, London.

WWF (1995) *WWF och turismen – Miljöanpassad turism and Ekoturism.* WWF Ecotourism Project, Sweden.

Tourism, Sustainability and the Social Milieux in Lake Superior's North Shore and Islands

17

R.J. Payne[1], Margaret E. Johnston[1] and G. David Twynam[2]

[1]School of Outdoor Recreation, Parks and Tourism, Lakehead University, Thunder Bay, Ontario, Canada, [2]School of Tourism, University College of the Cariboo, Kamloops, British Columbia, Canada

Introduction

Tourism is a traditional economic activity in the northern parts of the province of Ontario where fish, wildlife and wilderness have afforded opportunities for economic gain and personal recreation for over 100 years (Benidickson, 1982). This chapter addresses issues of tourism and sustainability from the perspective of the residents on Lake Superior's north shore and islands. The relationship between natural resource-based tourism and sustainability in this context should be easy to document. However, sustainable development, and the more recent term 'sustainability', has proved to be difficult to understand as it appears to mean all things to all people. Moreover, tourism, even that supported by the northern Ontario environment, is not immune to changes in economic, social and political conditions. These kinds of changes can alter the numbers and expectations of the clientele of tourism establishments, or can modify the rules governing other land-use activities that ultimately affect tourism. Such changes influence the sustainability of tourism as much as depleted fish or game stocks or the deterioration of the forest recreation environment. We seek to determine how residents of the north shore of Lake Superior view the possibility that tourism will become a more significant activity in their region. Furthermore, we are interested in examining how their views on tourism compare with accepted criteria for social sustainability in the use of natural resources.

© CAB *International* 2001. *Tourism, Recreation and Sustainability* (eds S.F. McCool and R.N. Moisey)

The region

In areas such as northern Ontario, where people's lives and regional economies are built upon the exploitation of natural resources, tourism has been promoted enthusiastically as an important addition to a limited range of economic opportunities (Smithers and Geissenger, 1991; Johnston, 1995). Tourism, it is hoped, will help to diversify a community's economic base, thereby providing some insulation from the peaks and troughs that are typical of resource-based economies. Tourism is also embraced for its promises of somewhat more stable employment opportunities, an important consideration when traditional hinterland industries, such as forestry and mining, are becoming capital, rather than labour, intensive. Tourism has been heralded in the past 25 years as the last hope for community stability or the best hope for continuing prosperity in northern Ontario. However, as shown in the Temagami area of north-eastern Ontario, enthusiasm for tourism, and especially for its non-consumptive varieties, is not universally shared across the north (Hodgins and Benidickson, 1989).

Tourism in northern Ontario remains problematic. Fishing and hunting continue to attract both tourists and residents; however, remote tourism operations are often resented by local people who feel that tourists get special access. Snowmobiling has increased with the establishment of long-distance trails. Ecotourism activities (e.g. canoeing, kayaking) are increasing as northern Ontario becomes more recognized as an ecotourism region (Twynam and Robinson, 1997). Wilderness areas, especially those in parks, continue to attract tourists who have interests in non-consumptive activities. The coastal hiking trail in Pukaskwa National Park, for example, provides wilderness tourism opportunities not available in more developed parts of northern Ontario.

Lake Superior itself is the key defining feature of this region. It is recognized as the world's largest lake. Management of the lake, shared between the US and Canada, has been facilitated by the creation in 1991 of the Lake Superior Bi-National Program. Under the Bi-National Program, Lake Superior's unique position in the Great Lakes watershed and its water quality are considered in combination, with the intention of demonstrating good management practices on the lake. The Bi-National Program's brochure explains that:

> Lake Superior is unique, a vast resource of fresh water that has not experienced the same levels of development, urbanization and pollution as the other Great Lakes. Because of this uniqueness, the International Joint Commission recommended that Lake Superior be designated as a demonstration area where discharges and emissions of toxic substances that are long-lived in the environment and build up in the bodies of humans and wildlife, would not be permitted.
>
> (Lake Superior Bi-National Program, 1998)

Since the programme's beginnings, considerable progress has been recorded in documenting pollution sources and in developing controls. Implementation of actions designed to reduce pollution is proceeding, albeit slowly. As the initial *raison d'être* of the programme is met, attention is turning toward expanding the demonstration status of lake-wide management by focusing more on the goal of sustainability. Issues of sustainability – in forestry, fisheries and tourism – are somewhat easier to define, given the low populations and environmental impacts of human activity on the Canadian side of the Lake Superior basin.

As the public profile of the lake has risen, Lake Superior has come to be viewed as a unique resource for tourism. Outfitters focus kayaking and other water-based activities on its shore zone, especially in protected parts of the north shore such as the Rossport Islands. Marketing associations have been luring power and sail boaters to the north shore with promises of 'wilderness cruising'.

Lake Superior's north shore and islands (Fig. 17.1) comprise an area of land and water from Terrace Bay/Slate Islands in the east to Thunder Cape at the foot of the Sibley Peninsula in the west. Determining the terrestrial boundary for the region is problematic. On the one hand, the edge of the Lake Superior watershed might be selected (see, for example, Skibicki, 1995); however, it is roughly 100 km inland and includes areas actively exploited for timber and minerals. On the other hand, the edge of settlement – not more than 10 km from the shore – offers an alternative; such an edge would represent a 'bioregional' boundary (World Resources Institute, 1992). The latter best describes local people's views.

The imprint of settlement in the region is most visible along the coast, where the Trans-Canada Highway (Highway 17 in Ontario) and the main line of the transcontinental Canadian Pacific Railway join the communities of Terrace Bay, Schreiber, Rossport, Pays Plat, Nipigon and Red Rock. Apart from these communities and isolated pockets of shoreline development, most land in the region is in public hands as Crown land that, in Ontario, the provincial Ministry of Natural Resources is charged with managing in a sustainable manner. Several of these communities have large pulp mills, testifying to the importance of the forest industry as employer and as influence in the region. The region has an identity ('the north shore') that is recognized by those living there as well as by other northern Ontario residents.

The region has been recognized by several organizations as possessing both outstanding natural beauty and ecological integrity. Attention from outside the region has come from Parks Canada, which has selected a candidate National Marine Conservation Area (Parks Canada, 1995, p. 85) centred on the region. Environment Canada and the US Environmental Protection Agency have identified the region,

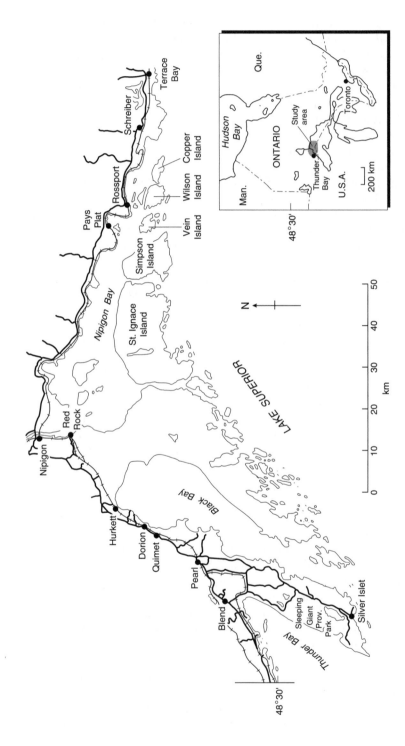

Fig. 17.1. Lake Superior's north shore and islands. Cartography by C.A. Chapin, Lakehead University Geography Department.

and especially the islands, as a 'Shoreline Biodiversity Investment Area' (Reid and Holland, 1997, p. 58). Both recognitions will contribute to the growing tourism promotion of the natural heritage aspects of the region.

Purpose and objectives

This chapter has two general goals:

1. To investigate residents' views of tourism along the north shore of Lake Superior; and
2. To compare those views with accepted criteria for social sustainability.

This section of the chapter introduces the study area – the north shore and islands of Lake Superior – within the context of northern Ontario. Then, the concept of sustainability, focusing on its social dimensions, is discussed and a position developed. A discussion on methodology explains the nature of the data as well as the quantitative and qualitative methods employed in collecting and understanding them. The presentation and discussion of the results follows. Finally, in a concluding section, the lessons learned about sustainable tourism in the region are presented.

Sustainability and its social dimensions

Sustainability in a social sense is deserving of special attention because, unlike its ecological and economic siblings, social sustainability more obviously involves people. For this reason, approaches to defining sustainability in operational terms that ignore people and their use of natural environments might be considered suspect. A sector-specific approach, for example, such as sustainable forestry, focuses on forest industry activities to the exclusion of all others. Even ecological sustainability, driven by the stress–response ecological model, places science and scientific knowledge far in front of the interests and understanding of local people. In the following section, we examine various approaches to social sustainability in order to prepare for our enquiry into how people in the region view it.

No term since the ubiquitous 'lifestyle' has captured the imaginations of social and natural scientists, as well as the public, in the way that the terms 'sustainable development' or the more recent 'sustainability' have. Some (Salwasser, 1990) see in the term a new paradigm for conservation; others see a retreat from protection and preservation (Noss, 1991). Indeed, the term has been bent into a variety of shapes and meanings: for example, sustained development and sustainable growth, in relation to resources; or, sustainable budget or government, in relation to public administration. Some enthusiasts (Ontario Hydro, 1990; Skidmore, 1990) seem to believe the term means 'business as usual'. As used in the Brundtland Commission report (WCED, 1987), sustainability loses its potentially analytical edge. That economic growth is necessary and that care ought to be taken not to diminish the biosphere's capability for future generations is a mere platitude. This definition is so weak that the idea of sustainable utilization, as set out in the 1980 *World Conservation Strategy* seems powerful by comparison.

The first *World Conservation Strategy* (IUCN *et al.*, 1980) made 'sustainable utilization' one of three main principles for the conservation of living resources. Sustainable utilization comprised not only the obvious economic dimension but also social and ecological components. If sustainable utilization and sustainable development can be equated, then it becomes possible to differentiate three interrelated dimensions of the term. Development which is ecologically sustainable does not disrupt the ecological integrity of a site or region; development which is socially sustainable does not alter the ways of life of people in a region; and development which is economically sustainable does not disrupt existing economic structures.

This view is open to a number of criticisms, not the least of which being that it is hopelessly naive in its understanding of how socioeconomic change occurs in a capitalist economy. However, this approach is significant for two reasons: it differentiates three dimensions upon which development of any kind will have effects; and it brings people and their forms of social and economic organization into conservation decision-making at a fundamental level.

In 1990, the IUCN and its partners discarded the term 'sustainable development', opting instead for the more analytical 'sustainability'. In the re-shaping of the World Conservation Strategy (IUCN *et al.*, 1990), sustainability comprises economic, social and ecological dimensions. This term, with all of its meaning and breadth, is adopted for the remainder of this chapter.

The Rio conference on Environment and Development in 1992 focused attention on implementing sustainability. One of the important outcomes of the Rio conference, Agenda 21, speaks of the necessity of integrating sustainability considerations into natural resource decision-making:

> Its successful implementation is first and foremost the responsibility of Governments. National strategies, plans, policies and processes are crucial in achieving this. . . . Other international, regional and subregional

organizations are also called upon to contribute to this effort. The broadest public participation and the active involvement of the non-governmental organizations and other groups should also be encouraged.

(United Nations Development Programme, 1992, Chapter 1.3)

While Agenda 21 recognizes that all sectors must play a role in achieving sustainability, the role of government is understood to be the backdrop against which contributions will be made.

This more practical interpretation of sustainability has spawned a number of initiatives to define and to monitor sustainability, some of which are applicable to tourism:

- codes of conduct;
- best practices management;
- ISO 14000 environmental management standards; and
- sustainability indicators.

Codes of conduct are found in widely different occupations, guiding the behaviour of occupational groups such as doctors, lawyers and accountants. In all cases, codes of conduct are based upon principles to which practitioners adhere. The UN Environment Programme (UNEP) recently published a report (UNEP, 1995) which identifies voluntary environmental codes of conduct for tourism being used in a number of countries (see also Mason and Mowforth, 1995). Codes of conduct for both tourism operators and tourists have been advocated more recently by the World Wide Fund for Nature through its initiative to develop principles to link Arctic tourism and conservation (Johnston and Mason, 1997; WWF, 1998). The importance of minimizing negative social and cultural impacts and of involving local people in tourism development to some extent is emphasized in most codes of conduct for tourism operators.

Another initiative with implications for tourism and sustainability focuses on best practices management. Sustainability is not necessarily a goal in best practice management: goals are as diverse as the activities to which the best practices initiative is applied. The reasoning for the best practices approach is straightforward: find examples of excellence in management and use them as exemplars to improve management elsewhere in that sector.

Harris and Leiper (1995) present a best practices approach to sustainable tourism in Australia. The authors surveyed large and small tourism operations to determine which ones were managing their diverse environmental impacts in the most effective ways. For example, the Great Barrier Reef Marine Park Authority was selected as an exemplar for its management of stakeholder involvement, educational activities and spatial/temporal zoning within its jurisdiction, the Great Barrier Reef. Another operation, Australia, received commendations for its efforts ensuring that supplies were purchased from local people in regions where it operates.

The utility of the best practices approach is well illustrated by The Ecotourism Society (TES) (1993) which not only has documented best practices in that segment of the tourism industry, but also has made the results available to operators throughout the world. A subsequent evaluation in Ecuador of the effectiveness of the best practices approach used by TES revealed that several areas needed to be addressed further (Norman *et al.*, 1997). These included the need for information about the importation of plants, animals and disposable products, appropriate interactions with local residents, and respect for local culture, customs and values. The evaluation indicated that nature tour operators needed to pursue local development programmes and to encourage their clients to become involved in and contribute to local community development programmes, and further, to put pressure on local accommodation establishments to meet the guidelines (Norman *et al.*, 1997). Best practices management can play an important role in helping individual (tourism) organizations find effective means to implement generic codes of conduct.

The ISO 14000 series of environmental management standards have been developed by the International Standards Organization to identify and monitor the environmental 'footprint' of any activity (Standards Council of Canada, 1998). The standards are not directed at minimizing environmental impact; rather, they are meant to provide guidance to organizations that wish to, or need to, show that they have taken steps to set goals for their environmental impact. Gale (1996) explains that submitting to the standards is voluntary, a fact that strongly distinguishes the ISO 14000 series from governmental regulations. Gale goes on to point out two other significant issues: the environmental management statement:

> is the document a company will follow for certification/registration with a third party and/or for self assessment and declaration of conformance to the standard. This means that the document is written in prescriptive language as an auditable standard: it contains 'musts' and 'shalls'. The objective is to develop a sound environmental management system. It is the system that is auditable, not the company's environmental performance (i.e. the outcome of the system).
>
> (Gale, 1996; emphasis in original)

The requirement for third-party intervention is notable. However, this third party is not the government: rather, in Canada at least, certification is facilitated by the Canadian Standards Association (CSA) which offers training for employees of companies interested in being certified under the standards. The employees, once certified by the CSA, are authorized to draw up the environmental management statement. Gale's final point is also important: any auditing focuses on the system rather than the organization's impact on the environment. The stated intention of the standards is to enable organizations to develop a system comprising steps for managing their environmental impacts. The advantage of such an approach is that, with a certificate of compliance in hand, organizations are able to assert to customers and to critics alike that they are exercising environmental care. Business organizations, especially, recognize that such certification promises access to important market areas. In tourism, it is likely that large organizations will be the first to be certified under the guidelines, although small firms exhibit the flexibility in operations to make such changes more easily.

Behind many of the practical developments in implementing sustainability are sets of principles that connect theory and action. One such principle-based initiative, the *Charter on Sustainable Tourism*, originated at a world conference on sustainable tourism in 1995. The charter is composed of 18 principles directed at governments and the tourism industry. Principle 1 states the relationship between sustainability and tourism concisely:

> Tourism development shall be based on criteria of sustainability, which means that it must be ecologically bearable in the long term, as well as economically viable, and ethically and socially equitable for local communities.
>
> (World Conference on Sustainable Tourism, 1995, p. 12)

Other principles stress that, for tourism to be sustainable, it must recognize and support local people and their culture (principle 3), it must be a cooperative venture (principle 4) and it must be part of an integrated planning and management system (principle 5). In these principles, all of the actors, including governments, are charged with responsibility for assuring the sustainability of tourism. The charter emphasizes that sustainability in tourism can be achieved only if tourism operators and governments cooperate with local people in areas where tourism is well developed or has great potential.

Another principle-based approach, the Bellagio Principles (International Institute for Sustainable Development, 1997a), does not focus solely on tourism; rather the principles are aimed more generally at development. However, they share with the charter a concern that local people and their interests be integrated into decision-making. Two principles make this position quite clear:

1. Openness: assessment of progress toward sustainability should:
• make the methods and data that are used accessible to all; and

- make explicit all judgments, assumptions and uncertainties in data and interpretations:

2. Broad participation: assessment of progress toward sustainability should:

- obtain broad representation of key grass-roots, social, professional and technical groups, to ensure recognition of diverse and changing values; and
- ensure decision-makers' participation, thus securing a firm link to decision-making and resulting action (International Institute for Sustainable Development, 1997a).

Principles such as these form the bases for scientific perspectives on sustainability. Furthermore, since sustainability is generally a policy or legislative goal, implementing it will require not only defining but also understanding cause and effect relationships in ecosystems. In these terms, achieving sustainability requires that the tools of science, scientific knowledge and scientific method are applied by agencies having environmental management mandates. Furthermore, since sustainability is first a public goal, achieving it presupposes that government agencies possess both the mandate and the scientific capabilities necessary to take an effective leadership role.

Scientific studies of sustainability, even those focusing upon tourism (e.g. McCool *et al.*, 1998) have generally been based upon the 'stress-state-response-indicators model' (Indicators Task Force, 1991; Lake Superior Bi-National Program, 1995; Lonergan *et al.*, 1996) which requires data about a variety of variables as well as the scientific knowledge to understand (ecological) relationships among them. Crucial requirements in the model are the establishment of baseline data to represent 'normal' ecological conditions and the identification of indicators through monitoring. Consequently, this approach, and its dependence upon experts, is often described as 'data-driven'. Environmental non-government organizations such as the World Resources Institute continue to do intensive research using this framework into indicators for biodiversity (Reid *et al.*, 1993) as well as for other significant issues.

The limitations of an apparently scientific approach to sustainability are illustrated well by Wilson (1997). He has described the controversy over the re-introduction of wolves into the Greater Yellowstone ecosystem as a clash between environmentalists and local people who resent such outside interference in their way of life. Wilson emphasizes that this clash goes well beyond wolves and ecology to involve differing levels of access to social power, differing views of the relationship between humans and nature, and differing ideas about private property (Wilson, 1997, p. 454). In the Yellowstone case, the point of view of local residents was ignored while the scientific perspective, focused on restoring ecological integrity, carried the day.

A mixed approach to sustainability, favoured by Canada's International Development Research Centre and the IUCN, seeks to engage 'stakeholders in defining the key sustainability issues affecting their lives, and [to define] practical ways of measuring change in human and ecosystem condition related to these issues' (International Institute for Sustainable Development, 1997b). This approach contrasts with the expert or data-driven one common in the stress-state-response-indicators framework in three significant ways:

- it recognizes the importance of people's customary and traditional knowledge;
- it views sustainability issues in a bioregional context; and
- it seeks practical solutions.

The importance of these first two features cannot be overstated. The 'discovery' of customary knowledge (i.e. knowledge accumulated by people such as fishers who use their understanding of nature in economic activities) and traditional knowledge (i.e. knowledge of nature that is deeply embedded in people's ways of life) by the scientific community represents an opportunity to bridge the gap between science and experience. Connecting science and customary or traditional knowledge, by no means an easy task, holds benefits for both scientists and local people. Furthermore, the gradual legitimation of customary and traditional knowledge provides support for management regimes in which local people have not only a voice but also a measure of control.

The second feature of this approach – sustainability issues in a bioregional context – supports the important role of customary and traditional knowledge. However, it also repudiates various sector-specific attempts (e.g. forestry or tourism) to come to grips with sustainability by acknowledging that both ecological relationships and people's relationships with nature operate over relatively large areas. Indeed, attempts by forest scientists (e.g. Baskerville, 1996; Duinker, 1996) to develop sustainability indices for forestry seem more concerned with accommodating environmental issues in forestry practice rather than integrating sustainability as a goal. The case for bioregionalism is put concisely by the World Resources Institute:

> Within a bioregion lies a mosaic of land or aquatic uses. Each patch provides habitats in which different species survive and flourish, and each has its own particular relationship to the region's human population. All the elements of the mosaic are interactive; the management of a watershed affects riverine habitats, farms, estuaries, fisheries and coral reefs. The components are also dynamic; each changes over time as rivers change

course, fallow fields regenerate, storms batter coasts and fires ravage
forests.

(World Resources Institute, 1992; emphasis in original)

People, in their social and economic diversity, clearly play a pivotal
role in a bioregion. Involving them in developing and monitoring
sustainability indicators would seem to be a rational course of action,
with benefits to all.

If sustainability is to be an attainable societal goal that is relevant
to tourism as well as to other endeavours, the following critical
features are required according to the literature discussed above:

- active involvement of actors, from local people to (senior) governments;
- judicious application of science tempered by the practical concerns
  of local people; and
- a spatial (rather than sectoral) focus, possibly concentrated at the
  regional level.

It is this community-based approach (Woodley, 1993) to sustainability
that seems to offer the best understanding of local people's feelings and
thoughts.

Methodology

The research reported here was completed during September–October
1997 among the communities of the north shore of Lake Superior for
the Superior North Community Economic Development Corporation
(Twynam *et al.*, 1997). The results from the forums concerning
people's views of tourism on the north shore and in the north shore
islands were also directed to the Boreal West Round Table (as part of
the Lands for Life land-use planning process) and to Parks Canada (as
part of the public consultations on the proposed Western Lake
Superior National Marine Conservation Area).

Six forums were held across the region, one each in Terrace Bay,
Pays Plat, Rossport, Nipigon, Red Rock and Silver Islet. The forums
were advertised on local radio and in the local press in advance. In
addition, known opinion leaders in the communities were invited to
attend. Attendance varied widely: 44 people turned out in the cottage
community of Silver Islet; only two attended the forum at Pays Plat, a
First Nation reserve.

Participants at each forum completed a questionnaire that sought
information on their involvements with, and attitudes toward, tourism
in the region. In addition, participants discussed questions and issues

about tourism in the region put to them by facilitators in each forum. These qualitative data were recorded in writing and on audiotape by the researchers.

Data

The data collected were of two types. Quantitative data were collected about participants in the forums in order to develop a participant profile and to determine attitudes towards tourism in the region. This approach produced 92 completed questionnaires. The surveys completed by participants at the beginning of each forum provide quantitative data, including social and demographic variables such as gender, age and length of residence in the region. In addition, participants responded to a Likert-style, 28-statement section of the survey, based upon the TIAS Scale outlined by Lankford and Howard (1994), on their attitudes towards tourism in the region.

Qualitative data were gathered in order to delve more deeply into tourism issues. Capturing the qualitative data was a three-step process:

- first, participants at each forum were divided into two groups, each with a facilitator who focused discussion through a series of predetermined questions and who wrote participant responses on a flip chart;
- secondly, *rapporteurs* (Payne, Johnston and Twynam) took notes during the discussions; and
- thirdly, each session was recorded on audiotape.

Analysis

The analysis of the quantitative data utilized frequencies in communicating a profile of the forum participants. More complex analyses, using principal components analysis, K-means cluster analysis and discriminant analysis in SPSS for Windows, were employed to determine if there were meaningful groups among the participants with respect to their attitudes towards tourism in the region.

Results and discussion

Background

This section focuses on the quantitative and qualitative dimensions of participants' views, feelings and attitudes toward tourism and tourism development on Lake Superior's north shore and islands, collected during the forums. Three forms of reporting follow:

- a description of the demographic and social characteristics of participants;
- a discussion based upon the responses to the attitudinal questions; and
- a discussion of the themes and issues voiced by participants during the forums.

Demographic and social characteristics of the participants

There were 95 participants at the meetings, 92 of whom completed the survey. As Table 17.1 shows, the majority were male (72%). Furthermore, most of the respondents were 35 years or older, with more than half between the ages of 35 and 54 (53.9%). Nearly 60% of the participants had lived in the region for more than 40 years. Twenty-one per cent of the participants owned a tourism business and 23% had a job related to tourism (Table 17.2).

Table 17.3 contains means and standard deviations of responses from forum participants to the 28 attitude statements concerning tourism in the region. Discussion of these findings focuses on three patterns of response:

Table 17.1. Socio-demographic characteristics of forum participants (*n* = 92).

Socio-demographic variables	*n* (%)
Gender	
Male	66 (72)
Female	26 (28)
Age (years)	
19–24	1 (1)
25–34	4 (4)
35–44	26 (28)
45–54	24 (26)
55–64	18 (20)
65–74	12 (13)
75+	7 (8)
Years lived in region	
0–10	10 (11)
11–20	8 (9)
21–30	13 (14)
31–40	8 (9)
41–50	18 (20)
51+	32 (35)

Table 17.2. Forum participants' involvements in tourism industry (*n* = 92).

Involvement	*n* (%)
Owns a tourism business	19 (21)
Has a job related to tourism	21 (23)
No involvement	52 (56)

Table 17.3. Forum participants' outlook on tourism in the region (*n* = 92).

Statement	1	2	3	4	5	Mean	SD
a. Tourism provides desirable jobs	29	51	6	6	0	1.88	0.80
b. My community should become more of a tourist destination	29	38	13	4	5	2.08	1.08
c. Tourism in my region has improved my standard of living	3	22	36	20	10	3.13	1.01
d. More outdoor recreation development is not desirable	7	10	15	35	25	3.66	1.21
e. I am against new tourism development which will attract new tourists to this region	3	7	9	37	36	4.04	1.05
f. Because of tourism, I have more recreational opportunities available to me	16	28	27	11	10	2.68	1.21
g. It is important to provide recreation facilities for local people rather than tourists	5	28	31	22	4	2.91	0.98
h. Noise levels from the existing tourism facilities are not appropriate for this region	2	5	22	37	24	3.84	0.96
i. Tourism has negatively impacted the natural environment in the region	3	6	14	47	22	3.86	0.97
j. I believe tourism should be actively encouraged in the region	33	38	11	6	4	2.02	1.07
k. Tourism has a vital role in the region	28	45	7	9	2	2.03	0.99
l. The benefits of tourism outweigh any negative consequences	14	29	18	18	11	2.81	1.27
m. Tourists are valuable	32	52	7	1	0	1.75	0.64

Table 17.3. *continued*

	Statement	1	2	3	4	5	Mean	SD
n.	The quality of public services has improved due to increased tourism in the region	7	28	35	15	5	2.81	0.99
o.	The region has better roads due to tourism	4	23	20	24	20	3.36	1.21
p.	Tourism has increased crime in the region	1	5	19	43	24	3.91	0.89
q.	There is more litter in the region due to tourism	3	18	24	33	14	3.40	1.07
r.	Local political turmoil has resulted from tourism development	2	12	35	34	7	3.36	0.89
s.	I feel I can access the decision-making process to influence tourism development in the region	8	41	27	12	2	2.54	0.91
t.	Developing tourism will provide more jobs in the region	25	53	11	2	1	1.92	0.76
u.	Tourists interfere with residents' enjoyment of the region	4	10	17	50	11	3.59	0.99
v.	Local authorities are right in promoting tourism in the region	20	51	12	7	1	2.10	0.87
w.	Long-term planning by regional authorities can control negative impacts of tourism on the environment	23	47	8	9	3	2.13	1.02
x.	I have more money to spend as a result of tourism	4	14	31	31	12	3.36	1.03
y.	Tourism will play a major economic role in the region	18	47	15	10	2	2.25	0.97
z.	I would like to see tourism become the main industry in the region	9	19	28	19	13	3.09	1.20
aa.	Shopping opportunities are better in my community due to tourism	5	23	36	20	7	3.01	1.01
bb.	We should not try to attract more visitors to the region	4	8	13	35	34	3.90	1.11

1, Strongly agree; 2, agree; 3, neutral; 4, disagree; 5, strongly disagree.

- statements with which there is general agreement;
- statements with which there is general disagreement; and
- statements with which there is a diversity of views.

There is agreement among residents who responded to the survey that not only does tourism have a place in the region's future, but also that it does now, and will continue to, yield positive economic benefits for local people and the regional economy. Statements *a, b, j, k, m, t, v, w* and *y* in Table 17.3 address these two issues directly. All of these statements feature levels of agreement in excess of 69%.

There is disagreement with a series of statements which suggest that tourism development ought to be restricted or that tourism has had negative social effects in the region. Statements *d, e, h, i, p, u* and *bb* address these issues. Disagreement with these statements ranges from a low of 65% concerning no more outdoor recreation development (statement *d*) to a high of 79% in response to a statement (*e*) suggesting that new tourism developments ought not to occur.

The remaining 12 statements reflect a diversity of views. In one group (i.e. statements *c, g, n, r* and *aa*), the majority of residents have chosen the neutral category, declining to commit themselves to agreeing or disagreeing with statements that focus attention on tourism's impact on local community life. In another (i.e. statements *f, l, o, q, s, x* and *z*), people in the region have agreed or disagreed cautiously but certainly not as strongly as they did with other statements. These statements ask the residents to reflect upon the benefits and costs of existing tourism developments and activities in the region. The general attitude that tourism is potentially beneficial, especially if those benefits are put in economic terms, is consistent with a major theme concerning infrastructure, attractions and services, discussed below.

Using principal components analysis (as suggested in McCool and Reilly, 1993), the 28 attitudinal items were reduced to seven dimensions that account for 69.8% of the variance in the data (Table 17.4). Interpreting these dimensions and their relative importance reveals that factor 1, the personal benefits of tourism development, contributes 38.6% of the explained variance. The second factor, tourism in the local economy, adds another 8.6%. The remaining five factors, accounting for 22.6% of the explained variance, can be identified in the following ways:

- factor 3 – the negative effects of tourism (5.6%);
- factor 4 – the negative views of tourism (5.2%);
- factor 5 – the need for planning in tourism development (4.2%);
- factor 6 – tourism and infrastructure (4.0%); and
- factor 7 – tourism and decision making (3.6%).

Table 17.4. Underlying attitudinal dimensions.

	Statement	Factor 1 (E-values)	Factor 2 (E-values)	Factor 3 (E-values)	Factor 4 (E-values)	Factor 5 (E-values)	Factor 6 (E-values)	Factor 7 (E-values)
a.	Tourism provides desirable jobs	0.07842	**0.81528**	0.09339	−0.09951	0.02081	−0.01904	0.07904
b.	My community should become more of a tourist destination	0.33957	0.39197	−0.32327	−0.36344	0.18589	**0.40817**	−0.27890
c.	Tourism in my region has improved my standard of living	**0.64540**	0.22945	−0.01875	−0.30026	0.02997	−0.08011	0.07068
d.	More outdoor recreation development is not desirable	−0.16557	−0.38428	0.24038	**0.71252**	−0.01790	−0.00938	−0.03076
e.	I am against new tourism development which will attract new tourists to this region	−0.16173	−0.26210	**0.45497**	**0.61974**	0.04036	−0.23057	−0.07075
f.	Because of tourism, I have more recreational opportunities available to me	**0.60755**	0.15293	−0.18096	−0.34317	0.24917	0.09255	0.05130
g.	It is important to provide recreation facilities for local people rather than tourists	−0.04201	−0.03467	−0.01482	**0.73803**	−0.21541	0.01692	−0.01260
h.	Noise levels from the existing tourism facilities are not appropriate for this region	−0.06971	−0.17891	**0.46047**	0.20772	−0.11448	**−0.52798**	−0.27710
i.	Tourism has negatively impacted the natural environment in the region	−0.24217	−0.13332	**0.43821**	**0.48234**	−0.13579	−0.35030	−0.22331
j.	I believe tourism should be actively encouraged in the region	0.31656	0.16615	−0.30188	**−0.45331**	**0.44215**	0.38419	−0.18318
k.	Tourism has a vital role in the region	0.36455	**0.46958**	−0.23092	−0.35796	0.33810	0.18553	−0.05873
l.	The benefits of tourism outweigh any negative consequences	0.32096	0.38246	−0.22588	−0.38842	0.35286	0.06554	−0.00780
m.	Tourists are valuable	0.20861	**0.52608**	**−0.47200**	−0.20981	−0.03776	0.33829	0.04327
n.	The quality of public services has improved due to increased tourism in the region	**0.63546**	0.27367	−0.04815	0.18155	0.21258	−0.13505	**0.40965**
o.	The region has better roads due to tourism	0.39264	0.04823	0.00569	−0.00444	−0.13592	**−0.71955**	0.01157
p.	Tourism has increased crime in the region	−0.10697	−0.09716	**0.75108**	0.01749	0.02618	−0.15725	−0.02811
q.	There is more litter in the region due to tourism	−0.10304	0.10867	**0.81716**	0.11854	−0.11611	0.12001	−0.05647
r.	Local political turmoil has resulted from tourism development	0.19808	−0.02990	**0.48916**	0.17954	**0.52620**	**0.41393**	0.08255
s.	I feel I can access the decision-making process to influence tourism development in the region	0.12037	0.10226	−0.12446	−0.08631	0.06065	0.07545	**0.85292**
t.	Developing tourism will provide more jobs in the region	0.24831	**0.62209**	−0.10617	−0.24644	**0.40942**	0.03037	0.23589
u.	Tourists interfere with residents' enjoyment of the region	−0.16996	−0.19937	**0.46169**	0.30347	**0.47721**	0.19284	0.01830
v.	Local authorities are right in promoting tourism in the region	0.35235	0.34018	0.25530	−0.20097	**0.46121**	0.37625	0.18860
w.	Long-term planning by regional authorities can control negative impacts of tourism on the environment	0.22634	0.20582	0.06552	−0.12146	**0.77913**	0.14773	0.10853
x.	I have more money to spend as a result of tourism	**0.68897**	0.06302	−0.01705	**−0.44518**	0.09359	0.05857	0.14048
y.	Tourism will play a major economic role in the region	0.36541	**0.70194**	−0.17851	0.04122	0.32297	0.04532	0.22340
z.	I would like to see tourism become the main industry in the region	0.34365	**0.53158**	−0.07133	−0.27133	0.17883	0.04326	−0.24549
aa.	Shopping opportunities are better in my community due to tourism	**0.73916**	0.24625	−0.28709	0.12453	0.11113	0.04326	−0.08152
bb.	We should not try to attract more visitors to the region	−0.11604	**−0.40588**	**0.47967**	0.35090	−0.17850	−0.18507	−0.15787

These dimensions illustrate that local people are ambivalent about how tourism development might affect their lives. While they appreciate the economic benefits, both for themselves and for the local economy, they worry about negative environmental effects. They are also concerned that tourism development may supplant their own way of life in favour of those of tourists. They suggest that sound planning, better infrastructure and assured access to decision-making processes of senior governments will ameliorate negative effects. When these dimensions are further analysed, their relative importance is further clarified. Using K-means cluster analysis and discriminant analysis, the participants were subdivided into three groups, the larger numbering 71 and the others, 11 and 10 respectively (see Table 17.5). The three groups differ substantially in their attitudes towards tourism.

The largest group expresses weak and rather ambivalent support for tourism development in the region. It hovers about neutrality on all the dimensions but one: planning for tourism development. Group members express scepticism that planning will be useful.

The other two, much smaller groups express more positive views. The second feels that planning can reduce tourism's negative effects. The third, apparently composed of people given to moderate support for tourism development in the region, feel that the positives outweigh the negatives.

Three of the seven dimensions, however, are largely responsible for the formation of the three groups (Table 17.6). The dimensions, in order of their importance in differentiating the groups, are as follows:

- factor 5: tourism development requires planning;
- factor 3: tourism's negative effects; and
- factor 7: tourism and decision-making.

These dimensions address the issues of tourism's effects and of how to control the effects, rather than whether tourism is economically beneficial in the region. Clearly, there is concern among the

Table 17.5. Attitudes to tourism – relationships among the dimensions.

Dimension	Group 1	Group 2	Group 3
Factor 1: personal benefits of tourism	−0.0675	0.0337	0.4424
Factor 2: tourism in the local economy	−0.0921	0.1938	0.4408
Factor 3: tourism's negative effects	0.1029	0.5136	−1.2952
Factor 4: negative views of tourism	0.1248	−0.4806	−0.3577
Factor 5: tourism development requires planning	−0.3819	1.8387	0.6890
Factor 6: tourism and infrastructure	−0.0387	−0.5612	0.8923
Factor 7: tourism and decision-making	0.1533	−0.0384	−1.0464

Table 17.6. Dimensions responsible for grouping.

Dimensions	Wilks' Lambda	Sig.
Factor 5: tourism development requires planning	0.42535	>0.001
Factor 3: tourism's negative effects	0.32966	>0.001
Factor 7: tourism and decision-making	0.25872	>0.001
Factor 6: tourism and infrastructure	0.21062	>0.001
Factor 4: negative views of tourism	0.18044	>0.001
Factor 2: tourism in the local economy	0.16372	>0.001
Factor 1: personal benefits of tourism	0.15265	>0.001

participants about how well local people will be able to control tourism development. This concern is at the heart of social sustainability.

The commonalities and differences identified in this discussion of the quantitative results set the stage for a more detailed exploration using qualitative data.

Themes concerning tourism among the participants

People's discussions concerning the role of tourism in the shore zone and islands of the north shore of Lake Superior revealed a number of major themes, three of which are discussed below:

- host–tourist interactions;
- tourism's environmental impacts; and
- tourism management issues.

The themes themselves are composed of dimensions that reveal the residents' far-ranging knowledge about the north shore and the islands, as well as their uncertainties about the future role of tourism in their lives and in the region. Their uncertainties are reflected in the often contradictory subthemes, especially under the main themes of host–tourist interactions and (tourism) management issues. Residents recognize that while increased tourism may bring them benefits, there may also be costs, in terms of environmental degradation, changes in lifestyles and loss of local control.

Host–tourist interactions
This theme addresses a common issue in areas where tourism plays a major role in local ways of life – the interactions between local people (the hosts) and tourists. Where tourists are seen by local people to be very different (i.e. in activity preference, in income or in attitudes toward nature) from themselves or to benefit from opportunities or

rights unavailable to them, distrust and even animosity may develop toward tourists. People on the north shore recognized that it might be a considerable challenge to balance the demands of the tourism industry with their existing (local) lifestyles. More specifically, residents expressed concern that, where facilities were developed in existing lakeshore communities, those facilities should be available to both tourists and local people alike. They also hoped that local people would garner the largest portion of economic benefits from tourism, expressing opposition to large-scale, transnational commercial tourism enterprises which would drain those benefits out of the region.

A significant component in this theme concerns the potential for conflict. While local people value hunting, fishing and camping, there is some recognition that tourists may prefer other, less consumptive forms of activity. Several people pointed to the potential for conflict between, for example, kayakers and power boaters. When one set of activities is identified with tourists and another different set with local people, the result may be negative host–tourist interactions.

Another dimension of this theme comprises the feeling among local people that tourists cause environmental degradation. Garbage and human waste near known campsites were attributed to existing tourists who possess neither the knowledge nor the sensitivity to act more appropriately.

A final element under this theme expresses a fear among local people that the Lake Superior shoreline and/or the islands will be rendered inaccessible to them because of private, tourist-orientated development. Local people feel strongly that they do not want to become second-class citizens in their own region and province.

Tourism's environmental impacts
A second major issue reflects the belief held by residents that increased tourism, of any sort, will cause unwanted environmental degradation. Local people have little doubt that large-scale tourism developments are sure to be accompanied by negative environmental effects. However, they recognize that even their preferred smaller-scale versions of tourism development could cause some environmental degradation. As examples, people in the forums pointed out the following environmental effects:

- conspicuous human waste associated with relatively low-impact camping on several of the islands;
- accumulations of garbage at similar sites;
- fouling of (drinking) water intake areas with effluent from boats; and
- loss of fish habitat when tourism facilities are constructed in the shore zone.

Local people were adamant that tourism developments ought not to despoil the natural beauty and integrity of the region. Some felt that any tourism development ought to be required to undergo an environmental impact assessment; others felt that tourism operators, especially those conducting business on the islands, ought to be environmentally sensitive and responsible.

While the concern for environmental degradation was general across the region, a dimension can be identified in which local people caution that concerns about environmental quality cannot stand in the way of all (tourism) development. These people argue that it will be necessary to find a workable balance between protection and development.

Tourism management issues

A third major issue is a large one, with several significant dimensions. People throughout the north shore stated that tourism must be managed in order to protect the natural environment, to maintain high standards in facilities and operations, to provide tourism benefits for the region, to discourage inappropriate activities and facilities and to achieve coordination of tourism development. Furthermore, they stated emphatically that local involvement in decision-making was imperative and that local control was highly desirable.

Local people outlined a variety of mechanisms through which such involvement and, perhaps, control could be effected. Among them were:

- the status quo;
- the private sector;
- user pay groups (such as snowmobile clubs);
- an existing marina marketing association;
- a regional tourism authority;
- a proposed National Marine Conservation Area; and
- a north shore regional government.

Residents declared that they expected senior governments (provincial and federal) to support their decisions concerning tourism development on the north shore and in the islands. They added that such support would be an improvement over the normal responses from senior governments: either ignoring them altogether when making decisions or confusing them with contradictory policies and actions.

The discussions in the region about tourism management incorporate a significant contradiction: regulation implies government; governments, especially senior levels of government in Toronto or Ottawa, cannot be trusted. Time and time again in discussions, people would argue for the regulation of tourism, only to realize with dismay that they were invoking government action and the accompanying bureaucracy. Many felt that entrepreneurs in the tourism business should be capable of regulating themselves. However, even these people seemed to doubt that tourism entrepreneurs, if left to themselves, would do so.

No issue better illustrated the uneasiness among local people with respect to managing tourism than the National Marine Conservation Area (NMCA) being proposed for the region by Parks Canada, the federal agency in charge of protecting representative examples of Canada's terrestrial and marine heritage. As a federal government agency headquartered in Ottawa, Parks Canada was seen to be far removed from the day-to-day concerns of life on the north shore of Lake Superior. Furthermore, the fact that national parks administered by Parks Canada were not available for the hunting or snowmobiling activities important to some of the residents suggested that an NMCA would institute the same set of regulations, barring them from using an area they used traditionally. Another group of local people saw in the proposed NMCA an ideal management structure which would ensure that tourism development would be regulated and managed, that environmental quality would be maintained and that local involvement in decision-making would be assured.

Residents pointed out that if senior governments were to be involved at all in managing tourism in the region, then those governments would have to be accountable for their promises and actions. Far too often in the past, local people claimed, governments promised jobs and other benefits that never materialized, from various forms of development.

Local people showed themselves to be very knowledgeable about the north shore and islands of Lake Superior during the discussions. Their knowledge covered such matters as safe anchorages, sites of natural beauty, land ownership and wildlife. Many indicated that they had visited a large number of the islands during the past 20–30 years. Such knowledge substantiates their wishes to remain involved, at the least, in decision-making along the north shore and in the islands. Moreover, it adds credibility to their desire to establish local control over tourism development in the region.

These findings illustrate several common issues confronting sustainable tourism. Local people exhibit a high degree of customary knowledge about the shore zone and islands. Perhaps most important, however, is the adamant belief among local people that they should have a voice in whatever tourism developments take place on the north shore of Lake Superior. Moreover, if they could find a suitable management structure, they would strongly favour not only a voice but also control over such development. Local people also feel strongly that any future tourism development must be appropriate, in their terms; by this, they mean that tourism development ought to be small in scale, sensitive in its environmental effects and considerate of their established way of life.

Prospects for sustainable tourism in the region

What then might we say about the prospects for sustainable tourism on Lake Superior's north shore and islands? There seems little doubt that, despite some disagreements over the role of tourism in the regional economy or the relative importance of consumptive versus non-consumptive forms of tourism, forum participants favoured the expansion of tourism. However, they took care to qualify their response by emphasizing that any new tourism development should be small in scale and should not occur on the islands. Furthermore, they maintained that a measure of local control and management of tourism was a requirement of their support for any expansion. While they were not able to agree on the appropriate means to effect management, they did prefer local forms over corporate and (senior) government varieties. When one compares their ideas and concerns with our adopted view of sustainability, local people in the region seem to be addressing tourism from a sustainable point of view. Their concerns centre on ecological, social and even economic dimensions of sustainability. Left to themselves, local people may well be able to implement a sustainable form of tourism in the region.

Neither the local people nor the region will be left to themselves, however; nor should they be. Recall that the Charter on Sustainable Tourism emphasized that not only local people, but also governments should cooperate to achieve sustainability. In Ontario, at present, there are indications that the provincial government does not take sustainability seriously as a public policy goal. Consider the evidence:

- the Ministry of Natural Resources was taken to court by a coalition of environmental groups over its sustainable forestry plans for the Temagami region of north-eastern Ontario and is judged to be at fault because it has not included, as required, measurable indicators of sustainability (Algonquin Wildands League *et al.*, 1996);
- the Ontario government, as part of its campaign to reduce red tape and to open Ontario to business development, has weakened or eliminated environmental laws and regulations since 1995 (Canadian Environmental Law Association, 1998a); and
- the Ontario government has pared government employment drastically since 1995, including a reduction of 2500 jobs in the Ministry of Natural Resources (Canadian Environmental Law Association, 1998b).

Elsewhere (Payne, *et al.*, 1999), we have argued that these policy directions will defeat sustainability, even though the Ontario Ministry of Natural Resources (OMNR) is currently undertaking a large-scale land-use planning exercise, which aims to reconcile conflicting land uses such as forestry, mining, (remote) tourism and protected areas in northern Ontario within a sustainability framework (Ontario Ministry of Natural Resources, 1997). The government's actions to weaken the regulatory regime and to reduce government employment have emasculated the OMNR's capability to develop and, especially, to implement such wide-ranging land-use plans. Without the provincial government's active and effective participation, achieving sustainability in any sector (e.g. forestry, tourism) or in any region in northern Ontario will be extremely difficult.

References

Algonquin Wildlands League and Friends of Temagami vs. Minister of Natural Resources, E.B. Eddy Forest Products Ltd., Agawa Forest Products Ltd., Grant Lumber Corporation, Elk Lake Planing Mill Limited, Algonquin Forestry Authority, Goulard Lumber (1971) Ltd., Midway Lumber Mills Limited, Birchland Veneer Limited, St Mary's Paper Ltd., Tembec Inc. and Mallette, Inc. (1996) *Judgement*: Ontario Court of Justice (General Division), Divisional Court, Court File No. 539/96.

Baskerville, G.L. (1996) Charting a course, and charting progress. http://www.mf.ncr.forestry.ca/conferences/isd/baskervilleeng.html

Benidickson, J. (1982) Northern Ontario's tourist frontier. In: Wall G. and Marsh J. (eds) *Recreational Land Use: Perspectives on its Evolution in Canada*. Oxford University Press, Toronto, pp. 155–174.

Canadian Environmental Law Association (1998a) Dismantling environmental laws. http://www.cela.ca/s-laws.htm

Canadian Environmental Law Association (1998b) Weakening the role of government. http://www.cela.ca/s-cuts.htm

Duinker, P.N. (1996) Indicators and goals for biodiversity in Canada's model forests. http://mf.ncr.forestry.ca/conferences/isd/duinkereng.html

Gale, R.P.J. (1996) ISO 14001 to tackle green triangle. http://www.web.apc.org/ecoeco/iso14000.htm

Harris, R. and Leiper, N. (1995) *Sustainable Tourism: an Australian Perspective*. Butterworth-Heinemann, Sydney.

Hodgins, B.W. and Benidickson, J. (1989) *The Temagami Experience: Recreation, Resources and Aboriginal Rights in the Northern Ontario Wilderness*. University of Toronto Press, Toronto.

Indicators Task Force (1991) *A Report on Canada's Progress Towards a National Set of Environmental Indicators – Final Report*. Environment Canada, State of the Environment Reporting, SOE Report No. 91–1, Ottawa.

International Institute for Sustainable Development (1997a) Bellagio Principles. http://www.iisd1.iisd.ca/measure/compindex.asp

International Institute for Sustainable Development (1997b) Compendium of sustainable development indicator initiatives and publications: IUCN monitoring and evaluation initiative. http://www.iisd1.iisd.ca/measure

IUCN, WWF and UNEP (1980) *World Conservation Strategy.* Gland, Switzerland.

IUCN, WWF and UNEP (1990) *Caring for the World: a Strategy for Sustainability* (2nd draft). Gland, Switzerland.

Johnston, M.E. (1995) Communities and the resource economy of northwestern Ontario. In: Tadel, C. and Suida, H. (eds) *Themes and Issues of Canadian Geography I/Beiträge sur Geographic Kanadas I.* University of Salzburg, Salzburg, pp. 107–115.

Johnston, M.E. and Mason, P. (1997) The WWF initiative to develop guidelines and codes of conduct for Arctic tourism. *Polar Record* 33(185), 151–153.

Lake Superior Bi-National Program (1995) Ecosystem Principles and Objectives: Indicators and Targets for Lake Superior. Discussion Paper.

Lake Superior Bi-National Program (1998) Lake Superior Bi-National Program. http://www.cciw.ca/glimr/lamps/lake-superior/

Lankford, S.V. and Howard, D.R. (1994) Developing a tourism impact attitude scale. *Annals of Tourism Research* 21(1), 121–139.

Lonergan, S., Ruitenbeek, J. and Gustavson, K. (1996) Selection and modeling of sustainability indicators for the Fraser River basin – final report. Report prepared for State of the Environment Directorate and Pacific and Yukon region of Environment Canada and State of the Environment Reporting, British Columbia Ministry of Environment, Lands and Parks.

Mason, P. and Mowforth, M. (1995) *Codes of Conduct in Tourism.* Occasional Paper No. 1, Department of Geography, University of Plymouth, UK.

McCool, S.F. and Reilly, M. (1993) Benefit segmentation analysis of state park visitor setting preferences and behavior. *Journal of Park and Recreation Administration* 11(4), 1–14.

McCool, S.F., Burgess, C. and Nickerson, N. (1998) *Toward a Sustainable Tourism and Recreation Industry in Montana: an Examination of Concepts and Industry Perceptions.* Institute for Tourism and Recreation Research, University of Montana, Missoula, Montana.

Norman, W.C., Frauman, E., Toepper, L. and Sirakaya, E. (1997) *Green Evaluation Program and Compliance of Nature Tour Operators.* http://www.ecotourism.org/textfiles/sirak.txt

Noss, R.F. (1991) Sustainability and wilderness. *Conservation Biology* 5(1), 120–122.

Ontario Hydro (1990) *Providing the Balance of Power: Ontario Hydro's Plan to Serve Customers' Electricity Needs.* Yorkville Press. Toronto.

Ontario Ministry of Natural Resources (1997) Lands for life. http://www.mnr.gov.on.ca/MNR/lfl/index.html

Parks Canada (1995) *Sea to Sea to Sea: Canada's National Marine Conservation Areas System Plan.* Ministry of Supply and Services, Ottawa.

Payne, R.J., Johnston, M.E. and Twynam, G.D. (1999) Tourism and sustainability in northern Ontario. In: Nelson, J.G., Butler, R.W. and Wall, G. (eds) *Tourism and Sustainable Development: Monitoring, Planning, Managing,*

Decision Making: a Civic Approach, 2nd edn. Department of Geography Publication Series No. 52, University of Waterloo, Waterloo, Ontario, pp. 237–266.

Reid, R. and Holland, K. (1997) The land by the lakes: nearshore terrestrial ecosystems. Background paper, State of the Lakes Ecosystem Conference 1996.

Reid, W.V., McNeeley, J.A., Tunstall, D.B., Bryant, D.A. and Winograd, M. (1993) *Biodiversity Indicators for Policy Makers*. World Resources Institute and the World Conservation Union, Washington, DC.

Salwasser, H. (1990) Sustainability as a conservation paradigm. *Conservation Biology* 4(2), 213–216.

Skibicki, A.J. (1995) *Preliminary Boundary Analysis of the Greater Pukaskwa National Park Ecosystem Using the ABC Resource Survey Approach*. National Parks Occasional Paper No. 6, Parks Canada, Department of Canadian Heritage, Hull, Quebec.

Skidmore, J. (1990) Canadian values and priorities: a multiple-use perspective. In: Bray, M. and Thomson, A. (eds) *Temagami: a Debate on Wilderness*. Dundurn Press, Toronto, pp. 65–68.

Smithers, J.E.P. and Geissenger, H. (1991) Polar tourism: an opportunity for environmentally sensitive economic development. In: *The Role of Circumpolar Universities in Northern Development*. Proceedings of the First Annual Conference of the Association of Circumpolar Universities, Thunder Bay, Ontario, 24–26 November 1989, Centre for Northern Studies, Lakehead University, Occasional Paper No. 4, pp. 102–114.

Standards Council of Canada (1998) What is ISO 14000 . . . questions and answers. http://www.scc.ca/iso14000/infobref.html

The Ecotourism Society (1993) *Ecotourism Guidelines for Nature Tour Operators*. The Ecotourism Society, North Bennington, Vermont.

Twynam, G.D. and Robinson, D.W. (1997) *A Market Segmentation Analysis of Desired Ecotourism Opportunities*. Great Lakes Forestry Centre, Natural Resources Canada, NODA/NFP Technical Report TR–34, Sault Ste. Marie.

Twynam, G.D., Johnston, M.E. and Payne, R.J. (1997) *Tourism in the Shore Zone and Islands of the Lake Superior North Shore: a Study of Residents' Views*. Superior North Community Economic Development Corporation, Thunder Bay, Lakehead University.

UNEP (1995) *Environmental Codes of Conduct for Tourism*. UNEP Industry and Environment, UN Publications, Paris.

United Nations Development Programme (1992) *Report of the United Nations Conference on Environment and Development*, (Rio de Janeiro, 3–14 June), Chapter 30. gopher://gopher.undp.org:70/00/unconfs/UNCED/English/a21_30.

Wilson, M.A. (1997) The wolf in yellowstone: science, symbol or politics? Deconstructing the conflict between environmentalism and wise use. *Society and Natural Resources* 10, 453–468.

Woodley, A. (1993) Tourism and sustainable development: the community perspective. In: Nelson, J.G., Butler, R.W. and Wall, G. (eds) *Tourism and Sustainable Development: Monitoring, Planning, Managing*. Department of Geography Publication Series No. 37, Waterloo, Ontario pp. 135–147.

WCED (World Commission on Environment and Development – the Brundtland Commission) (1987) *Our Common Future*. Oxford University Press, New York.

World Conference on Sustainable Tourism (1995) *Charter for Sustainable Tourism*. Lanzarote, Canary Islands, Spain (April). http://www.insula.org/carturi.pdf

World Resources Institute (1992) *Bioregional management*. http://www.igc.org/wri/biodiv/bioregio.html

WWF (World Wide Fund for Nature) (1998) *Linking Tourism and Conservation in the Arctic*. WWF Arctic Programme, Oslo.

Sustainable Tourism in the 21st Century: Lessons From the Past; Challenges to Address

18

R. Neil Moisey and Stephen F. McCool

School of Forestry, University of Montana, Missoula, Montana, USA

Ecotourism, nature-based tourism, responsible tourism and green tourism are all terms applied to what has been referred to as a gentler, more socially and environmentally sensitive type of tourism – one more in keeping with our shifting global focus from that of mass consumption to one more aligned with our role within larger ecosystems. Much of the debate within this book about the meanings of what we might collectively refer to as sustainable tourism reflects the larger discourse going on within the varied disciplines that study tourism. Sociologists, anthropologists, economists, business marketers and a variety of social and ecological scientists have recently been researching and describing the impacts of tourism on ecological and social systems, with the intent of demonstrating that there does indeed exist a type of tourism that can be more sustainable than current forms.

Cleary, the authors in this book reflect the larger social uncertainty about the meanings attached to the concept of sustainable tourism. Yet, these differences – conflict if you will – lead not only to more focused discourse but are necessary for the learning required to advance academic, entrepreneurial and social definitions of sustainability. Underlying much of the discussion is a common vision of what sustainable tourism is or should be. It is when we try to articulate those meanings that the discussion goes in as many directions as there are discussants, demonstrating the 'guiding fiction' character of sustainable tourism.

In the introductory chapter in this book, we outlined a series of pathways and pitfalls confronting tourism and its role in the world.

Each of the chapters addressed one or more of these by suggesting frameworks to examine many of the issues surrounding tourism development, examples of the pathways and pitfalls that places may have taken, and discussions of the role that tourism might play in our search for a more sustainable world and communities. As a whole, the chapters indicate that while we have learned a lot about attempting to implement sustainable tourism, there is much more for us to contemplate as we seek to choose appropriate pathways while avoiding potentially disastrous pitfalls. In this concluding chapter we raise some of the fundamental lessons learned in this examination of the pursuit of sustainable tourism.

The environment, culture and tourism

Tourism exists within, and in most cases is dependent upon, the environment in which it is located – whether this is the natural world or one that is man-made. In this sense, it is obvious that tourism can not be studied in isolation from the system in which it operates. In this book, we focused on tourism that tends to be located in more natural environments. In such environments, tourism developments do not always result in benign changes. Typically, it is the natural environment that tourists come to see. In addition, these areas are also rich in historic and cultural resources – these form the tourism product. So, it is within this context that tourism must operate. The tourism industry can either protect and maintain or it can exploit and deplete. One path leads to more sustainable options, the other to places we have all seen. It is a matter of establishing what trade-offs are associated with the options available and determining the acceptability of those trade-offs.

If the choice is based on understanding the relationship of tourism within a larger system, one where decisions are based on how tourism development might impact or enhance local cultures and environments, then we must understand these relationships and base decisions on their impacts and the objectives we are seeking. Of course, tourism is but one of many players within this system. To more fully understand the dynamics of the system, all players must be included within this process and, to some degree, all must be in agreement as to what they are trying to protect. In a sense, there should be agreement on what they and the system are trying to sustain. Clearly, this is a daunting task, for economic and social systems are filled with competing claims as to desired goals and methods, conflicting ideologies about capitalism (and its advantages and weaknesses), and frequently ill-defined judgements about what is important. Social discourse about sustainable tourism can help reveal otherwise hidden values, serve to organize social action, and suggest ways to develop linkages with other components of the larger social system.

It is within this context that we tackle some of the issues confronting tourism presented at the beginning of this book. Do the proposed frameworks provide clarification to such issues as tourism's role and responsibility within the context of sustainability, and do the case-study examples illustrate successful achievement of these objectives? Do such frameworks help organize discourse and force disclosure of hidden agendas (for sustainable tourism is as much a political act as an economic one)? If so, then the issues that illustrate the pathways to achieving sustainability, but also illustrate the pitfalls to avoid while on the way, provide a small piece of the roadmap to a more sustainable place.

Tourism and sustainability: guiding fiction or realistic end-state?

The oft-cited 1987 Brundtland Report provided the catalyst for much of the discussion concerning the issues of development and sustainability. But the report provided little guidance on how to achieve sustainability. In terms of direction for tourism development, much of the discussion still focuses on what role tourism should take. Does tourism sustain itself, sustain local communities, or should tourism's role be one of sustaining larger global systems? One can see that as the question moves from the local to the global, the relationships become more abstract and the answers further out of reach.

Rather than focusing on sustaining tourism or on tackling the larger issue of global sustainability, the authors in this book look more to how tourism might help sustain local systems (i.e. at the community level). Sustainable tourism is a more gentle form of tourism, one that is smaller in scale, sensitive to cultural and environmental impact and respects the involvement of local people in policy decisions. Clearly, the field of sustainable tourism is an area filled with norms and myths, particularly the focus on developments of smaller scales, yet there is much to be done to make existing larger-scale developments themselves more sustainable, particularly in energy and water consumption, waste generation, and in training, pay levels and benefits to employees. This raises an important question: can the benefits to the ideal of sustainable tourism be achieved more effectively by working with existing larger-scale developments than by constructing more smaller scale ones? To be sustainable, tourism in this context must 'fit' within the system and forge symbiotic relationships with other segments of the social and economic system. Visions and definitions of what tourism should sustain are critical to progress. Yet, the growing complexity of our economic and political systems points to the fact that action requires many actors with a variety of skills and capabilities, each sharing these definitions.

The role of sustainable tourism in this situation is illustrated in Fig. 18.1. Definitions of sustainability must be shared among three major institutional participants in tourism development decisions: (i) public agencies, which manage the natural resources and ensure their long-term health; (ii) the tourism industry, which provides an array of supporting lodging, eating and transportation services; and (iii) the local residents whose culture may form part of the attraction and may benefit from tourism development, but who may also pay certain costs associated with impacts on quality of life, physical infrastructure and services.

Each of the participants has a direct interest in sustaining their component but also an indirect interest in sustaining the other

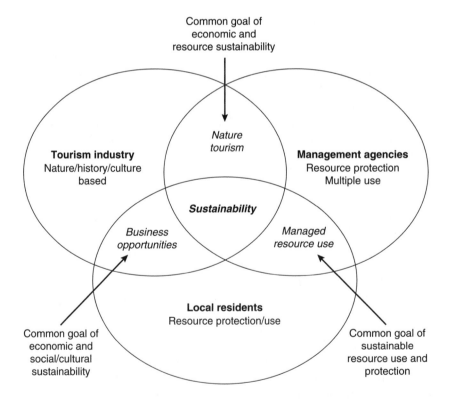

Fig. 18.1. Major participants in tourism development and their shared goals and opportunities for social, natural resource and economic sustainability.

components of the system, given the system's characteristics. While the tourism sector has an inherent interest in sustaining tourism, at some level there is the understanding that the tourism product is based on either the cultural or environmental resources. The community is motivated to sustain their quality of life, which includes such issues as a healthy economy and ecosystem. Public land management agencies rely upon the tourism industry to provide economic and political support, and the community is their constituency. If meanings are not shared, the linkages among sectors cannot be articulated and mitigation of negative effects cannot proceed. The efficacy of this mutualistic system is highly dependent upon shared definitions of sustainability.

Without shared meanings, sustainability does indeed become nothing more than a 'guiding fiction', leaving the participants with a moving target of an idealized end state, yet paralysed when it comes to taking action. Ioannides illustrated this within his longitudinal framework where, over time and scale, definitions of sustainability change in response to the development stage of a destination. Understanding where in the development process we are might provide insight into why participants may or may not embrace sustainability, engage in appropriate actions or develop meaningful discourse with other segments. Dawson's discussion of the Tourism Opportunity Spectrum provided another framework to assess what opportunities should be sustained and the impacts of alternative development scenarios in terms of sustainability.

Not only are shared meanings and definitions critical in achieving sustainability, but they must become institutionalized within each of the participants. Tourism operates within a complex and interwoven social, ecological and economic system. It would be foolhardy to assume that unless shared meanings were part of the underlying reward systems the incentives to achieve those meanings would exist. In other words, participants would be maximizing their individual rather than shared goals resulting in potentially non-sustainable solutions. The fragmented character of tourism – many small businesses, a variety of government institutions, each with differing mandates and procedures, and a diverse citizenry – means that those interested in sustainable tourism face a daunting challenge to organize venues where possibilities can be discussed.

Public participation: keywords for success?

A fundamental, but not sole, role of public participation is to inform decision-makers of the value systems under which various publics are operating. Achieving sustainability requires a variety of individuals, agencies and programmes, each operating under different value and reward systems and each bringing different and sometimes competing goals into the planning process. In a tourism context these players include tourism developers, local communities, government agencies, tourist representatives (indirectly through tour operators or local tourism business owners) and non-government organizations. The views of each must be represented, articulated and integrated within the shared definition of sustainability and how sustainability will be achieved. It is through the political process that this takes place. We note that it is only out of this process, iterative, difficult, complex and messy as it is, that shared definitions of sustainability will develop and evolve.

From a Western perspective, the majority of political systems are open processes that include public input or involvement. But even within these democratic systems, other influences operate to undermine participation. For example, widespread corruption can exclude the public in the decision-making process. In many countries, the political system is corrupted by money buying power. Problems are often ill-defined, power is not equally distributed, there may be structural distortions in access to information, and the sense of competing priorities may vary. In such situations, those most affected by development decisions are typically excluded from the process. In still others, the scientifically based, expert-driven, progressive-era models of planning tend to marginalize experiential and local knowledge. Achieving sustainability in such situations will require not only a restructuring of political power, but also the development of trust among participants in tourism development decisions.

Several authors discussed the need for changes within local and national political structures to enable participation in deciding tourism development issues that affect community sustainability. Weak or non-existent political structures and informal venues for political discourse not only diminish the likelihood for citizen involvement but ensure that important values will be neglected. What options are available if local values and politics do not favour public participation? Gender, economic well-being and social status also play a role in the social acceptability of political involvement. Under such social and political systems, achieving sustainability appears unlikely, if only because when groups are excluded based on gender, race or ethnicity, sustainable tourism loses its legitimacy. Tourism can bring about social and economic changes in communities dependent upon traditional industries and socio-political roles. Tourism tends to employ those less economically independent in the traditional natural resource industries. Economic independence engenders political empowerment, which in turn fosters enlightenment and participation within the political system.

An inequitable sharing of the benefits of tourism has been shown to breed a 'collective indifference' – tourism becomes less salient, which tends to stifle widespread participation. The community becomes less cohesive in defining the role that tourism plays in its development. This lack of community solidarity, in turn, determines not only support for tourism development but also the degree of citizen participation. Participation by only those positively affected by tourism will focus issues of sustainability on beneficial aspects of tourism – sustainability of tourism becomes the goal rather than a broader focus on community sustainability and resiliency. Thus, through neglect of authentic participatory processes, important elements of the tourism product, such as the friendliness of local people, are lost and anti-tourism attitudes and behaviours develop.

In broader circles, considerable discussion has focused on the role of science in defining sustainability. Science can provide information about the costs of decisions and the interrelationships between the various players, trade-offs between costs and benefits, and the potential impacts of alternative scenarios. But science can not decide what is 'right' or 'wrong' – these are value-based decisions ideally left up to all affected individuals. This leads to a paradox: can we integrate both science and values effectively into sustainable decisions? This in turn leads to additional questions. Is sustainability a technical or value/moral issue? What is the role of traditional knowledge in defining sustainability, and who decides the role of each? And, who gets to decide what will be sustained and how?

No one argues that participation is not important to integrate local knowledge or protect local values in the search for sustainability. Indeed, without participation, communities lose their identity – their sense of place. Lack of participation leads to inappropriate goal setting with little or no ownership in a shared vision of development options. Community solidarity is weakened. The pathway to sustainability becomes lost.

Linking planning with outcomes: decisions and trade-offs

Planning involves decisions about desired future conditions that involve trade-offs in both the short and long term. Sustainable tourism doesn't just happen, it occurs only with explicit decision-making processes that consider what futures are plausible and desirable and the pathways to them. In terms of tourism development, there are many options leading to multiple future conditions. Public involvement provides the 'reality check' in terms of outcomes, while the role of science is to provide information about causes and effects, trade-offs and consequences in the decision-making process.

In most cases, competing goals, lack of scientific agreement on cause–effect relationships, and agreement on the degree of acceptable change or impact characterize tourism planning in a modern context. These situations call for more inclusive and integrative planning processes, where emphasis is placed on mutual learning and consensus building. Planning for sustainability requires minimizing ecological and social impacts while maximizing economic and social benefits. But development implies impacts, which implies trade-offs. Developing appropriate organizing frameworks to understand these underlying relationships will lead ultimately to more sustainable decisions.

Several authors in this text (e.g. Leung, Dawson, Ioannides and Carmichael) have proposed a variety of planning frameworks or tools that diminish some of the uncertainties involved in sustainable tourism planning. For example, Leung and Marion suggested that the ecological impacts of tourism in remote areas can be quantified based on recreation ecology research. Dawson's discussion of the Tourism Opportunity Spectrum and Carmichael's holistic framework for evaluating developments both illustrated how a variety of tourism development options can be evaluated in terms of sustainability.

The potential impacts of tourism development imply trade-offs between participants, present and future generations, and where likely impacts will accrue. Collaborative rather than traditional planning styles increase the likelihood of fair and equitable decisions as they relate to current participants. Decisions in a collaborative context are borne by all affected parties. All those impacted directly, and to some degree those impacted indirectly, should have collaborative input into forming development goals. Evans and Litchfield illustrated some of these trade-offs, in terms of protecting certain natural areas by sacrificing others. But the important question remains: how should the benefits of tourism be weighed against its costs?

Sustainability implies the protection of future generations' interests. But the advocacy of these interests is dependent upon decision-makers in the present. By ascribing to the goals of sustainability, those in the present implicitly assume an understanding of the goals, needs, preferences, resources and relationships between these that may exist in the future. This most likely is not the case. Explicitly incorporating future opportunities is one of the strengths of planning for sustainability over more traditional planning approaches that ignore future costs and benefits or minimize them through the use of discount rates. Uncertainty in planning is unavoidable, but should not limit planning horizons. Yet, we are confronted with the question of who best represents future generations.

Indicators of success?

Given that planners, community members, the tourism industry and public agencies are in agreement on a sustainable course, how do we know if tourism development is contributing to sustainability without a set of measurable variables that indicate progress? The question is, what should tourism sustain and can we measure whether it is becoming sustained?

What tourism should sustain is a negotiated and agreed-upon outcome of the collaborative planning process. Through the involvement of interested and affected participants, a clear vision of sustainable development goals then drives future development decisions. Agreement on general indicators of sustainability is derived from these goals. Translating those general factors into specific, measurable, efficient, valid and reliable indicators is a key component in achieving sustainability.

A growing body of literature has focused attention on the concept of sustainability indicators in both the larger sustainable development context and, more recently, with regard to sustainable tourism indicators. Many issues have been identified, including: whether sustainable tourism indicators are compatible with broader indicators of sustainability; the role that scale (both spatially and temporally) plays in the interrelationship of indicators; limited data availability and comparability across spatial and temporal scales; and that many efforts to date have created ad hoc indicators with little theoretical or conceptual bases.

It is an appropriate role for science to assist in the identification and development of sustainability indicators. We do not know what the impacts of tourism are on larger spatial and temporal scales, nor what the relationships between many of the indicator variables are and how exogenous factors such as tourism might ripple through ecological and social systems. While many of the recent efforts to develop indicators of sustainable tourism have identified an almost infinite set of indicator variables, many decry the use of a standardized set of indicators but support the use of site-specific indicators. In either case, to be effective, indicators must measure progress toward sustainability.

Conclusions

The recent rise in the popularity of cultural and nature-base tourism, combined with an increased taste for the exotic, is changing the traditional linkages of tourism with social and ecological systems.

Tourism is fast discovering new and untouched areas of the globe – places that are ill-equipped to deal with the onrush of outside influences and impacts.

Sustainable tourism is the linking of culture and environment with one type of economic development. Each of these players is dependently linked, once realized this creates a symbiotic relationship, resulting in more sustainable development decisions. This is the concept we have presented throughout this text. More than ever, sustainable tourism is being viewed as a tool of social and economic development and as a method of protecting our cultural and natural heritage. Consensus on these goals among these players is a necessary, though not sufficient condition, for implementing appropriate actions.

While the chapters in this book pose many more questions than they answer, this is beneficial in the furtherance of the discussion of the meaning of sustainability, how tourism can help to achieve sustainability, and the pathways and pitfalls that lead to sustainability.

Index

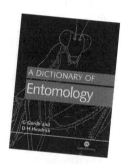
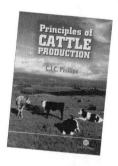